For C
[signature] 5/13/09

HUGH HEWITT

THE WAR AGAINST THE WEST

Crucial Conversations With The Most Informed Experts About Our Enemies, Our Defenses, Our Strategy and Our Leaders in the Long War Against Islamist Extremism

FEATURING INTERVIEWS WITH

Lawrence Wright • Norman Podhoretz • Douglas Frantz and Catherine Collins
Michael Ledeen • Dr. Ali Ansari • George Weigel • Mark Steyn • Dr. Walid Phares
Robin Wright • Timothy Weiner • John Bolton • Douglas Feith • Robert Kaplan • Dexter Filkins
Michael Yon • General David Petraeus • John F. Burns • Victor Davis Hanson

The War Against the West:
Crucial Conversations with the Most Informed Experts About Our
Enemies, Our Defenses, Our Strategy and Our Leaders in the Long War
Against Islamist Extremism
by Hugh Hewitt
Published by Townhall Press

Printed in the United States of America

ISBN 978-1-60791-069-5

www.townhallpress.com

Dedication

For Dean Barnett, 1967-2008

My friend, colleague, co-blogger and frequent guest host. Dean was an extraordinary man.

If we had a hundred Deans, the country would understand the stakes in this war, and would have come to that understanding with a lot of laughter along the way. He is greatly missed.

Table of Contents

Chapter 1.

Talking About The War Against the West

It will strike historians of the future as incredibly strange that most of the American presidential campaign of 2008 was devoted to subjects other than the war then waging against the West. If the West survives, its own chroniclers will say that survival owed nothing to the debates of the fall of 2008, focused as they were on the financial crisis and plunging stock markets, Governor Sarah Palin's wardrobe expenses and Barack Obama's vast fundraising prowess.

With only two weeks left in the campaign, Joe Biden did tell an audience to "Mark my words. Mark my words. It will not be six months before the world tests Barack Obama like they did John Kennedy. The world is looking. We're about to elect a brilliant 47-year-old senator president of the United States of America. Remember I said it standing here if you don't remember anything else I said. Watch, we're gonna have an international crisis, a generated crisis, to test the mettle of this guy."

John McCain tried in vain to focus attention on this candid admission of the state of the world, and launched an ad that used Biden's warning, but to no avail. In one of the great ironies of 2008, the overwhelming success of the "surge" in Iraq that John McCain had urged and George Bush had ordered had taken the battle for Iraq off the front pages while the battle in Afghanistan, still raging, is far more difficult to report or convey. A nation used to a constantly changing news diet became transfixed by the credit crisis and plunging markets, and debate about the war in which the West finds itself never really took center stage.

As Joe Biden predicted, however, it will be back on the front page. When it returns to our collective consciousness with the seriousness it deserves, we can only hope it is not with the same or greater ferocity as occurred on 9/11.

The best guarantee against another horrific surprise and the devastation that could accompany it is a commitment by American journalism

1

to reporting the war in all of its many complications. By "the war," I mean the worldwide struggle against Islamist jihadists willing to use violence and terror to overthrow any government in order to install a government based on their understanding of Sharia, whether those Islamists are of the most radical Sunni or Shia variety. The vast majority of Muslims around the world do not favor this war, and the long term hope of the West is in the triumph of peaceful Islam over the jihadists. That triumph is far off, though, and so the war with all its immense risks and awful carnage will go on for many years and indeed decades. Only by understanding the origins of the war can the West hope to endure and triumph in it.

It is the duty of journalists to explain this war to their audiences, as often as necessary, and with as much clarity as possible. In the course of hosting a daily three-hour talk show since July of 2000 I have tried to do that, and this book is one part of that effort. That effort often involves interviews with national security experts such as Frank Gaffney of the Center for Security Policy, Max Boot of the Council on Foreign Relations, Fred Kagan of the American Enterprise Institute, Daniel Pipes of the Middle East Forum, Andrew McCarthy, of the Foundation for the Defense of Democracy and author of <u>Willful Blindness: Memoir of the Jihad</u>, and Thomas P.M. Barnett whose book <u>The Pentagon's New Map</u> has shaped the thinking of a new generation of military officers and with deeply informed journalists from across the political spectrum, including E.J. Dionne and Thomas Ricks of the *Washington Post*, Jonathan Alter of *Newsweek*, John Podhoretz of *Commentary Magazine* and Bill Kristol and Fred Barnes of *The Weekly Standard* and Morton Kondracke of *Roll Call*.

One particular focus of mine, though, has been those men and women who, since 9/11, have produced books on the war that somehow comprehensively advanced my own understanding of the conflict. Many fine books have been written about various aspects of the war, but a number have reached the level of necessary and important contributions to the understanding of the overall struggle. I have tried to focus large amounts of radio time in concentrated fashion on these authors and books.

Dexter Filkins is one of our country's preeminent war correspondents, having spent most of the past decade in either Afghanistan or Iraq on assignment with The New York Times. I thus jumped at the chance to interview him for my nationally syndicated radio show when Filkins published his memoir, The Forever War.

At the conclusion of the interview, I asked Filkins to autograph my heavily annotated copy of his wonderful book. He more than obliged, writing "To Hugh: Thank you for the extraordinarily thoughtful discussion –it's the best I've ever had. And than you for all the great work."

Filkins was referring to just discussions about his recently published book, of course, and he had yet to be interviewed by the gold standards in my business when it comes to author interviews –Charlie Rose and Brian Lamb. But I hope it is not immodest to say that I get reactions like Filkins' from many, many authors and other interview subjects. Really, I do. There are many reasons why most authors and their publishers and agents view me as among the very best of interviewers at work in broadcast media today and seek out an interview with me. I want to focus on a few of them in the hope that this might breed some imitation among talk show hosts in the future, whether on television, radio or the internet.

First, I sell a lot of books and those who interview authors should try and do the same for their guests. With more than 120 affiliates across the U.S. including most of the major broadcast markets in the country including New York, Los Angeles, Chicago, Phoenix, Houston, Dallas, Philadelphia, Atlanta, the Twin Cities, Denver, Portland, San Diego, Cleveland, Orlando, Tampa Bay, and and San Antonio as well as far flung outposts from Alaska to Hawaii, an author can expect a far-flung audience of serious, book-buying people by appearing with me. They can also expect me to mention the complete title of their book often, and to provide an easy-to-find-and-use link to the Amazon.com listing on my blog.

But there's more to my popularity with authors than my impact on sales because there are much bigger platforms than mine. I am in only the second tier of radio shows devoted to news and politics when it comes to total audience, behind Rush and Sean Hannity, grouped with Laura Ingraham, Dennis Prager, Michael Medved, Bill Bennett, Glenn Beck and Dennis Miller. My reach into the book-buying public may extend a bit further and deeper than theirs because of the audience for my blog and for Townhall.com of which I am executive editor; but still my total number of listeners is far below that of Rush and some television appearances still sell more books than even the best radio interview.

The real reasons I attract the best authors of the most important books have to do with substance and style.

First, I prepare for interviews extensively, reading and rereading my subject's work and published articles, taking copious notes, and preparing a detailed outline. I do not rely on staff, though my producer Duane Patterson and engineer Adam Ramsey and long-time assistant Lynne Chapman are extraordinary compliments to my work; and my wonderful wife Betsy, known as the "fetching Mrs. Hewitt" to my radio audience, will contribute in run-up conversations about authors and guests with whom she is familiar.

Second, I am very, very experienced. I have been a broadcast journalist since December of 1990, spending five years as a weekend radio host for Los Angeles powerhouse radio station KFI and a decade as co-host of a nightly news and public affairs show for PBS's Los Angeles affiliate KCET –"Life & Times." I also conceived and hosted an eight-part series for national broadcast on PBS, "Searching for God in America," before launching my nationally syndicated radio show on July 10, 2000. Not counting conversations with callers, I estimate that I have done more than 10,000 interviews in my two decades as a broadcast journalist. That many interviews will teach all but the most block-headed many things

My third great advantage, driven home by my long time television producing partner Martin Burns: I Listen! Too often interviewers are wedded to an outline prepared by other people, and press on robot-like from question-to-question whether or not it makes sense, often ignoring amazingly interesting or provocative answers. Even hosts working from their own notes have a game plan from which they will not depart; and like an NFL coach determined to stick with his diagrammed first 15 plays, the interviewer simply moves from question to question. This is often because the interviewer lacks time, and must hit a mark that is ridiculously limited –a five minute interview, or even 10 are absurdly constrained frames in which to work. The reason I loved PBS and gave it up for radio, which I love even more, is that both places provide me the broadcast time within which to really work at getting the authors to convey with candor and clarity the essence of what they have to say. The long form is the best form, and the gift of time allows me to listen closely and pursue what I hear that surprises or engages or moves me.

Over the years since I began the radio show —years of war and deep political division and controversy I have kept accomplished individuals of all backgrounds and ideologies coming on to the show. Men and women of the left are harder to recruit for a variety of reasons, but authors will almost always show up in the search for book sales. Some brave elected Democrats have also appeared only to be surprised by the civility with which they are engaged. Most of nationally syndicated talk radio is actually very civil though deeply engaged in the important conversations and impatient with talking points.

This variety of guests and subjects has caught the attention of my audience and has powered the growth of the show into most of the major markets of the United States. Via podcasts and internet broadcasts, my audience is worldwide. I am often asked for transcripts and CDs of various interviews, and recently we opened the Hugh Store at www.hughhewitt.com to make the most requested interviews and other programming available.

But many, many listeners have asked for a book like this one devoted to this particular subject, and so, with the assistance of my staff, here it is.

Since 9/11 I have tried to conduct at least one extended interview with each author who has put out a serious book that is well received and admired by both supporters and critics of the war. Though I am myself a transparent political partisan, I did not intend in this series of interviews advance the interests of the Republican Party or to defend George Bush or John McCain or attack Barack Obama. Some of the interviews were very much intended to defend and support the "surge" strategy and the policy of seeking victory and stability in Iraq as part of an overall strategy for prevailing in the global war against jihadism before some segment of the jihadists could gain control of nuclear weapons, but they are not "political."

I call these books, collectively, "The Necessary Bookshelf," as each title on that shelf seems to me to be incredibly important to understanding how the world got to where it is today and to figuring out how to defend civilization against the barbarism of the Islamist extremists. In this volume I have included transcripts of the interviews I have conducted with the authors of these books as a short cut and yet another prompt to the readers to begin the reading that will equip them to help guide our democracy forward in the perilous years ahead.

None of these books sell in the way a good novel or even a trashy celeb biography sells. They are widely admired and receive positive critical reviews, but they just don't sell because Americans just don't get their information about the war that way –through long, densely written books no matter how well written or how incredibly important those books are. We are, by and large, a nation of listeners, which is why we are also making this book available on CD and MP3 podcast.

I do believe these interviews –the transcripts as well as the audio— make these authors and their books accessible to many people. I have always tried to conduct my interviews with the larger audience in mind. When I first began my career and broadcast late on Sunday nights over the 50,000 watt KFI clear channel powerhouse that could carry across the entire western United States, I would keep in mind a trucker on a long haul trying to stay awake and focused but not by being screamed at but by being transfixed by a conversation and by hearing asked exactly the question he or she wished would be asked.

That is still my approach, though now I try and put myself in the mind of the mother or father of young children, working hard to get ahead, saving some money and preparing to raise their children to lead good, productive and, crucially, God-fearing service oriented lives. When I talk to the experts, I want those parents (and secondarily, young adults just starting out in life) to hear a conversation about the world that is unfolding before them. I want them to hear answers to the questions that they would ask if they were in a studio with one of my guests.

I want them so badly to understand what it is we are up against, the nature of the peril, the necessity of alarm but also the dangers of panic and overreaction.

I hope this book and these CDs make that understanding easier, not just with regard to the authors and their books, but also about what has happened in recent years. To that end I have included some conversations with some of the clearest strategic thinkers at work in the world today, including my conversation with General Petraeus from the late summer of 2007, my conversations with *New York Times* reporter John Burns –one of the wisest, most balanced men I have ever inter-viewed—and an interview with historian and classicist Victor Davis Hanson, who more than anyone else at work today brings a perspective to this war that is rooted in the vast experience mankind has with war and the rise and fall of civilizations.

I have organized the interviews to facilitate the reader's/listener's understanding, so the interviews are not in the order in which they were conducted, but rather cover the sequence of the subject matter. We thus begin with the interviews that explain where the Islamist threat took root and why, and then follow with the books that chart America's deep failure to recognize and respond to the threat before it was upon us, and then on what has happened and why in the first years of the long war.

The very last conversation took place in closing days of Campaign 2008 with Victor Davis Hanson.

VDH happened to be close to my studio in the middle of October, 2008 as the Obama victory seemed very likely given the financial panic of those days and the inability of John McCain to speak into the roar of a media intent on using the crisis to catapult Barack Obama to the White House.

Professor Hanson spent two hours on air with me, and left any fair minded listener sober about the future and deeply aware of the past's warnings to America as it concluded the first presidency of the long war.

Chapter 2.

Three Conversations with Lawrence Wright

I picked up <u>The Looming Tower</u> soon after it was published and read it in a handful of sittings. It is a genealogy of al Qaeda –where it came from, what it believes, [what it would like to accomplish –which is rule the world in the name of Allah]—and how that world would look if the movement's masterminds were successful.

I went hunting for Wright soon after his book, which would win the Pulitzer Prize in 2006 was published, and have featured him since whenever he has added to his writings on al Qaeda in the pages of The New Yorker where he is a senior writer. Wright, like many of those I interview, is a man of the left who is clear-eyed about the enemy the West faces. Here are the interviews we have had.

Interview with Lawrence Wright
September 22, 2006

HH: If you're driving, you'll want to pull over. If you're in your house, you'll want to sit down. For the next two hours, I'm going to talk with Lawrence Wright, author of <u>The Looming Tower: Al Qaeda And The Path To 9/11</u>, about the nature of al Qaeda, where it came from, where it is going, what it did on 9/11, and what it did before and since. It's a conversation you really don't want to miss. <u>The Looming Tower</u> is now on best seller lists across the United States, widely hailed as the most comprehensive history of al Qaeda ever put forward. Lawrence Wright is a staff writer at the New Yorker, a fellow at the Center on Law and Security at New York University. He's the author of five previous books. He's a graduate of Tulane, and I'm pleased to welcome him. Lawrence Wright, welcome to the Hugh Hewitt Show.

LW: Hugh, thanks for having me.

HH: Great to have you. I'd like to begin at the end, if I could.

LW: Sure.

HH: John O'Neill, on the night before he is killed in the World Trade Center, after helping personally evacuate the kids from the day care center, had been out all night at Elaine's in New York, out to the China Club. And this retired FBI agent, turned head of the World Trade Center security, says to one of his colleagues out carousing and dining that night, "We're overdue."

LW: Yes.

HH: In the course of writing this book, Lawrence Wright, did any other similarly situated American counter-terrorism official tell you something similar to what O'Neill said on September 10th, or the early morning hours of September 11th, 2001?

LW: O'Neill wasn't alone. He was just one of the very few who really understood the nature of the threat, and what peril we were really in. There were people. John was a prophet in many respects, because as early as 1996, he was saying that al Qaeda posed a real threat to America, even though his director, Louis Freeh, for years afterwards, was reassuring the White House that al Qaeda posed no threat to the homeland. Michael Scheuer at the CIA was another one who was very aware of the danger of al Qaeda, and was constantly trying to alert his superiors. And there were people within the I49 squad, which is one of those squads that I particularly pay attention to in my book, who were really charged with finding bin Laden. There was some really good people in that squad, but they were thwarted, in many ways, by inter-rivalry among other intelligence agencies, and by their own superiors.

HH: Over the course of the next two hours, I want to cover a lot of that ground. But in the five...you've been writing this book for how long now, Lawrence Wright?

LW: Well, you know, I started on 9/11, so it's essentially a five year project.

HH: And it's incredibly well researched. You've had to travel the globe. And it's so comprehensive, that no matter what someone's politics, they're going to have to walk away from this saying this is a truly extraordinary and fair and balanced account. My question is in the post-9/11 world, as you've talked to other people, similarly situated to John O'Neill, do they think that we are once again overdue?

LW: You know, it's more complicated now. We were in a spot, Hugh, where…I've been reading the al Qaeda's memoirist, and their strategist recently. And they…al Qaeda itself says it was essentially eliminated after November/December, 2001. Although bin Laden and Zawahiri and the top lieutenants got away, according to al Qaeda, you know, 80-85% of their membership was captured or killed. And they themselves were scattered, and in disrepute all over the globe. So essentially, they were in a kind of zombie-like state. It's not something that they were surprised about in some ways. I mean, they had planned for the day when their leadership would be eliminated. They wanted to create a legacy of smaller groups, such as the ones that we've seen popping up, especially in Europe. You know, 8-10 people, loosely connected, if connected at all, but bound together by ideology, learning tactics over the Internet. This was all part of al Qaeda's contingency plan. And unfortunately, Iraq has given them a new lease on life, and provided a new training ground for al Qaeda, which they badly needed. So yes, we are in danger, although the threat levels, and the kind of chatter that preceded 9/11, aren't evident right now. That doesn't mean that there aren't lots of people that aren't trying to hurt us.

HH: A historical question. Do you believe, based on your researches, that there were other planes in the air on 9/11 that were part of the operation that were grounded, and did not carry through their missions?

LW: No. I don't have any evidence of that.

HH: Now the same question about three different groups. First group. Do you think most of the American political elite understand this enemy, even five years after the attack?

LW: No, I think that it's a tragedy that after five years...I'll speak especially about our intelligence community. We have such a poor grasp of who these people are, and what they want, and where they come from. And I'll tell you why. You know, we have reorganized American intelligence. We've added an entire new tier of bureaucracy with this directorate of intelligence. We have created an entirely new Department of Homeland Security. That has not added anything to our intelligence. What would help our intelligence is getting people on the ground that actually understand al Qaeda and where it comes from. If you go up on the 7th floor of the FBI, to take one example, an organization that made its reputation fighting the Mafia, and to some extent, the IRA, who do you find up there on the top floor? Irish and Italian Catholic guys. It's no wonder they were effective in fighting those organizations, because they come from the same neighborhoods. They speak the same language. They know who they're fighting against. But our intelligence agencies have an ingrained prejudice against hiring people of Muslim or Arabic background who really can penetrate those communities. When, for instance, Clinton told the CIA get him, you know, he gave a presidential directive. Get this guy. The CIA couldn't get him. They didn't have anybody who could get close to him, and they still don't.

HH: Second category. Does the American military elite understand this enemy?

LW: I think of all the branches of government, that the military is moving faster in terms of evolving its response to this threat than in any other branch of government. It's not to say that the military can solve the problem alone. I don't think it can. But you know, the military is really down in the weeds with the enemy, and they've learned a lot about the culture and how to adapt to it. So I feel better about the military's ability to understand the enemy, if not defeat him.

HH: Have you had a chance to read Robert Kaplan's Imperial Grunts? Along with your book, I think the two indispensable books, post 9/11?

LW: No, but I'll put it on my list. Thanks for the recommendation.

HH: It's about the military, and I think you're right about the "down in the tall grass" with them. Do any of the people who would be president, who are out already speaking, and there's a long list, Republican and Democrat, and I'm sure you've heard some of this. Do any of them strike you as being particularly aware of this enemy, and how and why it operates?

LW: No, I think that terrorism is a unique threat. And if you go back, for instance, to the pre-9/11 presidential campaign, Bush-Gore, they didn't talk about terrorism at all. And it's very difficult for any, either of the parties to really pose a clear, sustainable plan for dealing with terrorism. It's a long term, perhaps a generational problem.

HH: Do you think Bush understands his enemy in this regard, Osama and his lieutenants?

LW: I think that American intelligence and the administration are beginning to recalibrate. You know, the bravado days of bring 'em on, those are gone. And I think that in Bush's recent speeches, where he's directly addressing bin Laden and his policies, rather than avoiding the issue, I think are very encouraging. So I do think that there's an appreciation that's beginning to take root in the administration, of the nature of the threat, and what a formidable challenge they do actually pose.

HH: There's one anecdote in here, one bit of history of al Qaeda, which I want to get in before our first break, so that people understand. It's the boy spies...

LW: Oh, yes.

HH: ...about which I'd heard nothing. But it tells us about Egyptian secret police, it tells us about Zawahiri. If you could, in a minute and a half, tell people what that episode was.

LW: In 1995, Zawahiri, the number two guy in al Qaeda, and other Egyptian groups, attempted an assassination on Hosni Mubarek, the Egyptian president. It was part of their long term campaign against the Egyptian state. But that went too far. The Egyptians, the intelligence agencies, went to Sudan, where Zawahiri and his organization, al Jahad, were located. And they enticed a young boy, a 12 year old boy, into coming to watch some videos and have some sodas. And they drugged him and sodomized him and photographed the entire thing. Then, they told him that they were going to turn these photographs over to his father if he didn't cooperate. That could have been a death sentence for that boy. So he cooperated. He put microphones and listening devices in his parents' apartment. He brought home papers…he brought papers to the Egyptian spies. And he also recruited another boy, who was subjected to the same degrading treatment. And the Egyptians decided to use these boys to try to assassinate Zawahiri. They actually got them to try to plant a bomb outside an apartment building where Zawahiri and some of his leaders were going to meet. The Sudanese intelligence intercepted this…

HH: Lawrence Wright, before we went to break, we were telling…you were recounting the story of the boy spies kidnapped in Sudan in 1995 by Egyptian intelligence, sodomized, brutalized, turned against Zawahiri. And what happened to them?

LW: Well, the Sudanese intelligence intercepted this young boy as he was planting a bomb on behalf of the Egyptian intelligence officers. And Zawahiri found out about it, and he demanded to talk to the boys. And the Sudanese willingly handed him over, thinking they were going to get him back. Zawahiri put these two boys on trial. First of all, there was some objection about putting children on trial, but he had them stripped naked to see if they had pubic hair, which was an indication that they were mature enough to stand trial. And then, he convicted them and executed them, and videotaped the entire procedure to distribute among other followers who might be tempted to betray him.

HH: And how old were they?

LW: 12.

HH: To me, both the brutality of the Egyptian secret police, and the brutality of Zawahiri, come through in that in ways that lots of books fail to communicate, and we'll come back to that. Now I want to shift into a mode that's a little bit less forward looking, and try and get a condensation, if it's impossible, of where this movement came from. But I want to begin by looking at your author's note at the end, when you talk at great length about a number of different aspects. And at one point, you surprise me by saying "I've had to compromise on reporting things I believed to be true, but cannot prove." And you reference a Prince Turkey note.

LW: Right.

HH: You don't mean to say you didn't report anything you didn't believe was true, but that there were things that you thought you could not put in here, because they had not been adequately sourced, or were contradicted?

LW: Exactly. You know, there were plenty of tantalizing rumors, and sometimes, they came from rather authoritative sources. Like an example is, I was told by two different…well, Gilles Kepel and Olivier Roy, two French scholars of great repute, they're wonderful scholars; both of them had heard this story that in the battle of Jalalabad in 1989, when the Soviets had left, and the Afghan communists' government was trying to defend that city, bin Laden, and several of his supporters captured a garrison of troops who were out at the airport, and they cut them into pieces, and put them inside boxes, and sent them inside a truck to the garrison troops in Jalalabad with a note saying this is what happens to unbelievers. Well, that was interesting. You know, I mean, it was the first real evidence of this kind of bloodthirstiness that's so characteristic of bin Laden and his movement. I hadn't seen that before. But neither Gilles nor Olivier were present, and so I had to seek out people that were actually in the battle of Jalalabad that were with bin Laden, and Arab reporters who have covered it, and Afghan troops. I couldn't find anybody who would substantiate it. But I had two really good sources. And I just chose not to print it.

HH: And so, I tell that to people so that they understand that which does appear has been very, very deeply sourced, and we're going to get to that after one more preliminary. Also in the author's note, I owe a particular debt to Richard A. Clarke, who is a very patient tutor in the way of Washington. Now Clarke is a very controversial figure with my audience, with a lot of audiences. Not because of the work he did in the 90's, but the tales he told before the 9/11 Commission. Where do you assess his credibility, Lawrence Wright? I've had friends who worked with him on the NSC, close friends of mine, tell me Dick Clarke was always about Dick Clarke first. But that doesn't necessarily disqualify him from being better than most, not as good as some in the 90's.

LW: You know, when I first met Dick, it was right after 9/11. I was desperate to find a way to write about what had happened. I was looking at online obituaries that were streaming in, and I found this obituary for John O'Neill, whom we just talked about. And I thought, it made him sound like a disgrace, honestly, that he had been kind of forced out of the Bureau, and had become the chief of security at the World Trade Center, had died that day. And I didn't know what to make of him, but I decided this is the way I'm going to get into the story. That's where I began. And one of the people that had never talked to the press before at that point was Dick Clarke. He was very close to O'Neill. But when I called him up, he returned my call. And he said, "You know, I'm doing this because I want John's kids to know what kind of man he was." This is before most people knew the name of Richard Clarke. And he was very patient with me, because I didn't understand the inner workings of the National Security Council, or how the FBI and the CIA dealt with each other, or refused to deal with each other. He was remarkably candid. So I understand that many people find him a controversial subject. But in terms of being a tutor in the ways of Washington, you couldn't find a better one.

HH: Now I'm going to ask you, was the source for...there's a very compelling anecdote on pages 291 and 292, when the CIA finds bin Laden in the company of some United Arab

Emirate princes, who were out hawking in Afghanistan for an endangered bird.

LW: Yeah.

HH: And Osama is moving in and out of this camp, and Scheuer comes up with a plan, and the Pentagon readies its cruise missiles, and Dick Clarke says no, I'm not going to advance this one. We could kill the UAE royal family…

LW: Right.

HH: We could end up this way. Who told you that story? Was it Clarke?

LW: Well, it was Scheuer and Clarke. You know, both of them. Any time I found something like that, I'd try to talk to both parties. So I had both of them tell me about it.

HH: Now you have a neutral voice in this book. But looking back at that, ought they to have fired on that party?

LW: You know, the thing that Scheuer admits, he never could find bin Laden. He just knew he was there. He knew that bin Laden was coming in and out of that region. He couldn't see his camp. I mean, it was odd to me that he could see the falcons on the mast through satellite imagery, but he couldn't spot where bin Laden might be staying. So on balance, I feel like you have to have the man actually in your targets in order to pull the trigger. We've made mistakes before. I mean, you know, the CIA was under the impression, for instance, that bin Laden is a physical giant, which his friends say he's not. He's about 6' or 6' 1".

HH: And under the impression that he had kidney failure, that to this day, I didn't know was an urban myth until I read your book.

LW: Yeah. Well, there are many of these myths that I suffered from as well when I started. In 2001, after 9/11, when predator drones were going through Afghanistan, they shot down a man who was tall, because he was tall. Now it makes a difference whether your information is correct. But they found a tall man, and they killed him. If bin Laden's only six foot tall, then that poor fellow was the subject of a mighty dose of misinformation.

HH: And we've had misinformation about the Sudan aspirin factory, and before that, about...

LW: Oh, yeah. Many tragedies in the way.

HH: Many in this war.

HH: Before we turn to Sayyid Qutb, Lawrence Wright, there was a controversy recently about an ABC series, the Path to 9/11, a five-hour mini-series. Did you watch it?

LW: No. That speech is both nights, so I missed it.

HH: [From the accounts that you have heard...sometime, when you see it,] I'd like you to see it. It seems to me that you would find it very fair, if in one or two minutes, overdramatic because of the narrative you provided, which I read after seeing the movie. And it just seems it would be interesting to get your reaction to that. Let's begin with Sayyid Qutb, about whom a few people have heard, but not nearly as many, [as need to]and certainly [don't know] that he spent some time in Greeley, Colorado. . .

LW: Oh, great.

HH: (laughing) Yes, we've got a lot of Greeley listeners, so please tell them their history, and their involvement in the production of al Qaeda.

LW: Well, first of all, I want to thank the citizens of Greeley for being so hospitable to me when I was there. I had a great time. Sayyid Qutb was an Egyptian writer and educator who came to America in 1948. And it was a time when America's standing in the Arab world, Muslim world, was really high. And Americans' opinion of themselves was pretty high. You know, we were just on a post-war party, and really in a kind of triumphalist mode. Qutb saw a different America, and he spent much of that time in that little northern Colorado town, going to an education school there. For one thing, he was a very dark Egyptian, so he saw that racist side of America. One of his roommates recalls that they went to a movie. And at that time, Qutb loved American movies. And the theater owner said you can't come in, you're Negroes. And one of them said, no, no, we're not Negroes, we're Egyptians. And the theater owner said oh, very well, you can come in. And Qutb drew himself up and said well, if you will not let a black American in, this black Egyptian refuses to enter. So he saw that side of America. He was also really appalled, but also highly titillated by the sexuality that he encountered. He was a middle-aged, teetotalling Egyptian virgin. And I think that the kind of excited atmosphere, that he was so charged. When he writes about it, it's almost pornographic. And there was no bars in the city, because it was a temperance colony. You would think it would be a perfect place for him. But these farming ranch girls that would come in, and they were very frank about sexuality. They really unsettled him, and he thought that the preachers were in league with the devil, because there were these Church dances that were sponsoring dates between girls and boys. All these things horrified him. He went back to Egypt, and he wrote a book about his adventures in America that was very influential. But the book that really started things up was one that he wrote called Ma'alim fi-l-Tariq, which means signposts along the way, or <u>Milestones</u>, it usually is translated. And in there, he talked about how there was no pure Islamic society anymore. There was no way for a Muslim to be truly Muslim any longer, that we needed to purify Islamic society. And he called for a vanguard of Muslim youth to rise up and overthrow their infidel rulers, and create a pure Islamic society. That's the book that Zawahiri and bin Laden and all the future al Qaedaistas read.

HH: <u>Milestones</u>?

LW: <u>Milestones</u>. And there…actually, Hugh, there's a direct connection between Qutb's life and Zawahiri. The last man to see Sayyid Qutb alive before Nasser, the president of Egypt, hanged him in 1966, was…he's now a labor lawyer in Cairo. His name is Mafouz Azan. And he was also Qutb's lawyer, and his protégé. And the year that Nasser hanged Qutb, Ayman al Zawahiri was in a cell to overthrow the Egyptian government. He was fifteen years old.

HH: When we talk about Sayyid Qutb, Lawrence Wright, we're talking about Salafist fundamentalism, and Wahabist fundamentalism. We're not talking about Ahmadinejad's Shiia, 12th imam thing.

LW: Right.

HH: And there's not much about the latter. Before we go back to Egypt in 1950, which do you view as the greater threat to America at this hour?

LW: It's an interesting question, Hugh. They're both very dangerous in their own way. And I think that the real threat is that they are collaborating in certain ways. I've written about al Qaeda's master plan, its grand plan. And one of the things that al Qaeda would love to see happen [is to have happen,] is to have the U.S. and Iran in a real conflict, because it would accomplish things that al Qaeda can't do for itself. Like al Qaeda would love to destroy the oil facilities in Saudi Arabia and Kuwait. Iran can do that. al Qaeda can't. Al Qaeda would love to have Hezbollah activated against Israel and the U.S. Al Qaeda can't do that, but Iran can. So that's a part of their strategy, if they could accomplish it. So I think they're more dangerous together than they are separately. And we'd be really wise not to try to follow their playbook, which is to draw us deeper into conflict with Iran and Syria. And they're great readers of American political theory, and Paul Kennedy's book, The Rise And Fall Of Great Powers…you know that book?

HH: Yes.

LW: In there, he talks about imperial overreach. And this is central to their idea, of their plan for America, is to draw us deeper and deeper into these regions, so that our grip becomes less and less strong, and eventually, we're way too overextended.

HH: I don't want to digress too far, though. But if Ahmadinejad makes a speech as he made yesterday, and if I have it available, I'll play for you the end of that. Did you happen to hear…that he made on Tuesday. Did you happen to hear his…

LW: No, I didn't hear it.

HH: He closed it with a most extraordinary prayer that called for the 12th imam's urgent return. Would you ever want that government to have nukes, Lawrence Wright?

LW: You know, no. I don't want them to. But we were likely to see this happen, though, Hugh. We've already had, of course, an Islamist government in Pakistan that developed a nuclear bomb before Musharraf came into power. So although very dangerous, and their contacts with Hezbollah, I think, make it even more dangerous, it may not be something that we can actually stop. So I think we're going to have to find a way to negotiate our way out of this, because the alternative is not very rewarding, I don't think.

HH: Well, we'll have to come back to that a different day, because I don't want to lose the thread. We're back in Egypt in 1950…and we disagree, but we'll just put it aside.

LW: Yeah.

HH: Sayyid Qutb returns to Egypt, and this is the time when Faruq is so profligate, and such a disgusting figure. Nasser raises up his coups. They cooperate with Qutb, they fall out, and Nasser executes him. What's the effect on the Muslim brothers of this period?

LW: Well, you know, Nasser had thought he had crushed the whole movement. He rounded up as many of them as he could find, and threw them into these concentration camps. You know, I happened to live in Egypt during that time. I was there from '69-'71, teaching at the American University in Cairo. And I was there when Nasser died, and Sadat came to power. And Sadat made the unfortunate calculation that he could let these guys out of prison, and work out an agreement with them. I could see where he would think that, because he was an extremely pious Muslim himself. He had the prayer mark on his forehead, which was very unusual when we lived there. I mean, you didn't see women in hijabs or black abayas, and stuff like that, like you do now in Egypt. And Egyptians actually made fun of that prayer mark, although now, you see it everywhere. But he calculated that he was a pious Muslim himself, and that he could deal with the radical fringe that was so popular in the Muslim Brotherhood and other groups. But he completely miscalculated.

HH: When the secular Arab leaders miscalculated, and executed Qutb, or then Sadat let the brothers out of prison, you begin to turn to the story of Ayman al-Zawahiri, which in many ways, he's a much more evil character than Osama, though it's hard to put gradations on this. Tell people about where he came from, his background, and how he became the brains, possibly, of al Qaeda.

LW: You know, he is a fascinating guy. I don't know exactly who it would be. The family is not at the level the Kennedys or the Rockefellers, but they're really well known names in Egypt. The Zawahiris, on his father's side, were mostly doctors. His father was a professor of pharmacology, and his great-uncle was the head of al-Assar, the most prominent university in Islam, in Cairo, the oldest university in the world. And on his mother's side, the Azam side of the family, her father was a diplomat, founded a university in Saudi Arabia, had been the ambassador to Pakistan and Saudi Arabia. Her grandfather had founded the Arab League. So extremely prominent families on both sides. And so Ayman al-Zawahiri had a lineage that anybody in Cairo would have known about. He was himself a surgeon. And he was, as I said earlier, determined since a teenager to overthrow the Egyptian government, and had been working underground all of his life. In 1981, Sadat was assassinated by an organization that Zawahiri was associated with, and he was put into prison, along with more than…nearly 200 other Islamists. In that prison, he was really brutally tortured. And I think a lot of the brutality, the appetite for blood that is so characteristic of al Qaeda, comes out of that experience.

HH: Where did he go, Lawrence Wright?

LW: Well, he went, first of all, to Saudi Arabia. He went to work in a clinic in Jeddah, which was bin Laden's home town. And it might be that they met at that time, in 1984. And it would have been logical. One of my sources says that they did meet at that time, because both men, both Zawahiri and bin

Laden, were interested in the jihad against the Soviet invasion in Afghanistan. So young Egyptians were coming to Jeddah, where they were sent off to Afghanistan; and bin Laden was paying for that. So it could well have been that they met there. But if not then, in the next couple of years, they did meet in Bashawar in Pakistan, where the base for the resistance against the Soviets was established.

HH: And so he was, actually, quite the committed fanatic. He would travel back and forth to the front lines of the jihad in Afghanistan, and at quite considerable personal peril and expense to wage jihad at this point.

LW: This is bin Laden?

HH: No, I'm talking about Zawahiri.

LW: No, you know, the truth about Zawahiri is he didn't care about the jihad against the Soviets. He was only interested in overthrowing his own government.

HH: But didn't he go to the hospitals there?

LW: Yes, he did. But his real goal, Hugh, was not...he was a takfiri, which means one who excommunicates any other Muslim who doesn't believe as he did. And the takfiris excommunicated, in their minds, the entire nation of Afghanistan. They just didn't believe they were real Muslims. They were Sufis, for the most part. So they didn't take them seriously. What Zawahiri really wanted was to capture these young Egyptians, these idealists who were coming in to fight against the Soviets. He wanted to capture them and to train them, and then take them back to Egypt to overthrow the government. That was his real...

HH: But he's been a phenomenally, because of his personality, he has been phenomenally unsuccessful in molding his own terror network, is that...

LW: Yeah, you're absolutely right. He was not...he's certainly not a charismatic leader. But he did have a talent for organizing men around him. And when he met bin Laden, you know, sometimes, I think it must have been like Colonel Parker spot-

22

ting Elvis for the first time. He thought, you know, I can do something with this kid. Here was this wealthy, charismatic, young Saudi who had a dream, which was, at the time, he wanted to create a Muslim, an Arab foreign legion, something that could go anywhere and fight for Muslim causes. And mainly, he was an anti-communist organization at the time.

HH: This hour, let's begin, Lawrence Wright, with bin Laden's father, who comes out of Yemen, and simply by dint of extraordinary effort, builds a fortune of extraordinary size.

LW: You know, it's an amazing story, Hugh. And it's hard to understand Osama bin Laden without appreciating the figure, the titanic figure that his father is. Mohammed bin Laden walked out of Yemen in 1930 into Saudi Arabia. He was illiterate, he was missing one eye, and he was a hod carrier, essentially. And yet, he managed to build himself up a small construction company that eventually became the largest, privately-held company in the Middle East, and the largest construction company in Saudi Arabia. He built much of modern Saudi Arabia, the highways, the universities, the airports, the mosques, the schools. He renovated the holy mosque of Mecca and Medina. His hand is everywhere. You can't look around Saudi Arabia without seeing the bin Laden touch. And you know, he died when Osama was nine, and he'd divorced Osama's mother when Osama was around five. So Osama didn't know his father very well, but he lived in the shadow of this figure all of his life, and he was obsessed with kind of living up to that legend.

HH: And he began doing that by taking his part of the fortune, which was considerable, and establishing the base, al Qaeda, in Afghanistan, during jihad against the Soviets. Then quickly tell us where he moved from, because part of this is also the history of Saudi Arabia.

LW: Yeah.

HH: That's why the book is so compelling, and how their deal with the Wahabist clerics became sort of a suicide pact in many ways.

LW: Yeah, it's a fascinating tale, and one of the interesting anecdotes in the book is about the attack on the mosque in 1979.

HH: I didn't know any of this stuff, the French who convert to Islam in order to go in and try to pump poison gas in?

LW: It was a horrible fiasco in many ways. A group of radicals, in some ways, prototypes for the kind of al Qaeda thinkers that would be on the horizon, they seized the Grand Mosque during the Hadj. It was two weeks, the Saudi forces were struggling to evict them. It was a very bloody battle. It's hard to know, really, how many people died, but probably hundreds. And it wound up with the Saudis having to drill holes in the terrace above these warrens that were underground, and drop hand grenades in, to drive these people out. It was the bin Ladens, of course, the family's construction firm that had really built the mosque, and they, Salem bin Laden, one of bin Laden's eldest brothers, came out to help Prince Turkey al Faisal, who was the head of Saudi intelligence at the time, try to root these people out. And it's a little irony that bin Laden, Osama bin laden himself was actually arrested right after this. He was apparently coming from the family farm, which was near Mecca. And he was driving down a dirt road, leaving a trail of dust, and they thought, the authorities thought these were some of the radicals trying to escape. So he was held for several days. And at the time, he thought that this was a horrible desecration of Islam, but later, he came to believe that these were good Muslims. And much of what he says now about Saudi Arabia and Islam echoes the statements that these radicals made in 1979.

HH: Well, the extremist war against Saudi Arabia, itself a very extreme state when it comes to theological beliefs, begins, really, in '79 with this thing.

LW: Yeah.

HH: And somehow, bin Laden gets caught up in it, even though for a while, the Saudis thought he was doing great work.

LW: Yeah, and following...and 1979 was the earthquake year in Islam. You know, there was this Grand Mosque attack, and that was the year that the Shah fell, and the Ayatollah came to power, showing so many radicals that it is possible to take over a very important country, and turn it into a theocracy. And then, of course, you had the invasion of the Soviets into Afghanistan that same year. It just completely rocked the Islamic world. [And it was...] Bin Laden, like every young Muslim, was shaken by this, and the invasion into Afghanistan was particularly upsetting to him. And that's where eventually, he decided to put his energy.

HH: After the driving out the Soviets, and after the warlord period begins in Afghanistan, he finds himself in Sudan, as does Zawahiri. And in fact, it sort of underscores, both Sudan and Afghanistan, Lawrence Wright, that the Bush administration's policy of they cannot be allowed to nest somewhere, because all of the terrorists will find them. It's extraordinary how they've all met and eaten and supped together, and plotted together.

LW: You know, it's actually...and I see this as kind of a paradox, Hugh. Sudan was an open country for terrorists. You know, they had an Islamic revolution, and they opened their doors to anybody, any Muslim who wanted to come. And naturally, the ones who came were the ones that weren't invited anywhere else. And so even...you had Carlos the Jackal there, and Abu Nidal, and all these different terrorist groups. And you had bin Laden, who had some money to give them. And it was in...during the Clinton administration, in 1996, that it was decided that bin Laden posed a threat by just being there. And so American authorities put pressure on the Sudanese to expel him. And the Sudanese first of all said well, do you want him? And you know, we didn't have an indictment on bin Laden. There wasn't very much that we could do with him. At the time, it may be that he hadn't killed any Americans yet. So we said no.

HH: We being who?

LW: We being the State Department, and the NSC.

HH: Quite a lot of debate over whether or not President Clinton was involved in that decision. What do your researches tell you?

LW: Well, they did want to…you know, the Clinton administration clearly wanted to force bin Laden out of Sudan. They thought it was dangerous for him to be there. But the Sudanese argued, listen, he's going to go to Afghanistan. Here, he's under watch. Here, he has investments. You know, at least you know his address. If he goes to Afghanistan, nobody will be in control.

HH: But when…let me press you on this point. When Sudan offered bin Laden to the United States, and we said no, and you said State Department and NSC, do you think President Clinton was involved in that decision?

LW: Well, you know, it certainly reflects his administration's policies.

HH: Because he said something to the effect that he was. But that's a presser. You never can tell when they're talking off the cuff.

LW: Well, you know, I can understand their concern, but they weren't thinking about the fact the Sudanese really did have a point. You know, he's dangerous, but he's under our watch. Well, we did…they did, at our instruction, expel bin Laden. And on the way out the door, they picked his pockets.

HH: Oh, that is amazing, yeah.

LW: Yeah, he was never really as rich as we've thought. He was worth only about $7 million dollars, which was his share of the bin Laden construction company. And the Saudis had cut him off of that, and they also cut off his annual allowance, which on some really good years, amounted to as much as half a million dollars. His own investments weren't making any money. But nonetheless, they were substantial, and the Sudanese authorities divvied them up among themselves. Abu Rida al-Suri, who was bin Laden's business manager and good friend, told me in Khartoum that when bin Laden left there, he was worth about $50,000. But the intelligence agent who held the file on al Qaeda for the Sudanese government said he left here with nothing.

HH: Wow. Before we get to break, and we go to Afghanistan with bin Laden, we also have to introduce the blind sheik into this, because although he's in federal prison, in the harshest of lockdown conditions, along with Ramzi Youssef, he was, for a time, a competitor, a different franchise, operating with the same objective. How come he lost, in a manner of speaking, and ends up in New York, and bin Laden ends up in Afghanistan with Zawahiri?

LW: Well, you know, [bin Laden...excuse me] the blind sheik, Adbel Rahman, and Zawahiri were in prison together. [And they were...] Their efforts were very closely tied, but they were really competitors. And they had many quarrels in the prisons about the future of the Islamist movement. And they were always competitors, too, for bin Laden and his money. And in this sense, Zawahiri showed his organizational genius by surrounding bin Laden with his own men, so that he kind of captured him.

HH: So in effect, having the blind sheik, leaving him no choice but to go to America.

LW: Yeah.

HH: Lawrence Wright, bin Laden gets to Afghanistan, and all terrorist roads start to run to him, although the original relationship with Mullah Omar, as you recount, is somewhat strained, and at times, tenuous. But we failed to break it, the Saudis failed to break it, and he begins to flourish, and he runs these camps. And into these camps comes Khalid Sheikh Mohammed, and other terrorists who would be behind the embassy bombings, the Cole bombing, and ultimately, 9/11. How did we not see what was coming, when all terror suspects in the world are going in and out of bin Laden's camps, and talking to Zawahiri?

LW: It's a little mysterious, Hugh, at how badly we fumbled it, because when Zawahiri had come to America, and his own man, Ali Mohammed, a great story, had tried to penetrate American intelligence...actually did kind of penetrate American intelligence, and he had revealed the existence of al Qaeda in 1993. But that never got up to the top. And then in 1996, we get it from an al Qaeda defector, you know, straight from the real source, as bin Laden's former secretary. And he outlines the whole thing for us. And then in August of that year, bin Laden declares war on America. And then in 1998, he actually bombs the American embassies, after warning on CNN that he was about to do something drastic. So again and again, we were getting messages that this guy really posed a problem to us. And even after the American embassy bombings, there were people in American intelligence that just didn't take it seriously. It was only after that, that al Qaeda went on the State Department terrorism list. And even then, they weren't devoting that much attention to the real problem that al Qaeda posed.

HH: But in classic FBI fashion, they were after Ramzi Youssef. And they got him, because he had killed New Yorkers in the first World Trade Center attack. And to a certain extent, they were what? Chasing the minor capo in the organization, not seeing what was going on at the top?

LW: You know, I would say that after the embassy bombings… I have to credit the FBI with doing a wonderful investigation of that, and they got a lot of convictions, and they indicted bin Laden early on. So they did know, but there was not a real strong governmental effort to actually get him. As I said, we didn't have the ability, we didn't have the people on the ground. One of the heroes in my book is Ali Sufan, this 29-year-old Arab-American who was the case agent on the Cole bombing in October of 2000. And he was one of 8 FBI agents in the entire country who spoke Arabic, the only one in New York. And I'm afraid that hasn't changed. Last week, the FBI graduated a new class of fifty new agents, and only one of them speaks a foreign language at all.

HH: Right. Let's talk a little bit, then, about one of the most despairing passages, is the refusal of the CIA to work with the FBI, and the FBI's arrogance back to the CIA, the famous wall.

LW: Yeah.

HH: I played earlier Pink Floyd's number. That was actually part of the musical repertoire of the CIA. Explain to people how.

LW: Well, the best way to explain this is that I just mentioned Ali Sufan. When he and John O'Neill, and other investigators were looking into the Cole bombing, they uncovered evidence that was leading to several al Qaeda personalities into a meeting that had taken place somewhere in Southeast Asia, as it happens, Kuala Lumpur, in January of 2000. Three times, Sufan, the FBI, formally request through the director's office to the director of the CIA, formal request for information about that meeting. Three times, the CIA refuses to respond. Now there was no legal wall, or legal reason for them to do so. There's a culture that had grown up, they were very, very jealous of surrendering information. Just leave aside the fact, you know, that meeting in Kuala Lumpur was between the Cole bombers and two hijackers who would then come to America. Here was Ali Sufan and his team investigating the death of 17 American sailors, and the CIA essentially is obstructing justice. Well, of course, the CIA did know about that meeting. They actually asked the Malaysian authorities to surveil it. They had photographs. They found out that in January of 2000, two hijackers, two would...future hijackers, two known al Qaeda members, flew from Kuala Lumpur to Los Angeles, then went to San Diego. They knew in March of 2000, a year and a half before 9/11, that al Qaeda was in America, and they refused to tell the FBI.

HH: On this program, Christopher Hitchens, Vanity Fair writer, has asserted that on the morning of 9/11, George Tenet, upon learning of the attacks, said, "I hope it wasn't the guys in the flight school." Do you credit that? Or is that apocryphal?

LW: Hugh, I don't know how far up the chain the information about these two al Qaeda hijackers went. Certainly, there were people that were in the top of Alec Station, not Mike Scheuer...

HH: You've got to explain what Alec Station is to people.

LW: Alec Station was the virtual bin Laden station, that was recently abandoned. [But it was create...] It was to pursue and find bin Laden, set up in 1996. And there were people there that knew because of the following of the Malaysian meeting, and the participants there, they knew that these people had come into the U.S. I don't know how far it passed up. I could not get cooperation from the CIA to talk to the people that were involved.

HH: Would George Tenet cooperate with you?

LW: No.

HH: How about Sandy Berger?

LW: I talked to Berger, but very briefly. He wasn't very happy. (laughing)

HH: How about Janet Reno?

LW: I could never get her to call me back.

HH: Louis Freeh?

LW: We exchanged e-mails on several occasions.

HH: Do you think…you know, there's a cast of characters in the 90's, Reno and Freeh and Tenet and Perry and Cohen and Berger and Albright. Did any of them really believe there was a threat out there, in your estimate, Lawrence Wright?

LW: No, they say they do. I think that the people that really believed there was a threat, people know that they believed that. I mean, it was obvious with O'Neill, for instance.

HH: Right.

LW: He was publicly saying it. It was obvious with Scheuer. He made himself very unpopular in the CIA, because he was constantly hectoring them about what a threat bin Laden was. So if, for instance, Sandy Berger really felt that way, and if George Tenet had really declared war, as he says, you would think that there would be people that remembered that.

HH: But Scheuer and O'Neill are also hating each other with an intensity that springs off of your pages.

LW: It's such a tragedy. It makes tears come to your eyes. Here are two really powerful, insightful, driven men. I mean, driven… you rarely run into anybody in life who are so obsessed, and so compelling in their pursuit of bin Laden. And yet because of personal rivalries, and bureaucratic turf wars, they hated each other. And it was, for instance, when O'Neill put the FBI man in Alec Station, Scheuer just thought they were spies. That's the way he treated them.

HH: I want to go to our allies, and their methods, Lawrence Wright. We've touched on Egypt's, we touched on Saudi Arabia's. Can they ever kill off this extremism? Or do their methods inevitably bring more of the extremists to the fore?

LW: That's the paradox that we face, Hugh. You know, the kill and capture approach has…we've succeeded in killing and capturing hundreds, maybe thousands. But we've created as many more, or if not, even more. And it's…it is a truism that it is a battle of ideas. I think this is a long term conflict, that we're going to be dealing with for a good long time. And that it's al Qaeda, and the kind of Islamist radicalism, will only be defeated by creating a certain kind of hope in the Muslim world. You know, you can't spend a lot of time in that part of the world without coming to grips with the futility, the sense of helplessness and despair that's so characteristic of young people's lives there. I had…I couldn't get into Saudi Arabia as a reporter. You know, they wouldn't let me in. So after a year and four months, I realized I'd have to take a job, so I got a job teaching. It was the best piece of bad luck. I got a job mentoring these young reporters in Jeddah, bin Laden's home town. And so I got acquainted with Saudi life in a way that I could never have had the privilege of doing if I'd just been a reporter in a hotel room making my calls. And my reporters, just to give you a sense of what their life was like, there are no movies, no theaters, no plays, no nightclubs, no music, very few parks or museums, no political life at all, no political parties, no unions. There's very little to do. And there's very little for them, very few opportunities for them to express themselves in the world. And that sense of futility and helplessness is so pervasive. If you can fight that, if you can help them have more productive economy…

HH: But you're raising, Lawrence Wright, something that the Islamists don't want. They want that life, don't they? Isn't that the essence…

LW: It's the most perverse thing in the world, isn't it, Hugh?

HH: Yeah.

LW: That what does the Muslim world need to be liberated from? Well, from ignorance and from poverty, and from repressive political societies. Those are the things that would really bring hope to that part of the world, and equality with the rest of the world, which they…and would overcome the sense of humiliation that they constantly refer to. But al Qaeda doesn't offer that to them.

HH: And they don't want it. I mean, if you go back to <u>Milestones</u>, I think you did a tremendous service in portraying…this isn't born of poverty, in many respects, and you go through the hijackers. This is born out of religious zealotry, that desires that fierce asceticism that is very off putting to some, but intensely attractive to others, that they want to be martyrs.

LW: Yeah, yeah. There's one thing that al Qaeda does offer, is death. And you know, I've been thinking recently, from our point of view, al Qaeda is a terrorist organization. But if you look at it from the point of view of those who join al Qaeda, it's a suicide organization.

HH: Yeah, it's a death cult.

LW: And I was very affected by a remark a reporter, a Pakistani reporter made to me several years ago…his name is Raham Ali Youssef-I, and he had covered the war against the Soviets. And he came upon a contingent of these Arabs, and there weren't very many of them, and they had no effect on the war against the Soviets at all. But there they were, camped outside on a plain in white tents. And he said, "What are you doing?" You know, the Soviets will, their air force will see you, and wipe you out. And one of the Arabs said to him, but we came to die. And that's the culture in which al Qaeda was created, this sense of longing for martyrdom.

HH: And it's…when we come back for our next segment, it contrasts with John O'Neill drinking, out on the town at Elaine's, and eating until four in the morning, when the suicide attackers of 9/11 were ritually shaving themselves, and going through their suicide preparation. How the former can take on and defeat the latter, I don't know.

HH: Lawrence Wright, a couple of years ago, you wrote for the New Yorker, The Terror Web. I tried to book you a couple of times since then, but you've been all over the world writing The Looming Tower. The Terror Web was an eye-opener, in that al Qaeda metastasized after they lost their base, after the American invasion of Afghanistan, even as 80-85% of their people were killed. You closed this book with Zawahiri and bin Laden riding into Pakistan, escaping Anaconda. Have you followed, since you wrote the Terror Web for the New Yorker, which is available on the Web, the continuing iteration of the sort of metastasized al Qaeda?

LW: Yeah, I just recently did a piece for the magazine called The Master Plan. And I'd been wondering what al Qaeda's plans for itself were. And it turns out they're very easy to obtain. Most of them are published on the Web. And some of them are actually in English, although I had a lot of the work translated from Arabic. The plan is basically rather chilling, although it's self-justifying, it is highly propagandistic in many ways, but sometimes, it's a little chilling to see how it's unfolded, and what they have in mind. Their 20 year plan is to…they wanted to entice America into conflict with the Muslim world, and that begins with 9/11, and the first stage ends with the fall of Baghdad. And their idea is that young jihadi recruits will stream into Iraq and get training. And then, they'll go back to their own countries, and wage jihad against their rulers, and eventually pull down those governments, establish a caliphate. And in the year 2020, they will create an Islamic army that will wage a final apocalyptic battle with the unbelievers. That's their plan.

HH: They intend war.

LW: Yes, they do. The al Qaeda strategists, you know, intend this to be a battle to the finish. That doesn't mean that everybody that's drawn to al Qaeda has those kind of absurd, Utopian goals. There are people that go into it for very narrow reasons, and it could be combatted by addressing some of the intense political problems in the region. But it's gotten…it's fascinating to me to see how al Qaeda has evolved over time, from being an organization that…mainly, bin Laden's big goal was to get the American troops out of Saudi Arabia. You know, if you had sat him down in 2002, or early 2003, and said what's your goal, get the Americans out of the holy land. And then, the Americans got out. In April of 2003, the troops which were there to enforce the no-fly rule against Saddam Hussein, the American administration said you know, Saddam is gone, we're going to remove our troops. In May, the very next month, al Qaeda began its assaults on the foreigners housing compounds in Saudi Arabia. And it seemed a very clear statement that they weren't going to be appeased, or mollified by any moves in the direction of what was their stated goal.

HH: And so, they're not going to be appeased. They have this master plan, and to engage, obviously, in Iraq is one part of it. But although bin Laden was originally opposed, Zawahiri is very committed to weapons of mass destruction. Will they use those if they come into the possession of them?

LW: They certainly would. I mean, there's no reason for them to hesitate to use it. It's been a long term goal of al Qaeda to acquire a bomb, or any kind of weapon of mass destruction. Bin Laden himself was more wedded to the idea of the nuclear bomb. And Zawahiri was always interested in anthrax. That was one of the things he was very keen on. And there was another Egyptian, Abu Kabob, who was creating a kind of nerve gas, that was really…

HH: He's killing all the dogs, and watching them die.

LW: Yeah, it took the dogs five hours to die. But they've always had an interest in WMD. And I'm sure that if they had such a weapon, they would employ it as soon as they could.

HH: Now let me ask you. What do you think would be the consequences of a rapid, or an immediate withdrawal of American troops from Iraq?

LW: My fear is that Iraq will turn into an even wider scale civil war than it already has, under way, and that it might spill over into other regions. One of the problems with Iraq is although people are talking about dividing it, it doesn't divide up very easily. And so, the Kurdish area might, but other than that, there'll be just huge amount of conflict over territory and ethnic bloodletting. I don't know that we can prevent it. I just observe that that might well be the consequence.

HH: I also, in a couple of pages, I'm not going to make you too popular with some people. On pages 295 and 296, you review the history of Saddam's connection with al Qaeda, tentative, but not dismissive of it at all. Have the post-war documents that have begun to arrive changed your understanding of that relationship?

LW: Not at all. I think you know, I think it's pretty clear that Saddam had toyed with the idea of enlisting al Qaeda, and was rebuffed. [He had,] Saudi intelligence had told me that he had sent minions over to Sudan when bin Laden was there, between '92 and '96. And they flattered bin Laden, and told him he was the Mahdi, or the messiah of the Islamic world. And that didn't get him anywhere. And then we sent, again, when bin Laden went to Afghanistan, on both occasions, bin Laden expressed no interest.

HH: And so, Saddam wanted them, but he did not get them?

LW: Yeah.

HH: Now...30 seconds to our break. Is the Mubarak way, in your opinion, Lawrence Wright, the only way in the Arab world to deal with this?

LW: No, no. I don't think so.

HH: I'm glad to hear you say that.

HH: First, Lawrence Wright, thank you. That's a lot of time out of your schedule. I see you've given a lot of long form interviews. Are you surprised by the interest?

LW: You know, I'm really pleased, because people seem very hungry to understand this situation, and they want it laid out in context. They don't want soundbytes. They really want to understand what's going on.

HH: Against that backdrop, I need sort of a two minute sound-byte. What ought to be the strategy here, vis-à-vis, we'll put the Shiia menace aside in Iran, the 12th imam stuff, and just focus on al Qaeda, versus them. You get two minutes with the President. What's the speech?

LW: All right. First, fix the intelligence by hiring people who actually speak Arabic natively, and Pashto, and Urdu, the languages you actually have to, the cultures you have to work against. We're not going to understand…it'll always be a failure of imagination if you have people that simply aren't from those cultures fighting it. And secondly, I think that I believe in the democratization process. I don't abandon that. But it's going to be ugly, and it's not going to be always very rewarding. I think Hamas in the future, we'll see that again and again. But the thing about democracy that I genuinely believe is that it is an inherently moderating force. I think you can see that even right now with Hamas having to come to grips with being in power. They have to answer to the needs of the people. Turkey is a good example of a Islamist movement that has come into power and has had to adapt. So I say let them come to power through democratic processes, and it may not be pretty. But we can't control everything. But if we do have people who are democratically elected, then we've got a better chance to have real partners.

HH: Have you seen the rise within Islam of reasonable…I hope you understand, reasonable fanatics, people who are reasonable fundamentalists?

LW: Yeah, and it's funny you would ask it in that way, Hugh. You know, where they are, oddly enough, they're in prison in Egypt. There's some of the leaders of Gama Islamiya and even al Jahad, Zawahiri's old organization, have been…they've had a considerable amount of time to think things over, and they've been writing very stern articles and books about the failure of the radical and violent approach, and how it steered the movement into a catastrophe, and that how the actions of al Qaeda's suicide bombings, the murder of innocents, and all are against Islam. Those are the voices that people will listen to, and I think we should encourage that kind of dialogue, and find an opening to talk to them.

HH: Lawrence Wright, yours is a voice I hope everyone listens to, and a book I hope everyone buys and reads. The Looming Tower: Al Qaeda And The Path To 9/11. Thanks for a lot of your time. I very much appreciate it.

LW: Hugh, it was great. Thanks for having me.

End of interview.

Interview with Lawrence Wright
September 11, 2007

HH: It's Hugh Hewitt on a special edition, an anniversary of 9/11 edition with Lawrence Wright as my guest. Lawrence Wright, of course, the Pulitzer Prize winning author of The Looming Tower: al Qaeda And The Road To 9/11, perhaps the single most important book for any interested observer of al Qaeda to begin with and read. Lawrence Wright, welcome back to the program, great to have you.

LW: Thank you, it's good to be back on.

HH: Well, now it's out in paperback, and we're talking on the 6th anniversary of 9/11. In the six years since they launched the successful attack on America, Lawrence Wright, how is al Qaeda faring in the world?

LW: Well, it's a mixed report. You know, al Qaeda central has been, to some extent, reduced, isolated. It's been unable to accomplish many of its major goals, especially capturing a Muslim country, and restoring the caliphate, and creating a kind of theocratic law. That it's failed to do. But on the other hand, essentially after November, December, 2001, after the

Tora Bora battle, al Qaeda was pretty much a zombie. It was over. The war on terror was at an end, and it's been amazing to see how that organization has been able to reconstitute itself. It's now deeply rooted in a lot of countries where it wasn't present before. The banner of al Qaeda has been taken up by a lot of disaffected young Muslims around the world who hadn't been interested in it before. So on balance, I think it's as dangerous as it was before 9/11, but in different ways.

HH: What does the new bin Laden transcript tell you, the videotape that he released last week?

LW: Well, it's a peculiar document. For one thing, I'm always amused by his kind of commentary on American politics, and you know, averting to the Kyoto treaty and stuff like that, that you know, where he does this kind of second-rate commentary on the American political scene. I think that the message that he wants to get out is that he's still a threat, he's still relevant, and he wants…I think he's probably not capable of carrying out the high-scale attacks that he has accomplished in the past, but he wants us to think that. And so by rattling the cages periodically, he accomplishes at least keeping us unnerved.

HH: There is some concern always that he signals awakening of sleeper cells with this. Does that still concern intelligence agencies that you stay in touch with, Lawrence Wright?

LW: Well, it concerns me in that I know…the title of my book, for instance, The Looming Tower, was a quotation that bin Laden used three times in a speech that was found on the hijacker's computer, and I suspect that that was a go-ahead signal. So I am concerned that he may use, and Zawahiri as well, the number two man, use the public media as a way of communicating with his followers.

HH: Now Lawrence Wright, in The Looming Tower, which I listened to to prepare for this. I'd read it twice before, but it's a very different experience listening to it. I think it may force someone to slow down and absorb a lot that just flows out of this book. He has a theory of American character that posited we would run away as soon as we took a series of blows.

LW: Right.

HH: Is the anger towards Bush in this most recent document the fact that the one thing he thought he knew best about the West has just proven not to be the case?

LW: No, I think that he is frustrated that we're still in Iraq. And honestly, Hugh, there's a…I think al Qaeda's a little frustrated in Iraq as well, you know, they're still in Iraq. That's where al Qaeda's preoccupied, and where it's been pouring all of its resources in, and it doesn't have much to show for it, either. It's been frankly a draw. Al Qaeda's in a great public relations situation, whereas if we withdraw, then they can say that they won, and that they defeated the other superpower. And if we stay, then Iraq is still a beacon for disaffected jihadis who want to go join the war. So they are in an enviable position, but really, they haven't accomplished what they hope to do in Iraq.

HH: Now in yesterday's testimony, General Petraeus, in response to a question, affirmed that the largest number of jihadis in Iraq that are coming from outside of Iraq are still coming from the Kingdom, from Saudi Arabia.

LW: Yeah.

HH: What does that tell you about what has and has not happened since 9/11 in the Kingdom?

LW: Well, the Kingdom ran into problems with this in Afghanistan. There's a precedent for this. And you know, they funded it, they supported…and we did, too, they supported the Mujahideen, but there was a blowback in the Kingdom in the form of al Qaeda, and bin Laden's legacy. I am afraid that the Saudis are in the crosshairs of the next step of jihad. And you know, there's a reason why young Saudis leave the Kingdom to go fight the jihad, because they would rather fight it in their own country. And that's the goal of al Qaeda. They want to train these young men, and then turn them against the regimes in their own countries. It's a mistake for the Saudis to not clamp down much stronger on these young men who are leaving the Kingdom and then joining the jihad. But they're in a fix. They want to show their support for the Sunnis, and the Sunnis are under attack in Iraq. And so it's a real paradox for the Saudis.

HH: Lawrence Wright, earlier this week, I talked with Robert Kaplan, who's got a new book out on the American military. He spent some time in Algeria. Algeria succeeded in suppressing its Salafist insurgency. Why do they accomplish that and the Sauds can't?

LW: Well, Algeria's now having new problems with what is now called al Qaeda in the Islamic Maghreb, which has been able to pull off several very devastating bombings. So I wouldn't say that the story's finished in Algeria. And the Saudis have waged a very bloody war against their own Qaedistas in the Kingdom. Hundreds of Saudis have been killed at the hands of al Qaeda, and ex-pat workers as well. And I think that the Saudi authorities are a little surprised at how resilient the local al Qaedas are.

HH: Where is the money coming from? One of the compelling narratives in The Looming Tower is how bin Laden was stunned when the King arranged for him to be cut off and disappropriated of his family's fortune, and how broke he was.

LW: Yeah.

HH: Where's their money coming from now?

LW: To start with, they don't need very much. Let's go back to the Embassy bombings in 1998, two simultaneous bombings in East Africa, operated by a sleeper cell in Nairobi, which maintained itself on a fishing boat they ran. They were pretty much a self-supporting outfit. Then you have 9/11, which was, you know, it cost half a million dollars or less. So they were not talking about a lot of money, and one of, and Ayman al-Zawahiri wrote to Zarqawi, who was the head of al Qaeda in Iraq at one point a couple of years ago before Zarqawi was killed. And he asked for a hundred thousand dollars. Well, doesn't that figure strike you as being rather small?

HH: Yeah.

LW: And it's kind of pathetic. You know, we're stuck here, wherever we are, and we need the gift of a hundred thousand dollars. That's all he's asking for.

HH: Does it mean, then, that no matter how much pressure we put on the financial system, they will continue to be able to survive as long as they're alive, because it doesn't take much to go to a cave and eat tuna?

LW: Listen, when they went from Sudan, the whole movement essentially emigrated from Khartoum to Afghanistan in 1996, when we forced the Sudanese to expel al Qaeda and its followers. And they were really destitute. They were living on well water, and they were eating green pomegranates. They were really close to penniless. And yet it was during that period that bin Laden was able to organize al Qaeda, pull them together, and pull off 9/11. I don't think that they need a lot of money to be very damaging.

HH: Let me conclude this first segment with you, Lawrence Wright, by asking about the incineration holocaust talk in bin Laden's latest missive. What is that all about?

LW: I think he's playing to the fears of many Westerners about weapons of mass destruction. And you know, he may have access to that, I don't know. I don't think so. I think that the most damaging weapons system that al Qaeda has explored is anthrax. And if they could make a step forward in weaponizing anthrax, as they were trying to do in Afghanistan, then that would be really a serious note.

HH: Lawrence Wright, before we go to the franchises of bin Laden's original organization, I want to just spend a couple more minutes on this latest message from him. As you recount in The Looming Tower, there came a moment when Zawahiri and bin Laden turned their organization from its focus on a coup in Egypt and Zawahiri's vision and hostility to America, to a really anti-Christian worldview.

LW: Yeah.

HH: This latest missive is back to being anti-capitalist, and warning about global warming. Have they morphed? Or is it just any straw that they can grab?

LW: Well, that might be an interesting way of looking at it. You know, the truth is, they're commenting on the American or Western political scene, and they have absolutely no politics of their own. If you look through all those Harmony documents, which are the documents that American and Coalition troops captured after the battles of Tora Bora, there are thousands of pages of internal al Qaeda documents. They haven't got a single page in there about their own political agenda, because they don't really have one. They're not interested in politics. They're only interested in purification. The Taliban are a perfect example of what al Qaeda would do. I mean, they leave government to others. They're mainly interested in excoriating Muslims. So it's so weird and hypocritical when bin Laden talks about the Kyoto treaty, when no one has ever asked him to produce his own environmental policy. He's never thought about it.

HH: When you're reading through The Looming Tower, I am, I realize that Zarqawi might have been this brute killer, and that bin Laden might be this clueless person, but the sinister guy is Dr. Zawahiri. And has he grown more or less sinister in all these years?

LW: Oh, he's really unchanged. The thing that a study of Dr. Zawahiri's life will lead you conclude is that there was only one important...maybe I should say there were two important events in Dr. Zawahiri's life. One was that in 1966, Gamal Abdel Nasser, who was the president of Egypt, who had taken over in a revolutionary coup, hanged Sayyid Qutb, who was the philosopher behind this whole radical Islamist movement. He wrote a book called Ma'alim fi-l-Tariq, which means milestones. And he was close to Zawahiri's family. That was in 1966. And in that year, Zawahiri started a cell to overthrow the Egyptian government. He was fifteen years old. The other signal event in his life was that in 1981, he was arrested following the assassination of Anwar Sadat, the president of Egypt, Nasser's successor. And he didn't have much of a role in the assassination, but he was placed in prison for three years, brutally tortured, as many of these guys were, and I think that the appetite for carnage that is so characteristic of al Qaeda, and which separates it, really, from any other terrorist group in history, I think that comes from the torture that these guys, the Egyptians, endured in those prisons. And al Qaeda is fundamentally an Egyptian organization with a Saudi head.

HH: You know, I repeat to people all the time that although our allies in Egypt and Saudi Arabia may be waging war on terror, they may be doing the hydra head thing, given your remarkable account of Zawahiri's torture, and those with him. Back up for a second to Sayyid Qutb. Again, I often talk to audiences, and I recommend your book, and I say you'll be surprised to learn that al Qaeda got a big lift out of its years in Greeley, Colorado. Would Qutb recognize al Qaeda today?

LW: You know, I had the opportunity to talk to his brother, Mohammed Qutb, who lives in Mecca. And he came out of Mecca to talk to me, and he's in his 90's, he's a very interesting man. And he strongly feels that his brother's work has been misrepresented, although when I read it, it's a little hard for me to see in what way, because he really was calling for a purification of Islam, a return to the fundamentals, to the life of the prophet. And he felt that Islam could not be lived in a modern-day Islamic country, because they weren't living under Sharia, and the pure Islamic way. And he called for a new generation to spring up and overthrow these governments and institute Sharia and so on. That is the beacon that drew bin Laden and all these other young jihadis.

HH: But did he intend to launch Takfiri? Did he intend to have his...the fiction writers who he mentored in Egypt end up being the targets of al Qaeda, as you describe here.

LW: Yeah, yes, that's interesting. The word Takfir that you just used is very key to understanding this. It means excommunicating another Muslim. In other words, it's not enough to say I am a Muslim. You have to prove to me that you are a Muslim in my view. And it first in modern times came up when

Sayyid Qutb was in prison in Egypt. And he was in the Muslim Brothers. And a group of Muslim Brothers were held in a solitary cell by themselves, and the guards went in and mowed them down, because they were on a hunger strike. And Qutb was in the prison hospital when some of the wounded were brought in, and he said to himself, what kind of Muslim would do this to another Muslim? And his answer was, they are not Muslims. In other words, he declared them, he declared Takfir on them. It was up to him to decide who was a Muslim or not. And that seems justifiable in that instance, but it expanded to the point that when, for instance, al Qaeda was in Afghanistan, Zawahiri declared the entire country of Afghanistan to be Takfir. They were Suffis, for the most part, so they weren't true Muslims, the people they were ostensibly there to defend.

HH: Well then, it becomes a kind of rolling independent association of inquisitors without portfolio. They can…who declares that, and has that spread? Has this doctrine spread into other people declaring them Takfir?

LW: Yeah, it is an ancient heresy that goes back to the moment when the prophet died. And there were always Muslims who were declaring that others were not a part of the faith. And you know, the schism that exists today between Sunni and Shia goes back to that date. It's been a problem for that faith since its inception. And modern day Takfiris, like bin Laden, like Zawahiri, really believe in their hearts that they are saving Islam, and they are saving humanity by purifying it, by killing all the heretics. And you know, it's a religious cult that has attracted the attention of a lot of disaffected young people who want to have a way to express themselves. But essentially, that's what it is.

HH: I went to break, Lawrence Wright, by wondering whether or not in the six years that they've been on full display for the world, the Saudis knew about bin Laden before 9/11. Has the rest of Islam braced itself to deal with the Takfir heresy and with the al Qaeda menace?

LW: I think Islam is in a period of deep introspection, and it's unclear to me how it's going to be resolved. I think, however, that the answers will come in Europe, which that's where Islam is most at play, with the conflicts with the modern world and the West. It's, as I say, I'm not sure how this is going to work out, because there's a lot of turbulence right now in Europe, and I'm worried about what actions might occur there in the next few years. But Muslims in Europe are a lot freer than they typically are in their countries of origin to discuss matters of their faith, but they are also freer to be more radical. So it's a double-edged sword. That's why it's on such a high boil right now in Europe.

HH: Have the Saudis rethought their support for the Salafist and the Wahhabist approach to this, which as you point out in The Looming Tower, 90% of the missionary work is funded and conducted by Saudi mullahs who are not in the traditional mainstream of Islam?

LW: Saudi Arabia is going through some changes. They have moderated their textbooks, for instance. They've bridled some of the more outspoken imams. Bear in mind the clergy in Saudi Arabia, they're government employees. So to a large extent, I think, the government does bear responsibility for what is said in the Mosques on Friday. And I think one of the things that would help the most in terms of empowering the diversity within Islam, and the moderates, would be for Saudi Arabia to allow other forms of Islam to be practiced inside that country, especially in Mecca, where it used to be that the four great legal schools of Islam were freely allowed to teach and to practice. That's not true any longer. If Saudi Arabia would begin to open up Mecca to other forms of Islamic thought, then I think there would be a long...it would go a long way towards making Islam and Wahhabism itself more tolerant.

HH: Any sign of that happening?

LW: No, not yet.

HH: In The Looming Tower, you talk about how at his farm and his offices in the Sudan years, bin Laden would welcome Shia, and would discuss with them how to cooperate. And then Zarqawi launched the attack on the Mosque in Samarra, and this terrible civil war. Has that operational cooperation shattered now in the civil war within Iraq? Or does it still go on around the world?

LW: You know, there's some puzzling aspects to this. First of all, al Qaeda is an entirely Sunni organization. And of course, the Iranians are largely Shiites, and Iraq is largely a Shiite country. And it was never, Iraq was never really on bin Laden's list, at least, of likely countries for jihad, because he knew, you know, he'd be struggling against the Shiites. And it was Zarqawi who forced the issue, created this civil war with the goal of…although Shias are the majority in Iraq, they're a minority in Islam. And he wanted to create an Islamic civil war. Well, bin Laden had real reservations about that, and you see in some of the letters from Zawahiri to Zarqawi, he's saying you know, are you going to try to kill all the Shiites? Has such a thing ever been thought of? You know, he was incredulous. So they didn't want to precipitate the Islamic civil war that Zarqawi brought on. But now that it's engaged, I think that bin Laden has essentially endorsed it when he allowed Zarqawi to join al Qaeda.

HH: Lawrence Wright, on the day of the attacks six years ago, there were only a handful of Americans who really understood what this threat was. One of them, unfortunately, died with the Towers, John O'Neill.

LW: Right.

HH: What's the situation six years later? If you're grading American counterintelligence, and American intelligence agencies, do they know what they're doing yet?

LW: There have been some improvements. You know, the 2004 reform act has made some important changes, I think. The National Counterterrorism Center is an example of that, where CIA and FBI are made to work together. You know, they have to be there, along with NSA and other members of our intelligence community. But has there been measurable progress? Well, if you measure progress by capturing or shutting down al Qaeda leaders, no. If you measure progress by stopping any attacks inside America, yes. So it's a mixed picture right now, and I think it'll be easier to see in the next few years whether these reforms have really made a change. I do think that the intelligence community has been traumatized by what happened on 9/11, and also by the faulty information that led us into Iraq. And one member of the intelligence community said you know, we feel like the returning Vietnam soldiers, you know, that we've been ostracized by our society. And they're very conscious of the pressure to change and make changes in the way we gather intelligence. I don't think that we have come far enough, and I think you know, we've got a lot of changes left to make before we can really feel that we've adjusted properly to this challenge.

HH: You've alluded a couple of times to a concern that Europe may be the site of the next spectacular attack.

LW: Right.

HH: And I've seen the MI5 leadership say in Great Britain there are 5,000 active jihadis over there, and they've tried a few times. What's the certainty, if you have to bet probabilities here, Lawrence Wright, in your view, studying it as closely as you do, of another spectacular attack where the casualties are in the hundreds or the thousands, not the tens and the twenties?

LW: I think that's you know, very likely. It's easy to imagine, even using very low-tech weapons, how to create mass casualties. And certainly, that's been the goal of many of these foiled attacks. Had any one of several of these attacks that have been stopped in the last several months been able to be carried off, then we would have been talking about thousands of casualties. So it seems unlikely that we'll be blessed with a continued period of relative tranquility with all the activity that's going on right now.

HH: And when it comes to American counterterrorism, especially, have we developed the sort of skill sets when it comes to translation and monitoring that?

LW: No, no. This is a critical point. You know, one of the heroes in my book, Ali Sufan, was one of eight Arabic-speaking agents on 9/11. There are six now.

HH: There are six?

LW: But I want to interject right away that the intelligence community has awakened to the fact that this is idiotic, that you have to have people who natively understand Arabic, and Pashtu, and Dari and Urdu, and all the languages that they're struggling to manage. You have to have people who understand the languages and the cultures, and we're really handicapped. I talked to the head of the army translation corps, and he said you know, after 9/11, many Arab and Muslim Americans came forward and offered their services to American intelligence, and they were spurned. But the Army picked up many of those, and of course, what happened? They became interpreters in Iraq, the most dangerous possible assignment. He said after four years of serving their country, they can't get a job in American intelligence, because they're considered a security risk. Well, I want to ask, what other declaration of loyalty to they need to make?

HH: Well asked. Let me ask you about the American public generally. I know you lecture on this a lot. Do they understand the war that we're involved in? Or has, have we gone back to our holiday from history?

LW: Honestly, I was reading in the Times yesterday that 33%, I think, of Americans think Saddam Hussein was involved in 9/11. It makes me wonder. There's ample amount of information out there about 9/11, about al Qaeda. I don't know why Americans aren't more informed about the nature of this menace, and who they are, what they're up to, and what they hope to accomplish, and therefore how we should treat them. It's a little mystifying to me.

HH: Did you see the ABC mini-movie, television movie, The Path To 9/11?

LW: No, I was lecturing both nights, so I missed that.

HH: Well, it's being held at Disney. They're not putting that out there. What does that tell you about the seriousness when obviously, it would sell a lot of copies, but Disney doesn't want to put it out there?

LW: I don't know. I have been doing this one-man play called "My Trip To Al Qaeda", and I'm going to be doing it at the Kennedy Center in Washington at the end of the month. And the thing that always surprises me when I talk to audience members afterwards is they often say nobody ever told us this. And I can see that people feel misguided, misled, ill-informed. But I think American people have some responsibility to educate themselves on this subject.

HH: Oh, it's very frustrating, especially when it's been made easy, and I'm not shining you on here by your book. I've not heard of this play before, My Trip To Al Qaeda. How long have you been performing it for?

LW: Well, I did it at the New Yorker Festival last year, and then I did a six-week run in New York, and I'm going to do it here in Washington at the end of the month at the Kennedy Center. And that's probably it, though. I'm not an actor, and I can prove that. But I really have enjoyed doing it, and it's been a very rewarding experience for me.

HH: Lawrence Wright, you've probably spent more time than any American journalist studying bin Laden, Zawahiri, their organization. Do you have a clue yet on whether or not they'll ever give up?

LW: Well, the people you're talking about will never give up. The question is can we persuade the people that would be their followers not to turn to them. And in my opinion, this is a long, long term effort. I think of al Qaeda being really a function of the despair of a lot of young Muslims around the world. You know, the Muslim world is one-fifth of the world's population, but half the world's poor, and typified by repressive regimes. It's a world in which there's a lot of frustration, and their economies are very barren, and they have very little to offer their young people. Until those things are changed, then we're going to see radicalism in one form or another. Al Qaeda is one form of it. We may see other, I expect we will, other forms of radicalism in the future. So it's a matter of providing jobs and literacy and hope to regions which have very little of those items.

HH: Now you're sounding a lot like a Bush doctrine aficionado at this point. I don't want to debate Iraq on this, but I do worry, after reading The Looming Tower now, or listening to it once and reading it twice, that Egypt is the source of many of these problems, and Saudi Arabia, those two, and that nothing is happening in these countries to change it.

LW: Yeah, you know, and let me separate these two countries, because they're very different. I am a great believer in democracy, and that it is an inherently moderating force, and that this is the ultimate answer to the radicalism and the challenge that al Qaeda poses. But Saudi Arabia is not ready for a democracy. It doesn't have anything like a civil society. I mean, they don't even have movie theaters or night clubs or there's no political life at all.

HH: Women driving, as you describe…

LW: Yeah.

HH: …led to immediate suppression of those women.

LW: Exactly. So it's a very stark civil society, almost absent entirely. And so imposing democracy suddenly on that country would be a mistake. That's not true of Egypt. Egypt is ready. Egypt has an almost eternal sense of itself as a nation, unlike Iraq, which you know, Churchill drew up on a napkin after lunch. That was cobbled together. That's not true of Egypt. It has a tradition of politics. It has a tradition of parliamentary democracy. It is ready to return to a democratic state, and we should push hard for that.

HH: And that's the takeaway of this interview. I hope again, as always, to have you back, Lawrence Wright. It is always just very, very informative. The Looming Tower: Al Qaeda And The

Road To 9/11 in paperback now. You've got to read it. Lawrence Wright, thank you for being back on the Hugh Hewitt Show.

End of interview.

Interview with Lawrence Wright
May 30, 2008

HH: A special hour of the Hugh Hewitt Show, I'm joined again, and we're glad to have him back, by Lawrence Wright, Lawrence Wright the author of The Looming Tower, the very important genealogy, really, of al Qaeda, where did it come from, why does it believe what it believes, which won, rightly so, the Pulitzer Prize in 2006. He's also the author of many other important articles on al Qaeda and the terror networks, including the Master Plan in the September, 2006, issue of the New Yorker, The Terror Web in the August, 2004, New Yorker, and now a brand new piece in the June 2, 2008, issue of the New Yorker, titled The Rebellion Within. Lawrence Wright, welcome back to the Hugh Hewitt Show, great to have you.

LW: Hugh, it's good to hear you again.

HH: Let's start with a little history on the assumption that some of our audience is walking in from off-stage, and they really don't know much about this, so we can put the importance of The Rebellion Within into context. And I think we should probably start with the Muslim Brotherhood, and its leading theorist, Sayyid Qutb, when it got started, and Qutb's contribution to it, Lawrence Wright.

LW: Well, the Muslim Brotherhood was the sort of the grandfather of all of the Islamist movements. They began in 1928 in Egypt. And Sayyid Qutb was one of its major ideologues. He had come to America in 1948, and hated America at a time when America's standing in the rest of the world was really very high. And he spent two years in America, and went back and wrote some very influential articles. But the main thing that he did, the main thing he wrote, was a book called Ma'alim fi-l-Tariq, or Signposts Along The Road, which he published in prison.

And in there, he denounced the Muslim rulers, and said that all of the Muslim rulers are infidels, and he called for a vanguard of Muslim youth to rise up and overthrow them, saying that Islam could not really be practiced in current times because of the conditions that Muslims were living in. And it was that philosophy in that very book that bin Laden and Ayman al-Zawahiri, the number two guy in al Qaeda, read. That's the book that is at the basis of so much of al Qaeda's philosophy.

HH: Is it sometimes translated as <u>Milestones</u>?

LW: <u>Milestones</u>, yeah.

HH: Or <u>Signposts</u>.

LW: Yeah.

HH: Also, could you give us sort of the brief sort of history of Europe after the king is overthrown, the Nasser-Sadat-Mubarak approach to governing this massive Arab state, especially their relationship with fundamentalist Islam?

LW: Well, Nasser, when he came into power in 1952, he thought that he could broker a deal with the Muslim Brothers, and he worked with Sayyid Qutb. But they had such fundamentally different ideas about what they wanted, Nasser was essentially a secular socialist. And his interest was in creating this pan-Arab nation. Well, Sayyid Qutb had no interest in any of that. He was certainly not a secularist. He wanted to create a theocracy. Pan-Arabism didn't mean anything to him, because Muslims are not necessarily confined to Arabs. He wanted to create a caliphate that would include all Muslims. And finally, he wasn't interested in socialism. As a strict Muslim, socialism wasn't really interesting to him. It's not a part of their ideology. So they didn't agree on anything. And in 1954, there was an assassination attempt on Nasser by the Muslim Brothers. And after that, Nasser rounded up thousands of them, put them in prisons. Qutb was one of those who was imprisoned, and later hanged in 1966. And that was a critical moment in our story, because a young man named Ayman al-Zawahiri started a cell to overthrow the Egyptian government that year, and he was fifteen years old.

HH: Wow. And for the benefit of people who are more closely acquainted with European history, I've been developing an analogy that I use with folks, and I'd love your reaction to it, Lawrence Wright, that Qutb is really the Marx of the Islamic fundamentalism of this generation, and that if you look at Azzam and bin Laden as the Lenins, you've got maybe Zawahiri as the Stalin, and your new article deals a lot with the guy who's probably their Trotsky, Fadl.

LW: Uh huh.

HH: But it does have these generational...but the fountain is Qutb, and I think that's the key thing.

LW: Right.

HH: ...and that Zawahiri is radicalized. When does he meet Dr. Fadl, and can you tell people a little bit about Dr. Fadl at this point?

LW: Sure. They met in medical school in 1968. They were both teenagers, and they were both very precocious young men. As I said, Zawahiri was already involved in underground work in Cairo to try to overthrow the Egyptian government. And he met this young man, whose real name is Sayyid Imam al-Sharif, and he was probably somewhat ahead of Zawahiri in his skills and his devotion not only to his studies in medical science, but in the jurisprudence of Islam. Those were two things that he was very intent on learning. And eventually, Zawahiri drew him into his own little cell, and implicated him in the, they were rounded up after the assassination of Anwar Sadat after 1981. But Dr. Fadl got away before he was arrested.

HH: Now you write in The Rebellion Within about the astonishing capacity of Fadl. He has an extraordinary memory and an extraordinary grasp of the Koran, and of the Hadith, and is far the superior scholar to Zawahiri.

LW: Right.

HH: ...and doctor, it appears from your article.

LW: Well, he was making quite a career for himself as a young doctor, as a plastic surgeon. He specialized in burn injuries. And by all accounts, he was a superb physician.

HH: Zawahiri goes to jail in the roundup after Sadat is assassinated in '81, Fadl gets to Pakistan where he finishes the book, The Essential Guide for Preparation. Can you flash forward to '88? Zawahiri is out, and we've got pretty much all of the jihadists gathered in Afghanistan at this point, or Pakistan, perhaps, that region. And the big four get together, Azzam, bin Laden, Zawahiri and Fadl. Fill us in a little bit about Azzam and what comes out of that meeting.

LW: What we're talking about is the creation of al Qaeda, which was twenty years ago. This August will be its 20th anniversary, which is a long time for a terror group to stay in existence. If you remember, the Soviet Union had invaded Afghanistan in 1979, and nine years later, ten years later, they were essentially defeated, and they had announced their withdrawal. And it was bin Laden's dream to round up these young men who had answered the summons to jihad that Azzam had issued, he was sort of the godfather of jihad. And bin Laden wanted to round them up before they went home and create a kind of Muslim foreign legion that would pursue the Soviets into Central Asia, and he would also employ them against the communist government that was then in control of Yemen. So essentially, he created this organization as an anti-communist militia.

HH: It relocates to Sudan, though, the following year.

LW: It was after 1992, that they go to Sudan. That was because bin Laden had fallen out with the Royal Family in Saudi Arabia. The cause for that was that Saddam Hussein had invaded Kuwait in 1990, and he was massing troops on Saudi Arabia's border. And bin Laden had gone to the minister of defense and proposed that he would defend the Kingdom of Saudi Arabia with al Qaeda, which couldn't have been more than a couple of hundred guys at the time, and a hundred thousand unemployed Saudi youth, and the earth-moving equipment of his father's construction company against what was a two million man army with one of the largest tank corps in the world. And of course, he was laughed out of the office, but his real fear was that the U.S. and Western nations would come in to the holy land of Saudi Arabia, and that's indeed what happened, half a million troops. And in his reading of Islam, there should be no non-Muslims in the entire Arabian Peninsula. This was a sacrilege. And that's the basis of his argument with the Royal Family.

HH: And with about a minute to our break, we're getting up to 9/11 here. But they go to Sudan, the whole group of them, and Fadl's working on his second major book, The Compendium of the Pursuit of Divine Knowledge. But Zawahiri replaces Fadl as the emir, as you call it, of al-Jihad, the Egyptian-based terrorist group.

LW: Right.

HH: They've had a falling our by this point. Why?

LW: Well, they were always kind of edgy with each other. And although Fadl was the actual emir of the group, most of the members didn't even know it. They thought that Zawahiri was their leader. And in the early 90's, Zawahiri had begun to wage war in Egypt against the Egyptian government. And it was a complete catastrophe for his terror organization. The Egyptian government rounded up thousands of his followers, and threw them in prison. And you know, many people were killed, and the members of the terror organization called al-Jihad, which became the core of al Qaeda, they demanded their leader's resignation. And they were surprised to find that their leader was Dr. Fadl, who willingly left, because he was bored with this kind of action by now, and he'd finished his life's work, he though, in writing this book.

HH: Lawrence Wright, after Dr. Fadl, really the fellow who developed the ideology beyond Qutb of al Qaeda, including I guess the doctrine of takfiri – is he the guy who comes up with that?

LW: Well, you know, this is really key to understanding al Qaeda. Takfir, essentially, the word means excommunication. And it goes, it's an ancient heresy within Islam. There've been problems with Muslims declaring that other Muslims weren't Muslims since the early days of the religion. But in modern times, it really started with Sayyid Qutb, who was in prison when the government assassinated twenty-something Muslim Brothers in the prison, in a cell. They just opened up the door and shot them down. And Sayyid Qutb was in the prison hospital when some of the wounded were brought in, and he asked himself what kind of Muslim would do this to another Muslim. And his answer was they are not Muslims. Now that's what takfir means. He declared that they were not Muslims, that they were heretics, they were apostates, and that under Muslim law, they were deserving of death. Now Dr. Fadl picked that doctrine up in Peshawar, Pakistan, where he and Zawahiri and others were staging for the jihad against the Soviets. He expanded that in his second book to encompass any Muslim who, not just the leaders who were corrupt and were not enforcing Sharia as they believed, but any Muslim who lived under such a regime and didn't engage in jihad against that ruler. In other words, practically all Muslims were infidels in his point of view. And it gave al Qaeda the warrant to kill anybody that's in their way.

HH: And it led to atrocities like the Luxor massacre. Even though Fadl's gone to Yemen, Zawahiri's attempting though al-Jihad to overthrow the Egyptian government, and '97 marks the Luxor Massacre. That's takfir, is it not?

LW: Absolutely, yeah. Most of the victims were actually tourists, but about a dozen Egyptians were killed as well, and most of them were Muslims. So there was no discrimination in terms of who they were killing.

HH: Of course, Zawahiri goes with bin Laden now, Fadl's been sidelined to Yemen, and the blind Sheik is in America, and in jail, and so the leadership goes to Afghanistan. But then 9/11 happens, and Fadl says al Qaeda's committed group suicide. Did he disapprove of the action on a theological basis or because of its practical consequences?

LW: Well, actually, Hugh, this…the point of this argument is that there are two tracks.

HH: Yup.

LW: One is practical, you know, does it accomplish our goals? And in terms of 9/11, no. If you wanted to wound America and cause it to withdraw from the Middle East, the consequence is the opposite. You wounded America, but now we invade two Muslim countries, and we and the West are much more deeply engrossed in Middle Eastern affairs than we were previously. And then the second is theological – is this the correct Muslim practice? Are we doing the right thing? And what Dr. Fadl had sold in his previous books to young Muslims who were considering joining al Qaeda, is the philosophy that this is the only route to salvation. Islam has to be purified. No Muslim can go to Heaven without reestablishing the kind of pure Islam we stand for. And now, you know, one of his arguments, for instance, about 9/11 is indiscriminate killing is against Islam. And that was part of his reaction to 9/11.

HH: Now let's update it to where we are today. In 2003, Fadl was arrested in Yemen, and shipped to Egypt secretly. And this past year, he wrote a new book called <u>Rationalizing Jihad</u>, primarily composed in the Scorpion, within Tora prison…by the way, the Scorpion sounds like about the last place in the world anyone wants to be.

LW: Yeah, it is. Well, Egyptian prisons are infamous.

HH: And in this 2007, Rationalizing Jihad, Fadl, the author of so much, writes, "We are prohibited from committing aggression, even if the enemies of Islam do that, and there is nothing that invokes the anger of God and His wrath like the unwarranted spilling of blood and wrecking of property." Lawrence Wright, this must have sent earthquakes through al Qaeda.

LW: Well, yeah, you can judge their reaction by the fact that Zawahiri has responded in repeated videos, and has written a 200 page book trying to refute Dr. Fadl's arguments. And he's not the only member of al Qaeda. They've brought out every legion, you know, that they can to attack Dr. Fadl to try to dampen the argument that's going on right now.

HH: Now the obvious question will be, how much coercion is in Dr. Fadl's renunciation of his previous ideology? What do you think on this?

LW: Well, I don't know. I mean, the honest answer is that he's in an Egyptian prison, and they can do horrible things to him. On the other hand, he's one of many voices, some of which have come out of the prisons, and others of whom are free. There was a movement that has started in the Egyptian prisons in the 1990s, on the part of another organization called Gama'a Islamiya, or the Islamic Group. And they had begun, after years, decades of being in Egyptian prison, to reexamine their violent views. Now this is long past the time when torture and that sort of thing might have been used on them. And they began to write a series of revisions. Now, a lot of these guys are out of prison, and I've talked to them. And they are no longer under the kind of subjugation that they were in the Egyptian prisons. It's pretty clear that they have had a sincere rethinking of their previous views. And Fadl's views track theirs very closely. So yes, as Zawahiri points out, how can you take it seriously, it comes out of the Egyptian prisons. As he said himself, when Fadl sent a fax out to a London newspaper about announcing his book, Zawahiri said well, I didn't know they had faxes in the Egyptian prisons. I wonder if they're connected to the electric shock machine.

HH: Lawrence Wright, you taught at the American University in Cairo for many years, and one of the asides that I found so fascinating in The Rebellion Within is your sort of look at great intervals at what's going on in Cairo, and it's just getting worse and worse there.

LW: Yeah, it's a miserable period for Egyptians. And you know, they've been suffering for a long time. And a lot of the causes of the radicalism that has come out of that region are simply the political repression that's so characteristic of those regimes. Since Sadat was assassinated in 1981, you know, we're talking 27 years ago, the country's been ruled by one man, Mubarak…

HH: Hosni.

LW: Hosni Mubarak, right. And his son, Gamal, is standing in the wings. It's…and it's a place where food riots are going on now, the cost of living is increasing, people are feeling real despair. And the way the government responds to it is to round up, for instance, recently, 600 members of the Muslim Brothers, and throw them in prison for no reason at all, just to show, exercise their strength. It's…the people are really demoralized, and I don't know what might happen in the next few years there.

HH: What is the role of the grand mufti, am I pronouncing it right, Gomaa?

LW: Yeah, Sheik Ali Gomaa.

HH: Explain…he's in this…in terms of destabilizing al Qaeda's ideology, and at the same time, what does he represent in Egypt?

LW: Well, he is one of the top sheiks in the Islamic world. His job at, he's with al-Azhar, the university, kind of the Vatican, if you will, of Islam, and his job is to issue the fatwas that govern Islamic life, and there are five thousand a week that come out of his office. So it's a very time consuming job. But over the last decade or so, Sheik Ali has been going into the prisons and talking to the prisoners about their views of Islam, and pointing out to them the distortions in their thinking that have led to their violent actions. And so he's been guiding some of the revisions. Now I want to point out, he's essentially a government employee. And he's got an incentive in steering them towards his, the government's perspective.

HH: You also mentioned in The Rebellion Within the work of the grand mufti of Saudi Arabia who issued a fatwa in October of 2007, forbidding Saudi youth to join the jihad outside of the country.

LW: And then al Qaeda tried to kill him. Saudi authorities rounded up a bunch of young al Qaedaistas after that. They stopped a plot.

HH: And Sheikh Salman al-Oadah, who is another former bin Ladenist who's now rebuked him on television, are these outliers? Or do they represent a sort of generalized revulsion against al Qaeda?

LW: Well, I think that you're beginning to see a consensus developing not among moderate Muslims, but among radical ones, that first of all, these actions are not productive, and secondly, they are not Islam. They are indiscriminate violence, they... bin Laden and al Qaeda use principles that are opposed to the fundamental tenets of Islam. And this is an attack from within radical Islam itself, and that's why I think it's so significant.

HH: Have you read Michael Yon's new book yet, <u>Moment of Truth in Iraq?</u>

LW: No, I haven't.

HH: He describes in great detail the Anbar uprising, or the Anbar awakening, where the brutality of al Qaeda did more to turn the Sunni sheiks and imams of that region against it, and it's sort of a microcosm of what you talk about over the course of twenty years in The Rebellion Within. There's a self-correction built into radicalism, almost.

LW: Yeah, I mean, for one thing, Dr. Fadl's argument places the relevance of al Qaeda at question right now. Al Qaeda can't exist without terror. That's all it is. It can't really very well defend its philosophy. It's own philosopher has overturned the apple cart. And so the only thing that al Qaeda can do to demonstrate its relevance is to create some other radical, terrible, tragic action. And I think they're under a lot of pressure right now to do something like that.

HH: Lawrence Wright, Zawahiri did not take Dr. Fadl's new book lying down. As we mentioned earlier, he responded with a 200 page letter. And was it coherent? Or was it contingent and argumentative, but not persuasive?

LW: You know, he makes some good points, but he's really not a theologian himself, and so it's very difficult for him to respond to the jurisprudential argument that Dr. Fadl makes. He's not adept that way. He steers it mainly into politics. And his line is mistakes have been made, but mistakes were made during the Prophet's time, but jihad did not stop. And you can see that he's grasping at straws in some respects. For instance, he says well, you know, why blame us? Look at Hamas, for instance. They kill civilians indiscriminately with their missiles into Israel. Why don't you attack them, which is of course, he knows that that's a very touchy issue for a lot of Muslims who see the resistance movements in Palestine as having a kind of different moral standing.

HH: Two aspects of your summary of his letter struck me. One, his attempt to rationalize 9/11 as a response to the 1998 [bombing of the] pharmaceutical plant in Sudan. That just, that can't be persuasive, even to a radical jihadist.

LW: Well, you know, he says that the only difference between the bombing of, the American bombing of that pharmaceutical plant in Khartoum is that it was Muslims who died there. Of course, only one Muslim died there. Only one person died there. It was a night watchman. And in New York, it was infidels. And of course, many Muslims died in that attack. And what Dr. Fadl is pointing out is that it's against Islam to kill people indiscriminately, and it's against Islam to kill civilians. Zawahiri can't respond to those arguments, because there's no ground for him to do that.

HH: I was also interested in your summary, that he takes, Zawahiri does, time in his response to attack Hezbollah.

LW: Yeah.

HH: And this is, of course, there were some contingent operational agreements between Shia radicalism and Sunni fundamentalist radicalism, but Zawahiri's not buying that anymore, is he?

LW: You know, it's…he is being outflanked. I think that that's what's happening, is that al Qaeda is much less relevant now than it has been. And Hezbollah has really put itself forward as a major player in the region in a way that al Qaeda's simply been unable to do. And I think that there's probably some envy built into those remarks.

HH: Now let's talk a little bit about, though, where it goes from here. I'm reading from the last couple of pages of your article, is al Qaeda finished? "It is, of course, unlikely that al Qaeda will voluntarily follow the example of the Islamist Group and Zawahiri's own organization, Al Jihad, and revise its violent strategy. But it is clear that radical Islam is confronting a rebellion within its ranks, one that Zawahiri and the leaders of al Qaeda are poorly equipped to respond to. Radical Islam began as a spiritual call to the Muslim world to unify and strengthen itself through holy warfare. For the dreamers who long to institute God's justice on earth, Fadl's revisions represent a substantial moral challenge. But for the young nihilists who are joining the al Qaeda movement for their own reasons—revenge, boredom, or a desire for adventure—the quarrels of the philosophers will have little meaning." Expand on that, Lawrence Wright. What are the relative numbers here?

LW: Well, you know, when we talk about al Qaeda, al Qaeda central, the core of al Qaeda, a member of Egyptian intelligence puts a number at fewer than 200. American intelligence says they estimate between three and five hundred. But it's not a very large organization. It's much reduced from what it was. On the other hand, al Qaeda is a movement, and there are many affiliates that are connected to some extent with al Qaeda central, and then there are a lot of wannabes that are al Qaeda sympathizers. Those people, and I think especially among the wannabes, there are a lot of nihilists who are only in this for action. There's been some interesting European studies, especially a Dutch study, of this third generation of al Qaeda. And they're so much less focused politically than their forbear in that group. They have very poorly formed ideas about what they're up to. They're just striking out. And for them, I don't think they're going to care about what Dr. Fadl has to say.

HH: And so what is the, in that Dutch study, or in the other reading that you've done, how to combat that?

LW: Well, I think that one thing that we've done, I think the best thing that we've done since 9/11, is to model the behavior that we're doing right now with this magnificent election we're having, where we're really talking to ourselves about who we are and what kind of country we want to become. And I can tell you the Muslim world is fixated on it, because it's such an example of what they don't have, the opportunity to change their governments, to really reform their own countries. This has been a lesson that America has given to the rest of the world, especially the Muslim world, that I think is very valuable. And that's one way, I think the most productive way, that we can address this problem.

HH: You know, Robin Wright was a guest on the program after she wrote Shadows and Dreams. And I took away from that that I don't see much evidence of any kind of political opening in any of these Arab states. Have you seen any indication that there's political progress being made in any of these states, Lawrence Wright?

LW: Well, there was a period of time in 2005, really, when the Bush administration had put a lot of pressure on different Arab governments. And if you remember, there were votes in Iraq and Lebanon, Afghanistan, you know, it felt like a big change was coming. But that door closed. And also, we're not pushing on that door anymore.

HH: I want to thank Lawrence Wright for spending this much time with us again. The author of The Looming Tower has a brand new article in the June 2, 2008, New Yorker, which I very much recommend to you. It is called The Rebellion Within. I've linked it at Hughhewitt.com. Lawrence Wright, I want to finish by talking about Iraq. Obviously, there's word out of Mosul this week that even though there are some suicide bombings, that al Qaeda has lost its very last stronghold after a series of devastating blows between the United States military and the Iraqi Security Forces, and they've put up on some of their web sites basic hand-wringing over how did we lose Iraq, et cetera. How important is it to the destruction of radical jihadism that Iraq be stabilized, and become sort of that emblematic, if not a democracy, at least a non-repressive, I don't know, alternative to either Mubarak or Syrian strong men, or Saudi Arabian absolutism and moncharists? How important is Iraq now?

LW: Well, you know, there are two really important intellectual centers in the Arab world. One is Egypt, the other is Iraq. And the idea behind the invasion of Iraq, which I was opposed to, was to set up this model democracy that would then become a beacon for reform all over the region. It's going to be really hard to achieve the goal that we had set out, although now, I am in the awkward political position of being opposed to withdrawing. I think we should stay there as long as we can to try to hold this entity together until they are able to remain stable, create a fairly reliable electoral process, police force, and that kind of thing, and take care of themselves. I don't know if we can achieve that, but it's hopeful to see that Iraq has been, you know, I don't want to say that they've been put to death completely in Iraq, but they certainly are in retreat. And that's critical, because if al Qaeda won in Iraq, who knows how far it would go.

HH: Lawrence Wright, last question, what are you working on next? You know, I always look for your byline, and obviously, these are complicated pieces. Are you ever going to grow weary of charting this very extreme and dark side of the world?

LW: Yes, I am (laughing). I am weary of it many times. And I'm taking a little break. I'm doing a screenplay for Ridley Scott, and I've been working on a play about the making of the movie "Cleopatra" in 1962. So you can see that I'm trying to put a little distance between myself and the terror world.

HH: Well, you deserve it. You've done such great work. Thank you again for this piece, and for an extra hour of insight into it. Lawrence Wright, always a pleasure. Maybe we can talk about your screenplay sometime, "Cleopatra." Thanks for spending time with us.

End of interview.

Chapter 3.

A Conversation with Douglas Frantz and Catherine Collins

Today and for decades ahead the world worries about Pakistan and its growing internal Islamist movement and that movement's proximity to Pakistan's nearly 100 nuclear devices. As the world's least stable nuclear power, Pakistan scares not just its neighbor and historic enemy India, but anyone with any grasp of the perils of the situation.

Like Lawrence Wright, Douglas Frantz and Catherine Collins are not conservative ideologues. Far from it, in fact. Frantz was a long time staffer for the Los Angeles Times, rising eventually to become the paper's managing editor. Collins, married to Frantz, had spent years as a reporter with the Chicago Tribune. Together they brought enormous research skills and long experience with Pakistan to the question of how did A.Q. Khan establish his criminal network that successfully looted Europe of its nuclear secrets, transfer those secrets back to Pakistan and then buy the technology with which to first construct and then begin the export of the technology of mass killing to North Korea, Libya, and Iran and possibly other as-yet-unknown governments.

What the Nuclear Jihadist makes clear is that the spread of nuclear weaponry had very little to do with America and its allies, and everything to do with the ancient hatreds of the Asian subcontinent and the still deep wounds of the partition of India in the aftermath of World War II. Frantz and Collins give crucial history to the story that is as fresh as this morning's headlines while warning any reader or listener that predictions about the number of years before this or that country goes nuclear are never to be trusted.

Interview with Douglas Frantz and Catherine Collins
February 12, 2008

HH: You know, from time to time, books come out and I bring the author or authors onto the program for an extended interview. I did that a year and a half ago with Lawrence Wright when The Looming Tower came out. And I told you then it would win the Pulitzer, which it did in 2007. I've done it with other books, and I'm happy to do it again today. And if you are doing something, you'll want to sit down and just listen, or you're going to want to go for a long drive if you're in the car, and get stuck in a traffic jam, because this next program on The Nuclear Jihadist: The True Story of the Man Who Sold the World's Most Dangerous Secrets, and How We Could Have Stopped Him, is the only book since Helter Skelter to keep me awake at night. And I'm pleased to welcome Douglas Frantz and Catherine Collins to the program. Douglas and Catherine, welcome, it's good to have you on.

CC: Thank you.

DF: Thanks very much, Hugh. It's great to be with you, and thanks for that good introduction.

CC: Thank you.

HH: Well, it's a fascinating book, and I want to start by telling folks that you're a husband and wife reporter team. Douglas Frantz is now at Portfolio, formerly managing editor of the Los Angeles Times. Catherine's been a reporter for the Chicago Tribune, also written for the Times and the New York Times. They're both prolific authors. But this one is different. Let's start, and I'll go back and forth with you guys. Doug, give us a little background on how you decided to write this particular book.

DF: This is the fifth book that Cathy and I have done together, and it's by far the most complicated, and I think the most important. It started out, actually, Hugh, as an assignment for me from the Los Angeles Times. I was based in Istanbul as the first foreign investigative reporter in the history of the Times in early 2003, and I talked with John Carroll and Dean Baquet and Marjorie Miller, the foreign editor, about what topic I should tackle first. And we all agreed that nuclear proliferation was the most important issue facing the world today, because it intersects with so many other issues, including terrorism and our troubles with other countries. At that point, Iran wasn't really much on our radar yet. And so I started out doing a series of sort of long investigative pieces for the Los Angeles Times, and I came across A.Q. Khan and his activities as a rogue Pakistani scientist very early on in that process. And I worked on it for the Times for about two and a half years doing various stories. And near the end of the second year, it was apparent to Catherine and I [sic] that this was a topic that really needed more work. And so she started working alongside of me, gathering material for the book.

HH: Now Catherine, before we go any further, let me ask you not as a reporter but as a spouse. The L.A. Times calls up and says we'd like you to go to Pakistan. This is after the murder of Daniel Pearl. How did that news reach you?

CC: Oh, obviously, I was very concerned. But we stayed in touch, and you know, sometimes you do things that make you a little anxious, and you'd rather not do. But really, the more important thing is the story. And you have to take those risks sometimes, because this story was very important to get out, and to air these issues.

HH: Let's begin, then, by talking about after you told the L.A. Times you're going to write a book. Did they give you a book leave, Douglas? Or did you just say, "I've got to devote full time to this?"

DF: No, I've always balanced my day job with writing books. And I'm able to do that because Cathy and I work so well together. But no, actually, we had just started roughing out the outline of the book when I became managing editor in the fall of 2005. So they certainly didn't give me anything like a book leave. We had a lot of balls in the air for quite a while there until we finished this book. And I finished my job at the L.A. Times, too.

CC: You know, some people play golf or bridge or something. We tend to spend our evenings working on these projects, and weekends, too.

HH: That's a lot of excitement for an evening.

CC: (laughing)

DF: (laughing)

HH: Catherine, tell me a little bit about the reception of the book. Obviously, we're talking at the beginning of February, 2008. This is the initial time that the interview aired. The book came out in December, so it hadn't had a lot of time yet, but how's the reception?

DF: Well, it's been surprising. There's been a lot of attention in the press. We've done several big op-ed pieces. There have been very good reviews. The Economist, in early January, just gave us a four star review. It was very heartening. And yet, the sales are pretty slow. And I think as we've looked back over the history of books about nuclear issues, they, almost all of them, have sold pretty slowly. And as we puzzle over why, because of the good reviews, because the news has rolled out right on the cycle of this book with the problems in Pakistan, and the problems in Iran continuing, we can't quite figure out why this isn't selling better. But I think that nuclear catastrophe is an unthinkable prospect for most people, and particularly for Americans who tend to live in a cocoon, even after 9/11. And so people don't want to think about it, they don't want to read about it. But you know, we sure believe that they should, and that's one of the reasons why we're so happy to be on this show and to get to your audience especially.

HH: Well, I think it's going to develop legs, and I'll tell you why. The same thing happened with The Looming Tower, because it's a profoundly riveting read. I mean, it carries you along, page after page. It's a detective story. But it also has these implications about I didn't know that, and that changes my worldview. And Catherine, let me ask you, when you began this, did you know anything about Khan or what he had been up to until you dove in?

CC: No, I didn't. I just started to read Doug's stories, obviously, and you know, we'd talk at night about these, and over coffee and lunch, and pretty soon, he got me into the subject just as strongly as he was. It's a fascinating story. Dr. Khan is like the real life Dr. No.

HH: You're absolutely right about that, and he's a chilling kind of character. And let's start there. Actually, let's start earlier than that. Douglas, to get this set up right, I think we have to begin with the partition of India. Now people are going to sit there and hear me say that, and they're going to say, "what?" And in fact, it's all about the partition of India after World War II.

DF: You're right, Hugh. This is an integral action in history that's led to A.Q. Khan becoming this real life Dr. No. In 1947, the British partitioned India, and they created the state of India, and the Islamic Republic of Pakistan. Pakistan was set up as a refuge for Muslims. And tens of thousands of them began streaming into this new country of Pakistan, both East Pakistan and West Pakistan, at that time, divided by the thumb of India sticking up there. And A.Q. Khan was 11 years old during that period. And this had an impact on him that stayed with him his whole life, because he saw thousands of Muslims being persecuted and massacred by their Hindu rivals in India. And this affected him. It created a deep-seated hatred of India. He remained with his mother and father in India. They were living in Bhopal, and he remained there until 1952, when his father saw that there was no future for his young son in India. And so he sent him to join other family members in Karachi. And Khan, all through his life, has told this one small story about his trip. He was put on a train to leave India, and head to the Pakistani border. And the Indian police came through those loaded cars filled with Muslims. And they took everything of value – jewelry, money, you know, fancy clothing. Khan didn't have anything of value except for a gold pen that he had received from recently graduating from high school. And an Indian police officer reached into his pocket, and plucked out that pen. And that was a symbol for A.Q. Khan that really would drive him many years later, and make him become this rogue nuclear scientist who was determined to help Pakistan build its atomic arsenal, to protect it against its archrival, India.

HH: I'm talking with Douglas Frantz and Catherine Collins, authors of The Nuclear Jihadist, and we will be doing that for the program today. Do not go anywhere. You're going to figure out why I'm doing this. Catherine, do you think hatred for India is too strong of a term to attribute to A.Q. Khan? Or is that just what it is, unmitigated hatred?

CC: Oh, I think that's what it is. And what it did was it sparked a nationalism for Pakistan that he was able to put into play. After he did his college education his early years in Pakistan, he went overseas to Europe, as many people from that part of the world do, because the educational opportunities were better, and he did his advanced degrees in Europe, and eventually got his PhD and went work at this lab in the Netherlands called Urenco, where they were developing the latest ultra-centrifuges to enrich uranium. It was actually a joint project with the British, the Dutch and the Germans. And during that time period, India tested its first nuclear device, which was in 1974. And at that point, this restarted Khan's hatred of India, his own nationalism, and he realized just serendipitously that he happened to be sitting on a wealth of information that he hoped he could take back to Pakistan in order to help Pakistan jump start its own nuclear program.

HH: And we'll be going through that detail by detail. I think the key, though, at the beginning, for the audience to understand, is the depth of the animosity between these countries, because I just don't think most Americans have an idea of the scope of intense conflict along that border. Do you two?

DF: Well, I think we do. I've been up to that border, and Cathy and I have both spent time in Pakistan, and I've been to India as well. And it's a deep-seated hatred that continues today. They fight today primarily over Kashmir, which sits between India and Pakistan. It's the one part of that region that wasn't settled when the British divided, set the boundaries. But the Pakistanis and the Indians have fought three wars since partition in 1947, and the Pakistanis have come out on the short end of all three of those conflicts. And that was, and India is obviously a much larger country, a billion or so people there compared with 150 million Pakistanis. And so the Indians have a much larger army, and that really creates enormous fear in Pakistan. Their whole military perspective is facing east and looking at India.

HH: It's clearly colored by that.

HH: When we broke for our first break, and by the way, if you want to learn more, there is a web site, www.thenuclearjihadist. com. When we broke for break, we were talking about the fact that India and Pakistan have been at each other's throats since 1947 in the partition of India. We'll come back to the three wars between them, and we'll come back to Khan. But Doug, let me ask you for a second as well, to set up the American nuclear monopoly, and what Eisenhower did with Atoms for Peace, that was really part of unleashing this genie that then Khan managed to control to his own nefarious purposes.

DF: It was, Hugh, and that was one of the many surprises we found along the way in researching this book. In 1953, President Dwight Eisenhower created a program called Atoms for Peace. And frankly, like most people, I think, we've never really paid much attention to it. Atoms for Peace is a nice sounding word, and it connotes using nuclear energy for good to develop power, and for medical purposes, and other research. But as we looked into that, what we saw was two things. Eisenhower set up Atoms for Peace to mask the increase in the American nuclear arsenal. This was 1953, so dropping the bombs on Hiroshima and Nagasaki was fresh in the minds of Americans, but so of course was the rising Soviet threat. That's when people were beginning to build bomb shelters, and we'd start to go through these duck and cover drills in schools. And so Eisenhower wanted to build up the American nuclear arsenal, and to go to hydrogen bombs as well, but he wanted a cover so that the public wouldn't get alarmed. And so they set up Atoms for Peace, which was a program to send out nuclear research reactors to all kinds of countries. It was a way of spreading nuclear technology, it was a way of getting these countries under the American umbrella, the Western umbrella, if you will. And of course, the Soviets responded with their own program, and they began sending nuclear research facilities to countries within the Soviet sphere. So you had this competition to spread nuclear power at that time. I don't think anybody was really thinking that they were spreading nuclear weapons technology, but what we know today is that the line between civilian uses of nuclear technology and the military applications of nuclear technology is very thin, very porous, easily, easily breached, as we've seen in so many instances, from the Indians and the Pakistanis and the Chinese, to the Israelis and the North Koreans, and certainly very soon, the Iranians.

HH: Let's just jump ahead for a moment, and Catherine Collins, any doubt in your mind that knowing what you know from this book, and following the headlines, that Iran is poised to weaponize its nuclear capability if it decides to do so?

CC: Well, you know, that recent NIE report, the National Intelligence Estimate that came out, it was very interesting. And I think that some people missed the point of that. And the point was the report was largely about Iran's nuclear weapons program. And what it said was yes, in fact, Iran did have a nuclear weapons program, which they closed down in 2003; [which] what we feel is more important is that Iran's uranium enrichment program has continued unabated. And they are able to enrich uranium at a faster and faster rate. And fairly soon, we think, they will be enriching uranium at an industrial scale. And with some tinkering, that enrichment process could be altered in order to enrich uranium to the extent that it could be used for weapons. And at that point, that is the more difficult part of the process, at that point, the weapons program itself could be restarted, and Iran could be another member of the nuclear elite.

HH: That's why I want everyone who cares about this issue to read The Nuclear Jihadist, because you can't put the book down at the end and be anything except alarmed at the state of the nuclear program in Iran, and other places around the world, because it's so easily transformed into a weapons program. But again, I'm ahead of myself. I just wanted to give you a preview of coming attractions. I want to go back to Atoms for Peace, Doug, for a second. Can you set up for us what the Eisenhower scheme was? I think it was basically we'll give you the stuff we don't think you can mess around with, but we're going to keep the stuff like centrifuge design behind so you can't possibly weaponize. Is that a good layman's summary?

DF: Yeah, yeah, that's very good. That's well said. You know, they sent out small, small research reactors which would allow countries to become comfortable with the nuclear technology, to use it for medical research and scientific research. But these were very small reactors that couldn't produce enough highly enriched uranium or plutonium for a nuclear weapon at that point. [And so they kept…but another part of that, and] Cathy just reminded me, another part of that is that also as part of Atoms for Peace, we sent them the reactors, and we volunteered to train their scientists. And so thousands of Indian scientists, and Iranian scientists during the era of the Shah, and scientists from all sorts of other countries, came to the United States, and they went to Britain. And others from the Soviet sphere went to Moscow. And they learned nuclear technology. And what Eisenhower and his supporters and successive administrations weren't paying attention to was that this technology is easily transferable to a weapons program. But to go back to the part of your question again, Hugh, they did, the U.S. did try to keep track of the fuel. They tried to keep centrifuge technology as a top secret technology, and they refused to share it, even with their closest allies, the Germans and the British, which is how in the early 1970's, after Richard Nixon refused to share this technology with countries that wanted it to fuel, [they wanted the fuel] for their own civilian nuclear plants, the Dutch and the Germans and the British formed this consortium called Urenco so that they could develop their own centrifuges, and use that technique to develop fuel for their nuclear power plants. But it's a very, as we've said a couple times, a very thin line between developing it at low enriched levels for civilian uses, and highly enriched levels for weapons uses. So in a sense, the American policy of holding onto the fuel technology set the stage for A.Q. Khan's arrival on the scene in the mid-1970's.

HH: And let me ask you about that, Catherine, we've got about a minute and a half to the break, Urenco goes after centrifuge design, because the U.S. has a monopoly on it, and they begin to hire willy-nilly. And I'm just appalled at the level of detail which we can't go in here, of the security sloppiness. They let anyone go to work at Urenco, apparently, including A.Q. Khan.

CC: Well, it's funny, isn't it? They didn't exactly vet him very well. But they hired him, they were desperate. His skills were in metallurgy. He was a metallurgist. So they hired him to work with these highly specialized metals that are used in the centrifuge development. And they didn't clear him, hire him to work in the most secure facility at Urenco. But as time went on, and they needed his other skills, they just moved him around to more and more secure areas without increasing his security clearance. And he never went in for that full examination. And perhaps, someone might have taken note of his nationality, and that Pakistan had a program. But they just never did it.

HH: Now I'm going to do, in five minutes, Doug and Catherine, the hardest thing, but it's very, very crucial. In the book, finally, someone explained to me in the kind of detail that a layman, an interested layman, needs, the differences between how you make a bomb from plutonium processes and how you make a bomb through uranium processes, and why they're different, and which one's harder. And you can't possibly put it into a four or a five minute segment, Doug, but try and explain to people the two different paths to weapons of mass destruction, nuclear category.

DF: I will. I'll do the best I can.

HH: In five minutes or less (laughing).

CC: Here's to all scientists out there.

DF: (laughing) Well, [there are. There are, as you say,] there are two routes to a nuclear weapon. The United States and other countries have used both. The shorter, easier route is by taking the spent fuel from a nuclear reactor, putting it into a reprocessing plant, and turning it into plutonium. They reprocess these spent fuel rods, and turn out plutonium, which creates a very powerful nuclear weapon. But it also, that pathway, requires that you have an operating nuclear reactor, and it requires that you have this big, high-tech, major expenditure of a reprocessing facility to do that. And so that's the one route. The other route is to take natural uranium ore, and to enrich it through a series of centrifuges. Centrifuges are tall cylindrical machines, maybe they're six to eight feet tall, depending upon the type, and they spin at roughly twice the speed of sound. And they will spin for weeks, months, and sometimes years on end. And so they have to be very precisely balanced. And if you have an enrichment plant, all you need is this natural uranium ore. You put it into a process and turn it into uranium hexaflourides, and you can feed it into this series of centrifuges, which they call a cascade. And once you master the technology for these spinning centrifuges, you can turn them out. They're a dime a dozen, and you turn out thousands of them. And unlike needing a nuclear reactor and a big eyesore of a reprocessing plant, you can take your centrifuges, and put a thousand of them in a gymnasium, you can bury ten thousand of them in a tunnel in North Korea. They're much easier to hide. They don't have the kind of signature in the atmosphere that a reactor or reprocessing [plant] do, so it's more secretive. Mastering the initial technology is a little harder, but when you link these things in a series, and you spin the uranium gas, you turn out highly enriched uranium. And it's…actually, once you master it, you can turn it out, you know, you can make enough bombs, you can make enough to supply a huge arsenal in a pretty short order.

HH: Let's bottom line it. Pakistan had no bombs 25 years ago. How many do you think, or how many does the intelligence community estimate that they have now, Catherine?

CC: We've heard as little as fifty and as high as 120.

HH: And that's all from uranium enrichment, correct?

DF: Yes, it is. They don't have a plutonium project there, yet. It's interesting, because back at the start, they tried to do it the plutonium way, but the United States persuaded other countries to not sell them, in fact, the reprocessing technology and the reprocessing plant they needed. So they were thwarted there. And that's when A.Q. Khan came on the scene with his magic centrifuge technology, and he really brought them very quickly, and almost miraculously, into the nuclear weapons age.

HH: So [the two things you need, or actually,] the three things you need are uranium, and you need centrifuges, and eventually, you need a delivery system. And where did they get the uranium from, Catherine or Doug?

DF: They had their own uranium mines in Northeastern Pakistan. They have a fairly good supply there.

HH: And is that in unlimited supply, or at least as much as they need to continually produce more bombs?

DF: I think it was as much as they needed, Hugh. I've never heard of them importing uranium from other countries. In fact, I think on a couple of occasions, they may have exported some to Libya during Khan's dealings with Libya, but that's a little down the road for us, Hugh.

HH: And last question before the break, how many countries in the world do we think have uranium enrichment capacity sufficient to producing the gas, and then from the gas, the highly enriched uranium?

DF: Well, I'm not sure what that number is, but we do know that Mohamed ElBaradei, a little over a year ago, he's the director of the United Nations nuclear watchdog agency, the International Atomic Energy Agency, Mohamed ElBaradei gave a speech in which he said there are thirty or more countries that could essentially flip a switch and become nuclear powers, that they have the technology. Usually, it's going to be from centrifuges, but some of these countries have big reactors, and could reprocess it and turn into plutonium. But there are at least thirty and possibly more countries that could become nuclear states almost overnight, in a matter of weeks or months.

CC: He called them virtual weapon-states.

HH: Virtual weapon-states. That should be a sharp blow to your stomach, America.

HH: Catherine, let me go to you on this, because I'm going to leave Mr. Khan inside of the Urenco facility in Europe, and come back to India and Pakistan after partition. Can you tell us briefly about their three wars, and what they were fought over, and what India did in response to this?

DF: I've got to take that on, Hugh.

HH: All right, go ahead. I just keep going back and forth for the benefit of the voices.

DF: No, no, some of these, we've tried to sort of divide this up, because it was such a huge reporting task.

HH: Then I'm just going to ask the questions from here on, and you guys decide which one to answer it, okay (laughing)?

CC: Okay.

DF: Fair enough.

CC: We can see each other.

DF: That's true. We're within grabbing distance. The first war came in 1948, shortly after partition. It was a war over Kashmir. And the Indians just outmassed the Pakistanis and forced them down. In 1971, there was another critical war. Again, it was started over Kashmir. The Indian troops, the Pakistanis, rather, disguised some of their troops as commandos or as militants, and infiltrated into Kashmir, and started destroying some of the Indian settlements there, and the Indians massed for war. And within a matter of two or three weeks, this was from late '71, or early '71, I think, they routed the Pakistanis. And the rout was so thorough and so humiliating, that Pakistan was divided at that time. At that time, it had been East Pakistan and West Pakistan. And the Indians forced them to give up East Pakistan, which then became the new nation of Bangladesh. And Pakistan was whittled down in size and population.

HH: Doug, let me interrupt. What kind of casualties are we talking about in these wars?

DF: Oh, we're talking about 10,000-12,000 casualties, not huge numbers of casualties at this point. But again, the point is that for Pakistanis, this created in their minds the idea that India really wanted to blow them completely off the map, to get rid of them, because they divided the country now, and they'd created Bangladesh out of East Pakistan, and so the people who remained in West Pakistan felt very threatened.

HH: You know, I was reading the book, and I thought to myself, Pakistan at that time must have felt a little bit like Mexico to our south in terms of this juggernaut across the region, across the border. Was it that great of a disparity in the minds of the Pakistanis?

DF: Yes.

CC: Well, it was. And there are accounts of Khan in Europe, from friends of his, weeping over the results, weeping over the images that appeared in the newspapers and magazines, on television. And when European columnist would weigh in about the aggression initiated by the Pakistanis, he began writing letters to the editor, and would write letters to professors who had spoken out about this. This was a crucial moment for him, and he was furious, and he talked about, going on for weeks without being able to study properly, about this. But I wanted to reflect back to something you said earlier on, which I thought was a really good point. This is a conflict that Americans simply do not, are not aware of, or don't understand, because I think you're right about that, because so many Americans have not been to these countries, and these are conflicts that did not, unlike Iraq, let's say, these are conflicts that didn't have a personal impact on us.

HH: I agree with that completely, because reading it, it's vivid, it's easy to grasp, but I just don't know this, and I'm supposed to know stuff like this. So let's go back to '71. What happens after that, because I know there's a third war coming.

DF: There is, [and the critical, before we get to the third war,] the critical aftermath or after-event of 1971 was that the military ruler of Pakistan was thrown out, they had elections, and Zulfikar Ali Bhutto, a patrician, feudal Pakistani land owner, was elected to be the president of Pakistan.

CC: And this an important turn of events…

HH: Yup.

CC: …because Bhutto had been energy minister before that. And as energy minister, he'd been the first Pakistani to push for a nuclear weapons program. Initially, he'd been turned down by the Pakistani military, because they were afraid it would detract from their conventional weapons. But when Bhutto became prime minister in the early 70's, he was able then, at that point, finally, to begin his nuclear weapons program.

HH: [He must have been an amazing…of course,] he's the father of Benazir Bhutto, about whom most Americans are now aware. But he must have been an amazing man. The charisma that comes through in your book is of an extraordinary leader, though we can't approve of what he was up to.

DF: Yes, we have, I think, a wonderful scene in the book in the Pakistani city of Multan, where in 1972, he has summoned secretly…

HH: Yup.

DF: …all of the military and scientific leaders of Pakistan, and they're on the lawn of a beautiful, colonial house there, and there's a big tent covering them, and he gets up and gives a fiery speech about the need for never being overrun by India, never being humiliated like this again, and the only way to stop that is to have our own nuclear weapon, what he called the Islamic bomb. And so that really was the official beginning of the Pakistani nuclear effort. And it stalled for two or three years there until A.Q. Khan came back and really rescued it for Zulfikar Ali Bhutto.

HH: Okay, we've got about a minute to the break. Take us back into the India-Pakistan conflict after '71.

DF: Yeah, the next critical conflict came in 1999. It's known as Cargill, because that was a mountain high in Kashmir. And Pervez Musharraf was the military general in charge of that operation. He created this, he sent some of his commandos up to take control of this mountaintop. And again, the Indians came in and they massed about 400,000 troops on the borders. And at that point, both of these countries have nuclear weapons. The year before, in 1998, India and Pakistan had both tested nuclear devices publicly, and the Clinton White House was absolutely apoplectic. They were very worried that this third war was going to turn into the nuclear Armageddon on the subcontinent of India. And so they dispatched, gosh, I can't remember who it was, it was Gates, Bob Gates. I'm forgetting who it was.

HH: We'll come right back and we'll pick up that thread.

HH: Before I go back into substance, I'm just curious, have you two been approached by television or movies? Because this is a mini-series.

DF: No, we haven't. We're kind of disappointed in that, actually.

CC: Who would you make the hero?

HH: I don't know that there's a hero…well, maybe, you know who's a hero? Leonard Weiss, though my politics and his don't agree at all, is a pretty interesting character, and I know some of these guys on the NSC who went chasing these nukes. And I also think Heinonen is a pretty cool guy. But I just mean, it's fascinating how this happened, and it's a mystery. So no one's yet called up and said we want an option on this?

DF: No, nobody has. We're a little surprised. I mean…but again, perhaps we shouldn't be, because the sales have been kind of slow, too. It's a topic that you need to devote that kind of time and thought that you are to it on your show, Hugh, for people to really pay attention to this. [It's not,] you can't explain this in three minutes, and it's very easy for Americans to turn away from something like this. You know, this isn't Charlie Wilson's War.

HH: No.

DF: This is the real world, and this is, we think, the biggest threat going today.

HH: Oh, it's scary. I told my audience when we were getting ready for this show, I listened to this book. I got the I-Tunes download, and I listened to it when I was running in the morning, and I couldn't stop listening to it. [Now I'm remembering most…]I've got a hard copy in my hand to help me with the names, et cetera, but if you can listen to a book and remember everything in it, that's riveting. And so I'm just surprised. Now very quickly before we go to the hour break, India, meanwhile, while Pakistan's getting thumped by India, India decides to go nuclear. Why did they do that? Was that China? Or was it just in order to lord it over Pakistan?

CC: Well, it was China. These things never happen in isolation, and the funny thing is that India acquired nuclear weapons because of their concerns about China. And Pakistan acquired nuclear weapons because of its concerns about India. And this is a pattern that we've seen throughout history, and a pattern that alarms us today, because when ElBaradei warns that in addition to the nuclear states that we already have, if there are thirty virtual nuclear weapon-states out there, they don't go one at a time. When Japan, if Japan were to decide to flip the switch, a series of other countries would, also. These things happen like a domino effect.

HH: Let me ask you both in the minute to the break, we have a long segment coming up, I'm 51, so let's say I get my appointed

81

span of another 25 years. Do you think I'll see a nuclear weapon detonated in anger in the world?

DF: Absolutely. Absolutely. I don't think you have to live out your full, healthy life to see that happen. All the experts we talked to, Hugh, said it's not a matter of if, it's a matter of when. And it may not be a city in the United States. It may be a city in Europe, or someplace else. But it will happen. There's just too much clamoring, and this information is out there, and our controls over the fissile material are too weak. The probability is high, but we can lower it if we do certain things.

HH: I was afraid you were going to say that, because it's the conclusion I reached at the end of The Nuclear Jihadist, and I assume it's going to be Tel Aviv, actually, but we're talk about that when we come back.

HH: I gave a talk this week before a large crowd of center-right conservatives, and I said you've just got to read The Nuclear Jihadist. It's going to change the way you think about the world. And to summarize our first hour, if you're just joining us, after India was partitioned, it was bloody, it was horrible, and Pakistan developed an inferiority complex, and trauma-tized Pakistanis moved across the world. One of them was A.Q. Kahn. He's a metallurgist. He goes to Europe. Meanwhile, India nuclearizes, Pakistan loses two more wars, and Khan becomes convinced that he's got to help Pakistan survive its long-running engagement with India. And he has a friend in the form of...say it for me, Doug or Catherine.

DF: Zulfikar Ali Bhutto.

HH: Zulfikar Ali Bhutto. And we pick up the story in, and Khan is in Europe, and tell us what he does in Europe when he goes to work for Urenco. How does he get access to this? How does he know to steal it?

DF: Well, he started work there, as Cathy said earlier, as a metallurgist. But they had a great demand. They were really racing forward, this consortium, to develop their centrifuges. [And so they had.] The Germans had developed an advanced ultra centrifuge called the P-2. And they wanted, they needed these documents at the Dutch plant where Khan worked. They needed these documents translated from German into Dutch so that the Dutch workers could begin to implement the designs. And Khan had gotten his PhD in Germany, he'd studied there for many years, he spoke excellent German, and he spoke pretty good Dutch because he was living in Holland. And so they assigned him to this top secret facility called the Brain Box, which was supposed to be their most secure facility. And they let him go in there without the proper clearance at a time when most of the world knew Pakistan was beginning its pursuit of nuclear weapons. And they gave him twelve volumes of German designs to translate into Dutch. And it was like the perfect storm of a lack of security, because he had access to them, he was able to take his own notes, he was able to take these documents out of the facility, saying that he needed to take them home for his wife to help him with the translation, because she spoke better Dutch. And so he was able to copy all twelve of these volumes. And he offered then, in the end of 1974, to take them back to Pakistan. He went then at the end of that year, and had a meeting with Bhutto in Islamabad. But Bhutto wasn't ready for him to come back. He said go back and find for me the suppliers, the people who can provide us with the technology and the material we need to implement that design. And so Khan went back, and he spent another whole year stealing more designs, and lining up the suppliers who were going to help Pakistan jump start its nuclear weapons program.

HH: Now I want to pause here for a moment, because the people who ought to be reading this, I assume that this is being read far and wide within the FBI and other counterintelligence agencies, the CIA, and across Interpol and things like that. But anyone in industrial America really needs to take a hard look at this, because one of the astonishing things is the terrible serendipity of having Veerman in the same office as A.Q. Khan. And it's one of those terrible accidents of history that I just want to expand upon. You put a photographer with a spy, and presto, you've got a leak of the most enormous proportions.

CC: Yes, you do. And I think Khan is a very likable, pleasant person. And Veerman was a photographer, a technician. And he was thrilled when this foreign man came in with a huge smile, and treated him equally, and with respect. And they developed a very strong friendship. And Veerman was also so pleased when Khan expressed an interest in his work, and admired his photographs of this machinery as works of art. And eventually, he asked Veerman to help him buy a camera so he could do the same sort of work himself. [And Veerman later,] it took months before Veerman realized that he'd been duped, basically. And people…there are many accounts of co-workers seeing Khan writing notes in Urdu, and talking on the phone in Urdu, and he'd always smile at people and say no, I'm just writing letters home to my family. And he conducted this espionage in full view of many people.

HH: I also want to pause for a moment. I used to know a lot about the Soviets, and how they'd turn people around. And when I was reading The Nuclear Jihadist, [it all came…] there were three reasons you could get a guy to go to the other side. One was money, one was ego, and one was nationalism. And sometime you could blackmail them, but those were the big three. They all came into play with A.Q. Khan, and especially this ego. [I'm…] the portrait you two draw of him is of a man who needed to be important far beyond his daily life.

DF: Yes, that's right. There was an instance early when he was boy, his mother took him to a shaman, a fortune teller, who predicted that he would be someone who had a great destiny. And then again, just before he went to Europe in the early 1960's, he and a friend went to a fortune teller, and the fortune teller again predicted that Khan would do great things. Now whether these stories are true or not, they're stories that Khan told, and they certainly express his personality, and his belief that he was someone who was going to do important things. And as his power and influence and success grew, once he'd returned to Pakistan, and was helping develop the nuclear weapon, his sense of ego and Khan really began to explode. And that led him, I think, to the next sort of stage in his career, where he felt he was above the law, and he could sell this technology then that he'd brought to Pakistan, he could sell it to other countries.

HH: Let's stay for a moment on…is it Fritz Veerman?

DF: Fritz Veerman, yes.

HH: Yeah, Fritz Veerman, the photographer who shares an office. He goes over to Khan's house for dinner one night, and Khan loves to cook, et cetera, he is a devout Muslim, he doesn't drink, but they love food. And he's there, and he sees these binders that Catherine referred to, and he doesn't do anything about it. And I thought to myself, at that point, no one wants to be a snitch, but when you see highly classified documents lying around a house, ought he not to have acted in your opinion?

DF: Oh, my gosh, of course he should have. And Fritz Veerman, from the time we've spent with him in researching the book, is someone who's very tortured today about having failed to do the right thing. But there were two factors at play. One is what Cathy said. He admired Khan, and he treasured their friendship, because nobody else treated him very well at the labs. But also, there was this fear of his that he'd been such a help to Khan, he'd given him photographs, he'd showed him how to use his camera…

HH: Yup.

DF: He'd sort of had these suspicions, but never anything had come clear. And he was worried that when he blew the whistle, fingers might be pointed at him. And so he remained silent until after Khan had absconded with all of the designs and plans and the shopping list that he needed.

HH: Now that we've set this up, let's go back to what's going on in Pakistan. They start a plutonium project after this meeting you describe in the tent. It goes nowhere. And then Khan, quite amazingly, demands a meeting with the president of Pakistan, and tells him to put him in charge of the program, or he wants to come back and help. What happens?

CC: Well, this is a very smart move on Bhutto's part. They were pursuing the plutonium route, and [not getting,] not doing very well with it. And then when he's approached by Kahn, of course first of all, he's a little suspicious because he's well informed enough to know that this is a very difficult thing this man is proposing. But then he thinks, "Why not?" and so what he does is he uses Khan to develop a parallel program. So in fact, he's got two programs going simultaneously and the plutonium route, which he knows is not going to succeed, is sort of a diversion that allows A.Q. Khan's enrichment program to continue in secret. So one masks the other.

HH: And when he goes back, he sends Khan back to Europe, and he also sends along a very mysterious fellow, Butt is how I think you say it, Siddique Butt?

CC: Yeah.

DF: Yeah.

HH: Let's explain to the audience who he is, and his role in the Khan network in Europe.

DF: Yes, Siddique Butt was a junior physicist in the Pakistani scientific community, and he was actually at that 1972 meeting in Multan, where Zulfikar Ali Bhutto is exhorting the crowd to build this bomb for him in three years. And Butt was one of the people we were told by witnesses there, who stood up and said, "We can do it for you." We can do it for you. And so come 1975, late '74, when Bhutto sent Khan back to Urenco to get the plans, he set him up with S.A. Butt, and he assigned Butt to the [Embassy at the Hague, the] Pakistani Embassy at the Hague in the Netherlands. And he created, along with Khan, what became known as the Pakistani pipeline. They set up a series of front companies, and ruses, and used false invoices and that sort of thing, to buy the equipment that was on A.Q. Khan's shopping list. And they were very crafty about it. If they got thwarted in one country, and they were occasionally thwarted in the Netherlands particularly, they would go and find people willing to sell it to them in Germany, or Switzerland, Canada, some in the United States. And this Pakistani pipeline thrived for nearly a decade with S.A. Butt at its head, and A.Q. Khan running the levers from, [once he got back to] Pakistan. It was a very successful procurement operation. If Saddam Hussein had been as clever and as successful, I think he might have had a nuclear bomb before the first Gulf War, before we went in there and found his secret program.

HH: It's overwhelming. In fact, when Khan goes back and he just starts making a list and checking it twice of what he's going to need, that's the critical year. And when we come back from break, we're going to talk about why the West did not act, why they missed Khan as he got a shopping list together, so he could begin to dispatch around the world to get what he needed to build the bombs which he eventually did build.

HH: My guests, Douglas Frantz and Catherine Collins have [completely…we're blowing past] all the fascinating details which you really need in <u>The Nuclear Jihadist</u>, and you'll get them there. But the short form is, where was the West?

CC: Well, we were out there. The Dutch became suspicious about Khan and what he was up to, and there was a conflict within their government. The economic side would have been very embarrassed to disclose publicly that they had a spy operating in their midst. But the law enforcement side wanted to arrest Khan and charge him with espionage. So in order to resolve this dispute, the Dutch security police turned to the CIA and explained what the situation was, and said we want to arrest him. Do you agree with us? And to their surprise, the CIA said no. Let him go. We want to watch him, and we want to wait and see what he's up to. And so that was the first time that Khan was allowed to walk away from this, and walk away with all these secrets, and return to Pakistan.

HH: I was struck by the story in <u>The Nuclear Jihadist</u>, they had the search warrants issued. They were ready to raid his house. They were ready to arrest him and take all of his files away. And then they called it off. What the world would look like right now if that in fact happened.

DF: Yeah, I think the world would be completely different. I think Pakistan would have been delayed for years, and possibly decades, in its quest for a nuclear weapon, Iran would not be on the verge of enriching uranium on an industrial scale, North Korea probably would not have what we believe is a hidden enrichment facility somewhere deep in its mountains, and we wouldn't be so worried all the time before we go to sleep about whether al Qaeda or some other terrorist nut group has access to fissile material, or to the plans for a nuclear weapon. But A.Q. Khan turned out to do more damage than any other person or country when it came to spreading nuclear weapons around the world. And in 1975, he could have been stopped.

HH: Now let's back up a little bit and talk about the concept of dual use technology. It's in the newspapers a lot, it causes MEGO (M Eyes Glaze Over), because people just don't understand, I don't understand, I'm not putting anyone down, what it really means, and how difficult it is to enforce, and why the Congress, whether it's Senator Glenn, or Republicans, or anyone else, really can't get folks to get a good regime in place. Explain the peril of dual use technology, if you would.

DF: Yeah, it's…dual use technology is technology that can be used for civilian or military purposes. Therefore, it has a dual use. [And it…] there's a tension when it comes to a country wanting to buy that, it happened with Iraq, it's happened with Iran, it happened with Pakistan, because you try to buy, say, a lathe or a centrifuge, and you say it's for a textile plant, or it's for, as Khan said a couple of times, it's for a butter factory where we need to spin things around. And so we need the components for the spinners, and we only are using it for civilian purposes. And that's what we intend to do. And so there are economic incentives for countries to keep those export regulations loose and lax, so that they can sell the equipment for commercial purposes. But it's so easy with much of this equipment to turn it over into military uses. And so we need, obviously, a stricter set of laws that are better enforced, and we also need a mechanism by which countries around the world, the developed countries, share their knowledge of who is acquiring these dual use technologies, because if you look at the patterns of who's acquiring certain technologies, certain material and equipment, then you can discern whether perhaps they have something nefarious in mind. In dual use technology, it does sort of make your eyes glaze over, but it's the means that Pakistan used in large part to develop its own nuclear arsenal. And it's what helped Iran, and Iran is still out there on the market trying to exploit those loopholes now.

HH: So in the 70's, Khan bolts from Europe, he's acquired his shopping list, both parts of it and also where to find it, and Butt remains there. He comes back, and this takes a lot of money. And I have skipped over the Islamic Alliance, but I think we have to go back now and talk about how Pakistan, this dirt poor country at the time, manages to get together the resources to go shopping around the globe.

CC: Well, Bhutto went around and visited different countries and different leaders and, you know, hat in hand, [and] said do you want to be a part of this history? This is a ground-breaking, historic moment, and do you want to participate in this? Will you support us in our quest for this ultimate weapon? And in fact, he did get an enormous amount of support from Libya, from Saudi Arabia, and other places. They actually named a cricket stadium for Muammar Gaddafi.

HH: He was selling an Islamic bomb, was he not?

DF: He was, absolutely. At one point, Zulfikar Ali Bhutto justified Pakistan's nuclear program by saying we have a Christian bomb, we have a Jewish bomb, we have a Hindu bomb. Why can't we have an Islamic bomb? And so he found a receptive audience, particularly, as Cathy said, in Libya, where Muammar Gaddafi sent cash by the suitcase-full, to help buy this Islamic bomb for Pakistan, and the Saudis also provided money, and they provided in-kind oil to allow Pakistan to devote more of its resources to this program. And as a result, A.Q. Khan found himself with a blank check. And he later remarked that he was amazed at the greed of Western companies, and how they were lining up to sell him this technology.

HH: Now I think something we've got to make sure we let people know, when he comes back to Pakistan, he has a rival. And this will play into why he's able to get away with the privatization of his nuclear export after a period of time. He makes a play for complete and utter authority, and he gets it. Explain why he made that play and how he got it.

DF: Well, I think it was his ego at work here. I mean, [he promised,] he promised Zulfikar Ali Bhutto that he would have enriched uranium for him within three to five years. And for a backwards country like Pakistan, that was a bold promise indeed. But he found himself, in the first days, constrained because he was put inside the nuclear establishment of Pakistan, and it was run by a man named Munir Khan, who was no relation. And Munir Khan was more of a scientist, and he was also more of a straight shooter. And he was trying to bring Pakistan along on the nuclear level, pursuing a plutonium case, above board. He'd worked at the IAEA in Vienna before, and so he was Westernized. He really didn't want to send people out there breaking all the laws. And so A.Q. Khan was able to bring Bhutto over to his side when he went back and said, "I can't do it, and you're not going to get your bomb if you let Munir Khan do this. I need to have complete independence, no oversight for what I do, and I need a blank check." And Bhutto was desperate at that point to develop his bomb. India had tested its first device in 1974, which had inflamed A.Q. Khan, and drawn grave concerns in Pakistan. And so Bhutto was willing to give him this blank check.

HH: At this point, I'm asking Douglas and Catherine how did India get their bomb, and to explain for us how Khan set up Kahuta, and the role of President Zia in this.

CC: Well, there's interesting similarities and differences when you look at India and Pakistan. India also got its program by sort of surreptitious methods. It took a Canadian reactor that they were building with help from Canada, and it was a light water reactor. And they [were] managed secretly to divert that technology in order to develop a military program. [But the difference between India and Pakistan is that India was able…and by the way,] India also had thousands, I believe, of scientists trained overseas, many of whom were trained in the United States in order to do this. But the difference between India and Pakistan is that India was able to do much of this work indigenously, with local talent, and they were able to develop this equipment and this technology more or less on their own. Pakistan, on the other hand, had no indigenous ability to develop this technology to make the various bits and pieces of equipment that go into one of these plants. And so I think one of the curious things about Pakistan's program is that it's perhaps an early example of globalization that Pakistan's program was built, assembled with bits and pieces from countries all around the globe, from Canada and the United States and Britain and Switzerland and Germany. A lot of countries have participated, knowingly and unknowingly, in Pakistan's program, which at that point, even Khan would say didn't have the ability to make a decent bicycle, much less an enrichment program.

HH: Take us back to the India of 1974, when they explode their device under the desert. [Indira Gandhi is…] how shocked is the world, and how likely is it that we've got similar shocks coming up on us soon?

DF: Well, the world was completely surprised by that, taken by surprise. The CIA didn't see it coming, nobody saw it coming. And the Indians just blew up that desert with one device that they called, oddly, a peaceful nuclear explosion. Now that seems to me like a contradiction in terms, the ultimate oxymoron. But the world was taken by surprise by the Indian program. And you make exactly the right point looking forward, Hugh, that we're in for these surprises, I fear. I mean, we talk, I'm getting ahead of ourselves, but we talk at near the end of our book about a missing shipment of critical equipment, and where did it go, missing bomb plans, where did they go? We may be in for a very rude surprise one of these days.

HH: And that's…we will get there. I do know what the payoff on this book is, which is alarm, but intelligent alarm. Let's go back to Kahuta, and explain to people what Khan did there.

DF: Yes, when Khan got his blank check from Zulfikar Ali Bhutto to build this enrichment plant, they immediately set to work at Kahuta, which was about forty miles southeast of the capitol of Islamabad in Pakistan, in a very remote area, Kahuta was a village of no repute. And they began building this huge nuclear enrichment facility there for A.Q. Khan. [They called it, I don't even know what they called it initially, but] in 1977, as construction was well under way, Zulfikar Ali Bhutto was ousted by Mohammed Zia ul-Haq, who was a military general, who took power in 1977, and he began the very distinct Islamization of Pakistan, if you will. He brought in all of these madrasas that would wind up training the soldiers for the Afghan war, and fighting the Indians in Kashmir. And so Zia took over the power; but for A.Q. Khan, it was like nothing had changed, because he just went from one patron to the next. He began to adopt a more Islamic demeanor, he began to wear a quasi-military uniform, and so Zia kept him going with the same blank check, and allowed him to build Kahuta. And Kahuta was turning out so successful that in 1981, Zia went out to this then-huge, vast complex, with thousands of employees, covering hundreds of acres, and he dedicated it as Dr. Abdul Qadeer Khan Research Laboratories.

HH: You know, what struck me is that Khan was very much to the Pakistani nuclear program as Admiral Rickover was to the American nuclear submarine program. Every person hired, every detail of the program, completely under his thumb, and it showed.

HH: I want to stay for a moment on the nature of Khan at Kahuta, because as I mentioned before break, he's like Rickover. He interviews everyone that gets hired, he approves every invoice, he searches out every part and parcel, a villain, but an amazingly talented one.

CC: Well, yes. You see, I don't think he was a brilliant scientist. One of his own professors said he was no Einstein. But his genius seemed to be his ability to bring together all sorts of different people, and get different things going all at once, and get them all to work in unison. You know, usually, when you start a new factory or a new program, you would run a little test program, and then you'd set up a pilot, and then you'd start doing the main program, you know, one step at a time. Khan did it all at once and jumped in. He risked everything. He took enormous risk in order that this would succeed. And he brought people from around the world. He recruited scientists from Europe and from North America, and brought them back, appealing to their nationalism. And he was able to bring all this together, weave it all together into a successful program.

HH: Now he also does this with the protection of Zia, and the United States basically has to turn a blind eye, because the Soviets invade Afghanistan, and as depicted in Charlie Wilson's War, incompletely I believe, but nevertheless there, President Zia's our guy during this conflict. He's arming the Mujahideen, and we're helping him. So we really can't crack down, can we, on Pakistan's nuclearization?

DF: No, we can't. I mean, you mentioned earlier in the show, Hugh, the one critical year. And I thought we were going to talk then about 1979, because I think that really is the critical year. Jimmy Carter is the president, he had run in part on a campaign plank that called for stopping the spread of nuclear weapons. He'd been an officer on a nuclear submarine, so he knew something about the topic. And in April of 1979, there were press reports, and the U.S. had a lot of intelligence reports that Pakistan was making unexpected progress on its nuclear program with its enrichment facility at Kahuta, and that A.Q. Khan was the man who was behind this. So in April of 1979, Carter imposes very tough sanctions on Pakistan, and he sets about diplomatically trying to persuade American allies to stop the flow of this dual use technology we've been talking about into Pakistan. And [things sort of,] it looks like we may put the brakes on Pakistan's nuclear program. We might not have stopped them, but we could have delayed it by many, many years. But in December of that same year, the Soviets invade Afghanistan, and Zbigniew Brzezinski, who's the national security advisor to President Carter, tells him explicitly, in a memo that we quote from in the book, that we have to reverse our sanctions on Pakistan, because we need them more to help funnel money and arms to the Afghan resistance. So [that, so] Carter agreed, they pulled back the sanctions, and for the next eleven years, the United States turned a blind eye to Pakistan's steady, fast march toward joining the nuclear elite. You know, we just let them go right on ahead. We let Zia go right on ahead, because he was our guy. [And Zia,] we made a couple of attempts to try and persuade him to slow down. But Zia was a smart man, and he knew that once the United States didn't need Pakistan anymore after the end of the Afghan war, [that he would abandon them.] The United States would abandon them. And so he was more determined than ever to develop that nuclear program.

HH: Now when that is going on, obviously, they are our crucial allies in the destruction of the Soviet Union. But when does the fatal contact with North Korea begin?

DF: 1993 is when we place it in the book. In December of 1993, [A.Q. Khan by that time,] Kahuta's up and running, A.Q. Khan is turning out all the enriched, highly enriched uranium that Pakistan needs for its nuclear weapon. They have nuclear weapons galore by then. All they have to do is turn a final switch, and they could have tested them at any time. But A. Q. Kahn has sort of worked himself out of a job, because he succeeded so quickly and so thoroughly. And yet he has an ego that is inflated beyond all means. He's the public face of the Pakistani nuclear program, and so he's filled with hubris, and he wants to do more. And so what he wants to do now is develop a missile that will help deliver this nuclear payload he's built.

CC: So what he does...I'm sorry...

HH: Go ahead.

CC: He goes to Benazir Bhutto, who's been brought to office for the second time, and they'd never gotten along very well. She was very suspicious of him, but she remembered his relationship with her father. And he went to her and said I understand you're going on a mission to China. Would you mind stopping along the way to pick something up for me in North Korea? And she's hesitant, but she agrees, because she wants to, she recognizes her need to get along with the military this time around, and she's helping that by establishing a better relationship with Khan, that he would be an advocate for her. So she agrees to go to North Korea, and they hold a big state dinner and parade, and she comes back with these plans that he's been wanting. And she brings them back to him, and hands them over, and warns him that they have an agreement with India not to develop this sort of thing unilaterally, that he is not supposed to develop it until India does the same. But he takes the plans, and he does exactly that. He proceeds and develops them immediately.

HH: You know, in the middle of all this, you tell the story, the very convoluted story of Pakistani politics. Zia is killed in an airplane crash, which also kills the American ambassador and senior other American official. It's very suspicious. And the military intervenes, but then they allow elections to come back. And everyone's on the take in Pakistan. I don't mean to say literally everyone, but it does seem as though it's just a given that corruption is going to be part of this, and Khan's getting rich. That's the point I want to point out. Khan's not just doing this for the nationalism. He's buying up properties and hotels and all sorts of things.

DF: Yeah. [We trace, I mean,] the book sort of follows this interesting arc of A.Q. Khan's life, and you can see at various points how his motive changes. He goes from a nationalist and ardent patriot in the mid-70's and early 80's. But as he accumulates power and success, he wants more. And so then he becomes very wealth driven, very greedy, and he wants more and more influence. And so he's skimming off the top. At the same time, you know, Bhutto's husband, Mr. 10%, is skimming off the top, too, when she's in there in her first term as prime minister from '88-'90, and then again from '93-'96. And widespread corruption is endemic.

HH: It's the rule.

HH: Next hour, we're going to talk about how Khan went private after he got Pakistan into the nuclear club, [how he went private.] To set that up, I wonder, we've got to go back one more time and tell people, the rest of the world isn't standing still. We talked about India going nuclear, but of course, we believe Israel went nuclear long before that, and we know that Iraq was trying to join them.

DF: Yes, absolutely. Saddam Hussein, throughout the 1980's, was using a procurement network set up of front companies and false invoices throughout Europe and the United States to buy technology to develop his own nuclear weapon. And at the time, Iran and Iraq were locked, of course, in that very brutal war they had with a million deaths on each side. And near the end of that war, in 1987, Iran also decides that it would like to revive its nuclear weapons ambitions, which at first surfaced during the Shah's era in the mid 1970's. The Shah wanted to obtain nuclear technology, and the United States was more than willing to sell it to him, because he was our ally. But in '87, of course, things were a little different in Iran. North Korea is as actively and secretly pursuing a nuclear weapons program during that period, and Israel has a nuclear arsenal by that time for sure.

HH: [And how…and] you talk about the double standard of the nuclear ambiguity. America's pretty comfortable with Israel having its arsenal, and pretty comfortable with Iran getting its capacity. And Pakistan plays that against us.

DF: Yes, I think that's exactly right, and it's one of the points we try to make in this book, that this double standard is in fact a double-edged sword. In the Ford administration, the United States was very willing to sell the entire nuclear fuel cycle to the Shah of Iran. And among the people who were backing that were Henry Kissinger and Donald Rumsfeld and Dick Cheney and Paul Wolfowitz. And that's not right. We shouldn't separate friend and foe here in terms of acquisition of nuclear power, because it's such a thin line between nuclear power and nuclear weapons, and we can see very clearly what happened with Iran in 1979, when the Ayatollah came in, and they had the Iranian revolution. They went from friend to enemy overnight. And had we sold them the nuclear material that we were willing to before then, they would have, be sitting on a nuclear arsenal today.

HH: And when did we start selling Pakistan the platform for delivery, the planes?

DF: That came up in the 1980's. We were allied with Pakistan in trying to force the Soviets out of Afghanistan. They were playing a big role. And they wanted a lot of things from us. And the Reagan administration was willing to sell them F-16's, which they were not supposed to use to deliver nuclear weapons, but it became quite clear from intelligence that they were working on the kind of firing and electronics they needed to use them to deliver them.

HH: In the first two hours of this program, we've covered sixty years from Khan's birth in pre-partitioned India in 1936, through his emigration to Europe, his return with nuclear secrets, the establishment of a top secret program, the proliferation of Pakistan, of nuclear capacity under the uranium enrichment program. And here we are in the mid-90's, they've got the delivery system, they've got the bomb, India's got the bomb. And this is when it metastasizes. Doug Frantz and Catherine Collins, let's pick up the story of when does Khan go rogue in the eyes of the Pakistani government, looking backwards? When does he decide to get rich by exporting weapons of mass destruction?

DF: That's a tough question, and a difficult one to parse when you look at when he goes rogue in the eyes of the Pakistani government. We do know for a fact, we prove conclusively in the book, that in 1987, Khan was part of a small group that sold the first centrifuge parts and components to Iran. They had a secret meeting in Dubai, the Iranians paid $10 million dollars to obtain these plans and components from A.Q. Khan, and from three of Khan's European suppliers. So they set that up. And now Khan's take out of that $10 million dollars was $2 million dollars, according to banking records that we have seen as part of our research. The question, though, Hugh, is was he then a rogue? Or did the Pakistani government know what was going on? And I believe we certainly can prove, perhaps not conclusively, but we believe that there were elements of the Pakistani military and intelligence communities that were aware that Khan was providing this material to Iran, because Iran was a potential ally for the Pakistanis at that time. The war in Afghanistan was winding down, Zia was seeing the day when the Americans would walk away from Pakistan, and so he was looking at the possibility of building an alliance with Iran, Afghanistan and Turkey, four Muslim countries. And trading this nuclear technology to Iran may have been part of that deal. We certainly believe it is. We don't have, I think, conclusive evidence, so I wouldn't say he was a rogue at that time, but it was the first time that he had reversed the flow, and gone from a buyer on the black market to a seller of the same technology.

HH: This takes us inside the rather convoluted world of Pakistani government and politics, because you mentioned the military, the ISI, the ISI part of the military, you've got a separate, stand-alone nuclear agency, and you've got civilian governments going on. Can you just line out the sort of complicated dance that goes on within Pakistan every single decade between these various elements?

DF: [What people need...]the one single fact that sorts all this out for you when you look at Pakistan is this – the military is always in control. From 1947 on, certainly after the death of Jinnah, the founder of Pakistan, the military has been in control. There have been various civilian governments, but they've operated to various degrees as puppets. The country remains controlled by the military. We've seen that, certainly clearly, over the last eight and a half years with Pervez Musharraf, a military general until very recently, running the country. We saw it with Zia. But even the civilian governments [were] in power, like Benazir Bhutto and Nawaz Sharif, it was the military that was pulling the strings. And the military and the ISI, which is the preeminent Pakistani intelligence agency, the Inter-services Directorate, they're synonymous. The ISI is part of the military. You don't have the separation that you have here in the United States between the Defense Department and the Central Intelligence Agency. They're all one, they all control everything.

HH: You two have been studying this for so long, let me just get this out of left field, a question. What's your degree of confidence in the control of Pakistan's nuclear arsenal? Is it secure?

DF: You know, we may disagree on this a little bit, so I'll try to go first and get my point across. I think that the arsenal is secure in terms of militants are not going to be able to raid these facilities and walk away with a working nuclear device. The Pakistani military is arrayed in great numbers around these sites; many of them are secret sites. I think they're arrayed there to protect them from raids by the Indians, and in their darkest moments, by the Americans. I think that the concern over the security of the nuclear arsenal in Pakistan comes into play should the government fall, should Pakistan flip over the edge into the status of a failed state, and an Islamic faction takes control of the government. The Islamic powers in the military or the intelligence agencies rise up and take control, and then, they may be willing to use one of these nukes, they may be willing to sell it to their friends in al Qaeda or the Taliban. That's the lack of security that concerns me, something that comes with Pakistan falling into chaos, and a big, dramatic change in government.

HH: When we refer, Catherine or Douglas, to the Pakistani nuclear arsenal, and when we say American nuclear arsenal, we all have in our mind images of silos opening, and missiles coming out, or cruise missiles launching from the SS boomers out there, or B-2's dropping packages. When we refer to the Pakistani arsenal, what are we referring to?

CC: Well, we're referring to bombs and warheads. And they're very carefully hidden. The Pakistanis want to maintain control of their own arsenal, and they don't want their friends, the Americans, to know precisely where they are, or how to get to them, and they've been very reluctant to have any input from other countries in terms of securing them. They want to maintain control of them themselves. And that's not an illogical attitude to take.

HH: Now when we refer to bombs and warheads, obviously they imported missile technology from North Korea. And we all watched North Korean missile tests. They're not very good, but they also have these Phantoms, which are pretty good. But isn't the Indian Air Force capable of dropping them? I mean, does India really worry about the capability of Pakistan to get through?

DF: I think India does worry and should worry. [They have,] Pakistan has not only the Ghauri missile, which A.Q. Khan developed from the North Korean designs, but they have their own indigenous missile designs, and I think they could launch enough nuclear warheads that it would be impossible for the Indians to knock them down. And India is very close. I mean, obviously, they share a thousand mile border with Pakistan, and so, you know, these missiles don't have to travel very far to reach every Indian city of any size. And the same with the F-16's. The Indians [may be, they] have far superior forces; they may be able to knock down most of them. But you only need one to get through to Delhi or Mumbai, or some other city like that to cause a conflagration.

HH: One more question, what's the size of the Indian nuclear arsenal now?

DF: I think it's about the same size as Pakistan's. It might be slightly smaller, actually, but we're concerned that the Indians may use this technology that they're getting from the United States to increase the size and the power of their nuclear arsenal, you know, in this deal that the administration has cut with India to strengthen our ties with them by giving them access to more of our civilian nuclear technology.

HH: Okay, let's go back to Khan. When he either goes private or partially private, he has three customers that we know about: North Korea, Libya and Iran. Where's he doing business with them? Take us inside the network a little bit. They can't fly into Karachi and do deals with him. Where's he making his trades?

CC: Khan's passport must be one of the fattest in the world. He's traveled all over the world, to dozens of countries repeatedly in order to do this. He did this, and it's unusual, because normally, a nuclear scientist in any country would have to let people know where he's going, and there would be some monitoring of his travels and activities, and where the people with whom he was meeting. But Khan was able to travel, you know, unaccompanied and at his own will.

DF: And they set up the hub. The hub for the network was set up in Dubai.

CC: Yeah.

HH: That's what I was getting at, yeah.

DF: That was where they did the first Iranian deal in '87, and eventually in the early 90's, Khan moved there, he bought an apartment there, he installed a mistress in another apartment, and he hooked up with a Sri Lankan businessman who ran a computer company named B.S.A. Tahir. And they set up their main operating in Dubai. And Dubai was a great choice, because it's sort of a modern day Casablanca. It's a black hole. What goes in there one way comes out a whole other way. It's a major shipping port on the Persian Gulf with very lax customs regulations. And so it was perfect, both in terms of location and looseness of laws for somebody like Khan to set up in a series of warehouses there, where they could bring this material in from Europe or South Africa or Malaysia or China or Canada or Spain or Japan, get it in their warehouses, and then send it off to Iran or to Libya, not so much with North Korea. He really just used the Pakistani Air Force to ferry his centrifuge technology to North Korea in payment for the help with the missile plans.

HH: Is it fair, to compare this, he's an architect, he has all the drawings upstairs and in his briefcase, and he just orders into a warehouse his production materials and trans-ships them to where it's going to go?

DF: Yes, I think that's exactly right. I mean, you know, it's a little more complicated, of course, but that's the basic outline of it. And when he couldn't get things that he needed for, say, Libya, Libya was a major project for Khan, as he struck a deal with Gaddafi in 1997…

HH: Doug, hold that thought. We'll go to break. I'm going to come back, and the Libya example is exactly where we're going next, because it is the most chilling of stories, and we know most of it.

HH: Now, this segment may be the most important, because I think Libya, Gaddafi as customer, Libya as market, is a stand-alone example of what Khan was doing that could very well have been replicated in other markets that we don't know yet have occurred. And let's start with that, Douglas and Catherine. What you know about Libya, could it have happened elsewhere that we don't know about now?

CC: Oh, definitely it could have. It was Khan and his network at their [most, at] their pinnacle, let's say. He approached the Libyans in 1997, he had a sort of a sales meeting in Istanbul, one of our favorite cities, and he proposed to them this off-the-shelf bomb factory. And we believe he received $80-100 million dollars for this transaction. And for that, he was able to bring his operations across Europe and South Africa, Spain, Malaysia, all together, and free to buy, through this main office in Dubai, he was able to start shipping literally hundreds of tons of material, of pieces of this factory, to Libya over a six year period.

HH: Now first question, someone else could have done this as well, let's say Saudi Arabia, let's say Egypt, let's say Malaysia. Any country that wanted it probably could have done the same deal, correct?

DF: I think so. I think so, Hugh, and you know, we touched on it earlier in the show. In our reporting, we discovered two very alarming things, the most alarming things to me. And they are that there's a missing shipment of centrifuge components and machine tools used to manufacture centrifuges, and there are missing plans for an actual Chinese-tested, Chinese-developed nuclear warhead. [These are,] electronic copies of these plans are missing. So this shipment is missing, these electronic plans are missing, nobody knows where they went. And there's a list of likely suspects. I mean, we don't know who they are. I mean, we've tried hard, and certainly people with more resources than we have have tried. You know, the list of likely suspects, Syria, certainly, the Israelis bombed something in Syria in September, the Saudis have always been on that list. They helped to finance the Pakistani nuclear program. They've expressed an interest in acquiring nuclear weapons in the past. They bought some Chinese missiles capable of carrying nuclear warheads. And then there's the unknown. A.Q. Khan and some of his scientists had dealings with al Qaeda. Two Pakistani nuclear scientists were meeting with Osama bin Laden in August of 2001, and talking about how to develop nuclear weapons for al Qaeda. So that's the part of this book, and the part of our reporting that keeps both of us awake at night.

HH: And I put it down, and I immediately thought Chavez in Venezuela, because you need a lot of cash, you need capacity, industrial capacity, and you need the ability to hide something. [I'm not...]I don't doubt that al Qaeda was meeting with them. I read with fascination your details. But I thought about the rogue states out there who have the kind of cash that you need to hide such a thing, and that's Chavez.

DF: Oh, that's fascinating. You know, it hadn't even occurred to me, but now that you say it, it makes all the sense in the world. And what's worth pointing out here is that A.Q. Khan is under house arrest. He's been under house arrest for almost exactly four years now. But his network still exists. And as long as there's a customer, these people, these suppliers, these greedy people who will sell anything to anyone, are popping up. They're still there. The network has not been shut down. Many of the people who worked with A.Q. Khan are still out there and still trying to sell their wares.

HH: Okay, let's go back to Libya. What exactly did they buy? And over what period of time? And how far along was the Libyan program when we invaded Iraq?

DF: Well, that's a good question, and they started sending material there in 1997. We have a really interesting description of a meeting between Khan and two senior Libyan officials in Istanbul in '97, where they strike a deal to do this. Now they were supplying the full range, they were going to build a centrifuge plant in Libya to enrich uranium. He gave Libya the atomic warhead plans that he had gotten from the Chinese, so they could develop their own warheads. They were setting up a plant to turn uranium ore into this uranium gas that you feed into the centrifuges. It was going to be there, a do-it-yourself atomic weapons plant. And they started in '97, they shipped hundreds of tons of material in there. It came from all over the world, from Japan, from South Korea, from Spain, from Singapore, from Europe, from all over the world. There was a huge factory outside Johannesburg, South Africa, that was part of the Khan network that was devoted to developing a big element of the Libyan plan. They developed it, they made it, they put it into eleven freight containers, and they were getting ready to ship it by sea to Libya. Khan set up a special factory in Malaysia to manufacture the centrifuges for Libya. I mean, the whole ball of wax was going to be there, until it came unwound at the end of 2003. And it came unwound because Muammar Gaddafi in part was frightened by what he had seen happen in March of 2003 to Saddam Hussein, when the American troops rolled in there. But Muammar Gaddafi also, I think, had come to realize that a nuclear weapon was something that he was spending too much money on, and if he ever wanted to get back into the good graces of the international community, he had to agree to give up his nuclear weapons program and his chemical weapons program.

HH: Let's talk a little bit about that, because that is an unsung episode in American foreign policy. And the people who brought that deal to fruition in the British and American governments deserve a hat tip. Yes, I believe the invasion of Iraq, there are accounts out there that Gaddafi called Berlusconi and said I give up, I want to get rid of this. But then, there's a lot of steps between the desire to give it up and get free, and actually getting the stuff out of Libya. Fascinating chapters.

DF: Yeah, I think that's some of the strongest reporting in our book. We were able to really get inside that operation. We take readers inside the negotiations between the Americans and the British, and the Libyans. And the Libyan negotiations were led by Seif Gaddafi, Muammar Gaddafi's son and designated heir. And so we see those negotiations going back and forth .And Gaddafi has spent, now, $80-100 million dollars building up this nuclear weapons program. He wants to have it to be a regional power. He wants to have it to be taken seriously. Perhaps he wants to have it to protect himself from turning out like Saddam Hussein, and getting overrun by the Americans. But the Americans, and a guy who's the deputy director at the CIA right now named Stephen Kappes, was the chief American negotiator. The chief British negotiator was an Arabist named Mark Allen from MI6. They do deserve medals, and they've probably gotten them in some secret ceremony. They played a big role in persuading Gaddafi to give up his weapons program. But the final straw occurred in October of 2003, when the Americans were able to seize a shipment of centrifuge components manufactured at a Khan-sponsored factory in Malaysia. They seized them on their way to Libya, and they seized them with the help of a man from the inside of Khan's network who had been recruited by the CIA in what we think was a very important recruitment, and a very important element of our book.

HH: You're going to have to read it. Even if you listened from the start, you have no idea of the stuff I have left behind. I feel like I'm bailing water here. But I do want to spend some time on the denuclearization of Libya, because you take us inside that operation, and I read about it in the newspaper, [it's never conveyed to me.] This is a huge deal, and you have this, I guess he's a retired Army colonel, who's overseeing it like a traffic cop, trying to get all this stuff out of Libya before they change their minds. And you've got the IAEA inspectors who won't even look at the plans, because they're barred by law from looking at warhead designs. It's a complicated ballet, and it came off.

DF: Yeah, it did. It was a major intelligence success for the United States and Britain, and it was also a very carefully orchestrated opera. The performances are amazing. The retired Army colonel you mentioned, Donald Mahley, is at the State Department with his then-ambassador rank, and they sent him over, because he was a nuclear weapons officer in the Army, to supervise the deconstruction of this massive nuclear facility that Tripoli was in the midst of building. They had stashed hundreds of tons of equipment all over Libya, in abandoned schools, in empty warehouses out in the desert, you know, and they were just preparing for the day when they brought it all together in their plant. And Mahley went over there with the orders, as you say, to take it all apart and get it out of there before Gaddafi changed his mind. And toward that end, they picked the most sensitive infomaterial, these nuclear weapons plans, the bomb plans we've been talking about, the warhead plans. They were in two shopping bags from an Islamabad tailor shop. That was how A.Q. Khan had delivered them to the Libyans. And Mahley wanted to get those out of there as fast as possible. He wanted to get prototypes for the most advanced centrifuge machines out of there as quickly as possible. And so he was able to get [American,] a big American aircraft freighter in there to take the first load out. But the second load was so huge that they had to get a giant ship in to fill it up with the more hundreds of tons of this equipment. It was a massive, a massive effort, and a successful one.

HH: And you convey the sort of grinding pressure. They're afraid Libya's going to turn on it, because Gaddafi's mercurial. That's a gentle way of describing it. And they can't get the trucks through. They basically have to get the dictator to shut down Tripoli, don't they?

DF: Yeah.

CC: Yeah, they do. It's a very difficult city, apparently, to navigate during the day with large trucks. And they tried repeatedly to do it, and they were way behind on the delivery schedule. So finally what they did was they told everyone they had to stay home, and they shut down the streets, and they cleared them out for these big trucks to go through all at once.

HH: Now I want to emphasize one thing. We didn't know he had this, did we?

DF: Of what period?

HH: Prior to 2003, did we know what Gaddafi was up to?

DF: Yes. Yes, we did. We did. Remember, we mentioned a couple of minutes ago the recruitment of a guy inside the Khan network.

HH: Oh, that's right.

DF: That happened in 1999 or 2000. We're not just sure. But he was a Swiss technician named Urs Tinner, who played a central role in Khan's network, both first in Dubai, and then later in Malaysia running the factory out there, manufacturing the centrifuges for the Libyan program. A CIA agent nicknamed Mad Dog had recruited him, and he began providing information to the Americans about what Khan was selling to Libya. We have, what's that great quote in the book, Cathy?

CC: You know, Tinner's relationship with Khan didn't start, though, in '99 or even 2000. Tinner had known Khan all his life. He was the son of one of Khan's very early hires, Friedrich Tinner. So they'd known each other since [the early, since] the mid to late 70's. The Tinners are from Switzerland, and they provided valves for Pakistan's program. And then later, as Khan opened the network up, they provided valves, these very technical pieces of this equipment for the centrifuges, they provided it for all the countries.

HH: Did we know how far advanced he was? And did we know that he had plans for the warhead, Gaddafi?

DF: No. No, we didn't know that he had the warhead plans, and we were uncertain about how far advanced he was. And there remains a dispute over how, whether Gaddafi ever would have had, really, the skilled workers and the infrastructure necessary to build a bomb. There's a significant group of people who think that he could have been within two or three years of having a bomb, and there's another group who looked at what was going on, and looked at the lack of skill of the Libyan workers, and they suspected it would have taken many more years, and many more tens of millions of dollars.

HH: I read not long ago, and interviewed Ambassador Bolton about his <u>Surrender Is Not An Option</u> memoir. And Bolton's in your book, and I'm not sure you guys think much of Bolton, because he's so hammer-headed about this sort of stuff. But he had the measure of the Iranians. I don't think he actually had the measure of the IAEA as perhaps you folks do, because he's very disparaging of them. But I'm very impressed with how they go after, when they're on the ground in Iran, the evidences of the uranium hexafluoride, and their technical abilities. But we really don't know what Iran has to date, and the IAEA really can't force their way on that country and find out what Khan gave them, can they?

DF: No, you're right. The IAEA acts with the consent of the host country. [We know,] we know a lot about what Iran has, Hugh. We know that Iran has 3,000 centrifuges installed at Natanz, which is a plant [in central,] a huge, underground plant built 75 feet underground, with concrete roofs to protect it from any bombing by the Israelis or the Americans. We know that inside those giant halls, they have 3,000 centrifuges, which will soon be operating at full speed. We know also that A.Q. Khan and his network provided them with a lot of information about how to build a nuclear weapon. We don't know whether they've done that or not. [And we also,] What we don't know about Iran is whether Khan gave them the same atomic warhead plans that he gave to Libya.

HH: What do you think about…that's the question. What do you think? What's your hunch?

DF: You know, my hunch is yes.

HH: Yeah.

DF: He gave them to them. Why would he give them to Libya and not give them to Iran? Both of these countries have exactly the same goal. It's just illogical. And you know, what? We could get that question answered if this administration would push Pervez Musharraf and cash in that $10 billion bucks.

HH: I'm coming back to that, because I absolutely agree with you on the fact that we've got to get to Khan. But in terms of not only the Natanz facility, one of the other things I took away from The Nuclear Jihadist is they could have a bunch of other facilities with centrifuges up and cascading, and we wouldn't know about it, would we?

DF: No, you're exactly right. As we said earlier, these are very easy machines to hide, and there are a lot of people we spoke with in the research for this book who believe that Iran has a secret parallel military program. And you're right to say the IAEA has been successful there, but there are areas that are off limits to the IAEA, just as there were in the early 1990's when Saddam had his hidden nuclear program going on. You know, there were areas that were off limits to the IAEA. Since then, the IAEA's authority has been increased somewhat by countries that signed something called the additional protocol, which gives the IAEA quicker access to suspicious facilities. But even then, Iran has not signed the additional protocol, they've not ratified it, and they've not allowed IAEA inspectors access to everything inside their country.

HH: So the day could arrive, possibly, and I'd like to kind of get your calculation of odds, where Iran, like India in 1974, tests a device underground somewhere in their vast desert, and we really shouldn't be surprised, although we will be.

DF: I think you're right. It may well happen, and we won't be surprised, and certainly, anybody who reads this book won't be surprised. But you know, I don't think that Iran needs to test a nuclear weapon. We can look at Israel, and Israel has never openly tested a nuclear weapon. There were some suspicions about a test in the Indian Ocean, but Israel has never tested a nuclear weapon. It's enough, in a way, that the world knows Israel has a nuclear arsenal. And it will be enough, in a way, that the world knows Iran has a nuclear arsenal. We will have to treat them differently, and it's also going to mean that their neighbors are going to be a lot more concerned, and it's going to be that domino effect that Cathy spoke about earlier in the show.

HH: Let me ask you both, obviously, Khan is under house arrest, and…well, let's quickly get to that. Why is he under house arrest? Why did Musharraf put him there?

CC: Well, in late 2003, after the seizure of the BBC China, the United States finally went to Pakistan and said look, this is enough.

HH: That's the ship, right? That's the ship…

CC: Yes, that's the ship. Sorry, that one's the ship that they seized, from which they took out the five containers containing the equipment for Libya. And that was the final straw. And they went to Musharraf and said look, you really have to stop this. And because of that, Musharraf was able to confront Khan, and he had him arrested, and he was forced, eventually, to confess on national television. But immediately afterwards, Musharraf pardoned Khan, and treated him as a national hero. And he's still thought of that way on the street. And since then, Khan has been under house arrest in his home. In the beginning, it was a very, more severe type of arrest. He was not allowed to leave the home at all, he did not have access to newspapers and computers. His dear friend and biographer said that it was a very extreme punishment for a man who was used to being out in the public as much as Khan was. But [he,] since then, the terms have been softened somewhat, and he's been out more. But most importantly, aside from the idea of whether or not he should be punished, is the idea that here is a man with all the answers. He is the one man in the world who can tell us precisely to whom he sold this information, these materials, who his clients were, and who the suppliers were. He can tell us precisely who has what, and where our concern should be. Yet this administration has not pressured Musharraf in order to make this man available. And we're not advocating enhanced interrogation. We're advocating that someone should sit down and have a serious conversation with him. And if the Americans or Europeans or another country are not the right people to conduct this interrogation, perhaps a neutral international organization like the IAEA would be an appropriate place to begin this discussion.

HH: A minute to the break, and our last segment coming up. Is it possible that in fact, that interrogation, that conversation has happened, but for reasons similar to those that the CIA exercised when they did not arrest Khan in Europe all those many years ago, we've chosen not to make that public because we're watching the network?

CC: You know, you're not the only person who's brought up that possibility. Yeah, that, certainly, that could be a possibility. But think about this. This network that Khan ran is supposed to have another fifty people in it. And only a half dozen have been rolled up and been caught in the judicial system in various countries around the world.

HH: I know.

CC: There are a lot of people out there still doing business. And if someone had had this conversation with Khan, one might expect to have heard more in terms of the prosecution of other elements of his network.

HH: Good point.

HH: I want to thank you, Douglas Frantz and Catherine Collins, not just for spending all this time with me, but for the book, The Nuclear Jihadist. My hat's off to you. You probably don't know this, but I'm not exactly the world's greatest fan of the Los Angeles Times. But...

CC: Oh...

DF: (laughing) I know that.

HH: Shocking, huh? But this is just an extraordinary bit of reporting. And I don't know how you did it, but I want to finish by talking about the nuclear clock, because that's where you folks finished. And it's just very alarming that it's moved forward because of one man. It's hard to imagine one man could do this.

DF: It is. It is hard to imagine, but A.Q. Khan changed the rules of the nuclear game forever. You know, the first nuclear age was about the great powers facing off against each other, the Soviet Union and the United States. And that was terrifying. But at least then, everybody knew the rules. In this second nuclear age, which A.Q. Khan ushered in, in the age really of A.Q. Khan, you know, there's no return address for a nuclear weapon, so there's no deterrence. This bomb could come in a backpack, in a briefcase, or in an ox cart, or in a shipping container. And we've seen, through A.Q. Khan, the privatization of the atomic bomb, the outsourcing of the bomb. And that makes it much more frightening, because of this deadly legacy that he has really spread around the world. And we talked earlier about the likelihood of a nuclear explosion in anger. [And it's...]the probability is high, but it's not inevitable. There are steps that can be taken to at least lower the odds, and give us a better chance of surviving without this most horrific of catastrophes.

HH: Here's my last question. I'd like both of your thoughts. If that bomb goes off somewhere, whether Tel Aviv or India or somewhere else, that Pakistan either uses directly, or has exported because of Khan, will A.Q. Khan be sad? Or will he be satisfied?

CC: Oh, dear, what a thought. [I would...silent.] I would think that if it were to go toward furthering his world vision, perhaps he'd derive some satisfaction of that. If he felt that the bomb were used in a justifiable manner, maybe he'd be okay with that. It's just hard for me to imagine that anyone could welcome this sort of thing, because you know, these are weapons that really, while we have them, they really can't…from your mindset and my mindset, they just can't be used.

HH: Right.

CC: They've always been a deterrent. But they're not something that someone actually uses.

HH: Well, you opened with the quotes from John Hersey, but Doug, you've got about thirty seconds. Do you think he'd be sad or satisfied?

DF: Well, I think he'd be satisfied. I think that he is so egomaniacal, and he's got such a narrow worldview now, that he would be satisfied if India or Israel or some American city were wiped off the map.

HH: That's the chilling bottom line, and the reason why, folks, you really ought to buy The <u>Nuclear Jihadist</u>. Thank you Douglas Frantz and Catherine Collins.

End of interview.

Chapter 4.

The Threat from Iran: Interviews with Michael Ledeen and Ali Ansari

It is always dispiriting to hear Americans casually confuse Shia and Sunni, demonstrating again and again why our allies and friends in the Muslim world must be endlessly amazed by our collective inability to get the most basic of key facts down and absorbed. Imagine if an outsider to the long struggle in Northern Ireland didn't know the difference between Catholics and Protestsants? How seriously would we receive proposals on the future of the conflict from them?

Two of the authors I have interviewed specialize in the Iranian theocracy. Michael Ledeen is perhaps the longest running one-man alarm bell in the world, and his book The Iranian Time Bomb covers in great detail the rise and rule of the Ayatollah Khomenei and his successors. Dr. Ali Ansari is by striking contrast much more sympathetic to the Iranian theocrats but no less detailed in the picture he paints of the regime. Both interviews are crucial to understanding Iran's role in the long war.

Interview with Michael Ledeen
October 4, 2007

HH: Special hour now on the Hugh Hewitt Show, a conversation with Michael Ledeen about his brand new book, The Iranian Time Bomb: The Mullah Zealots' Quest For Destruction. Michael, always a pleasure, welcome back to the Hugh Hewitt Show.

ML: Hugh, thank you so much. I love you, you know that.

HH: Well, you're awfully kind. I love this book, and I'm going to be talking about this book a lot over the next few weeks, because I think people need to read it, beginning with the idea we've got to remember who Khomeini was, that the revolution wasn't because the Shah was too oppressive, but because the Shah was too liberal. Give people a walk back as to where Khomeini came from and what he stood for, Michael Ledeen.

ML: Well, he hated the Shah because he saw the Shah as the agent of Western feminism, really, in a way, because what got Khomeini more excited than anything else was the very thought that women could teach boys in school, that women could participate in government, that women were increasingly having equal rights, that they didn't have to cover up their heads, and so forth. And that just drove him crazy, and they were among his first targets when he took over in 1979. He threw the women out of the boys' schools, he banned them from high office, and he required this humiliating costume that they all have to wear.

HH: There's a lot I did not know about the revolution in your book, The Iranian Time Bomb. One of those is that the Republican Guard, the vanguard of the Islamic Revolution, had been trained by Fatah. Has that been known for a long time?

ML: Well, I wrote it years ago. I originally learned it from this fabulous man, Ion Mihai Pacepa, who has a new book out on the Kennedy assassination. And he was at the time the head of the Romanian intelligence service, and they knew about it, because they worked so closely with Arafat on behalf of the KGB. And then I heard it again from an Iranian who was actually present in the training camps starting in the early 70's in Lebanon, where Arafat was training the Revolutionary Guards. And remember, once Khomeini came to power, the first foreign dignitary to visit Tehran and be honored by the new regime was Arafat himself.

HH: Now like other fascists, Khomeini, you recall and write in the book, used the mass plebiscite to sort of legitimize his dictatorship.

ML: Right.

HH: Has that ever since been challenged? Did they ever come back and ask for a second re-up on the revolution?

ML: No. In fact, it's the opponents of the regime who call for referenda. They're the ones who say, "Let's have a referendum on the form of government that the Iranian people want." And the regime won't have it now, because they know that most of the people don't want them.

HH: Can you briefly describe for us, as you do in the first chapter, how that government operates in Iran now, the role of the supreme leader, the judicial council, the president, and the Revolutionary Guard?

ML: Well, you know, Ahmadinejad has gotten so much press, because he's such a colorful character, that people have lost sight of the fact that it's a clerical fascist dictatorship. And there's a man named Ali Khamenei who's almost never referred to, but his job title is supreme leader, which tells you something about how important he is. Presidents come and go. There have been exactly two supreme leaders in the nearly thirty years of the Islamic Republic, and they're not elected at all. They're chosen by a committee of their peers, and that committee is generally chosen by them for the most part, although there are these phony elections that they have. So that's the way the system works, and the desires of the supreme leader are enforced upon the society by the secret police, and by the Sharia courts, the Islamic tribunals. And one of the first things Khomeini said when he came in is no more of this Western justice system where you get appeals and justice is delayed, and all of that. No, the case gets to be heard by an Islamic judge. The Islamic judge rules, and that is that. And that's one reason why you have so many of these executions, public executions, women stoned to death, opponents of the regime thrown into prison for extended periods of time, tortured and sometimes killed. So it's a very ugly system.

HH: Now the judicial council, can you describe what its role is when it comes to elections?

ML: [Well, when it comes…] you know, elections in Iran are charades. They're not elections. And lists of candidates are submitted to these commissions, and the commissions go through them and eliminate anybody they don't want. So President Kahtami, for example, who's universally held up as a great example of a moderate, he was number, I don't remember the number exactly, but something like number 231 on that list. The preceding 230 were unacceptable.

HH: Wow.

ML: So every candidate is screened, every list is filtered, and anybody who's anybody in Iran has been effectively chosen by the regime, whatever the charade of elections.

HH: I'm getting ahead of myself, but you mentioned towards the end of the book there is concern now that Ahmadinejad and the Revolutionary Guard have built a state within a state, one that is advancing, really, a second Islamic Revolution. Can you expand that, Michael Ledeen?

ML: [Yeah, this one,] there are a lot of scholars who believe [this, who believe] that there was an easing of the repression for a few years, and that Ahmadinejad and his cohorts who all come from the Revolutionary Guard's organization, which is one of the more fanatical military wings of the regime, that they decided that this had to be rolled back. And consequently, they are imposing a kind of new terror on the people.

HH: I'm talking with Michael Ledeen, author of the brand new best selling book, The Iranian Time Bomb. I've linked it at Hughhewitt.com. I really recommend you get this if you want to know what this conversation is all about. But back up to Ali Khamenei, Michael Ledeen. What are his ambitions, what's his knowledge of the sort of extent of Iranian terror from Khobar forward?

ML: Well, you have to keep in mind that the Revolutionary Guards, which is the main instruments of assassination overseas and of supporting foreign terrorist organizations like Hezbollah and Islamic Jihad and al Qaeda, that this organization reports directly to Khamenei. It does not go through the government, and it certainly doesn't go through the regular military. So every major operation that's undertaken by the Revolutionary Guards goes through Khamenei personally, and is approved by him personally.

HH: So is it fair to say that the Revolutionary Guards is sort of a combination of Gestapo and SS answering directly to the supreme leader?

ML: Yes, I think that's exactly right, and just like the SS, they swear a personal oath to the supreme leader, and their commander sits in on all the important strategic discussions held by the supreme leader.

HH: Now within the Revolutionary Guards, there are some divisions like the Quds force. I first heard about the Quds force from General Abizaid, oh, a year ago talking about the Iranian incursion into Iraq.

ML: Yeah.

HH: How big, generally, is the RG, and within it, the Quds?

ML: Well, the RG is somewhere between 400,000 and 500,000 people. It's a pretty big organization. And the Quds is much smaller, because Quds operates only overseas. Quds has no domestic role at all. So that's why the various Iranians that we've been arresting in Iraq and in Afghanistan, and sometimes they get caught in Lebanon, they're Quds people, because they're foreign operatives.

HH: Now you refer often in the book, The Iranian Time Bomb, to the senior Mullahs, many of whom are just absolutely ruthless, like Khalkhali and others that you draw quick pen portraits of. What's the Mullahcracy's number? How many Mullahs matter?

ML: Well, the easiest way to think about Iran is that it's a country of between 70 and 80 million people. It's a very big country. And of these people, [probably, well, for sure,] 70%, which is to say about 50 million of them, hate the regime.

Some of those people are actually Mullahs. Some of them are even grand ayatollahs, like the Ayatollah Montazeri, who's been under house arrest now for about fifteen years. In fact, what's always called the holy city of Qom, which is sort of headquarters for the senior ayatollahs, has the lowest participation in elections, and there are upwards of three thousand of these people imprisoned in Qom. So there's actually a religious opposition to the regime, because they think Khamenei is illegitimate, and they don't want an Islamic Republic. They want something more like what Iraq has. So I would say that of the Mullahcracy and their non-turban, secular allies, you can probably count, what, 10 million people, something like that.

HH: Okay, and if you're talking about the government that matters, are we talking a hundred mullahs, or are there five hundred mullahs? How big is the established order that holds this fascist dictatorship together?

ML: No, there's thousands of mullahs, not hundreds. Thousands.

HH: Okay, that I didn't know. A key observation, Michael Ledeen, they are not nationalists, but theocrats. You write, "To ask them to think like a nation state is like trying to use negotiations to convince the Pope that he should think of himself as the grand duke of Vatican City rather than the Vicar of Christ on Earth." You quote Khomeini extensively on this. This was just...I guess I knew this, but I really didn't. It's not a nation state.

ML: No, no it's not. Khomeini has the great line, which is [anybody...] "I'm not here to fight for Iran, I'm here to advance Islam. And anybody who is in it for Iran is a pagan." That's pretty strong language.

HH: It is. It's also an insight into what we're up against, because it's not going to respond to the typical carrots and sticks that nation states do.

ML: No, so when a Rafsanjani or an Ahmadinejad says we're going to bomb Israel as soon as we get atomic bombs, and even if the Israelis respond in kind, so what? Suppose they wipe us all out? We would have killed half the Jews, and there'll still be more than a billion Muslims.

HH: Michael, this segment, I want to talk about the export of the Islamic Revolution, Khomeinism, actually. And I want to begin with the birth of Hezbollah, and with a name I'll bet you not one in a thousand listeners knows, Imad Mughniyah. I hope I'm pronouncing it correctly. Can you tell folks who he is?

ML: Imad Mughniyah is the operational chief of Hezbollah. And Hezbollah, which is an Iranian creation, totally an Iranian creation, which responds directly to Tehran on all things, Imad Mughniyah is the guy who coordinates and leads, and often participates in their operations. And Imad Mughniyah's the guy, for example, who organized the bombing of the Marine barracks in the American Embassy in Beirut in 1983. And until al Qaeda, he was the number one guy on our list of most wanted terrorists around the world.

HH: Well, for 25 years plus, then, he's been killing Americans and orchestrating the killing of Americans.

ML: Yes.

HH: Where does he hang out?

ML: He floats back and forth between Lebanon, Iraq and Iran. And for example, the 9/11 Commission found him on an airplane from Saudi Arabia to Iran, and then to Beirut, accompanying some of the 9/11 terrorists. It's fascinating.

HH: Now Hezbollah, can you describe for people…obviously, they waged war on Israel last year, and at just about the late summer of 2006…but they have been waging war on the West as an extension of Iran for 30 years?

ML: Yeah, certainly since the Islamic Revolution in Iran. They've killed certainly hundreds, and probably thousands of Americans. They were involved in everything from the Khobar Towers bombing to the al Qaeda bombings of the American Embassies in East Africa, and on and on. And it turns out that lots of al Qaeda people were trained in Lebanon by Hezbollah. So they served that function for Iran as well.

HH: Not only has Iran armed Hezbollah in Lebanon, they've armed the Bosnians. I was unaware of this, this episode, and evidently, the Bosnians have now, like a malignancy, spread out from inside Bosnia.

ML: Oh, the Bosnian story is a huge story, and you're right. Very few people have looked at it. But there's considerable literature on it. The Bosnian government, and the Serbs in particular, found handbooks, training books that were used by Iranian terrorists to train other Islamic terrorists in the Balkans in the 1980s, and I mean, they had an extensive network. And probably that network was part of the network organized by Zarqawi, who we eventually killed in Iraq years later.

HH: I was coming to the Zarqawi connection, because although he is a Sunni extremist who would think that every Shia is Takfir, and especially the Iranian Khomeinists, nevertheless he, too, accepted assistance from [Iran], and [that's] well-documented in this book. Is that widely recognized or acceded to, Michael Ledeen, in the people who study Iran specifically?

ML: No, because most people buy into the meme that Sunnis and Shiites can't work together. It's one of the great myths of our time. So even though [the Revolutionary Guards were...] the super-Shiite Revolutionary Guards were created by the super-Sunni al Fatah, which came right out of the Sunni Muslim Brotherhood, they think it's impossible to find Sunni al Qaeda and Shiite Hezbollah working together. And so nobody can believe that Zarqawi was operating out of Tehran, even though a year before 2001, the German and Italian governments had evidence showing that Zarqawi was operating a European-wide terrorist network from Tehran, [and they have hundreds of intercepts that...] and this is public evidence at public trials in both Germany and Italy.

HH: One thing that was not news to me, because I have read The Looming Tower by Lawrence Wright...

ML: Right.

HH: ...is that while al Qaeda nested in Sudan, and bin Laden was there, that a facility by Hassan al Turabi, there was, in fact, Iranian and Hezbollah contacts with, and assistance to al Qaeda, both in Sudan, and later when they went to Afghanistan in the planning of the African Embassy bombings.

ML: Yes, exactly right. It goes back to the early to mid 90's. It's been going on for a long time.

HH: So when someone steps up and says, "Oh, but he bombed the Golden Mosque," what's your response, Michael Ledeen?

ML: Well, it wouldn't surprise me if it was the Iranians who bombed the Golden Mosque. [They love...] People say, "Well, why would they kill their own people?" and I say, "Look at Iran. They kill their own people everyday. Every day."

HH: Oh, true.

ML: Back when Allahpundit had his own blog, and was called Allahpundit.com before he went to work with Michelle Malkin at Hot Air, he once had a letter from somebody saying, "But why are they killing their own people?" and he replied, "Don't these people understand that's the whole point? They often kill their own people."

HH: They are also embarked upon destroying Lebanon. To what ultimate end? Is that just to create a colony state of Iran, Michael Ledeen?

ML: Well, there's two goals. They intend to dominate the world, eventually. So this is one more stepping stone. But the immediate objective is the destruction of Israel, and they hope to close in on Israel from both sides, Gaza and the West Bank on the East, and Lebanon on the North and West.

HH: Does anyone dispute that Hezbollah and Iran are arming Hamas, even though that's a Sunni terrorist organization?

ML: I don't think so. I think everybody accepts it. I think even the intelligence community in the United States, which has fought against this for decades, now accepts that, I mean, certainly Petraeus says that openly, and our military guys do, that Iran is arming both sides in Iraq today. They arm both Sunnis and Shiites.

HH: You also point out in the book that recent evidence shows that not only are they arming the Iraqis on both sides, they're now arming the Taliban again.

ML: They were always arming the Taliban. I mean, that's old news. Back before we went into Afghanistan, we had evidence that they were arming the Taliban, and that in fact, they sent Iranian hunter-killer teams into Afghanistan to kill our guys.

HH: [Would you...] Is it now obvious to everyone that this has been an open war at least since Khobar, and if not since Khobar, in the last two years in Iraq? Does anyone dispute this, Michael Ledeen?

ML: Yeah, I think they do, because they all argue, [they all argue] that we can negotiate our way out of this, that we can make a deal with the Iranians. I don't see how you can make a deal with somebody who's been waging war against you for thirty years, and who says every day, "Death to America."

HH: [Now my...] I share your disappointment with Secretary Gates' hedge, because obviously, you esteem his abilities. Why do you imagine he refuses to state the obvious when he is, as you say, one of the greatest analysts we've had working in this area in the last, you know, generation of analysts?

ML: Well, this administration is a mystery to me in many ways. But I imagine that what happened is that Secretary of State Rice is insistent that we follow the diplomatic track all the way down to the bottom, and that therefore, premature evidence of the Iranian role in various murderous activities gets in the way of negotiations, and gets in the way of making a deal. [As I...] one of the main points of <u>The Iranian Time Bomb</u> is that every administration since 1979 has convinced itself that it's possible to make a deal with these people, if only we'd find the right combination of carrots and sticks. And every one of them has come to grief. It has failed every single time. And so I say,

"Look, Einstein's definition of a crazy man is somebody who keeps doing the same thing, hoping to get a different result this time."

HH: This segment, Michael Ledeen, I want to focus in on the fact that American presidents, as you said last segment, have always fallen prey to the temptation of the grand bargain, and I blame this, to some extent, on my first real boss, Richard Nixon, for establishing sort of the China lure out there, the myth that you can Nixon-to-China in different settings. And they all want to, whether it's Carter or Reagan or Bush, do it with Iran. It won't work.

ML: No, it won't work.

HH: Carter began it, and he tried, and this came as a surprise to me, he armed the Mullahs and pleaded with the Mullahs, rather than resisting the Mullahs.

ML: Yeah, well, [he wanted,} he had various reasons. First, he was completely misled on the nature of Khomeini. Nobody in the American government at that time understood what a monster Khomeini was, and how terrible this regime was going to be. Secondly, he desperately wanted to show that he had not lost Iran, because if it turned out that Iran had fallen into the hands of these evil people, they were afraid in Washington that they were going to be blamed for it. And so in a lot of the cables back and forth, you find people saying you see, we haven't lost Iran after all, we can make an agreement with these people, these people are reasonable, we can work with them, etc. And then as time passed, and it became more and more urgent to deal with the Iranian threat in one way or another, all the diplomats argued that anything can be negotiated, and we can negotiate it with these people too, just have patience.

HH: Even after the hostage crisis and the embarrassment of Carter, and the freeing of the hostages on the first day of the Reagan administration, one would have thought that Reagan and Bill Casey and George Schultz and the rest of them would have been on guard against this, but as you recount, Reagan fell for it, too. Can you tell our audience how?

ML: Well, Reagan was sucked into the Iranian matter by the hostage crisis. The various Americans were taken hostage by Hezbollah, which is to say by Iran, and then it became possible to negotiate with the Iranians to ransom out some of the hostages. And so they got involved with that, and once they were involved in talking to them, then they said well, now we're talking to these people, we can talk about broader things. And in fact, from the very beginning, the Iranians kept on saying, you know, "Let's reach some kind of modus vivendi, because we don't have to hate one another." Remember, there was still a Soviet empire then, and the Iranians were very active against the Soviet empire. And there were actually things on which there was convergence of interest between the United States and Iran, namely the Soviet business.

HH: But after the interregnum that is Bush 41, and after Iran-Contra, everyone leaves it alone, arrives Bill Clinton, and again, falls for it hard, for the temptation of the Iranian thing. And why the Albright apology? It's one thing to hope for something, but it's another thing to embarrass yourself in the quest for that which isn't being delivered.

ML: Well, you see, what happened was that in the meantime, Khatami, the so-called great moderate, had become president. And so all the experts in the State Department and the intelligence community went to Clinton and Albright and said everything's changed, Iran is now a moderate country, now is the time to go all out to normalize relations. And so we did all these terrible things. We enabled the Russians to sell nuclear technology to Iran, and to sell weapons to them. In open violation of American law, we permitted the Iranians to smuggle weapons into the Balkans, which made it possible for them to set up their terrorist network there, and to expand it. And then you know, we let the Iranian wrestling team into the country, the usual symbolic gestures, we eased some of the banking restrictions and so forth. And Khamani spit in our faces. And my grandmother always used to say when somebody spits in your face, don't pretend it's raining.

HH: (laughing)

ML: But once we were committed to that negotiating track, we just plowed on. And Mrs. Albright even apologized for things we hadn't done, let alone things we had done. She said she apologized, for example, for helping Iraq in the Iran-Iraq war, when the first assistance we gave went to Iran, not to Iraq. And I think that on balance, we helped the Iranians more than the Iraqis.

HH: Well, W. originally called it spit and not rain in the Axis of Evil speech in early 2002, but after that, became, in your argument in The Iranian Time Bomb, befuddled or, I don't know what happened to him, but certainly less than serious about regime change. Is that changing back now, Michael Ledeen?

ML: Not that I can see. I mean, I read all these fantasy stories in the New Yorker and so forth, that claim we're going to bomb the whole country. No, the latest version is no, we're just going to bomb some military targets. I don't think we're going to bomb anything.

HH: Michael Ledeen, you quote the great American scholar of Islam, Bernard Lewis, as saying we are at a real turning point, and he likens it to the fall of Rome, the time of the discovery of America, and it really goes down to an image you have on Page 201 of a cabinet meeting called by Ahmadinejad where they all pledge allegiance to the 12th Imam.

ML: Yes.

HH: It's surreal.

ML: Isn't that a great scene?

HH: Explain to people what was going on there.

ML: Well, Iranian Shiites, so-called twelve Shiites, believe that their messiah, a little boy who vanished in the 9th Century to escape his assassins, has been living ever since in the bottom of a well in Iran, and that at the end of times, he will reemerge and lead them to greatness and glory, and a successful jihad against all the infidels. They think that time is now rapidly approaching, and so this cabinet sat down, wrote a contract with this little boy, signed it, had it hand carried to that well and dropped down the well so that the Mahdi, the 12th Imam, would know that he had a loyal government in Tehran.

HH: Now when you bring up stuff like this to apologists for Ahmadinejad, they say oh, he's not really in power. But in this chapter as well, the what is to be done chapter, you point out that the Revolutionary Guards and he are very, very tightly connected, and are building an even more radical state within an already radical state. Is the West much aware of this?

ML: I don't know what the West is aware of. I don't think anybody in the West is in any serious doubt about the intentions of this regime. I think that they all know that this is a lunatic fanatical regime that intends to first destroy Israel, then expand throughout the Middle East, and ultimately, attack all of us. I don't think anybody has any real doubt about that. But it's a step, a big step, from recognizing that fact to taking action against it.

HH: Now Michael Ledeen, you point out we need to provide hope, information and material support, and people have to read the book to get the details on that. It's the most detailed expression of soft aggression against Iran in the hopes of spurring a counter-revolutionary revolution, and you have lots of documents in here about the number of times Iranians have tried this and been murdered or tortured for this. I think that was a revelation as well. This goes on all the time. People do try to fight back against this regime all the time in Iran.

ML: Think Burma. Look at Burma.

HH: Yup.

ML: Who would have thought that the Burmese people would rise en masse against their regime? And yet, it happened. Who would have thought a few months before the Ukrainian revolution that Ukraine would have a democratic revolution? Nobody. And yet, in Iran, not a week goes by without some big demonstration against the regime, without people standing up and saying, "Down with the regime, let us vote, let us elect our own people, let us create our own form of government."

HH: Now you do point out you are against a major military attack, and you advise against using the CIA. Can you explain to people why that is your position on both counts?

ML: Well, the CIA is the easy one. Nobody in Iran trusts the CIA, and they will run away, for the most part, whenever a CIA person approaches them.

HH: This goes back to Mossadegh?

ML: Mossadegh is I think not a big part of it. I think it's just looking at the way the CIA operates, and the things the CIA says, and horror stories about...I mean, the CIA has several times created some sort of network inside Iran. They've all been rolled up. They just don't trust them. They have no confidence in them. And whether that's justified or not is way above my pay grade, but it's what they think. They do trust the military, so you know, let some guy with a lot of medals on his chest show up and start talking to some Iranians, and it'll be better. How to do it? Just the way we did it to the Soviet empire. Support the people. But it has to start with the President coming out and saying we want an end to this regime. That has to happen, and no president in 28 years has said it.

HH: What about the reaction to bombing on the nuclear facilities, Michael Ledeen? If the President, supported by Europe, even, and France is making these noises, certainly...

ML: Yeah.

HH: ...says we cannot allow the wide-scale enrichment of uranium, and that happens, what will go on inside the country?

ML: Nobody knows. That's the simple answer. It'll depend on lots of other things. It'll depend on the context, the background, what is said, how it's explained, it depends on a million things. There was a poll a couple of months ago, I don't know what it's worth, but it was a fairly extensive poll taken by telephone from Washington by Farsi speakers calling Iranians, and one of the questions was how would you feel about being bombed? And the answer was basically, if you're going to bomb us to get rid of the regime, okay. But if you're just going to bomb us to get rid of some nuclear facilities, no. So that's some kind of an indicator, and I like that result, because it coincides with my policy advocacy, but I don't know if it's true.

HH: How tenacious a military capability do the RG's possess?

ML: Well, not so great that the regime thoroughly trusts them, because they're purged all the time. The top RG people are replaced with amazing frequency. And a spectacular number of military aircraft containing high-ranking RG officials crash in Iran, and I don't think maintenance is that bad.

HH: And a number of them disappear.

ML: Yes, they do.

HH: Now maybe into Western hands, and maybe just disappear...

ML: Yeah, well, some of them, we've had some number of RG defectors in Iraq. And there's this spectacular case of General Asgari, who was one of the highest ranking of all the Revolutionary Guards, one of the two people who created Hezbollah, who was organizing the smuggling network from Syria into Iraq via Turkey, and he just disappeared several months ago, and nobody knows where he is. I don't know where he is.

HH: Now Michael Ledeen, one of the interesting meditations in The Iranian Time Bomb is the dilemma that Prime Minister Maliki faces, and I thought it was provocative, that if he was certain we were staying, and we were seeking regime change, he could become the sort of Shia official that we need in that region. Can you expand on that?

ML: Well, thanks, Hugh. I think that every leader in the Middle East, and I took Maliki because his name is better known than others, but every leader in the Middle East looks at their future, and says well now, what's going to happen here? The Americans are going to leave, whether it's next month or next year or five years from now, but they are going to leave. And the Iranians are going to stay. So I'm going to have to take out insurance with regard to the Iranians.

HH: Thank you, Michael Ledeen, for spending an hour with us. A couple of big questions to conclude this time together, the book is <u>The Iranian Time Bomb: The Mullah Zealots' Quest For Destruction</u>. It's brand new, on best-seller lists in bookstores everywhere. I've linked it at Hughhewitt.com, it's available at Amazon.com, the last name is Ledeen. Michael, if insipient populist counterrevolution comes to Iran, will the Revolutionary Guards simply sit up and mow them down in the streets?

ML: It depends on where and when, and how it happens, and it depends on how many people there are. If it's a thousand people, the Guards will shoot. If it's 10,000 people, it's less likely. If it's 100,000 thousand people, it's possible, but unlikely. And if it's a million people, they'll join the revolution. So it all depends. HH: And looking ahead to the near time, Khamenei is ill, as you detailed...

ML: Yeah.

HH: ...inoperable cancer. He will be replaced by this council out there. What do you expect? A 12th Imamist? Or a return to sort of the mercantile Rafsanjani, make a buck and move along guys?

ML: Well, but Rafsanjani...Rafsanjani is a mass murderer. He's wanted for murder in Europe.

HH: I agree, I agree. But he's not as...

ML: And so what's the difference? Yes, I mean, some of them are more mercantile than others. Rafsanjani has extensive land holdings in Southern California, where he produces pistachio nuts, for example. They're very busy. And they're all exporting their money, by the way, Hugh, which is one of the main indicators of a regime that does not expect to last. Who will replace him? I don't think it much matters, because whoever replaces him is going to be a man of the regime. It'll be just another one of them.

HH: And just as committed to the export of Khomeinism?

ML: Yes.

HH: Concluding then, when you talk to the Bush people, I was with the talk show hosts when we were talking with the President a couple months ago, and I brought up Ahmadinejad and this regime, and I can't quote what he said, but we all had the impression that there's a vigorous effort to combat this regime underway. You don't seem to share that, Michael Ledeen.

ML: I don't see it. I mean, I just don't see it. For one thing, Voice of America and Radio Farda, which were our two main broadcasting tools, have been terrible on broadcasting to Iran. They've just been awful. I mean, they've put on critics of Bush more often than friends of Bush, they've put on people who criticize the pro-democracy policy and all of these things, instead of giving the Iranian people what they need, which is news about Iran, conversations with people who have successfully participated in democratic revolutions elsewhere, and all of that. So not even that is happening.

HH: You know, that was very dispiriting when I read it in The Iranian Time Bomb. Who controls that?

ML: Well, there's a board of governors that's appointed by the President. We just got very lucky, because they had to replace the top guy on that board, and the new one is Jim Glassman, who's a friend and colleague of mine at AEI, and has been a publisher all his life, and who is really outstanding. So I expect that will start to get better. But we're not supporting Iranian groups. We're not actively engaged in efforts. And above all, the President doesn't say we want an end to this regime. That's the main thing.

HH: Hopefully, your book, The Iranian Time Bomb, will do that. Michael Ledeen, thank you.

End of interview.

Interview with Dr. Ali Ansari
October 14, 2007

HH: A special hour of the Hugh Hewitt Show. As the United States and the West moves towards a confrontation with Iran, I think it's important to make sure that we know the perspective from every side. And to do that, I am joined today by Dr. Ali Ansari. Dr. Ansari is a member of the modern history faculty at the University of St. Andrews in Scotland. He holds his doctorate from the University of London, he writes often for the Financial Times and the Independent of London. His book, <u>Confronting Iran</u>, is a very highly regarded best seller in Great Britain. It's made quite an impact on me. I enjoyed it quite a lot. Dr. Ansari, thanks for joining us today.

AA: Very good to be with you.

HH: Let's begin by getting it out there. You're not unsympathetic to the idea that Iran has a great deal of reason to be suspicious of America. Can you explain to people why that is?

AA: Well, I think a lot of it is historically founded. I mean, the relationship between Iran and the West, broadly speaking, including, you know, Britain and other countries, but then more lately the United States, the relationship has not always been positive. And I think in the Iranian historical mindset, they're repeatedly told, of course, that their one near experience with democratic government in the 1950's was terminated rather abruptly by a U.S.-British intervention which overthrew the government of Dr. Mohammed Mossadeq in 1953. So that is basically repeated very heavily within sort of the Iranian history books, and they're basically told that subsequent to that, the autocracy of the Shah was supported by the United States, and this had a very bad effect on the political development of the country, and obviously on the lives of people in general.

HH: And there's clearly no denying it. In fact, the new book by Tim Weiner details in great paragraph after paragraph the CIA's overthrow of the legitimately elected government of Iran in 1953.

AA: Yeah, I mean, and also, it's an open secret in many ways. I mean, a lot of the CIA's own documents have been released, so it's fairly well known, and it's quite clear that there was quite heavy involvement. And there's a lot of debate about the precise role of the Americans and British, and the way in which indigenous Iranian groups obviously helped with the overthrow of Mossadeq, quite a legitimate historical debate. But I think in the popular mood, in the way that people see it in Iran, they see it as obviously an intervention by the United States in their domestic politics.

HH: And then comes the second great break, though, and this is, of course, the Islamic revolution of 1977 and '78.

AA: That's right.

HH: And did Jimmy Carter really even have a clue what was going on, Dr. Ansari? Spending New Year's Eve with the Shah in '77, and then standing by as he was toppled, and then inviting him into the United States, it seems almost feckless on President Carter's part.

AA: Well, I think, you know, the fall of the Shah really did take the United States by surprise. And part of it was really because [so much had been,] so much dependence had been placed on the character of the Shah himself. I mean, many people [felt,] including many observers in Britain, for instance, felt that the Shah now was in a position he was confident about, and he was in a position really to do things himself, really to make the decisions that needed to be taken, and I think from Carter's perspective, Carter very much felt that it wasn't his role to make decisions for the Shah. And they had this view that really, the Shah had to get on and do things, and nobody really anticipated that the Shah would suddenly go into this sort of stupor and be unable to act for about 18 months. I mean, it was a very, very curious position, that people were constantly expecting the Shah to act and to make decisions, and he never did.

HH: You can't second guess history, but speculating a bit, Dr. Ansari, if Gerald Ford had won the election in '76, or even if

Nixon had not fallen from power from Watergate in '74, would events in Iran have run to the same conclusion, though not necessarily via the same course?

AA: It is a difficult one to judge on. I mean, it's certainly true that many people in Iran have argued that sort of Iranian governments, and certainly the Shah, always felt better, more comfortable with Republican administrations. They certainly built a very, very close relationship with the Nixon administration. Clearly, he had to adapt himself and adjust to the fact that there was a Democrat administration in office at the time. But I think probably by the end of the 70's, by the mid to the end of the 70's, the Shah was really operating on his own timetable. He had various agenda that really had nothing to do with the Americans. And ultimately, it's difficult to see how these various things would have not developed in the way they did. And really, the key individual in all this was the Shah himself, and there was very little that any other country, or any other power could have done.

HH: In a passage in your book, <u>Confronting Iran,</u> and by the way, America, the book is linked at Hughhewitt.com, and I really do recommend you read it in companion with Michael Ledeen's new book. Together, they're just comprehensive in their treatment here. Page 94, "The failure of the hostage rescue mission, televised in all of its horror, with Iran's hanging judge, Khalkhali, gloating over the burned and charred bodies of U.S. service personnel in the Iranian desert, increased the anguish and desperation of the Carter administration while encouraging the radicals and empowering the revolution. There was nothing like success against the United States to convince doubters that Khomeini was indeed a providential savior." That which works gets repeated, Dr. Ansari. Is that initial burst of anti-American fever so satisfactory to the mullahs that they've had to try and replay it again and again and again?

AA: Well, unfortunately, one of the things about the anti-Americanism, of course, is that it [has been,] it has been replayed. And one of the aspects of the revolution is that it has been unable to move on from various aspects of this ideology in the early 80's. There was a case to be made. One could argue that the new Iranian state had to make a break with the allies of the Shah, had to make a clean break in many ways. But I think one of the big debates that's been going on in Iran, really, for the last, I would say, at least fifteen to twenty years, has been how do you manage this relationship with the United States, can we afford to be in a position of perpetual antagonism and confrontation? And unfortunately, as you indicate, there are those who think that you know, this perpetual antagonism of the United States is just too good a political tool to lose. I think this is very short term. I think it clearly can't last, but it is sad, but true that there are groups in Iran, and certainly among the more radical revolutionaries, who think that this is a state that will continue, and that actually is to Iran's benefit in the long term.

HH: Now last week, General Petraeus, as well as Great Britain's own Lt. Col. Patrick Sanders, commander of the 4th Battalion, the Rifles, bluntly accused Iran of shipping the munitions and the expertise...

AA: Sure.

HH: ...to kill Americans and Brits into Iraq. Do you agree with their assessment, Dr. Ansari?

AA: Well, I think the evidence that's coming out is that clearly, the Iranians are following a sort of dual policy in Iraq, one which is elements of, certainly, the Revolutionary Guards, which are there to put pressure on, and antagonize, that basically encourage the Americans to leave. Now again, it's one of those policies in Iran that has a lot of detractors. I mean, there are a lot of detractors who are opposed to this policy. They can understand, in a sense, those people who basically say that this confrontation with the United States is basically a sort of a proxy war with the United States, and that they must engage as far as possible to keep the Americans engaged in Iran, so they don't move on to bigger and better things in Iran, for instance. I mean, that's one of the arguments they have. And I think it's quite clear that Iran was always going to have an interest in

Iraq. It's just a pity where I suspect that there are those who feel that they can push their intervention, their own interference and their own intervention in Iraq a bit further than maybe we would like.

HH: Now you've been studying Iran as long as anyone I know, with the possible exception of Michael Ledeen, who's maybe been at it as long as you. And he has opinions about this next subject [that] I'd love to get yours. Is it possible for IEP's and EFP's to be shipped into Iraq from Iran, and for the Quds forces to send people there without the supreme leader, Khamenei, knowing?

AA: I don't…in my view, this sort of behavior, it's highly unlikely. I mean, what the supreme leader would generally do, the way he works is he would sanction broad policy, the details of which would not be of relevance. I mean, the details of which he would not deal with, particularly. Now ultimately, he would have to sanction a policy of that nature, and I don't think something which is of such importance to Iran's position on the international stage could be done without his knowledge, if not or with his approval on particular details. But certainly, I think the broad strategic aspects of policy, yes. He would have to know and he would have to approve.

HH: So as America and Great Britain, and to a lesser extent, France, determines how it's going to conduct itself over the next year, vis-à-vis the nuclear program, they have to do so assuming that Ayatollah Khamenei has been fully approving of a policy of intervention in Iraq by Iranian Revolutionary Guards that results in the death of Americans?

AA: I think we have to…yeah, I think we have to accept it in as much as Ayatollah Khamenei, as the supreme leader, is not increasingly centralizing power within his own hand. I mean, there's very little doubt that that's what he's doing. Originally, the position of the supreme leader was not meant to be an individual who intervened in the day to day activities of politics or international affairs. But effectively, in the last few years, that's exactly what he's done. He's become a much more interventionary political figure, rather than simply a sort of religious spiritual figure. And I think on issues of this sort of magnitude, particularly with the confrontation with the United States and the West, that he would be informed, and he would certainly sanction or give his approval of these actions.

HH: Professor Ansari, when we went to break, we were talking about the supreme leader and his position in the government. Michael Ledeen argues he had to know about the Khobar Towers bombing. Do you agree with that assessment?

AA: Well, I think this is where myself and Michael Ledeen would probably differ on this particular point, in that on the Khobar bombing, I mean, as I put it, the evidence has yet to materialize on that, for Iranian involvement. If you assume that the Iranians were involved in the Khobar bombing, then he would have had to know. I mean, it would be very unlikely that he wouldn't know. The key question is whether we accept that that…that there isn't, you know, solid evidence and concrete evidence of that involvement.

HH: Now the United States District Court in the District of Columbia has awarded $2.6 billion dollars against the government of Iran for their complicity there.

AA: Sure, sure.

HH: So you don't believe that's persuasive, or not necessarily?

AA: Well, in my view, I mean, these things are very difficult to judge. I mean, there have been, yes, there have been a number of court cases where these have come through. But it's quite interesting that you'll find that there's often opposition even among the administration to these court judgments, and that they're not necessarily based entirely on all the evidence that's available. But nonetheless, I mean, yes, I mean, I can see that that is something that is very much believed in certain circles, if we were to accept that these things were going on, or that the Iranians were actually involved in something, that these were not indigenous Saudi groups, for instance. I mean, that's the other thesis on that part of the al Khobar bombing. If we were to accept that, that sort of thing, it's unlikely that the civil senior leadership would not have known about it, certainly.

HH: Now one of the fascinating aspects of Confronting Iran, your book, that I found so different from what I ordinarily consume is the degree of independence you attribute to Hezbollah in Lebanon. Can you expand on what you see as the relationship?

AA: The way I read it, and this is…I think we in the West tend to ascribe far too much rationality or sort of structured bureaucracy and organizations in the Middle East. A lot of the way in which these organizations operate is you have to look at it almost like an extended family. So of course, the link between Hezbollah and Iran is there. Of course it exists. And of course, there's a fairly tight relationship on a number of different levels. But to give the sort of assumption that direct orders are given from Tehran, and adhered to off in Lebanon, that's just not the way it works. Often, there's a situation where Hezbollah will act more independently, a bit like a sort of a cousin or a second cousin listening, taking advice, often taking handouts, and maybe a few directions, but not necessarily always doing as they're told. I mean, that's…it's a different type, a more complex type of relationship. And I think we automatically read sort of a much more structured relationship in there. And I've tried to take a comparison from, if you look at the United States and Israel, for instance, very good friends, getting along very well, oversee a lot of financial help, military help, but it's not necessarily true that Israel always does as the United States wants it to do, for instance. I mean, sometimes, it does things the United States doesn't like. I mean, this is very much a sort of parallel situation.

HH: Clearly, but are you…that one strikes me as a little a bridge too far, analogy wise, because I tend to believe, and tell me if I'm wrong…

AA: Sure.

HH: …that if Khamenei and the Iranian government wanted Hezbollah to stop, for example, the war on Israel and the…

AA: Sure, sure.

HH: ...that they could enforce that discipline, whereas the United State could never tell Israel...we could try and persuade Israel, but we could never stop Israel from acting in their own self defense if we wanted to.

AA: [Well, when I...I mean,] I would agree that, you know, that Iran probably has more of an influential role, but where I would suggest that in recent years, the relationship has become more distant. I mean, I would certainly agree with you that, say, if we were to go back ten years ago, or fifteen years ago, Iran would have a far more, a far more direct influence on Hezbollah's actions. These days, I would certainly agree that if there was a general peace in the Middle East, or if there was a general sort of agreement in the Middle East, Iran could, I think, bring an enormous amount of pressure to bear on Hezbollah to desist from its activities in southern Lebanon. But say, for the sake of argument, and Israel then took a pot shot at Hezbollah, then Hezbollah would react almost without any indication of whether Iran wanted them or not.

HH: Okay.

AA: I mean, that's the difference, really. But I agree. I mean, there is, certainly, clearly they're a certainly far stronger influence.

HH: Now this is really the rub of the whole conversation, Professor.

AA: Sure.

HH: A million people in the streets of Tehran a few days ago chanting death to America again, death to Israel. What's that, what are we supposed to make of that?

AA: Well, I mean, I'm not sure if a million people would be out there. Certainly, there are large crowds who will get out there, and a lot of...you know, we have to accept there are some people who really believe it. They will come out for true ideological conviction. But there are also, I would suggest, you have an enormous number of people who come out because it's in their political interests to do so, and because it's also in their economic interests to do so. I think you'll find, if you were to compare now with say ten or even twenty years ago, certainly twenty years ago, that the level of passion involved in this chanting is not quite as genuine as it used to be. I mean, people simply aren't interested. But there are sort of structural reasons within the Iranian state, if you offered people free handouts, rations, coupons and so on and so forth, as long as they attend various demonstrations and various meetings, then they tend to come out. I mean, there's a huge underclass in Iran, and a lot of them require, or feel it's in their interests, to really participate in these meetings. And you know, as I said, there are those who continue to believe it, apart from the sort of foot soldiers in the revolution. But I have to say that they're diminishing year by year, and [I certainly,] the demonstrations that have been held recently, pro-government demonstrations to do with maybe anti-American, anti-Israeli or anti-British and others, the count of those who go are much, much more modest.

HH: Well, let me ask you as a citizen of Great Britain…

AA: Sure.

HH: That sounds to me like what might have been said when the Brown Shirts were moving through Germany in the 30's, that there's a tendency not to want to believe the worst, and then to end up having to deal with the worst. Why is that analogy not a good fit here?

AA: Well, there's a number of reasons why that analogy doesn't work. First of all, I would say that it's absolutely, I think, right that you can find people in Iran who hold extremely distressing views. And I would count the current president as one of them.

HH: Right.

AA: And you know, I think that many of them occupy some unfortunate positions, and they're vocal in their opinions, and some of them have extremely nasty views. But in terms of the numbers of people in the population, the numbers of people who hold these views, I think they are a relative minority in the population. In fact, you know, a fairly small group. The other thing is that the analogies that are often brought with sort of 1930's Germany are misplaced [in the sense that you don't, we don't really...] 1930's Germany and contemporary Iran are completely different types of societies and space. One was sort of a dominant industrial economy in the 1930's with a very mechanized economy, a very powerful state, intellectually very advanced. Iran is not an industrial economy, whether they'd like to think of it, is not. I mean, as much as they try to puff up their sort of nuclear advances, the fact is their economy is not driven by industry. It's not as organized. It's not as efficient. And as much as people in Iran, and certain people would like to have a sort of totalitarian bent about them, the actual way in which society works in Iran wouldn't allow them to do it. So in that sense, I think those fears are misplaced.

HH: Professor, last segment, we were talking about President Ahmadinejad.

AA: Sure.

HH: Do you believe that he believes the return of the 12th Imam is imminent?

AA: He's certainly very obsessed with the idea. I mean, that is certainly true that he's extremely obsessed with the idea, and he does in many ways, as far as I can see, he thinks that the 12th Imam is coming soon, apparently.

HH: Well, how widespread is this particular variant of Khomeinism? I know that this cult was disapproved of by Khomeini himself, but it's back now.

AA: It was. I mean, there's an lot in the orthodox clergy who find these sort of ideas very worrying for a number of reasons in the sense that if the 12th Imam returns, of course, then all Islamic law is abrogated, because we start a new age. If you do that, of course, everything goes topsy-turvy. I think his views, his obsession with the return of the 12th Imam is something that disturbs quite a few people in Iran, and many people who are quite central to the establishment, it has to be said.

HH: Now who do you suspect, because obviously, he answers to Khamenei, the supreme leader, but Khamenei is said to be quite ill. Who is supposed to be the person that will replace Khamenei as you assess the mullahs in waiting, so to speak?

AA: Well, there are a number of contenders from both right and left in the political spectrum in Iran, and of course, by the way, right and left doesn't have an equivalence in the West. But certainly, there are a number of contenders. But at the moment, it seems to me that if Khamenei was to pass away, a leadership council would be established either to select the new leader, or in actual fact to replace a single leader with this sort of leadership council which would include a number of senior clerics and political figures. And the key figure in this is the form of former president Hashemi Rafsanjani.

HH: Now you mentioned last segment, and it's in your book that in recent years, the supreme leader has intervened in the way, for example, to crush the liberal press law.

AA: Sure, sure.

HH: ...that had never been anticipated. Is there any turning back that institution? Or is it now, you know, institutions rarely give back power that they've managed to get a hold of.

AA: Well, absolutely, and I mean, I think this is one of the most fundamental constitutional crises in the Islamic republic. There's a whole idea of this supreme leader was meant to be a sort of supervisory figure who maintained the morals, and you know, really the fanatical background of the faith. What he's really turned into, [what he's turning into] is an Islamic monarch. I mean, he's an Islamic king in many ways. And what he does is he intervenes in everyday activities. And you're quite right in saying that once you cross that Rubicon, it's very difficult to turn the clock back. So I think this is one of the most central problems facing the Islamic republic at the moment. And ultimately, I think a lot of focus will be made on what happens when Mr. Khamenei departs this mortal coil, and they want to see a successor. There's a lot of pressure on Iran to say we don't need another one of these now. What we'd really like is to strengthen the sort of regular republican organs of government. This is where, this is what we need to strengthen, not these sort of more transnational bodies. Transnational bodies simply are unaccountable. I mean, that is the major problem with the supreme leadership, is there's no real way of holding it to account.

HH: One of the best arguments, we're going to come to the nuclear program after the break, but one of the best arguments I've heard against military action, [against military action,] is interfering with and radicalizing this replacement of the supreme leader in the next round. Do you agree or disagree with that assessment?

AA: I think that there is certainly a worry that if you get involved in a very heavy-handed military way in the process in Iran, that what you are going to do is radicalize the population, put it behind the more radical elements of government. It is absolutely true from someone like Ahmadinejad, who's made a right pig's ear of the economy in Iran, would like nothing more than to get in an international crisis on a massive scale, because in a sense, he feels, I mean, I have to say I think it's a bad assessment on his part, but his argument would be that the radicals feel that the more you can build up the tension, the more you can focus people on international threat, and certainly the United States. The more the United States plays to that role, the better it is for us, because then, people don't pay attention to the economy. They pay attention to other things. They pay attention to international crisis. So I think the way in which the West, and the United States in particular handles this situation, it's got to be extremely delicate, and it's got to be extremely nuanced.

Professor, you've got this great portion of your book at Pages 169 and 170...

AA: Sure.

HH: ...that details the long list of assassinations the government of Iran has ordered, carried out, outside of their country's borders. We've got Ahmadinejad talking about flash of light and denying the Holocaust, and you've got the resupply of Hezbollah and assassinations in Syria.

AA: Sure.

HH: Why shouldn't we conclude that this is a rogue regime that simply cannot be allowed to have nukes?

AA: [Well, I mean, I think there is…I mean,] there's certainly a strong case, and I meant Iranians, actually, who would agree with this in many ways, that Iran is not a country that at the moment, you want the development of nuclear weapons. I mean, I think it's one of the things that's very interesting, for instance, that the Iranian government itself will not publicly proclaim that it's going after such an option, even let alone near developing those weapons. I think if you want to look at the sort of stability argument, or whether Iran is stable, or whether Iran has ambitions or others, there are probably many other countries, to be honest, in the region who in a comparative sense could certainly hold a torch to Iran on these features. I mean, I don't think Iran is unique in having a government that certainly wants to assassinate its opposition abroad, or holds view that we don't like. It just so happens that their kind of president holds views particularly repulsive on a number of different levels. But he may not be here next year, so that's something that many people are hoping for, I think.

HH: Didn't they take assassination as state policy to an extent that no one has ever practiced it? I mean, they went everywhere and got everyone that they wanted to kill.

AA: Well, I mean, I think there are other states that have practiced it. I mean, I think basically, the Iranian state has concentrated on effectively assassinating its dissidents that are their own problem, mainly Iranians. But I mean, Iranians have been the main victims.

HH: Right.

AA: …of the Islamic republic. There's no doubt about that. But I think if you look at other states in the region, they also have been quite active in assassinating or getting rid of unlikable people toward their social side of the state. It's a question of your perspective, of course. If you look at actually the grand total, in many ways, of the number of republic assassinations abroad, and they'd probably...are not, in constant terms, more than a number of other states do.

HH: Well, I know...and probably a reference, no doubt, to Israel's policy of seeking out and killing terrorists.

AA: Israel among others. I mean, I have to say there are a lot of others, too. I wouldn't just want to lay the door at Israel. I mean, there are many other countries that practice it. It's not something that I would endorse by any stretch of the imagination, but it happens. I think we have to accept that.

HH: But is there any comparison to, say, the targeting of, and killing of Shapour Bakhtiar, a former prime minister in exile of no particular relevance or harm to anyone? Is there...do you have an analogy to...

AA: Well, I mean, you know, I think that in the post-revolutionary period, one of the things that the revolution has failed to do, it is to reconcile itself with its past. It's gone after people it's felt has been anti-revolutionary. Revolutionary governments have tended to do this in the past, unfortunately. I mean, I agree. I think it's a complete waste of resources to go after people that frankly I don't think are any threat to the Islamic republic. The fact is, a number of people, unfortunately, among the radical revolutionaries, the sort of Jacobins of the Islamic revolution felt that they had to go after certain people. And I think it was...I think that they're still living with the consequences of these disastrous actions. There's no doubt about it.

HH: Are there some, as you put it, Jacobins in Iran who would welcome the chaos that would follow from any kind of a nuclear attack on Israel, even if it was destructive of the Iranian regime?

AA: I don't think there is any, I don't think there are many, or perhaps as far as I'm aware, any senior Iranian people who would be interested in a nuclear attack on Israel. I mean, I don't think that is something that they're seriously considering. I do think, however, that there are people who think there would be a lot to benefit from turning what is a very intensely cold war with the United States into something more hot. I mean, that is my worry. My worry is that confrontation with the United States is going to take on a different level because there are people, certainly in Iran, who think this is not a bad thing at all.

HH: What about the flash of light rhetoric, and gone in a whisper, about the state of Israel? What do you think Ahmadinejad is saying there?

AA: You mean the flash of light when he said to the General Assembly, and he thought he had a halo, actually?

HH: No, when he said that Israel would be gone in a flash of light.

AA: I must…I haven't encountered that particular phrase that he said, but I mean, I think his arguments are basically that we've got to call a spade a spade. I think a lot of people have tried to sort of explain his comments in a more nuanced way. They think with Mr. Ahmadinejad is what you see is what you get, and he speaks his mind. And his argument is that the state of Israel eventually will disappear, like the Soviet Union disappeared, like South Africa disappeared, the Apartheid South Africa. So that's his argument. And he feels it's inevitable that he thinks it's, you know, sort of almost a divine will. And he talks about it, almost sort of as he was reckless about it. And there are many people in Iran who think he's rather stupid saying these things. In truth, I've spoken with clerics who've written some very damning articles about him, and said that he's just wishful thinking on a number of these things. But certainly, I mean, with Ahmadinejad, I don't think there is any merit whatsoever in trying to explain his comments in a somewhat more sophisticated way, because this is not a sophisticated man, [which he thinks.]

HH: But if there…if he had control, Professor Ansari, of nuclear weapons, would he want to use them against Israel, damn the costs all around the world?

AA: No, I honestly don't think he would be of that caliber. First of all, it's very unlikely he would be in control of any nuclear weapons in Iran anyway. But even if he did, he's not of that, he hasn't…that would not be his modus operandi, and he's never really been of that ilk. The use of nuclear weapons, I think, still does have sort of a stigmatizing effect in Iran. I mean, I think people like the idea, because it empowers them, it makes them feel more secure, they feel they have a deterrence force.

HH: Could rational people come to a…

AA: Until there's intent to use, I don't think there's any…

HH: Could rational people come to a different conclusion as they look at Ahmadinejad, and assume that he has allies like himself inside the RG, that there are people who would welcome that exchange?

AA: There are…I mean, some people have come to that assessment. All I can say is from my perspective, and my assessment of what's going on in Iran, that there are, as far as I'm aware, no people who have ever come and made…I've never certainly read anything, I've never talked to anyone who's actually thought of using nuclear weapons in an offensive capacity. I mean, that has simply not come up. They come up with all sorts of other things that they think they would like to do, perhaps, and irritants and provocative actions and confrontational actions. But the use of WMD, I mean, you have to remember that this is very interesting. In the Iran-Iraq war, when Saddam Hussein was using chemical and biological weapons against Iran, Iran did not retaliate in kind.

HH: As we went to break, you were saying that in the Iraq-Iran war…

AA: The Iran-Iraq war, yes.

HH: They did not retaliate, from which you extrapolate a, what, an appreciation for life, an abhorrence of weapons?

AA: It's not necessarily an appreciation of life that they didn't use…I mean, I actually think the…I agree with you that in many ways, life can be very cheap, but not on absurd levels. But the fact is that they didn't at that time [they experienced it, they didn't at that time] retaliate using weapons of mass destruction. They did not use chemical or biological weapons against the Iraqis, whereas they were victims of it. So there is an argument, and I think it's one that you can make, that the Iranians are by and large very reluctant to use these types of weapons.

HH: And last question for you, what do you see as the consequences of United States, with or without its allies, Great Britain, France and Germany, massive air strikes upon the nuclear facilities of Iran? What would follow next?

AA: Well, first of all, I'd have to say I think they would be very disastrous for Iran. I mean, first and foremost, I think this is something that in Iran, they don't fully appreciate the consequence of what a mass air strike would be. And depending upon the level of the air strikes, of course, one assumes that the Iranians would retaliate in some way or form. I mean, I think they'd find themselves probably quite crippled in some ways, or it would be quite difficult to retaliate in the ways that some of them are saying. But certainly, just in the sure terms of the anarchy that may be created in this very, very strategic part of real estate located between Afghanistan and Iraq, I think the consequences for the Persian Gulf region as a whole would be potentially catastrophic, and I think there would be quite large economic aftershocks in the Western world as well. So I think these things all have to be factored in before anyone goes down this route.

HH: When you say catastrophic consequences, can you expand on that a little bit?

AA: Well, I mean, you've got to bear in mind that the Persian Gulf, I think, what is it, like 60% of the world's oil goes through the Straits of Hormuz. Dependency on that Persian Gulf oil is increasing rather than decreasing, and that if Iran collapses in a sort of state of political anarchy, or refuses, there's no central control, people start to retaliate, there's a very strong possibility that the Straits themselves could be closed. If the Straits were closed, then you have a knock on, in effect, their oil supply. Then of course, I think oil prices would go right through $100 dollars a barrel at the very least. At that is going to have an effect on the economies of the West.

HH: We've only got a minute, Professor.

AA: Sure.

HH: Is there a chance of counterrevolution there?

AA: I think there are possibilities of a sort of counterrevolution on the level that some of the people in the West would like. It's probably very small at the moment, but there is a huge amount of discontent. And I think the longer, actually, that Mr. Ahmadinejad stays in, the greater the chances of popular upheaval. There's no doubt about it.

HH: Well, I want to thank you very much for an hour well spent, Professor. Fascinating book, <u>Confronting Iran</u>, fascinating conversation, hope we can get you back again sometime.

AA: Thank you very much.

End of interview.

Chapter 5.

The Strategic Overview

In recent years a few authors have moved beyond the necessary telling and retelling of the history of how the Islamists –both Sunni and Shia—came to be and rose to power and have tried to communicate the strategic peril the West confronts from the global jihadist movement and from the demographic and cultural tides that are flowing in the world. Three of these authors are men of the right, and very different men at that.

George Weigel is an accomplished Catholic theologian and biographer of both John Paul II and Benedict XVI. His book, <u>Faith Reason and the War Against Jihadism</u> is a short introduction to the religious roots of the long war and how the West is ill-equipped to confront the new menace.

Norman Podhoretz is an aging lion of the anti-communist movement, one of the famed "neoconservatives," many of whom broke from their leftist colleagues in the tight-knit world of East Coast intellectual elites in the '60s and '70s to urge vigorous opposition to the Soviet Union and the moral equivalence of those decades that saw little difference between the foreign policies of the U.S. and Stalin's heirs. Podhoretz did not assist in the triumph of one vast effort against evil to stand on the sidelines as another erupted. His <u>World War IV</u> was the result of his return to the lists.

Mark Steyn is the most popular guest on my radio program, and with good reason. The man I call "columnist to the world" is wildly funny and always possessed of the keenest insight and colorful delivery. Steyn's learning is vast and extends across all fields. Steyn has taken to calling himself a "demographics bore," but of course he is anything but. His <u>America Alone</u> is a call to study the numbers when it comes to populations and immigration patterns. What we knew as Europe is sinking, Steyn concludes, with consequences deeply troubling for America.

Dr. Walid Phares is one of the world's leading authorities on Islamist terror, and his researches have tried to put numbers on the size of the threat so that the West can more easily grasp the extent of the menace.

Finally, Robin Wright is very different from the first three authors mentioned. To begin with, she is a woman. Second, she is from the left. Third, she works for what many on the right now brands as the "MSM" –main stream media, most recently the Washington Post. Fourth, and most important, she is an optimist about some of the regimes of the Middle East. Her Shadows and Dreams is a first person account of the state of all the key states in the epicenter of the long war's many eruptions.

Interview with George Weigel
January 3, 2008

HH: It's odd on the eve of such an important political day to stop talking about politics for an entire hour. But it really isn't [talking about,] not talking about politics, but the context in which this very important year of politics is unfolding. Joining me is George Weigel. He's the distinguished senior fellow of Washington's Ethics and Public Policy Center. He's a Catholic theologian, one of America's foremost commentators on issues of religion in public life, as well as the biographer of both John Paul II and Benedict XVI. George Weigel, welcome to the program, good to speak with you.

GW: Thanks very much, Hugh, good to be with you.

HH: Thank you. I don't have many one-sitting reads, but I sat down on the day after Christmas, and read Faith, Reason and the War Against Jihadism: A Call To Action, your brand new book in one sitting. I've since been back through it. It's very startling, it's very stunning, and it's very well done. What led you to write it, George Weigel?

GW: About a year ago, Hugh, I gave a lecture here in Washington called the Things We Can't Not Know: Five and a Half Years After 9/11, in which I tried to pull together the nature of the conflict in which we find ourselves, ways to think about dealing with that, and some policy proposals. That was so well received at the time, this is, as I say, a year ago, that I decided to expand it into a small book, which I hoped would, frankly, raise the level of conversation in an election year. This is a one year book. Its intent is to get our fellow citizens thinking outside the sound-byte box on what I believe is one of the two great contests for the human future at work in the world today, the war against jihadism, the other great contest being the struggle to get some legal and regulatory framework around biotechnology. In both cases, what's at stake is nothing less than the future of freedom, the future of human dignity, and we just haven't gotten serious enough about this, it seems to me, as a country. So I wanted to identify the roots of this, explain why our enemies behave with such passion, and with such a sense of self-sacrifice, and then suggest some ways that over the long haul, we can prevail in this contest for the human future.

HH: George Weigel, I think you have succeeded, and I urged on my blog a couple of times this week, and I'll be urging on the show, people interested in politics have got to get the book, but also give it to influencers so that they can reset how they're viewing this election, because it's really got to be about the issues in this book.

GW: I agree. I mean, I think it's just, frankly, appalling that everybody, and I mean people of the sort that you and I would be inclined to support, as well as others, have simply not, in the first instance, named the problem, and in the second instance, are spending an enormous amount of time arguing about who was right or wrong about Iraq, and when were they right or wrong without locating that in the context of this larger struggle against jihadism, which I believe has been going on for at least ten years. [I think you can, I mean,] if you want to pick a point where we can say that al Qaeda in particular declared war on the United States, it was almost ten years ago in the bombing of the U.S. embassies in Kenya and Tanzania. That didn't get our attention, and so we had the suicide attack on the USS Cole in the Port of Aden a year later. That didn't get our attention. And then we had a huge hole in the ground in Lower Manhattan, and one side of the Pentagon blown up. That should have gotten our attention. It got our attention for a while, but it hasn't kept our attention.

HH: And I've got to point out that one of the reasons is you write about the default assumption of people confronting this that it can't be happening this way...

GW: Right.

HH: ...of not taking the theology of our enemies seriously. And I think that is the default assumption especially of the mainstream media. And as a result, any effort to wake them up to this has fallen on deaf ears. They don't want to believe that theology matters.

GW: Yeah, it's really a large part of the problem, both in the United States and in Europe, the sense that secularization is the future, people can't possibly be motivated in ways that shape history anymore by religious conviction, and this is a huge obstacle to victory, because unless we understand why it is that people are willing to make great sacrifices, we will not be able to propose nobler ideas that lead the people of the West to make nobler sacrifices in order to defeat this threat.

HH: I want to read from the very beginning of the book, Page 8, on the complexity of the situation facing us, because I think this is one of the things that voters have to keep in mind as they cast their ballots this year, is just how difficult the situation the U.S. finds itself in. I quote now from George Weigel's brand new book, Faith, Reason and the War Against Jihadism, "The war is now being fought on multiple fronts, with more likely to come. Many are interconnected. There is an Afghan front, an Iraqi front, an Iranian front, a Lebanese-Syrian front, a Gaza front, a Somali front, a Pakistani front, a North Africa-Magreb front, a Sudanese front, a Southeast Asian front, an intelligence front, a financial flows front, an economic front, an energy front, and a homeland security front. These are all fields of fire. Some kinetic, others of a different sort, in the same global war, and they must be understood as such." George Weigel, that requires enormous capacity on the part of our leaders, our elected leaders.

GW: Well, great issues ought to test our great personalities to seize the opportunity to defend the cause of freedom. And as I indicate at the end of the book, Hugh, I think this can be a great moment of national renewal. We shouldn't look at this as simply one in a series of problems to be solved, but rather if we were to gather ourselves, to make the kind of arguments for the free and virtuous society that we're going to have to make, if we gathered ourselves to understand better, more comprehensively the role of religious and moral conviction in public life, if we rationalized our homeland security policies so that political correctness was not driving the bus, but the safety of the American people was driving the bus, if we began to defund jihadism by getting serious about alternatives to petroleum as a transportation fuel, all of these are aspects of a genuine process of national renewal for the United States. So if I were a candidate for the presidency, I would cast all of this as an opportunity, that great challenges present great opportunities. And I believe the American people are willing to rise to the occasion.

HH: Before I go through with a few brief words about each of the fifteen key lessons, I've got to say as well, the optimism I took from the book, and it wasn't a lot, there's a lot of pessimism I took from the book, but the optimism comes from Benedict XVI's willingness to start the conversation, and his capacity to do so in the right frame of mind. That is…the speech that drew so much criticism was in fact, maybe a turning point in the way the West wakes up and addresses this issue.

GW: Well, it's also a turning point, it could be a turning point in the Islamic world. I frankly find it impossible to understand why the default position on Pope Benedict's speech at Regensburg, you're referring to…

HH: Yes.

GW: ...in September of 2006, why the default position remains the Pope made a terrible gaffe. The Pope did not make a terrible gaffe. The Pope accurately described the twinned threats of faith detached from reason, so that you can believe that God commands you to do the irrational, like blow up the World Trade Center, and reason having lost faith in itself, so that the West no longer has the capacity to say here is why religious freedom, separation of religious and political authority in a state, civility, tolerance, democratic persuasion rather than coercion, here is why these things are morally superior. Those are the two sides of the great culture war in the world today, and the Pope hit it right on the head.

HH: Yes, he did. We've got a minute to our first break, George Weigel.

GW: Sure.

HH: Your first point is that the great human questions, including the great questions of public life, are ultimately theological. I agree with that. I think probably a majority of Americans do. But I don't see a lot of people who are influencers in the media believing that.

GW: Well, if one is dealing with people of a secular cast of mind, I think you could even rephrase that and say substitute for theological issue of transcendent moral value.

HH: Hold that thought, George Weigel.

HH: Mr. Weigel, as we went to break, we were talking about how theology matters so much. Lesson Two in your book is, "To speak of Judaism, Christianity and Islam as the 'three Abrahamic faiths,' the three religions of the book, or the three monotheisms, obscures rather than illuminates. These familiar tropes ought to be retired." As soon as I read that, I said oh, you're going for broke here. You're going to break the china.

GW: (laughing)

HH: I mean, no one's allowed to say that kind of thing, are they?

GW: (laughing) It's a challenging statement, but I think it's true, and I think serious Muslims with whom I've been in conversation would not find that an unacceptable formulation. The relationship that Islam has in its own self-understanding to Christianity and Judaism is simply incommensurable with how Judaism understands Christianity, and Christianity understands Judaism. In fact, this trope of the three Abrahamic faiths has no foundation in Islamic thought. It was invented by a French Catholic Arabist in the late 1920's, who taught it to a generation of graduate students who then spread it throughout the world. And it's one of these things that we become so familiar with because it's used so promiscuously, that we then say wait a minute, what are we saying here? What does this mean? I'm a great believer in serious inter-religious dialogue. But inter-religious dialogue, as one of my Muslim colleagues, interlocutors has said to me, is not Kumbaya. It begins with the acknowledgement of serious differences, and tries to find, in this case, moral points of contact.

HH: You're also a great believer in clarity, and I think you make an argument in Lesson Three that, "Jihadism is the enemy in the multi-front war that has been declared on us, that can't be refuted." I am pleased that both Romney and Giuliani refer to the enemy as jihadism, as being a particular variant of radical Islam that the Takfiris embraced that says we can kill anyone at any time for any reason, because we're right. And is it going to travel, do you think? Is it going to catch on?

GW: I hope so. I think it captures the reality of the situation, historically, which is that an intra-Islamic civil war that has to do with Islam's very difficult encounter with modernity, and particularly political modernity, and such ideas as the right of religious freedom, or the separation of religious and political authority in the state, that intra-Islamic civil war in which Muslims declared jihad on their own, and for the sake of purifying the house of Islam, that is now broken out into the wider world. The second reason why I believe jihadism is the appropriate description of what it is we're fighting is it's what the enemy calls himself. And I believe in taking people seriously...

HH: Yup.

GW: ...when they call themselves this. It is objected, it will be objected, it has been objected in the past, that the great majority of Muslims do not accept the jihadist definition of what the demands of Islam are. That is both true and completely beside the point. The fact is the jihadists believe that this is what their faith requires of them, and that's why they behave the way they do. And if we don't recognize that, if we indulge this weird, Victorian reticence about using the J word in public, then we are disarming ourselves in the face of an enemy who believes he has very serious warrant for what he is doing.

HH: I also found the next lesson very important. Now I have read Lawrence Wright and Victor Hanson and Mark Steyn, so I knew about this. But a lot of people don't realize, as you say, that jihadism has a complex intellectual history, the chief points of which must be grasped in order to understand the nature of the threat it poses to the West. Most people think this is a movement out of a few caves in Waziristan, when in fact it's virulent at this stage, but it goes back hundreds of years.

GW: No, it draws on early Medieval Islamic thought, it draws very heavily on modern Egyptian Islamic activist thought. Lawrence Wright does a wonderful job in describing this in human terms. Mary Habeck, whose book, <u>Naming The Enemy</u>, I commend to everyone. It does a marvelous job of tracing the history of ideas here. How do you get from a guy in 12th Century Spain to the caves of Tora Bora, and ultimately, to Ground Zero? I drew on her work, and tried to condense all this in a way that without losing the essence of it, connects the dots so that people understand this is not something, as you say, that has simply arisen out of the fever swamps on the Pakistan-Afghan border, but has a real history, and a cultural history behind it that we have to understand in order to contest it properly.

HH: And Lesson Five is that the jihadists take their history very seriously. Now it's a history that rejects a lot of Western assumptions, and about the progressive understanding of history. But it's a history that they hold very near and dear to their heart, and they don't give up. No matter how much we think it's insane for them to carry on about the reconquista, they do.

GW: Well, here's their problem, and it's a deeply rooted one, and it's one that the inter-religious dialogue, the genuine inter-religious dialogue, has to focus on. Mohammed was his own Constantine. There was no separation of religious and political authority in Islam from the beginning. This has made the Islamic encounter with modernity immensely difficult. It has also created an image of the future in the minds of jihadists in which they are defending the god-revealed truth of how humanity ought to live. And that's a tough one. I mean, if we don't understand that that's what's at the root of this, then we are not even at first base.

HH: George Weigel, we've got a minute to the break. You don't mention in <u>Faith, Reason, and the War Against Jihadism</u> any particular sense of the future. What do you think are the odds in the near term of a calamitous event, and by that, I mean a weapon of mass destruction wielded by the jihadists?

GW: I take very seriously what was done in Spain to try to interrupt or influence their election several years ago. I'm looking at Pakistan, as everyone else is right now. I hope we have got our homeland security act together, but I consider it an absolute certainty that there is going to be some effort, hopefully squashed, and hopefully, we'll never know about, but an absolute certainty that there will be an effort by jihadists to influence the United States election next year.

HH: I think you're right.

HH: George Weigel, Lesson Six, we're not going to get through all the lessons, I'm trying to bait the hook here...

GW: Sure.

HH: ...is one which is going to be profoundly upsetting to some of your readers. "It is not Islamophobic," you write, "to note the historical connection between conquest and Muslim expansion, or between contemporary jihadism and terrorism.

Truth telling is the essential prerequisite to genuine inter-religious dialogue, which can only be based on the claims of reason." Your friend and mine, Mark Steyn, is being persecuted, and maybe prosecuted, in Canada for truth telling that has been labeled Islamophobic. It seems to me almost a conscious strategy on the part of some Muslims to render this conversation out of bounds.

GW: Well, that kind of activity's only made possible because countries like Canada have gone so far over the Niagara Falls of political correctness that they're willing to abrogate free political speech. I'm afraid there's a fair amount of that in Western Europe today as well. The prerequisite for serious inter-religious dialogue is a frank acknowledgement of differences. Tolerance does not mean ignoring differences, as if differences don't make a difference. Tolerance means engaging difference with civility and respect, but with a clear understanding of your own moral values as applied to politics, and why they're worth defending. That's the only kind of dialogue that's going to support those Islamic reformers, and they do exist, who wish to create an Islamic case for civility, tolerance and the free society as we understand it.

HH: Where do you find them?

GW: Primarily in the United States. It's not unlike the Christian-Jewish dialogue, which has prospered in wonderful ways in America over the last forty years. Why? In part, because Jews are secure in America in the way that they have not been in much of the Western world for the past 2,000 years. I think that the same is true of the Islamic interlocutors I've found. They tend to be here, not in Cairo, not in Rawalpindi. They tend to be here. That's okay, because [this is,] this country remains the center of historical initiative in the world at this moment in time. And if this kind of conversation that I'm describing could be put together here, then it might be exported. But I think that's why. I think it's a question of being secure in a political community that has real grounds for living civility and tolerance.

HH: And will protect you if you attempt to do so. GW: Yes.

HH: Lesson number Seven, George Weigel. "The war against jihadism is a contest for the human future that will endure for generations." You know, that is true. It's hard for Americans to think in terms of generations. As Nixon used to say, the Russians, the Chinese thought in terms of centuries, the Russians in generations, and Americans in terms of next year. It's very tough to get people to think in terms of that kind of a commitment.

GW: It is, but it's also never been explained to the American people in those terms. There's a kind of deprecatory attitude on the part of political leaders that suggest that well, the American people really can't handle this. If we described it as jihadism, they'll go crazy. If we say we're going to be doing this for the next twenty years, they won't believe us, they'll throw us out of office. I think the American people are much more mature than that. I think the American people know that by Divine providence, as some would have it, by accidents of history, as others would have it, we are the principal defender of the freedom project in the world today. And in all of this alleged dissatisfaction and angst that we hear about so much in polling data running up to the frozen wilds of Iowa and New Hampshire in the next few days, I've heard very little about summoning people to a great enterprise. I think that's what people are waiting for. They're not waiting to be pandered to. They're waiting to be summoned to greatness. And the candidate who can do that, who can describe the reality of this without overhyping it or underplaying it, who can say this requires a generational commitment from all of us, and who can figure out some way to get the Democratic Party, or at least some elements of it…

HH: In the game, yeah.

GW: …in the game…

HH: Mr. Weigel, you're a theologian, and I think it's providential that we've had George Bush and Benedict XVI in their respective positions, and before that, John Paul II. But does the Roman Catholic Church, which has a necessary leadership role, because it does represent so much of Christendom, do they have the bench strength behind Benedict XVI, because he brings a unique ability to these times, as he's demonstrated over the last two years.

GW: I think that's a fair question, Hugh, to which the answer is I hope so. We will see what impact the Pope's clarity of mind, as demonstrated at Regensburg, and as I believe he will demonstrate when he addresses the UN in April, we'll see what impact that has on others. I think that the Church is very, very aware, Church leadership around the world is very, very aware of the perilous condition of Christian communities, Orthodox, Protestant and Catholic, in the Arab Islamic world. I think the Church is increasingly aware that robust defense of those communities, rather than the appeasement of Arab fashions, is the only path to safety for those communities. So I think this is moving in the right direction, but I hope the Pope takes it further when he comes to the United States in several months, and particularly when he talks to the UN, because he can say these things that we've been discussing in a way that no president, prime minister, party secretary, governor, senator, whatever, can say, and he can put stuff on the table in a way that no political leader can do.

HH: Can he demand, will he demand of his bishops and priests and loyal laymen that they take seriously that which needs first to be taken seriously? I know he's speaking out to the theologians of the world, but will he ask his brother bishops to do the same?

GW: I think that on the question of religious freedom, which is where the rubber hits the road on this for Catholics, and indeed for Christians living in the Islamic world, I think the Pope has made very clear that he expects everyone in the Church to be a defender of religious freedom of everyone.

HH: Right.

GW: Religious freedom for Catholics is not a matter for Catholics only. It's a matter of the defense of the basic human rights, and I think the word is out that everybody needs to get with the program on this.

HH: There were very few, [as] cheering things toward the end of the year, as the picture that emerged from Baghdad, Mass being resumed at the Copt Church there with Shia in attendance. And that takes me to Lesson Ten. "In the war against global jihadism, deterrence strategies are unlikely to be effective, because it's almost impossible to deter those who are committed to their own martyrdom. And the lesson just before that, in the war against jihadism, the political objective in the Middle East and throughout the Islamic world is the evolution of responsible and responsive government, meaning that we're only going to get this thing resolved if religious freedom becomes part not just of the Western canon, but of the Muslim canon. Is that possible?

GW: At least religious toleration.

HH: Yes.

GW: I mean, ultimately, I would like to see an Islamic case develop for religious freedom the way there is a Catholic case developed, which took some 200 years to do. For the moment, I'd be happy to settle for religious tolerance for a real separation between religious and political authority in the state, for an understanding that the imposition of sharia law on non-Muslim communities is an offense against Islam itself. That would be a step in the right direction. I use this phrase responsible and responsive because I think the experience of recent years suggests that using the D word all the time, democracy, while I am an enthusiastic supporter of the democratic project, probably, like three Abrahamic faiths, obscures more than it illuminates. There are going to be different forms of democratic self-governance in different cultural situations. What's emerging in the Emirates right now is an interesting new form of responsible and responsive government. What could emerge in Iraq is going to inevitably be a distinctive form of responsible and responsive government. I think that language is probably better suited to the long haul strategy that we need to implement.

HH: You were very persuasive in that argument, that democracy does not mean Western Constitutional style democracy. It does mean much, much more than that. But I want to ask you, I doubt you're aware of Father Fessio on this program a year ago relayed a lecture he'd heard the Pope give to his students, saying the trouble with Islam is of course that the Koran is the word of God, not an interpretation, something you deal with here. And I don't know how you get past Dhimmitude, George Weigel, which you discuss at length in this book, towards genuine religious tolerance. Do you think those two can coexist?

GW: Well, it's an issue, Hugh. I mean, the question that Father Fessio was referring to the Pope referring to, I actually discuss in the book, and that is while Jews and Christians believe that the Hebrew Bible and the New Testament were inspired by God, the Islamic claim is that the Koran was dictated, syllable by syllable. Inspiration leaves room for the activity of the human author, and therefore, leaves room for interpretation by subsequent generations. Dictated means it means what it says, period, that the black letter text is the meaning. Now where there is room in Islam for development is in jurisprudence, in the interpretation of legal canons, not only in the Koran, but in other forms of Islamic sacred writing. So that's worth, it's worth working on, on that side, on the jurisprudential side, on the kind of arguments about the interpretation of laws. But are we going to get a form of Koranic exegesis, interpretation paralleled to what Jews and Christians do vis-à-vis their scriptures, that's, I would think…

HH: It's problematic. I'll be right back with George Weigel.

HH: Mr. Weigel, let me close by asking you if you share one bit of good news with, an assumption that I have, and that is, I've got a virtual bookshelf which I consider to be the books that are indispensable, and they've got Victor Davis Hanson and Mark Steyn on there, and Lawrence Wright and Robert Kaplan, and Norman Podhoretz, and recently, Douglas Frantz and Catherine Collins' new book on nuclear jihadists, and now your book. And I'm beginning to think maybe the intellectual capacity of the West is beginning to rush reinforcements to the battle of ideas that just weren't there in the first three years. Do you see that happening?

GW: Yeah, I do, Hugh, and I think it's heartening, because the people you just mentioned are not all out of one political camp at all. [I think there is, as you say,} the reinforcements are coming. The question that really needs discussing in this campaign and in the next administration is how do we translate this increasing understanding we have of the problem into effective public diplomacy for dealing with it abroad, because believe me, broadcasting Britney Spears on Arabic language radio stations is not the answer.

HH: That was horrible to read, as you described it, yeah.

GW: I mean, unbelievable nonsense we've been doing on this front, unbelievable nonsense. This has got to stop, we have got to get into the argument game, let the free market take care of the broadcasting of entertainment, such as it is, to that world. Let's let Americans tax-supported overseas broadcasting, in both radio and television, demonstrate the benefits of freedom, the fact that you can have serious arguments without cutting each other's throats, the fact that democracy works to enliven religious conviction. [Let's stop getting,] let's stop being paranoid or defensive about the fact that America is a robustly religious society. Why can't we explain that to the rest of the world? And the fact that that emerges precisely out of democratic freedoms and the civility and tolerance that they promote, that's what we ought to be explaining to the world, not Eminem and J-Lo and Britney.

HH: And I think you've done a great, great service in making that argument, and hopefully it will spread and soon. <u>Faith, Reason, and the War Against Jihadism: A Call To Action</u> is the brand new book by George Weigel, it's available at Amazon.com, bookstores and of course, at Hughhewitt.com. George Weigel, thanks for joining us, I look forward to talking to you again in the future.

GW: My great pleasure, thanks for your help.

End of interview.

Interview with Norman Podhoretz
January 17, 2008

HH: Pleased to welcome now back to the Hugh Hewitt Show Norman Podhoretz, editor emeritus of *Commentary Magazine*. Mr. Podhoretz, welcome back, always a pleasure to speak with you.

NP: Same here, Hugh.

HH: I read with great interest your new article in *Commentary*, Stopping Iran: Why the Case For Military Action Still Stands. And I linked it on the Hugh Hewitt web site. But I wanted to talk with you in depth about it, because it's vitally important. Let's cut to the chase at the beginning.

NP: Sure.

HH: Do you think President Bush needs to authorize air strikes against Iran now?

NP: Yes, I do. The question is whether he will, although [I thought,] I was pretty confident that he would before the National Intelligence Estimate came out in early December. I still think in the end, he will order air strikes before he leaves office. But I am, as the NIE would say, I offer that prediction now with only low to moderate confidence.

HH: Well, I agree with your assessment of what has to happen, and I agree as well with being less confident than I used to be. But in your piece, you remind us, though, on the day the NIE came out, the President went back into the dock of history, and basically doubled down, it will not happen on his watch. Doesn't that encourage you, Norman Podhoretz?

NP: Absolutely. And you know, he has said several times before the NIE, that if we allow Iran to get the bomb, people fifty years from now will look back at us the way we looked back at the men who negotiated the Munich agreement in 1938, and ask how could they have let this happen. And I've always wondered why Bush would have put himself in the historical dock that way, if he intended to be convicted. And when he reiterated exactly the same point in his press conference the day after the NIE came out, he said it's not going to happen on my watch. I didn't know how else to interpret it but that he was determined to stop them. And he must know by now that the only way to stop Iran from getting the bomb is to bomb their nuclear facilities. Negotiations, sanctions, haven't worked, and will not work.

HH: Now let's cover a couple of the very troubling aspects of your new article, and again, I will relink it at Hughhewitt.com. One is the demoralization of the foreign policy establishment, previously pledged to carrots and sticks, and now apparently resigned to a nuclear Iran. That's very dispiriting. You live in Manhattan amidst the Council on Foreign Relations people.

NP: Yeah.

HH: Explain to folks how you came to the recognition that they'd lost their collective will.

NP: Well, I came to that recognition in the course of a debate I had on the Jim Lehrer New Hour with a young member of the foreign policy establishment, youngish member of the foreign policy establishment. And I expected him to attack me for being a warmonger, because I had said that sanctions and negotiations wouldn't work. And I also expected him to assume, as almost everybody in the world had been doing, that Iran must not be permitted to get the bomb. Instead, he tacitly acknowledged that the sanctions and diplomacy hadn't worked, and wouldn't work, by saying that well look, we can live with an Iranian bomb. We contained the Russians and the Chinese, who were much more powerful than Iran would be, even with a nuclear weapon, and we can contain the Iranians. I was very surprised to hear that, because I say, it was a tacit admission that the means by which people like that were claiming all along that Iran could be stopped were no longer seen as effective by them. But instead of drawing the logical conclusion that the only thing we could do now was to resort to what Bush had been calling the last resort, namely bombing them, he said we could live with the bomb.

HH: Now, they're obviously retreating into a theory of deterrence, which is inapplicable. Since your book came out, <u>World War IV</u>, two more books have come out that matter a great deal, <u>Faith, Reason and the War Against Jihadism</u> by George Weigel is one of them.

NP: Oh, yeah.

HH: He explores, as you did, the nature of the theology at work in Iran, and it's simply not deterrable, is it, Norman Podhoretz?

NP: No, it is not, and people who know far more about Iran than I do, like Bernard Lewis, who probably knows more about that part of the world and about the culture of Islam than anybody on the face of the Earth, believes that you cannot deter a people who are not only ready to give up their lives for their religious beliefs, but eager to do so. And I think that if you add that idea, that religious ideological passion to the idea, the assumption within Islam that what matters is not the nation-state, nation-state is a pagan creation in the eyes of Islam. What matters is the realm of Islam, and what has to be protected and defended, and whose interests have to be paramount. It's the reality of Islam that transcends all national borders, which is like Khomeini, the Ayatollah Khomeini once said that he doesn't care if Iran goes up in smoke, so long as Islam prevails.

HH: You also quote the alleged moderate, Rafsanjani, saying you know, we can wipe out Israel, and they might use nukes, but that would just produce some damage in the Muslim world. And then you quote Anthony Cordesman, a very serious guy, about what happens if Iran goes nuclear against Israel…

NP: Yes.

HH: And it's a devastating, chilling--but I think absolutely necessary to get in front of people--prediction.

NP: Yeah, well, when Cordesman's study came up with a grisly scenario, ten to twenty million dead, if Iran gets the bomb, he anticipates, as I do, that this would vastly increase the chances of an outbreak of a nuclear exchange that would not be confined to Israel and Iran. He thinks it might be confined only to the Middle East. I don't. I think it would spread. But in any event, even if it were to be confined to the Middle East alone, he believes that Egypt and Syria and Iran would all pretty well be wiped out, whereas Israel, contrary to what Rafsanjani said, would survive, just barely. And he backstopped that contention with, by pointing to the relative size of the two nuclear arsenals. But however it were to come out, it would be, [it's, you know,] it's thinking about the unthinkable, except that I believe that by allowing Iran to get the bomb, we would be bringing the unthinkable much, much closer than it ever has before.

HH: I think you're absolutely right about that. And now let's talk about the American political elite. Are they willing to even indulge this kind of thinking? It seems to me that, and you cite 1938, we're in 1936. They're unwilling to think about what the other side can and will do in serious and sophisticated ways.

NP: Well, it begins to seem that way, and it is very disheartening, because at least the foreign policy, the old foreign policy establishment up until recently at least took the position that we must not allow Iran to get the bomb, and believed that it could be stopped by means short of military force. Now that it doesn't believe we can stop them, even by non-military means, it's unwilling to contemplate the use of air strikes, and so it's trying to talk itself into the idea that we could live with an Iranian bomb. And this certainly is the climate of opinion that one detects in the body politick, except for one reassuring fact, which is that I think all the Republican candidates for president, except of course for Ron Paul, have insisted that the military option is on the table. And both Senator McCain and Rudy Giuliani, the candidate I support, have said pretty explicitly that you know, the only thing worse than bombing Iran now is to allow Iran to get the bomb. And both have said, "Not on my watch." So assuming that there's enough time for President Bush to basically kick the can down the road, one of those candidates should become president, there's a hope that he would take the necessary action. But I fear that there's not even enough time for that, and I think Bush knows that. [I don't know how...]

I mean, my guess is that he knows that, and that this is why I believe he will act. He's a man who knows evil when he sees it. He's shown the courage in the past to face up to evil, and to contend with it. And I think this is a case in which his determination and his moral clarity would face the ultimate test. And I believe he's going to pass it. At least I pray that he will.

HH: Let me agree with you, and set the table a bit closer. You're a Rudy guy, I'm a Romney guy. And you quote John McCain, and I approve of this, the only thing worse than bombing Iran is letting Iran get the bomb. I'm not a big fan of John McCain's, but he's right about this. Do you expect that the top five Republicans, if George Bush were to act in March or April, and that means Huckabee, Thompson and the other three we've mentioned, would all come out and stand shoulder to shoulder with the President, and declare that it was a necessary and important thing to do? Because that might be the moment of greatest political defense for the President to act, and I'm hopeful that's what we're headed towards.

NP: Well, that's a great question. I would certainly hope that they would stand behind him, and it would, by the way, be in their political interest to do so, because [they would,] Democrats would stick them with the responsibility for it anyway. And so I would hope that they would have the simple moral and political courage to back him. I mean, I think that the five minutes after the first bomb were to fall on the Natanz nuclear facility in Iran, there would be a motion to impeach the President. And it would probably go forward. But...our only hope of avoiding a really horrible domestic political situation would be for the Republicans to stand firm.

HH: Norman Podhoretz, the new book out by Douglas Frantz and Catherine Collins called <u>Nuclear Jihadist: the True Story of the Man Who Sold the World's Most Dangerous Secrets, And How We Could Have Stopped Him</u>, have you had a chance to read that yet?

NP: No, I haven't. I read the Weigel book, which is wonderful, by the way.

HH: I agree with you. This book charts in such amazing detail, there is simply no credible way to believe that Iran is not on the brink of going critical. They've got everything they need, they've had it for years. A.Q. Khan gave them everything they need. Libya was far ahead. And our CIA comes up with this NIE. What is going on inside of our intelligence agencies?

NP: Well, you know, the CIA throughout the Bush administration, at least since the invasion of Iraq, has been clearly opposed to the President's policies, leaks have been streaming out of the CIA at strategic, political moments which are calculated to undermine, or even sabotage his policies. And I think this NIE is just [the, it wasn't a leak, but it was just] the latest in a series of efforts by the intelligence community, which has now been politicized in an anti-Bush direction, to stop him from taking military action. Because you know, the very first thing everybody in the world said when the NIE came out was well, this takes the military option off the table. It's now impossible for Bush to do it, even if he still wants to. And I believe that was the intention of the people who wrote this summary. This is not the full NIE. You know, the full NIE is 99 pages long, and it's still classified. But this summary was written basically, drafted by three guys who came originally from the State Department, and who have records of hostility to Bush's policies. And I believe that the way they framed it was calculated to have exactly the effect it had, which was to tell everybody there's nothing to worry about, even though they hedge their bets by saying well, to be sure, Iran still has the possibility, and we can't say for sure that they're not going to resume this program that they've allegedly halted. But they knew damn well that by leading with the assertion that it had suspended its weaponization program in 2003, that this would be interpreted as meaning that well, they're not only not hell bent on getting a bomb, but they're probably not even interested in getting one any longer.

HH: Well, it's like Hitler saying he'd suspended his territorial ambitions in 1938, after swallowing Czechoslovakia.

NP: That's exactly right. He said he had no further demands, territorial demands to make. And that led Neville Chamberlain to come back and proclaim notoriously, "Peace in our time." And you know, I think the same kind of mistake is being made now, because you know, appeasement was not in itself a dishonorable diplomatic tactic. I mean, it was based on the idea that if you're negotiating with another state, and they had grievances, some of them might be legitimate, if you satisfied those grievances, you could avoid war, you would appease them, you would make peace. And if you were dealing with a traditional conflict between states over a negotiable issue, that might have worked. But the mistake that Chamberlain and Daladier and everybody in the West except Churchill made, was mistaking Hitler for such a statesman. Hitler was not interested in making a deal or in satisfying certain grievances. He wanted to change the international order so that Germany would be the dominant power. Iran has the same ambition now, beginning with its push for hegemony in the Middle East, and extending to Europe, and even to eliminating our influence over its designs, its religious political designs. And we, and now the foreign policy establishment is telling us, and most of the elites are telling us, that well, you know, despite the way Ahmadinejad talks, you can't take that seriously. This is, they have, you know, we can deter them, because they're not interested in blowing, having their country blown up, and they are actually, well, the NIE itself says they respond to a cost-benefit analysis, which is nonsense.

HH: Norman Podhoretz, it is, and it's almost soft bigotry on the part of Western elites to impose upon Iran a less chauvinistic view of the world than they have. They are expansionist. They're Muslims who believe in Islam.

NP: And of course, the Western elites are tone deaf when it comes to religion. They don't believe that anybody can take a religious eschatology as seriously as Ahmadinejad and most of the other mullahs do.

HH: Two more questions, and then I know you are traveling. First of all, in your article, Stopping Iran, you point out that some Americans are hoping we can outsource the dirty work to Israel.

NP: Yeah.

HH: But that's not going to happen, and we can't expect Israel to do that. Explain a little bit, would you?

NP: Well, I don't say it's not going to happen, because I think it might conceivably happen. The problem is that the Israeli Air Force, superb though it is, would, according to a very important study issued a year or so ago by two guys at MIT, the Israelis, if they undertook this mission, could only succeed if every single detail went right. And you can't expect that to happen, because you know, if you have no margin for error whatsoever, it's not going to work. And if the Israelis did it, or if we left it to the Israelis to do, first of all, we'd get blamed, because they would be regarded as our surrogate. But in any event, we could have the worst of all possible worlds, that is they could fail to damage the Iranian program, and at the same time, the world would totally turn against us. So my conclusion is that if Bush doesn't do it, the Israelis may feel they have to, because here, how can they sit there and let a country that has sworn to wipe it off the map, sixty years after the first Holocaust, a second one being prepared, they would be forced to act. And I fear, as I say, that they would not be able to pull off as difficult a mission as this. We, on the other hand, could, even if we made some mistakes. We have a much larger margin for error. So it would be better if we did it, and let the Israelis off the hook.

HH: And when do the Israelis, according to your best sources, suspect that Iran reaches the point of no return?

NP: Well, officially, they say 2009, which as we have to remind ourselves, is only a year away.

HH: Yeah.

NP: There are those who think [it's even,] we have even less time than that, and maybe eight months.

HH: Last question, and this goes back to your yeoman's work during the years of Commentary's rallying of the West against the Soviets, is that in your analysis, there's quite a lot of noting in America, fear of Iran. And that here we are, we're on two of their borders with America's expeditionary forces, our military is mobilized and highly trained, and we've got a wartime leader, and a population that has generally supported victory. And yet we're afraid of Iran? That suggests something even deeper unnerving to me than Iran getting the bomb, which is the failure of the ability to resist.

NP: [Well, we have, there are large numbers of people in this country, we don't know how many, I mean,] it would seem from the last election, that the country is almost evenly divided between people who realize that we're in a war, and that we have to win it, if our civilization is to survive and flourish. And there are those who think that this is not a war, this is just, in John Kerry's words, a nuisance that we can live with like…he uses illegal gambling and prostitution, that it doesn't rise to the level of a military challenge, and that it's ridiculous for us, the greatest power on Earth, to worry about a country, a relatively poor country like Iran, which at best would have a couple of nukes, and we have hundreds or thousands or whatever. So this is their attitude, and I think this is simply a cover for the kind of semi-pacifist passions that have invaded large sectors of our population. But thank God, not the whole country.

HH: Norman Podhoretz, thanks for a wonderful piece, Stopping Iran: Why the Case For a Military Action Still Stands, and for spending time with us today. Again, folks, <u>World War IV</u> is a must-read, it should be on your bookshelf, and we look forward to talking to you again, Norman, sometime in the near future.

NP: Thanks a lot, Hugh.

HH: Bye, bye.

End of interview.

Interview with Mark Steyn
October 19, 2006

HH: And a special hour of the Hugh Hewitt Show today, on the 19th day of October, 2006, with Mark Steyn, columnist to the world. We're going to spend an hour, because the more we talk about the central themes of Mark's new book, <u>America Alone</u>, the more likely you are to understand the importance of voting, perhaps even to buy the book and send it to someone who's on the fence. Mark Steyn, good to talk to you.

MS: Good to talk with you, Hugh.

HH: How is the book doing, by the way?

MS: Well, an hour ago, I happened to be alerted to the fact that it was number two in Canada, which is amazing, because you can't get it in any bookstores there. The monopoly bookstore chain only ordered three copies, because they couldn't figure out who was interested in it. And I showed this to my little girl, who was staggered to discover that at number three was the final book in the Lemony Snickets Series of Unfortunate Events series, and she was shocked and appalled to see that Daddy's appalling, boring, grown-up book was outselling Lemony Snickets. So I've seen off that loser Snickets, and he's finished, and he's through. He's over.

HH: (laughing) Now you only have to get Woodward out of the way. That's what I'm hoping for, is when you pass by Woodward.

MS: I know. Again, that's the thing. You know these so-called independent bookstores that they have...

HH: Yes.

MS: And wherever they are...I got an e-mail from a reader in Vermont who went into a bookstore in, I think it was Montpelier, Vermont, and asked if they had the book, and they said no. And the guy recommended the Woodward book instead. And my reader said, "I don't think you really understand what I'm looking for."

HH: Well, that's a little bit of bookstore malpractice, is what that is. I notice you're number 11 on Amazon.com, American edition, so congrats on that. [It's selling healthily, and I think it's...]I saw today where the former head of the Republican Party said that when Republicans are talking about the issues, they win elections. When they talk about process, they lose elections. America Alone is about the number one issue out there. And although you call it doom-mongering, it's really sort of very sober, but witty, analysis. Doom-mongering, yes, but necessary doom-mongering.

MS: Yes, I think it's about...it's not just about the big issue out there, but I think it's also about how the big issue connects with the small issues, because I understand that if you're someone who's not earning a particularly huge salary, and you're living in a part of the United States where there aren't a lot of great jobs, and health care is pretty expensive, and you've got a lot of problems, and you've been finding the $3 dollar a gallon gas hard to come by, and all the rest of it, that it's easy to say that a bunch of mullahs, or Kim Jong Il isn't relevant to the problems that you're confronting in your life. And what I try to do in the book is actually to make the case that [America, compared...]America's domestic situation, compared to almost anywhere else in the world, is enviable. And so it staggers me that Democrats think they can run on the economy. You know, unemployment is 4% in the United States. 4%. It's permanently double that in the European Union. And in France, they get all excited if it occasionally dips under double figures for three or four weeks at a time. They live with permanent high unemployment. You may get annoyed...you know, gas is down to, I don't know what it is now, $2.40, $2.30 a gallon, and people were annoyed when it was $3 a gallon. It's $5.80 in Germany. It's just gone down to $6.30 a gallon in the United Kingdom. You know, compared to almost anywhere else on the planet, the U.S. has a robust economy. And so when the Democrats say that this country needs to become more like Europe, that has enfeebled Europe to the point where it can no longer resist the threat of Islamism, and in fact, the annexation of that continent by Islam. The two...the little issues that affect everybody's daily life, and the big issue, are intimately connected.

HH: Now I want to go to the biggest issue of all. It's demographics, and it's fertility. And I would refer people [...you don't have your copy out, I do,] to page 54, the marriage rate and the fertility rate in the United States, Denmark, Netherlands, UK, France, Germany, Italy. Mark Steyn, this is the heart of the book. It is a dire, dire future for Europe.

MS: Yes, it is. [And it's an interesting...] it really is an interesting point to me, because people occasionally say, "Oh, well, you're just making predictions. You're just making predictions." No, I'm not. I'm actually dealing with the reality of now. In other words, if there's only a million Italians born in the year 2006, you can't have two million Italian 20 year olds in 2026. The most reliable twenty year indicator is the demographic one, because you know exactly who the adults are going to be in 20 years time. They're the people who are the children now. And Europeans simply are not having children. They're not having children. And what happens, I think, when you get to a particularly advanced kind of welfare democracy, in which every aspect of life is guaranteed for you by the state, socialized health care, cradle to grave welfare, is that life becomes like a sort of endless summer school vacation. And you live in a kind of permanent present tense, in which you're sort of severed from all the kind of primal impulses of society, including the most basic one, which is having children, and thereby ensuring the future. Because you know, the public pensions liabilities... we talk about social security going bankrupt here...in Greece, the public pensions liabilities by the year 2015 are going to be 28% of GDP. Well, that's total societal collapse, not a mild accounting problem.

HH: Not only that, you talk about the age dependency ratio, in places like Canada and the United States, forget Islam for a second, and militant Islam, and all the other things. No one's going to be here to take care of us, Mark Steyn.

MS: No, that's right. That's right. [And I think that is the…]I think that's what's interesting when you read some of the developments in Japan that I address, because Japan hasn't got any immigrants, Muslim or Hispanic or anything. The Japanese don't really like immigrants. They just want to be Japanese surrounded by Japanese. And yet, they have also given up breeding. And you notice this Southern frenzy now to develop…first, they've developed…there's no market for dolls in Japan, so the toy manufacturers have gone out of business, because there are no little girls who want to buy dollies and dress them up and play with dolls anymore. So they developed dolls for adults. They basically developed dolls that can make simple human conversation, to keep the old people company, and in effect, be the grandchildren that they don't have.

HH: Wow.

MS: And in a way, this is an incredibly poignant scenario. And obviously, the next stage is they're going to try and make more sophisticated models of these things, who can turn down the beds, and put a pot of tea on at the old folks home, because there aren't going to be any […there aren't going to be any] people to staff the old folks home.

HH: Or they will come from the third world, and primarily from Muslim countries.

MS: Well, again, that's true. I think the interesting question is, eventually, the birth rate will fall all over the planet. So if you're like a successful entrepreneurial go-ahead guy from Chile or Singapore, why would you say go to a place like Europe, where you're going to be working around the clock, and paying 60% tax rates, to support basically a geriatric native population? You'd be much better off, I mean, I would imagine that if you are that talented Chilean, or Singapore guy, you can write your ticket almost anywhere on the planet, and you'll want to come to somewhere where there are more people your own age, which would be the United States or Australia…

HH: Yup.

MS: And where your economic opportunities aren't crushed by the tax burden of having to support this vastly swollen geriatric population of Jacques and Pierres and Gerhardts, and so forth, who expect to be kept in luxury for the rest of their lives.

HH: Now Mark Steyn, as I was reading again <u>America Alone</u>, I read it when it was in galleys, and it's sort of depressing, actually, though it's very amusing. I had just begun listening to Jared Diamond's…the collapse of civilization book, and [it's…] the contrast strikes me. He writes about the Montana economy, and the threat from tailings from mines long closed. And it's just […it's] silly. The collapse we're staring at is a real deal that is demographically driven, and ideologically powered. And it's not on the front brain of most of the left.

MS: No, I think that Jared Diamond book is…if this guy's as clever as he's made out to be, then that book has to be a brilliant satire, and it will be hailed as such in centuries to come, because he's basically looking at why societies collapse, and he picks some very curious examples as well, you know, Easter Island, which isn't what one has historically regarded as a major civilization.

HH: Exactly.

MS: But he picks these…

HH: Greenland…

MS: I mean, the idea that if not for a quirk of history, Easter Island would now be on the G-8, and have a permanent seat at the U.N. Security Council, is a little hard to swallow. I don't think Easter Island's odds of being a major world power were ever very good to begin with. But he talks about, he basically picks societies, and the whole thing is this environmental…you know, deforestation is what causes everything to collapse.

HH: Right.

MS: And it's completely ridiculous. In fact, the one example where you could say deforestation played a role, which is in the Arabian desert, I think is the one he steers well clear of, because

I think the fact of the matter is that you could make a strained argument that deforestation is a very deep root cause of jihad if you wanted to. But the reality is that it's not about trees. I say in the book, it's not the tree, it's the family tree. Russia is as forested as you can get, and it's a dying nation, because it's running out of people.

HH: A deeply diseased and dying nation.

HH: Mark, your colleague at National Review today, and a guest on this program, Jonah Goldberg, wrote a column saying the Iraq war was a mistake. And I shake my head, both at the profound wrongness of that, but also its timing. And it seems to me, as we come up to this election, so much is in the balance, that it's almost hard to overstate how badly things could go with a Democratic majority.

MS: Yes, and I think it's simply a mistake to argue about whether a war is a mistake. Once you're in it, I think the best thing to do is to win it. And obviously, it's not easy. Nobody said wars are easy. And that's why I think in fairness to Jonah, who is a very agreeable person, and I'm sorry to see him join the great flock of molting hawks, because I think it's grossly irresponsible to argue the case for a war, and then three years later, to decide oh no, maybe it wasn't such a good idea after all. I'm sorry, it's...right now, what is at issue for everybody but the Iraqi people, is American credibility. And by that, I mean I think I said in the book somewhere that if you happen to be living in Fallujah, or you happen to be living in Tikrit, or you happen to be living in Basra, the Iraq war is about the Iraqis. But if you are living in any other country in the world, the interest in the Iraq war is in the credibility of the United States, and its ability to be a credible superpower in the 21st Century. And we know what happened in Vietnam. Vietnam had incredible long-term consequences, in part because people drew the conclusion that the United States was just this sort of effete sissy, pampered, corpulent, lazy kind of late-period Ottoman sultan, puffed up on his cushions. And if you gave the guy a little tiny pin prick in his toe, he'd just squeal in pain, and you wouldn't have to bother defeating him, that in other words, the United States is not a credible superpower. And that's where I think Jonah's making a mistake in going through this all over again.

HH: The heart of the book, to me, <u>America Alone: The End Of The World As We Know It</u>, and again, it's linked at Hughhewitt. com, is this excerpt:

"So we have a global terrorist movement, insulated within a global political project, insulated within a severely self-segregating religion, whose adherents are the fastest growing demographic in the world. The jihad, thus, has a very potent brand inside a highly-compartmentalized, and very decentralized network, much, much more efficient than anything the CIA can muster."

That's profoundly pessimistic, though I believe accurate, Mark Steyn.

MS: Yes, it is. I mean, I think if you look at the trouble the KGB had to go to, to plant sleepers in the United States, they had to establish fake identities for these people. They had to leave them there for decades, so that they could [...to] establish the credibility of these identities. They had to go through an awful lot of trouble, the clichés of the spy thriller genre, the dead drops in the park, and all the rest of it. And you don't have to do anything with this, because these mosques, these radical mosques, are on Main Street. They're on Main Street in every town in the United States, and in Canada, and throughout Europe. That is a huge advantage to any ideological project. Can you imagine what things would be like if Hitler had had high schools all over the North American continent, if there'd been a Hirohito High in Portland, Oregon, the way there are radical mosques there, and indeed, even jihad training camps there?

HH: Now let me ask you, do you think a lot of the complacency in the West comes from a not so well concealed racist view that these Muslims simply can't compete with us?

MS: Yes, [I think it's hard ...] I think it's hard for people to take them seriously as an enemy, because after all, we've got guys living in caves. I mean, Osama bin Laden, who is the face of this enemy, lives in a cave in some part of the Afghan/ Pakistani border, supposedly. And that's hard for anybody to take seriously as an enemy, because we've got better planes, better bombs, better guns. You know, Bill Clinton was basically doing terrorist shtick in his speech the other night...

HH: Right.

MS: ...mocking the way...oh, the Republicans, they're trying to scare you, they're trying to tell you there's a terrorist on every corner who's trying to kill you. In other words, there is no enemy. There's nothing to worry about. But the Muslims look at us, and they think you know, those tanks, those bombs, those guns, all that money, all that technology, it's no advantage. In a long struggle, put your money on will and manpower.

HH: And they've got both of those.

MS: Exactly. [They've got...] they're churning out millions of young men. And if you know, I mean, everybody knows this, that says statistically, and even in the most law-abiding community, it's the...even if there's someone stealing beer and cigarettes from the convenience store, and that's the only crime there is, it's generally committed by young men in their teens and twenties.

HH: Yup.

MS: And so that's what Islam has millions and millions of, young men in their teens and twenties. They've got millions of them in Yemen, they've got millions of them in Pakistan, and they've got millions of them in Europe.

HH: And they don't have cars, they have AK-47's.

MS: Yeah.

HH: Let me ask you, Mark Steyn, you suggest here that Benedict may well...I don't know if you were joking with us or not, may well have picked his name, anticipating what he foresaw for Europe. Do you really think that was on his mind?

MS: I do think so.

HH: Explain then what could be the motivation behind Benedict's choice of name.

MS: Well, you know, he named himself after the original Benedict, who was the man who basically saved dying civilization, and preserved the best of it, through the Dark Ages in Europe. He saved the best of Greek and Roman civilization, effectively fused it with Christianity, and laid the foundations for the modern age, the modern world we live in, which is the continued inheritance of our Judeo-Christian tradition, connected back through the Roman Empire, and to the Greeks. In other words, a seamless chain of civilization running back thousands of years. And the reason that he did…that we have that, is because one very brave man, as I said, the original Benedict, helped preserve the best of Greek and Roman civilization when it might have been lost to posterity. So in a sense, we owe the modern world to that man's foresight and understanding. And I think Pope Benedict did not choose this name by accident.

HH: And do you think this Benedict is undertaking the project [that…] and moving with the speed he needs to?

MS: Well, I think he has thought about this, and I think he realizes that [the challenge…]if the challenge for his predecessor was bringing freedom to Eastern Europe, then the challenge for Pope Benedict is really to see if you can rouse Western Europe. And if you can't rouse Western Europe, then what you have to do is try and find some alternative nesting place for Christianity, until whoever gets real again in Western Europe, decides that they're ready again to embrace their own inheritance, and their own culture.

HH: Mark, I was perusing your reviews at Amazon.com during the break, and my favorite one was laughing our way into the dust bin of history. And unfortunately, it's true. [It is…obviously,] it's marked by your sense of humor, but it's so gloomy. You do, however, say at the end, say look, we can submit to Islam, destroy Islam, or reform Islam. We're not going to do one or two, and the reform is not up to us. But you do have ten specific ideas. I like number ten, myself, strike militarily when the opportunity presents itself. Has that opportunity presented itself, vis-à-vis Iran. I don't know if you saw Ahmadinejad's latest.

MS: Yes, I did, and I think…the reason I say that is because obviously, the United States and a handful of serious allies, have the best militaries in the world. The trouble is, they don't have the opportunity to use them terribly often. And when they do use them, and this is, I guess, what Jonah has in mind in Iraq, that they often wind up using them for things that they're perhaps not intended for, such as in the case of the U.S. military in Iraq for perhaps longer than Jonah wished for, a little bit of colonial policing, that is not really what the U.S. military's purpose is. So you have to think to yourself, well, what can they do, and what can they do well? They're very good at actually just going in removing people who are trouble, and ending that trouble. And even if what then comes after is, as the naysayers would see it, a different form of trouble. That, in itself, is better than just letting a dictatorship establish itself, grow more permanent, develop nuclear weapons programs, become a bigger and bigger threat. And I think, for example, Darfur in Sudan is a classic case in which it would have been easy to do some bombing raids on the Janjaweed, and just make these guys realize that if they carry on, macheteing people to death, and raping villages, that they're going to get bombs dropped on their encampment and killed. And I think the tragedy is that America's enemies have figured out that it has this fantastic military, but it's like a beautiful car. You don't take it out of the garage very often

.

HH: And the molting hawks are adding to this. I analogize Jonah's call today to the argument that after Pearl Harbor, and after Hitler had declared war on us, that we would ignore him, that we wouldn't respond to him, because he actually hadn't hit us yet, and as a result, ignore Britain's pleas to form the grand alliance. Mark Steyn, Ahmadinejad, for the benefit of our audience, said today that Israel is a counterfeit and illegitimate regime that cannot survive, and that the Zionist regime is counterfeit and illegitimate, and cannot survive. The big powers that have created this fraud regime and allowed it to commit all kind of crimes to guarantee their interest…by the way, he said this on state television in a live broadcast. [There is no…] we can't miss the significance of this, can we, Mark?

MS: Well, I think we can, in fact. I think if you read the elaborate and almost absurd contortions that people go to in the Western press to explain why this man does not mean what he says, I think that is […I think that is] a very dangerous path to go down, not even necessarily just in terms of Iran, because everybody else who's sitting around, and they're saying, "Well look at this, look at this." This guy is going on TV, and he's announcing to the world that he is in favor of the nuclear annihilation of a neighboring state, and nobody does anything about it. He got on a big plane to New York, he came to New York, he stayed in New York, and he gave a big speech in New York, a man who threatens the nuclear annihilation of millions of people. He was treated as just any other head of state.

HH: Right.

MS: [And I think a lot of…] there's roughly twenty or thirty countries who would like to be in the situation that Iran and North Korea are in. In other words, they're failed states that are nuclear states. This guy, Ahmadinejad, he was sitting next to the president of Sudan, he's saying well, when we're a nuclear power, obviously what we're going to do is give it to our pals like this guy here, and he indicated the president of Sudan. Now does anyone want the Sudanese regime, that loves slaughtering millions of its own people, to also have the opportunity to slaughter millions of other people, too?

HH: Yeah, that is the question.

HH: Mark, how important are these elections?

MS: Well, I think they're critical, because I think to effectively repudiate the Bush administration, which is how it would be seen domestically, would be seen around the world as in fact a repudiation of the broader American will, and broader American determination. So I think that would be serious, not because there aren't legitimate differences about the war, and about fighting this enemy, and long term strategy, but because you'd be electing a party that simply has no useful contribution to this. I don't think it's possible to take Nancy Pelosi and Harry Reid, the Democratic Party of these two people, and Howard Dean seriously on this issue. They have not engaged seriously with it. And as I said on the domestic front, they're wedded to the solutions that have in fact turned Europeans into a weak continent that's sort of mortgaging its future to deeply hostile forces every passing month.

HH: Mark, we're at the end of our time together. It flies by. I just want to once again tell America, <u>America Alone: The End Of The World As We Know It</u>, by my friend and colleague, Mark Steyn, is in bookstores. It's at Amazon.com. You can get an autographed copy if you want at www.steynonline.com. And you might be able to read his signature.

MS: It's gotten worse since last week, when you were complaining about it.

HH: I don't know that that's possible.

MS: My arms are bleeding stumps now.

HH: But it is indeed a get out the vote effort [beyond...] without parallel. Mark Steyn, always a pleasure. We'll talk to you again soon.

MS: Thanks a lot, Hugh. See you next week.

End of interview.

Interview with Dr. Walid Phares
September 13, 2007

HH: This hour, I'm starting with one of the preeminent experts on jihad in the world. Walid Phares is my guest. He is with the Foundation for the Defense of Democracies. He has a brand new book out called <u>The War of Ideas: Jihadism Against Democracy</u>. Mr. Phares, welcome back to the program, good to have you.

WP: Thank you for having me on your great show.

HH: Now I have not yet read the new book, but I got an e-mail from a very close friend of mine who said I must, and I will, and we'll spend an hour on it. But I thought I'd talk to you today because of the arrests in Austria, Germany, Denmark, and the bomb that did not go off in Ankara in the last week. What is going on in the jihadist movement right now?

WP: It is much wider than that. Let me begin here at home in the United States. We've seen the arrests of those who became the cell, the Fort Dix six. But more important, the two Tampa jihadists who were caught on the East Coast, and then were moved to Western Europe, where there have been many arrests, including the famous one in Germany, and then of course the last string now starting from Scandinavia down to Turkey. And put next to that the videotape of Osama bin Laden. The bottom line, Hugh, is that basically, they want to score a victory, because their state of affairs is not that good. I have detected on their chat rooms, in the chat rooms and web sites, that they have a lot of questions, including after the videotape was aired by Osama bin Laden. Many jihadists are asking what have we done in Afghanistan? We're not back to Kabul? In Waziristan, we're under pressure by the Pakistani Army, we lost in Somalia, we lost even in tiny Lebanon. And in the Sunni triangle, the tribes are rising against us. We've got to read it from a wide perspective. The al Qaeda is instructing all their networks, either directly or indirectly, in Europe, the West and in America, to strike. Get them a victory.

HH: And so do you believe this to be a time of great peril across the West and in the United States?

WP: Yes it is, because when the jihadists, radical jihadists are cornered, remember the Nazis when they were on the defeat side, what did they do? They sent all their terrible weapons, V-1, V-2's, and everything they got under their hands. Now you're going to have a comparable situation whereby because they're not scoring on that side, because of the surge, also because of many other issues, they would want to have a strike in the West. And look how many videos they have issued. I mean, they may have been waiting for three or four victories or strikes in the West to accompany them with videos. We are at the fourth video now, and yet they haven't been able to do it, so it's frustrating for them, it's dangerous for us.

HH: Dr. Phares, I'm sure you're acquainted with Lawrence Wright's The Looming Tower, and I assume the war of ideas the same way. I have been rereading it because of where we are and what's going on, and there's a period of time when Osama bin Laden retreats to Afghanistan, consciously modeling himself on the travels of the prophet, away [from battle] having been routed in his initial victories, to a time of introspection. Can [bin Laden] hold onto that, and can he maintain the myth that he's reenacting the prophet's journeys for this long against this many defeats?

WP: Since day one, Osama bin Laden felt, projected, told his followers that basically, he is only copying the acts and the facts and the deeds and the statements of the prophet to attract the highest number of devout Salafists. Now the problem with bin Laden is that his health is not that good. That's different from where Mohammed was, Prophet Mohammed was as his example, wrongly taken from history. But nevertheless, he is now trying to appear as much as he can, and actually, on Al Jazeera, the analysts have said that the new bin Laden, the one who is very calm, and he is addressing the nation to umar, almost as a caliph. He's trying to project that to his own followers.

HH: And is it succeeding?

WP: It will always succeed with his followers. That's the difference. Now you have those who are diehards with him. The minute they see him, they're very happy. But with whom I call now the realist jihadists, those who are younger, who go online, who are still anti-West but want some scores, these are the ones who are raising all the questions I've been talking about. So with those, he's not that much succeeding unless he delivers victories and strikes.

HH: Now I doubt there are many people who have spent as much time as you have, Dr. Phares, in studying the jihadist movement. Can you give us a guess, your best estimate, of how many jihadis there are who believe in violence, and are willing to sacrifice themselves in the cause?

WP: Let me call them, that's a new word, I'm breaking it right now, the pre-jihadists, meaning those who have been recruited and indoctrinated to the ideology, to Islamic fundamentalism, if you want, or jihadism. I'm afraid to say they are in the millions, the pool. Those who have crossed the line to become jihadi activists, meaning terrorists in our legal language, meaning those who are ready to either sacrifice themselves or engage in confrontation, we're talking about in the hundreds of thousands. Those who have linked up with al Qaeda, you know, go from circle to circle, probably somewhere around 30,000 around the world.

HH: And how many at each level do you believe to be in the United States? Let's start with the 30,000 hard core members or affiliates of al Qaeda.

WP: Let me begin from across the Atlantic. The British are monitoring, that's the British government numbers which are the lesser numbers, obviously. 1,500 in the UK who could become suicide bombers. In the United States, no government has yet dared advancing any numbers, experts, and among them, would dare to say that at least, we're talking about 3,000 of those who are jihadi, ready to action. How many potential suicide bombers? Every single time we catch a cell, the two or three members are suicide bombers. So at least in the hundreds.

HH: All right, and then of the number who are jihadi activists in the United States?

WP: Well, jihadi activists, you're talking at least, I mean, these are rough numbers based on different types of estimates, somewhere between 5,000 to 10,000.

HH: And in terms of pre-jihadi recruits, people who are indoctrinated in the Salafist extreme ideology?

WP: Well, every time there is an attempt at research to see how many people believe in that trend, any time there is an attempt for polling, then you have the Wahhabi activists and all sort of lobbies that say oh, this is discrimination, and they're trying to pick who is thinking in that way, so it's very difficult. But you've got to double or triple the original number I gave, about 30,000, probably.

HH: All right. And now, so we've got 30,000 problem cases down to a hardcore number of hundreds who could be suicide bombers. Of those two men who were arrested in the South, any doubt in your mind that they were terrorists?

WP: No, no. I mean, explosives, and linked to Sami al-Arian, without having an organic link. And you know, all I ask in the media from the government is tell us what kind of literature they had on them, because if they have explosives and jihadi literature, I mean, you don't need a political scientist for that. It's easy. But the government this time did not release the kind of literature they had. I don't know why.

HH: Now what is the explanation for the way the government has treated the Fort Dix six, it's vanished from the headlines, these two arrested in the South. Why so circumspect? Are they afraid of copycats?

WP: There is this, there is also something that is beyond our realm. Who is advising government on how to treat it? Who in the Homeland Security, national security, and other type of circles that deal with that, is telling…not just whom, but what are they telling the government to do? Not to treat it as a jihadist movement, not to treat it as a terrorist movement, but as only individual criminals? For what reasons, we don't know. We really don't know.

HH: Has anyone engaged in this conversation with you? The Homeland Security cabinet secretary, Chertoff, or anyone?

WP: Not the secretary himself, but I have testified many times to DHS, to the FBI, to Congress, even DOD, and there are a lot of discussions back and forth, a lot of intelligent people out there. But again, when it reaches the level of lobby groups that can reach out to Congress, or reach out to the administration and say hey, we cannot discuss those issues, this is theology, this is not terrorism. And you know, my school tells me no. This is ideology, and we need to discuss it. We need to inform the American citizen of what's going on. This is where the real debate begins.

HH: Now I'm really baiting the hook for the longer conversation after I've absorbed your new book, The War of Ideas. But is it possible to turn the Salafist edge back on itself? Is it possible to win that war of ideas? Or just do we have to wait and watch it run its very destructive and horrible course?

WP: No, absolutely, we can begin the war or ideas. At this...we have not. And then we can, with time, turn the tide and win it. But we have not even began the real steps such as discussing it openly in Congress, have the right legislation for it, and have huge funding that is going in all directions, but not in the right directions, that is to fund the NGO's, women's movements, students movements, and all the intellectuals who in the Arab and Muslim world, including in the Diaspora, are completely anti-Salafist, pro-democracy. We have not begun to talk to them.

HH: Dr. Phares, are we breeding terrorists by fighting the war in Iraq?

WP: Basically, the terrorists, the jihadist becomes terrorist regardless of us doing anything. It's an ideological process, and by the fact that we are responding, basically what we are doing is mobilizing the American public to realize that there is a threat, and give us the resources, and then mobilizing those who are against the jihadists to join the ranks. I've been asked many times about the growth of al Qaeda, is it growing or not. Yes, it's growing, but it's growing because of the billions of dollars that regimes in the region, Iran, Saudi Arabia, Qatar, and circles in those regimes have been funding and creating the madrassas. The jihadists are the result of the madrassas, with the United States or without United States. They were producing those jihadists even when we were supporting the Mujahedin in Afghanistan against the Soviet Union. It's only them who decided after 1990 to turn their weapons against the other remaining infidel power.

HH: Dr. Walid Phares, I will get The War of Ideas quickly. We will have you back and spend an hour or two talking about this very important subject. Thanks for a short notice interview today after the arrests in Austria.

End of interview.

Interview with Robin Wright
March 18, 2008

HH: It's a special broadcast. Sit down, get your pens out, get ready to take some notes. I've got a very special guest. Robin Wright may be America's most experienced reporter abroad on the nature of the Arab world. She has reported for the Washington Post, the L.A. Times, the New Yorker, the Sunday Times. She's won all the journalism awards you could possibly want. And she's got a brand new book out, Dreams and Shadows: The Future of the Middle East, which is as comprehensive and riveting an assessment of the region that you will find. And Robin Wright, welcome to the Hugh Hewitt Show, great to have you.

RW: I'm delighted to be with you.

HH: Now if I recall correctly, are you a daughter of Ann Arbor?

RW: I am.

HH: Yeah, I took my tax from Doug Kahn, and not from your father. But boy, would he be proud of the way you wrote this book. This is an amazing piece of work here.

RW: Well, I'm honored that you know the family connection.

HH: Well, let's start with a little bit about you to put this in the light for the audience. You've been in 140 countries. When did you start reporting on the Middle East?

RW: I first landed in the Middle East on October 6th, 1973, which was the day the war, the fourth Middle East War broke out. [I landed there by…]the timing was accidental, but it also got to the point that it was a harbinger of my career. I covered more than a dozen wars, most of them in the Middle East, and to the point that my father once said to me that he wouldn't go to Bermuda on vacation, because he was sure there'd be a coup d'etat.

HH: (laughing) The fact is, though, it's odd for women to be able to have the access. As I went through <u>Dreams And Shadows</u>, you've sat down with Nasrallah. You've been in the room with Ahmadinejad. You've interviewed Khamenei. This is very unusual for a woman reporter to get that kind of access to the senior figures in Islam, is it not?

RW: Well, I think you'd be surprised at how many female foreign correspondents there are these days. It's true that I've probably been covering the region longer. It just means I'm older. But I think that it's surprising to me that I think there's such an appetite in the region to be listened to, that when people sit down and hear folks out, that they give them the time. I remember I went to see, after losing a lot of friends at the first embassy bombing in 1983 in Beirut, which was the first attack by a suicide terrorist, I went to see the man in Iran who was allegedly behind a lot of it. And I was told I wasn't allowed to speak with him, I could only meet him. But when I said I wanted to ask one question, he said what was it, and I said I wanted to know what the successes and failures of the Iranian revolution were. And two and a half hours later, I had to excuse myself, because I had another appointment.

HH: Wow. That is remarkable. Now I want to begin with some generalizations. And for the benefit of the audience, in the first hour, I'm going to focus primarily on Lebanon and

Palestine, hour two, Egypt and Syria, and hour three, Iran, Iraq and Morocco. But the big generalization question at the beginning, Robin Wright, I put the book down after reading it this weekend, and was just stunned by the pervasive cruelty of the region. Now I'm a student of dissident literature. I've read Vladimir Bukovsky and Armando Valladares out of Russia and Cuba, respectively. But still, the savagery of this stuff, whether Driss Benzekri in Morocco, or Riyadh al Turk and Riyad Sayif in Syria, the butchery in Hama, the crackdowns in Egypt. What's the name of the prison there? Lazoghli prison? Is this the worst that it gets in your experience, Robin Wright?

RW: No, unfortunately, it's actually been worse. But the reality is that you have a region, it's the last bloc of countries to hold out against the democratic tide that has swept over the world over the last three decades. It has some of the last and most autocratic regimes. Especially with the fall of the Taliban in Afghanistan, Saudi Arabia remains one of the most autocratic and difficult countries in the world. And yet, it's one of our allies. It's going to be a difficult period of change, probably harder than anyplace else, probably longer than any other region, and potentially more violent. It's going to be a difficult period. But I do think that the process has begun, and that's the point of the book.

HH: Is there something about the conditions of living in the Middle East that makes people more brutal, though, than say, in other regions of the world?

RW: Well, not necessarily. I mean, if you're implying that Islam is more violent as a religion than any other, I don't think that's fair. Clearly, in its current incantation, and the current leaders of some of the movements, it's more violent than potentially many past eras. The reality is, though, that what makes the region brutal is first of all, the current leadership, and the fact that it has ostracized, outlawed, exiled, or even executed a whole generation of democrats, liberals, nationalists who might pose some kind of serious opposition, which in many cases, has forced people to turn to Islamist movements, or even Islamist extremist movements, because there's no alternative. And we get caught up in that process, in part because the United States is seen, or the West is seen as a prop that holds these regimes up, whether it's because we buy the oil of the sheikdoms and emirates and sultanists of the Persian Gulf, or because we have allies in, like Hosni Mubarak in Egypt, who's been important to the peace process, but has certainly not been interested in creating peaceful democratic conditions at home.

HH: You know, I wasn't implying Islam, because obviously, you go to an Islamic country like Indonesia, and there's nothing like this. But Hama, the massacre by Assad of what, thirty to fifty thousand of his own people in Hama, Syria? That's sort of unprecedented since the Nazis, isn't it?

RW: Well, you think about what Stalin did in Russia, in the Soviet Union. There have been terrible massacres. And there are, you know, South African rule during Apartheid was hardly gentle when it came to black opposition. There are a lot of people in the world, in Latin America, the military dictatorships that have long histories of brutality. Clearly, because we're learning a little bit more about what's happening inside a lot of these countries, we're hearing a little bit more about the scope of their repression.

HH: Let me ask you about Iran, and then we'll go into them country by country. Are we on the brink of a confrontation with Iran that you think is going to go violent, other than…obviously, the Quds forces have been operating in Iraq, and we've had attacks from Iranian-sponsored terrorists for a long time. But I mean, a state to state confrontation, Robin Wright?

RW: I think last summer, we saw the drumbeats of war in Washington, with the same kinds of people who were advocating a confrontation in Iraq, advocating to confront the Iranian regime because of its nuclear program, and for other reasons. But I think the National Intelligence Estimate in the end of last year, indicating that Iran stopped the weaponization program, the weaponization potential of a nuclear weapon in 2003, pulled the rug out from under the carpet of those who advocated military strikes on Iran. I think it will be very difficult for the Bush administration to generate any momentum, given the fact that the international community is not enthusiastic, our military forces are stretched thin already with Afghanistan, Iraq and other commitments, that the U.N. would take, I think, a pretty strong stand against it. I think the best the administration can hope for is international economic sanctions as a main tool. But it is clear that Iran is going to remain a chief priority of whoever assumes power in the United States next year.

HH: How dangerous do you think a nuclear-armed Iran would be, Robin Wright?

RW: It's a very good question, and I think it depends on who's in power. The reality is that Iran wants, I think, a nuclear capability. Does it want a nuclear weapon? I think it would like to have the sense that it's in the same category of countries. After all, five of the eight nuclear powers in the world are either on its borders or very close by. And it feels threatened, because as an Indo-European people, the Persians are not Arabs, they feel like they're outsiders in that part of the world. They feel vulnerable in the aftermath of Iran and Iraq. But do they want a weapon to use? And I think there are some serious questions about that. One of the things that struck me when I interviewed the defense minister in Iran a few years ago, he said if only we were as naughty as the North Koreans, maybe we'd be receiving American aid. In other words...

HH: Sure.

RW: If they had a weapon, that the outside world would pay attention, and be offering them perks, basically, to give it up.

HH: But if we...and we've got about a minute to our break, Robin Wright, if they did, to the satisfaction of all the intelligence world, seemed to be on the brink of a acquiring a nuclear capability, weaponizing their missiles, would you think the West would have to act against them?

RW: That's a very tough call, and I wouldn't want to have to be the one to make it. It will be one that certainly Israel will be very nervous about, the Gulf Arabs will be very nervous about. My speculation at this point is that there would be serious efforts by the outside world to try to push for some kind of, whether it's a security arrangement that the grand bargain, which offers Iran the security it feels it needs or deserves, to try to preempt that. But it may well get to the point that there's some kind of tough decision to be made.

HH: Robin Wright, to set up our conversation about Palestine and Lebanon, I want to start with the very basic question. In your opinion, is radical jihadism metastasizing or contracting? And by that, I mean radical Islamists who are willing to use violence up to and including suicide violence in order to further their perceived agenda.

RW: There's no question that it's metastasizing in the sense that there are al Qaeda cells now operating in virtually every Arab country. But at the same time, one of the things that struck me in going back to the region after covering it for 35 years, trying to get an assessment of what's going on inside countries, is the sense that people are growing increasingly angry or frustrated with militant Islam as a potential solution, because while the al Qaeda cells can destruct, they can't provide constructive alternatives to the challenges of everyday life, be it jobs, education, some kind of independent future, housing, health care. There's a recognition, and we've seen this even in Iraq, where the trial sheiks in Anbar Province, the most volatile of all Iraq's regions, turned on al Qaeda after fostering them, aiding and abetting them, because they were just too brutal. The tribal sheik that turned the movement had lost his father and two brothers to al Qaeda. And there are people who were increasingly angry. And the tribal sheik, Sheik Sattar, mobilized not only his peers to form an awakening council, but also recruited 90,000 Iraqis, Sunnis, to form a police and a military unit to push al Qaeda back. So I think this plays out in so many regions, where they're tired of the violence themselves, and they're tired of living in fear.

HH: Let's start with the portrait where it hasn't turned around yet, which is on Gaza and on the West Bank. Hamas has been linked to fifty suicide attacks since 2000. Your account of Hamas is just brutal. But Gaza still looks to be worsening, not improving. Do you concur with that assessment, Robin Wright?

RW: Oh, absolutely. I think that Gaza is a…the living conditions, where something well over 70% of the people have to rely on handouts in order to get basic food to survive on a daily basis, that's a miserable existence. That's the kind of thing you see in the poorest part of the world. And the Palestinians have always been the most educated, the most self-sufficient, the best prepared to take care of themselves. So this is a real travesty.

HH: Now you write in the book, <u>Dreams And Shadows</u>, no one saw Hamas' triumph at the ballot box coming, and that Fatah did things like run too many candidates, just basic mistakes in political land. If it was to rerun again, do you think Hamas would still win the majority in parliament, Robin Wright?

RW: It's a very good question. I think the numbers would be very different. Who knows about who'd come out with the majority, but even Hamas didn't fully anticipate that it would win. There were calculations that it would be the largest opposition in parliament, but you know, very few of them understood until the very last couple of days that they might actually win the thing. There were terrible mistakes. I think that given what's happening in Gaza, given the fact that all the public opinion polls show that both Israelis and Palestinians still want a two-state solution and a peaceful outcome, that you might see a different vote. It would depend very much on who's running. But one of the things we don't understand in the United States in looking at that election is that people voted to reject a party and a leader who had dominated Palestinian politics for a half century. So the election was important in a sense, going beyond the Hamas victory, because they were saying no to those who'd controlled their lives for so long. That's a major breakthrough, changing the status quo. Getting beyond one party that's dominated for so long is pivotal to the transition in the region.

HH: One of the things that didn't leave me feeling at all cheery is the fact that when you went to Beirut to talk to Osama Hamdan and other representatives of exiled groups, that they are adamant. Israel must be destroyed. Not necessarily all the Jews, although that's a fine point to Israelis, but that...are they ever going to reconcile to the U.N.'s decision of 1948, Robin Wright?

RW: That's a very good question. I think it's the $64,000 dollar question when it comes to the future of the Arab-Israeli peace process. Hamas is very much like the PLO was in the 1980's. It has a number of different ways of thought, a number of different kind of factions within Hamas. There's some who are prepared to engage in what's called a hudna, or a cease fire, where there would not be a formal peace, but there would be a cessation of hostilities. That's the best that's on the table at the moment. But there are others, like Osama Hamdan, who believe that they should go back to Palestine, and those Jews who want to stay can, but it'll be one man, one vote, and therefore, given the demographics, there will no longer be a Jewish state. So there's a full range of opinion within Hamas. And it's clear that it will not be a party to the peace process. It will not be tolerated by Israel, the United States, the Europeans, the U.N., until it takes the same steps that Yasser Arafat did in 1988, in renouncing violence, and recognizing Israel's right to exist.

HH: So what do you see happening there? You know, every day rockets fall, the Israelis move in, the international press gets excited, the secretary of state goes over, people pledge cooperation, then it starts again, only worse.

RW: Yeah, I think that's a fair description. I think the reality is that the Bush administration cannot expect to make any headway by the end of the Bush administration's term as they set out to do with the Annapolis conference last year. The realities on the ground, and the events on the ground, which is always true, overtake diplomacy, and they have yet again. You have no longer just two parties, the Palestinians and the Israelis in these talks. You have two very different Palestinian groups that control each one of them a half of what was once the Palestinian Authority.

HH: You write on Page 57-58 that al Qaeda is definitely in Gaza. To what level, do you think?

RW: You know, I don't know, and I think that most of the al Qaeda cells are actually very, very small. One thing that is striking in terms of the hope for the region is that they are able to dominate headlines, because their acts are so violent. But in fact, their numbers are very small. They do not represent probably even one percent of the population in terms of the active cells carrying out these atrocious bombings.

HH: 30 seconds to our break, do you think Hamas leadership knows who they are and where they are, and are allowing them to remain as the Taliban did? Or are they operating independent of Hamas?

RW: I think they're probably operating independent, and I suspect some of the Hamas intelligence people have suspicions about where they are and who they may be, but I also suspect that in the true Taliban way, or al Qaeda way, they're moving around all the time and hard to track.

HH: Let's turn to Lebanon, Robin Wright. I am fascinated by Nasrallah. This is the best portrait I've read of him by a Western journalist. How much time have you actually spent with Nasrallah, the head of Hezbollah?

RW: Well, I've spent a lot of time with Hezbollah, dating back to the five years I lived in Beirut. And I saw the emergence of Hezbollah in the attack on the American embassy, two American embassies and the Marine compound, where I lost a number of friends. And it was because of that trend emerging, the first Islamic extremists, that I set out to understand who was responsible. And I wrote one of the first books on Islamic extremism. I went to Iran to track down the militants, and Damascus, and I followed that all the way through to tracking the Taliban operating in Afghanistan. Nasrallah, I spent some time with in 2006, just before the war between Israel and Hezbollah, and talked to a lot of his aides, a lot of the senior members of Hezbollah, to try to understand where it's headed in the future.

HH: Now you're very clear-eyed about the history of Hezbollah, and you talk about the Argentinian attacks, you talk about their attacks on the American embassies, and of course the Marines, and about his rhetoric. In fact, Nasrallah's rhetoric, on Page 180, from the 1998 Ashoura celebrations, Israelis are descendents of apes and pigs. I mean, this is a man who is a fanatic. Is that fair?

RW: He is definitely a fanatic. He is one of Iran's most active arms in expanding the revolution, exporting the revolution throughout the region. He clearly is a force to be reckoned with, even in Lebanese politics.

HH: Well, given all this, his extremism, what does his rise to almost Nasser-like status, and if that's a fair comparison, I take it from you, that after the 2006 war, which we'll discuss in detail, he's become the galvanizing, sort of superstar face of Islamic radicalism.

RW: Well, one of the problems for us as a nation, as the chief broker on Arab-Israeli peace, is that Hezbollah has achieved more in a tangible way than all of the peaceful politicians have managed to. It forced Israel to withdraw after its invasion of Lebanon in gradual phases until it left completely without any kind of peace treaty, without any kind of guarantees. That was the first time any Arab country, community or faction had managed to force Israel to back down. In 2006, it was one of the longest clashes between Israel and an Arab neighbor, and Israel came out with very little to show, and there's still two Israeli soldiers held by Hezbollah almost two years later.

HH: But it was a tremendous, as you point out, he even admits it was a tremendous miscalculation. He had no idea what he was getting into when they launched the operation that led to the 2006 war. But it didn't hurt him, it seems like. It might have hurt a lot of Lebanese Shiites, but it didn't hurt him.

RW: Well, it didn't kill him, but at the end of the day, Hezbollah paid a price in public relations inside Lebanon. He's a very charismatic figure, and appeals, interestingly enough, not just to the Shiites of Lebanon, but to many others, including a good handful, or more than a handful, many of the Christians I met who admire the fact that he was standing up for the Arab world in a way that the Arab politicians had been unable to. So he had a following, but I think the fact that there was such huge devastation in Lebanon, and enormous loss of life for a small country, led a lot to question. And certainly, he is now operating totally from the underground again.

HH: Yeah, you write here there's only one solution for Nasrallah, quoting a senior Israeli official. Do they intend to do to him what they did to Imad...

RW: Mugniyah?

HH: Mugniyah.

RW: I suspect that Mugniyah's assassination was a harbinger of what could happen to Nasrallah. But you know, I'm not in Israel. I don't know.

HH: What is the aftermath of Nasrallah if he is removed, if he is assassinated? Is there anyone of his stature standing behind him?

RW: Well, there's what they call a Shura council, basically a body of senior clergy who advise, it's like a cabinet that advise Nasrallah, and he has a deputy named Qassem, and he would probably succeed Nasrallah.

HH: Does Nasrallah have the potential to go Arafat, or engage the process as the way Arafat did, whether sincerely or not? Well, let's hold that thought until we come back from break.

HH: Robin Wright, when we went to break, I had asked does Nasrallah have the potential to mainstream, in one word, the way that Arafat did after Oslo? What's your thought on that?

RW: It's a wonderful question, Hugh. And I guess one of the things that has struck me in looking at Hezbollah is how I remember it when it was a clandestine cell, and engaged only in violence. No one knew who its leadership was or its members. And we've seen it evolve. And in 1992, it decided to run for parliament. It set up a huge infrastructure in Lebanon of health clinics, schools, farm co-ops. It is the second largest employer after the Lebanese state in Lebanon. There is clear cut movement toward becoming a mainstream political body. But until it gives up extremism, clearly, it's going to continue to be viewed by the outside world, first and foremost, as a terrorist group. I think down the road that there is a lot of debate within Hezbollah about going mainstream, engaging just in peaceful politics. But clearly, that's not going to happen until there is some kind of full, comprehensive peace with Israel.

HH: Now clearly, they are deeply intertwined with the Iranian mullahs, and you make that very, very clear here. But are they independent of them, or do they have to dance to that fiddle?

RW: A little bit of both. I think they're clearly dependent on Iran and Syria for arms. They give it the kind of muscle that makes it the only militia still standing in Lebanon after all others have been armed in the aftermath of a truce in its civil war eighteen years ago. But I think that Iran does not call all the shots when it comes to Hezbollah, and that Nasrallah has become such an entity, and Hezbollah's such a force in Lebanon, that he makes many calls himself when it comes to the political decisions of the group.

HH: When you [talk,] write in <u>Dreams and Shadows</u> about their rebuilding plan after the 2006 war, $12,000 dollars per household, that's a huge amount of money. Where is it coming from?

RW: Ah, that's where it comes from, Iran. Hezbollah allegedly has its own investments, would you believe, and its own money producing organizations, including some that are allegedly, or reportedly involving illegal activities. But it also has a lot of business interests as well now, and it has many Shiites who contribute. There's a tradition within Islam, and tradition within Shiite Islam, to hand over a certain part of your income for charity, for groups and clerics you support. And so Hezbollah makes a lot of money off its own followers.

HH: You obviously have a great affection for Beirut and for Lebanon. And for those of us in the U.S. who only know it through movies, like Caramel or something like that, it seems [a] very odd, it seems like four or five different countries. [What's going to...] what's your estimate of what it's going to look like in ten years? Will this confessional system of almost spoils endure?

RW: Well, you have seventeen recognized religious sects in Lebanon that all have a claim, under a power sharing formula, to some role in government. And that's not just in parliament. That extends all the way to the civil service down to kindergarten teachers and police on the street. So everyone has some vested interest in the system. Confessional? I think there will always probably be some balance, the idea of one person, one vote will be hard to entrench, because [there's long,] the whole creation of Lebanon was based on a formula that involves splitting power and guaranteeing the Christians, now in the minority, will have a guaranteed role. It used to be 6-5, Christian to Muslim. Now it's a 50/50 split in all positions of power, and all civil service jobs. So I suspect there will be some formula in a decade, or even the next generation. But it's clear that finding a mechanism for co-existence, [and...but] while still opening the way for all parties to feel they're fairly represented given the changing demographics is at the heart of the situation. What gives me hope is the fact that I lived through five years living in Beirut of a civil war. Today, you have a real crisis, the failure to elect a president since November, several, more than a dozen times postponed the election, and yet Lebanon has not slipped back into civil war.

HH: That is very optimistic. When we come back, we're going to be talking about Christians in the Middle East, especially in Lebanon and Syria. My guest is Robin Wright, her new book is Dreams And Shadows: The Future Of The Middle East, magnificent, put out by the Penguin Press, it's at Amazon.com, I've linked it at Hughhewitt.com. When we come back, we'll talk about that a little bit more. [When I...] Robin Wright, before we get to break, you write about Nasrallah that, "He's not a thief," that this is one of the key elements to his popularity. Is that a definition for new success in the Middle East? Are everyone going to have to be understood by people as not corruptible?

RW: Well, the interesting thing about Iran is that Ahmadinejad was elected in large part because he was seen as Mr. Clean. He was not a corrupt cleric. And this is something that appealed to people. No one knew in, [you know,] the two week long presidential campaign, what his foreign policy was, or what he was like, how hard line he was. But people were looking for someone who was not wearing a turban, and was not associated with the early days of the revolution, and might clean up society. No one in Iran, I think, bargained on how hard line he would prove to be.

HH: But do we know for sure that Nasrallah is not skimming the way that so many of these other corrupt leaders in the Middle East have been skimming?

RW: I don't know personally, but there is a sense among a lot of Lebanese that he has not pocketed millions or billions into a personal account, and that he leads a simple life.

HH: I also found amazing that his son died in the war, and that this is another source of legitimacy for him, that he did not spare his own family this sort of sacrifice.

RW: And not only that, he didn't talk about it with others who broadcast the fact that he had lost his son. He made no special provisions to get his body back from Israel. It took over nine months in a prisoner swap.

HH: We're going to discuss Egypt and Syria, so don't go away. In the last hour, Iran and Iraq, the big two. But Egypt is actually the big one, and we'll talk about that after the break. Robin Wright, one of the things I appreciated is that you dealt occasionally throughout Dreams and Shadows with the Christian community in the Middle East, often overlooked, often persecuted. How is it faring generally? Is it just going to be erased from history in the Middle East after years and years of oppression and shrinkage?

RW: You know, I don't think so. One of the things that's striking is [that] the diversity that still exists in the region. Ten percent of Egypt is Coptic Christian. At least a fifth, and some say a quarter of the Palestinian community is still Christian. Now many of the Palestinian Christians have fled elsewhere. Just as many Palestinians have left. But there are, the diversity of the communities in the region, when you look at how many are in Lebanon, how many are in Syria, the place where the first organized Christian Church was formed in Antioch. I was there for an Easter Sunday, and I was struck by how many Easter bunnies and chocolate eggs I found in the stores in downtown Damascus. So there are still minority communities, but then that's true everywhere throughout the region. I mean, how much do we hear about the Jewish Kurds, [that there are...] the Jewish Moroccans? There are a lot of minorities scattered throughout the region. The largest Jewish community outside Israel, ironically, is in Iran.

HH: Right, right. But do the new Islamists accord any kind of religious protection? For example, in Gaza, are there any Christians left at all in Gaza?

RW: You know, it's a good question. I don't know the answer to that. I think that most of the Christian communities are in the West Bank – Bethlehem, Ramallah...

HH: And how about Nasrallah's Hezbollah? Are they accepting...I mean, he's got an alliance with Aoun that you write about here, but that's a political alliance. How about in the south of Lebanon? Are there any Christians left?

RW: Yes, there are some Christian communities left in the south. And it's interesting that, as you point out, Nasrallah has this alliance with former General Aoun, one of the right wing Christian leaders in Lebanon. And [they,] in fact, Hezbollah had backed Aoun as the candidate for the Christian presidency in Lebanon.

HH: Is that a party of one, though? Is Aoun about the only Christian leader that's aligned with Hezbollah? Or are there others?

RW: He's the main Christian leader aligned with Hezbollah, yes.

HH: You've got so many contacts over there. Are they optimistic about some sort of a settlement, Robin Wright?

RW: On the Arab-Israeli conflict?

HH: No, on the Lebanese political stalemate.

RW: Well, this is another tragedy in the Middle East. Just like we know what the Arab-Israeli solution is, is a two state solution, both sides accept that, it's just a matter of working out the specifics. The same thing is true in Lebanon. They had a candidate for president, a former general. Both sides have agreed on it. It's the power arrangement around it that still has to be sorted out. So yes, I think there is a resolution. The danger is it may take a long time to get there.

HH: Robin Wright, last hour we talked generally, and about Palestine and Lebanon. I want to begin this hour with the longest segment in any hour by talking about Egypt, because it's a revelation, really. Egypt is the largest Arab country by far, and yet very little is reported on it. It's in every story, but very little is reported on it. And I don't think it was always that way. But what level of American awareness of Egypt do you think exists?

RW: Well, Egypt is a microcosm of our whole perspective on the region. One of the reasons I went back and spent a year looking at what's going on in all 22 Muslim countries and Israel, was because we know so little. We made a colossal mistake in Iraq in not understanding [what] the dynamics inside the country. We relied on a group of exiles, the leader of whom had not been to Iraq since 1958, when he left as a teenager. And so what I was trying to look at was inside countries like Egypt, what are the dynamics? Who are the actors? How is the political situation being redefined? And I found a very interesting array of people in diverse fields, totally disjointed. It's not any kind of big plot, but they all felt individually motivated to do something, and have certainly changed what's going on inside Egypt.

HH: You write on Page 72 that no people in the Arab world have a greater sense of national identity or pride than Egyptians.

Does Egypt lead the Arab world, Robin Wright, in a way that Nasser sought to do forty years ago?

RW: I think that's always been true. It constitutes roughly a third of the Arab population. It's been a political trendsetter. It was the one that made peace with Israel first. There's a saying in the region that books are written in Egypt, printed in Lebanon, and read in Iraq, reflecting the fact that a lot of the ideas and energy emanate from Cairo, particularly.

HH: Now there's an extended conversation in your book about the attempt by Hosni Mubarak, very carefully, very calibrated over a period of years, to replace himself with his son Gamal. And you write about the authoritarians, the democrats and the Islamists. And here's the authoritarian with the son, even as Saddam Hussein had planned to give to his mad as hatter boys the power in Iraq. What is your impression of Gamal?

RW: Well, my sense is that the Mubarak family has decided they want to create a dynasty at a time that dynasties are a dying breed elsewhere in the world. And Gamal is a man who is very different from his father. Hosni Mubarak, who's now ruled Egypt longer in a six thousand year history than anyone but two pharaohs, came from a village, he worked his way into power through the air force. He was a pilot. He studied in the Soviet Union. His son, by contrast, has always grown up in either the presidential palace or government housing. He was educated in Europe. He is not a man who's experienced anything from the streets. I doubt he's ever taken a taxi. And he is among the privileged elite who doesn't really have a sense of what's happening on the streets of Egypt anymore.

HH: Does he have a charisma of the sort that Nasrallah did, or even that Sadat had? Again, Sadat a very privileged figure, came up through the military. Does Gamal, looking ahead ten or fifteen years, is there someone here on whom the West can rely to stay in power?

RW: Well, that's a different question whether he has charisma.

HH: True.

RW: I don't think he has any charisma. I don't think that he has built up a following of young people around him that would give someone hope about new openings in Egypt, or stability, necessarily, in Egypt in the long term. He shows every indication of following the policies of his father, which you know, you think about Hosni Mubarak, he finally allowed a couple of years ago someone to run against him for the presidency. He won overwhelmingly, but his chief opponent was arrested shortly after the election took place, and he's still in jail. So the idea that there's any prospect of the Mubarak dynasty actually opening up Egypt is pretty limited.

HH: Well, it reminded me, as I finished the chapters on Egypt, of Iran, '76-'78, where you've got a number of different currents below the surface, you've got an Islamist movement, although it's Sunni, obviously, not Shia as it was in Iran. And you've got pressure for change that could quickly spiral into the kind of a revolution that we saw wrack Iran and endure to this day. Am I off in seeing parallels there? Or is that real?

RW: You know, I think the interesting thing about Iran is that the Sunnis particularly, but even the Shiites don't want to see a replication of the Iranian revolution. It did not bring stability to Iran. It was not welcomed by the outside world. It's been under sanctions now for almost three decades, that it has not answered the questions of daily life that so many people want, whether it's again, education, jobs, housing. [And that was…] it will, I think, remain a peculiarly Iranian phenomena. I don't think that people want revolution, but I do think that there is greater danger that the longer the autocrats rule without some kind of prospect of opening, there is a greater danger of violence taking place.

HH: Now you talk extensively about the Muslim Brotherhood. And this audience knows a lot about the Brothers, because Lawrence Wright's been a guest here a lot of times, and we've spent a lot of time talking about it. Do you believe Mohammed Habib when he tells you that if there is a free election, the Brothers would win 60% of the vote in Egypt?

RW: You know, I don't know the answer, and I don't think there are any polls that show. I doubt that if it were held tomorrow, that the Muslim Brotherhood would win 60%. The reality is that the vast majority of Egyptians don't vote. They don't believe in the system. And so when you say 60% of the vote, that's 60% of a minority of people who feel motivated to vote. The Egyptian government certainly isn't going to allow the Muslim Brotherhood to run that many candidates. They've not run candidates in every district when they run for parliament. But [it] clearly, because the regime has, again, outlawed, isolated, put under house arrest or executed the traditional opposition groups, the liberals, the nationals, the democrats, they've left very few alternatives but the Islamists. And in many ways, the Muslim Brotherhood's performance in elections in some ways allows the government to say, "See, there's a real danger. Unless you support us, you're going to get those Muslim Brother leaders in power," when I don't think necessarily the Muslim Brothers would win, at least in the short term, an overwhelming majority.

HH: You know, it's a very sympathetic portrait of the Brothers. They run hospitals, they take care of the poor. They're obviously quite committed believers. But at the same time, you write in a later chapter that no Arab country's every going to be able to reform until and unless it deals with women in a way that we consider to be legitimate, the West considers to be legitimate. Are the Brothers committed to that, in your opinion, Robin Wright? Or are they traditionalists when it comes to the role of women in Islam?

RW: Clearly traditionalist when it comes to the role of Islam. But they do have women who've run for office. They've taken some steps, beginning steps to include them in policy decisions. [They're not, you know,] Muslim Brother women members are not just wives and daughters. They do play a role in the party. But I would quibble with your description of it as being a sympathetic portrayal of them. I tried to get into the inner workings of them to see exactly what impact they're making. And like Hezbollah, like Hamas, they have set up social institutions in a country where people can't get reliable health care from government institutions.

HH: You see, I think that's admirable. I think they actually go out and do other than blow up things. They actually take care of people. That's why I meant sympathetic in that regard.

RW: Right. Well, and they've renounced violence, which is a beginning. But they still do not recognize Israel's right to exist.

HH: It's interesting, on Page 111, you call their position on violence two-faced. What do you mean by that?

RW: Well, when it comes to their own policies, they have abandoned the days of militancy, for which the party was once known. And yet they believe that it is justifiable to attack American troops in Iraq, because they see them as an occupation force. And they believe it's justifiable to attack Israelis in Gaza or the West Bank, because they are occupation forces.

HH: Are they playing us, Robin Wright? Will they achieve power and then go radical? It's really the same question I asked you at the beginning of this segment, but it's the most important one.

RW: You know, I think what we've seen is an evolution of some of the Islamist groups. And I think that they don't always speak with one voice. There are factions within. As there are with Hamas, there are as well with the Muslim Brotherhood. There are those who understand that whether they like it or not, Israel's around to stay, and that they have to play by the international rules, that violence is not a way to assume power and create credibility on the ground, or ensure enduring power. Will the Muslim Brotherhood turn radical? It depends on the conditions, but my sense is we've turned a corner in the renunciation of violence, and one can only hope that over time, if they are constantly prosecuted and persecuted by the Egyptian government, that they'll begin to play even more by the rules, international standards.

HH: Robin Wright, how's the book been received? It's comprehensive, I know you were on Charlie Rose last night. Generally speaking, is it getting the attention of an interested public? Or is the American people just so exhausted with Iraq and all things Arab that they're not paying much attention?

RW: Well, it's gotten wonderful reviews so far. It was on the cover of the New York Times Sunday book reviews section on March 2nd. I've been speaking to groups across the country, lots of media. I think there's a real appetite. I think people in the aftermath of Iraq are concerned about what happened, and I think that even though we're in overdrive in fatigue when it comes to Iraq, that there is an understanding that our future depends in part on the stability in that region, on the future of that region. There's an awareness that not just because of oil in Iraq, that we are going to be the protector of many of these vulnerable sheikdoms in the Persian Gulf, that stability in Lebanon is crucial to our interests, that what happens in Egypt is pivotal to ensuring the future of Arab-Israeli peace. There's just a lot of things…you know, unlike Vietnam, and I'm a Vietnam-era baby, we could walk away as a nation from Vietnam with a terrible loss and not have it affect us for decades to come. Whatever happens in Iraq and the Middle East will affect us, not only for decades, but for generations, maybe a century or more.

HH: When you hear, someone as experienced in the Middle East as you are, when you hear the political conversation, both on the Democratic and Republican side, are you appalled or are you encouraged by the level of knowledge or ignorance that you hear in there, in these conversations among electeds and would-be electeds?

RW: Well, I think the Bush administration still hasn't learned a lot of the lessons, basic lessons that happened because of Iraq. Vice President Cheney in Iraq this week has talked about that it was still worth the initiative, and that he's still hopeful that things are going to come out smoothly. I wish I shared that optimism. I think that a new administration may help the United States with the outside world, because it will have someone else in power. President Bush is so closely associated with the failure in Iraq, and its aftermath, and the failure to achieve peace despite big promises on the Arab-Israeli conflict, that a new face will help, but it will also depend on which face it is.

HH: You know, I'll come back to that next hour, because I'm more with John Burns and Robert Kaplan, guests on this program who believe that it is not only worth it, but that it could work there, and it sounds like you're more of a pessimist in Iraq than those, but I don't want to get out of turn yet. But I was talking about, for example, Sylvester Reyes gets elected to the chairmanship of the House Committee on Intelligence, and he doesn't know the difference between a Sunni and a Shia.

RW: (laughing) Yeah.

HH: Is that common, or is that...

RW: Yes, it's horrible. I mean, particularly on the Hill, the level of ignorance is gut-wrenching, you know, especially when they're appropriating billions of American taxpayer dollars on a monthly basis for the war in Iraq, and not to understand just the essentials of this part of the world.

HH: Well, one of those most puzzling of countries is Syria, and I loved your introduction, Damascus is the oldest capitol in the world, and ever since human history has been written, it's been there to record it. Was that Mark Twain?

RW: Yes, it was.

HH: Wonderful stuff, but it's also the most rigidly repressed. Can you describe for people what life in Damascus is like?

RW: Well, Damascus is a very cosmopolitan city, but it is also one in which there are secret police at every street corner, in every hotel, and every government building listening to the words of most visitors, as well as all politicians. The corruption is horrendous. The traffic cops move from corner to corner, and they will stop cars that are driving quite legally, and [tell,] make up some charge. And it's a way of exhorting bribes from taxi drivers or just ordinary people, so that they don't have to go to court and pay a ticket. They just buy off the policeman for doing nothing wrong. It's just a place where you feel the heavy hand of government in the same way you did in the Soviet Union.

HH: Now you write about the secret police following you around on your most recent trip there, and you made a complaint to one of the cabinet members. Did it stop, Robin Wright, after that? Or does it continue?

RW: No, it continued. And the fact is that I had a young Syrian woman who was helping me, and she used to get calls on her telephone saying well, what did Robin Wright do today? And would you like to come in and report on her activities, and what she was told, and who she met with?

HH: Now the Alouites, who are the Assad family's tribe, about 12%, I think you write in <u>Dreams and Shadows</u>, and do the Shia consider them to be heretics? Or do the Shias embrace them as sort of a Methodist equivalent of a Lutheran?

RW: Oh, well, that's a good comparison, actually. A lot of Shiites consider them an off-shoot. Some of them consider them heretics. But they are within Shiite Islam. And that's why the king of Jordan, King Abdullah, worried about the Shiite crescent, or the Shiite arc, stretching from Shiite-dominated Iran into Shiite-majority Iraq, into Shiite-ruled Syria, into Lebanon, where the largest of seventeen communities is Shiite.

HH: Now Bashar Assad comes back to take over after his father dies, the brutal Assad, and there was a Damascus spring. There was a Damascus hope for a movement. And it's all come to naught, hasn't it?

RW: That's true, but the reality is that there are still people struggling to make a difference. You know, we went through, in 2005, what was known as the Arab spring, as you called it, and this was a period where we saw the Lebanese take to the streets to force the Syrians to end 29 years of the military occupation. And we saw Iraqis turn out three times and make the purple ink-stained finger popular, turned out in every larger numbers in three elections. But that movement, that period, was quashed by both the autocrats and the extremists. And I went back to the region to get a sense, in part, of whether we were back at square one. And what I found was no, in fact, there are still an extraordinary number of activists. One of my favorite stories involves Riad Turk, a man who was the Nelson Mandela of Syria.

HH: Right.

RW: And he was imprisoned over and over by the Assad regime. And the third time he was picked up, he was fifty years old, he was held in a room the size of an elevator, with no toilet, no window, no furniture, no bed. He had no paper, no pencil. He was never charged, never knew whether he was going to be tried, total isolation, no word from his family, no access to a lawyer. He kept his sanity with nothing to do, no books to read, by taking the uncooked kernels of rice from his soup at night, and building during the day, with all those kernels, little geometric designs on the floor of his cell. And he was held that way for 18 years. And when he was released at 68, what did he do? Not go home and go into obscurity with his family, he continued to speak out and to call for the end of totalitarian rule. And what happened? He went back to jail.

HH: He went back to jail. It's one of the most brutal chapters and dispiriting ones as you think about those grains of rice that he's now using again.

HH: Robin Wright, you write about Syria, "Syria will be one of the two most difficult regimes to democratize. The other is Saudi Arabia. Their government's hold on power is absolute, people have the fewest rights or avenues of action, the secret police and public fear are the most pervasive. The two regimes have spawned sufficient support networks through family and corruption, and by playing upon cultural traditions." So how do you break that? You've got some very courageous people, Said and Turk and these others, but what happens to give you hope in Syria?

RW: Well, as I said, Syria, as you noted, Syria's going to be a very difficult place to crack. You said it was a dispiriting chapter. In fact, I find the political dissidents in Syria to be among the most hopeful cases. Despite the obstacles, they're willing to put their lives on the line. One of them wrote a new constitution for Syria to give people a sense of what the alternatives would be, what freedoms might look like. Another one wrote something called the Damascus Declaration, calling for regime change, and mobilizing 90% of the opposition behind it. There are dozens of people who are doing these very brave things. It always takes critical mass, but one of the goals of this book was addressing a challenge I had from a friend who said are there any Lech Walesas in the Middle East, referring to the leader of the Solidarity Trade Union movement in Poland, who helped end communist rule in Poland, and then bring down communist rule across the region. And so I went in search of them, and I think strikingly, there are lots of emerging Lech Walesas, but it takes time to bring change. And it's going to be more difficult and more time consuming than anywhere else in the world. But I do think that there are the beginnings of people who are changing the political debate, and putting pressure on regimes like they've never faced before.

HH: Well, take a guess for us at why Syria is doing things like allowing Islamist radicals, and I mean the Assads have been at war with the Islamists, brutally for a long time, to cross the country relatively freely to go make jihad in Iraq against the Coalition? What were they doing with the North Koreans as far as we can tell? And why an alliance with Iran to resupply Hezbollah? It's just a radical set of actions.

RW: Well, look at it in terms of its strategic interest. It lost, with the end of the Soviet Union, it lost that major ally to prop it up. And what it's doing now is it's meddling in Lebanon, it's facilitating foreign fighters going into Iraq, playing spoiler on the Arab-Israeli peace process. It makes itself an important player, when this is a country with virtually no assets, in deep economic trouble, serious opposition at home. But it makes itself an important player through its foreign policy, its regional actions.

HH: But what about the North Korean connection? Doesn't that just court massive retaliation? [Is that just...] you write

about the hubris of the Syrians, that they have always felt themselves to be at the center of the world, even when they haven't
been at the center of the world. Is that an expression, a treaty
with North Korea over nukes?

RW: Well, remember, [what we...] we don't know a lot about
that story. I wrote one of the first stories about it. There was a
facility that the Israelis attacked in September. No one told us
where it was or what it was, but through a process involving
weeks of reporting, and looking at satellite imagery and so
forth, we found a facility that clearly, the Israelis believed was
the beginning of a nuclear reactor, which would have given
Syria a potential down the road to use it for other purposes. We
know that there were North Koreans on the ground, reportedly, working at that facility. But there are more questions of
what we don't know. It's been there since 2001. What's striking
is that no one had picked it up in all that time.

HH: And given the aftermath of that, do you expect, has the
Assad regime pulled in a little bit? Or has it continued to be as
aggressive prior to the Israeli attack?

RW: Well, I think it learned a lesson. The interesting thing was
there was no retaliation, and I think that's one of the reasons
the Israelis decided not to make a major case of this to the
international community, that they didn't want Syria to take
revenge in a way that might start yet another Middle East war.

HH: And the attack on Imad Mugniyah there, also in the Syrian
capitol, have they detached themselves from other terrorists?
Are they beginning to see a downside to being the home away
from home for every mass murderer on the globe?

RW: No, unfortunately. And the reality is yet again, it becomes
a haven for extremists in part because that raises Syria's value,
the value of a country that has strategic placement, but has no
real assets to speak of, except the extremists and the misadven-
tures it gets into in neighboring countries.

HH: Yesterday, I was speaking with Senator McCain, Robin
Wright, as he was in Jordan headed towards Israel. And Israel is

not…it's in your book, <u>Dreams and Shadows</u>, but it's a reflection, not a stand alone chapter. Can you tell us why you went about it that way?

RW: Well, I went back to all 22 Muslim countries as well as Israel to try to get a sense of where the region is headed. And at the end of the day, I concluded that there were seven places that are going to be the most important in showing where the activism is leading, showing where the new movements are, identifying the new kinds of people engaged in politics. Israel is the most vibrant country in the region. It's arguably the most vibrant democracy in the world, when you consider it's about the size of Connecticut, and has such a huge political spectrum, much wider than our own, when it comes to mainstream parties, their parties included in its parliament. And its future will be determined, in many ways, by the likes of Syria and Egypt and the Palestinian Authority and Lebanon, in terms of its security, its economic future, and all the things you care about even in day to day life. I also didn't include a country like Saudi Arabia, because I felt that it was not a place, in fact, none of the Gulf countries were, where you see the dynamics have changed, that a crises of change beginning to take place with the new actors. There are some signs, but not many.

HH: You know, that's very interesting about The Kingdom, because in many respects, they're the bankroll for the Islamist radicalism, although Iran is obviously doing it as well, and they're our ally, Robin Wright.

RW: Well, there are an enormous number of inconsistencies when it comes to U.S. policy in the region.

HH: Yeah.

RW: Much of it dependent on our dependence on oil. The reality is that we would have probably less dangers from extremism if we did not have the kind of energy dependence on some of the world's most autocratic regimes. al Qaeda, after all, targeted us in part because its main focus is actually the kingdom of Saudi Arabia. We are seen as the prop that keeps the Saudis in power.

HH: Now, but going back to Israel and Saudi, if Israel is pushed to the wall again, at what point do you fear that they will simply attempt to go Roman, to settle it? They played a half war, in essence, and they lost 150 soldiers, a terrible toll for Israel in the summer of 2006, as you detail, nasty, horrible fighting, and the toll on Lebanon was hard. The next time, do you think that they go for the paralyzing blow against both Hezbollah and against the people who are the money bags?

RW: The problem is how do you hit them? I think there are some in Israel who would very much like to eliminate Hassan Nasrallah, the chief of Hezbollah. But how do you find him? They thought they had crippled Hezbollah seriously in Lebanon in 2006, and yet Hezbollah lives, and they're rebuilding in the south. And there are those who contend that Hezbollah is better armed today than it was even on the eve of that war. It's not so easy to go for broke.

HH: But do they have a choice? At some point, what I'm trying to dig at, is do you think Israel has reached the end of its rope? Because as they sit there and they watch, they watch Syria…if they believe 100% of your book, as I do, they watch Syria repress everyone. They watch Nasrallah assume a position of strength in Lebanon. They see Hamas growing crazier and more fanatical. They see Iran getting closer to a nuke. It's desperate times for Israel, and I think deservedly, they have a right to be panicked, Robin Wright. Do they?

RW: Well, every one of the problems that you cited is a different issue. It went after Iraq's nuclear program in 1981 at Osirik, because it felt a security threat. It may well feel that security threat again against Iran at some point. Lebanon and Syria are very different issues. What does it go for? Does it try to bomb the presidential palace in Damascus? To what end? So that Syria mobilizes against Israel? So that you rise up the Arab world? That's not a viable option. And I think the interesting thing is the polls show, in Israel, that the majority of people do want a two-state solution.

HH: But that...if Hamas doesn't want a two-state solution, or the Brothers don't want a two-state solution, or Syria doesn't want a two-state solution, it doesn't matter. That's what I'm getting at, is are we reaching the point where all of the hopes and best wishes of elites, whether Western elites or Middle Eastern elites don't matter against the hard and flinty gaze of a Hamas or a Hezbollah radical?

RW: Well, I don't think that Israel has the option to go after all of them, however exasperated it is. It is a very small country surrounded, as it likes to point out quite often, by a sea of hostile Arab regimes. Things are not what they were ten years ago even, that in the last four years, the Arab League has offered a proposal to Israel that would recognize its right to exist, offer trade relations to basically form a kind of regional bloc that you'd see in the European Union. Clearly, the terms are not acceptable to Israel, because it calls for going back to the 1967 borders. But the fact is that the Arabs no longer talk about the return of all Palestinian lands. And even regimes like Saudi Arabia, which introduced this proposal, do not talk any longer about the Zionist entity in their language. There's a recognition of the word Israel, and its right to exist. So there...you know, we have crossed a threshold in many ways from the days of absolutely and existential challenges. And however reluctantly, there is a recognition that the countries in the region are there to stay.

HH: Is that true for Hamas and Hezbollah?

RW: I think to a certain degree, it's true with Hezbollah. I think its primary focus is ending the conflict, making sure that Israel does come into Lebanon again, getting back its political prisoners and so forth. With Hamas, it's a bit different. Hamas has not recognized Israel's right to exist, and that's a far more problematic formula to solve, or dilemma to solve, because the best it's offering is a cease fire, and that's not acceptable to the outside world or to Israel.

HH: It's not enough.

HH: A special broadcast continues next hour with Robin Wright as we cover Iran and Iraq, the two biggest countries, and Morocco thrown in as well. Before we go there, though, Robin Wright, in <u>Dreams and Shadows</u>, there's so many vivid portraits of Arab leaders, that I was thinking about Sadat. I'm old enough to remember Sadat and the amazing trip to Israel, and his assassination, et cetera. Are there any Sadats left? Abdullah doesn't strike me as one, and I look around the Middle East and I wonder, Maliki appears to lack a certain charisma. Are there any Arab leaders willing to risk all for peace?

RW: Hugh, that's a great question, and the answer is that there is not a single leader in the Middle East, in the Arab world, in the Muslim part of the Middle East, that is in sync with the will or the wishes of their people, particularly on domestic issues. Peace is a different part of their foreign policies, and I think that there are many in the region who are now willing to accept Israel's right to exist under certain conditions. But I think that the tragedy of the region today is that at among the leaders of the countries, there are no people like de Klerk in South Africa, who recognized that Apartheid had to go, and Nelson Mandela had to be freed. There are no Gorbachevs as in the Soviet Union, who wanted to open up to perestroika and glasnost.

HH: When you talked about the Cedar Revolution, there were obviously millions of Lebanese who demanded a return to sanity. But out of that came leaders that Syria just rubbed them out. Is there any backlash among the Lebanese against that sort of violence that would lead them to almost take up arms against Syria?

RW: Oh, I think there is, and I think that's one of the reasons you see a stalemate over the presidency, that there are those who want to make sure that Syria is blocked from exerting its enormous influence in the country. You see protests and demonstrations, all peaceful, though, to try to make sure that Syria doesn't have the last word on the power sharing arrangement in Lebanon.

HH: Is the Lebanese army a real army?

RW: It's becoming better, but it's, you know, it has a long history of being factionalized as well. I remember living in Lebanon in the mid-80's, when the army just fell apart into its sectarian groups. I think that there's been an effort, and training by the outside world, to try to make sure that this is a much more professional army.

HH: Robin Wright, I want to start our third hour, primarily about Iran and Iraq, by reading from Page 330, a few paragraphs. You're describing your meeting with the Council on Foreign Relations, and President Ahmadinejad during a U.N. visit. "The diminutive president waived briefly, sat down quickly, was intent on business. Islamists often preface public remarks at public appearances with 'in the name of God, the most merciful, the most compassionate.' But as he did in his United Nations speech, Ahmadinejad added an additional line. Oh mighty Lord, he intoned, I pray to you to hasten the emergence of the promised one, that perfect and pure human being, the one that will fill this world with peace and justice. The promised one," you write, "is the missing Mahdi, the twelfth and last of the original Shiite imams descended from the Prophet Mohammed. He disappeared in the 8th Century. Shiites pray for his return the same way that Jews await the Messiah, and Christians await the Second Coming. Shiites believe the Mahdi is in a state of occultation, or hidden by God, and will return to cleanse a corrupt world on judgment day. After the revolution, the main Tehran boulevard that cuts across the entire capitol was renamed for the expected one. Ahmadinejad has a deep devotion to the Shiite messiah. Our revolution's main mission is to pave the way for the reappearance of the 12th imam. . . . Today, he said we should define our economic, cultural and political policies based on the policy of Imam Mahdi's return." Now Robin Wright, that's just horrifying.

RW: (laughing)

HH: That's just scary as scary can get, isn't it?

RW: There are far more scary exchanges I had with him, so yes, it is scary.

HH: Now the one thing that I've tried to read about Yazdi and on this, the one difference between millennialism among Christian and Jewish and the 12th Imam school is that they believe they can accelerate the return of the 12th Imam via the introduction of chaos into the world. Is that your understanding as well?

RW: Well, look, there are different understandings about conditions. Not everyone agrees with Ahmadinejad, needless to say. There is a strong belief that there will be the return of justice when the Mahdi comes, but that's a common belief in the major monotheistic religions.

HH: But what about, do you have an understanding of what he believes is the role of people on Earth in paving the way, as he put it, for the return of the Mahdi?

RW: I will be the first one to tell you that while I've talked to him twice, I have less understanding of him coming out of those meetings than I had going in. [This is a man who, you know,] one of the people at the first meeting I attended with him was Maurice Greenberg, a well-known American industrialist, who survived the Holocaust, lost family members to the Holocaust. And he said to Ahmadinejad at this meeting, how can you deny the Holocaust? It's the best documented contemporary event. And Ahmadinejad said to him, so, you say you lost family, how old are you? And Greenberg said I'm 81. And the president said well, congratulations. You see? You're alive, as if all the reports about the Holocaust amounted to nothing, they were make believe.

HH: It's a wild story, yeah.

RW: It's a wild story, unbelievable.

HH: Now you also write, I didn't know this, that after the CFR, before Columbia, he went home and he wrote about it on his blog, and he apparently believes that, what, you folks are part of the international Jewish conspiracy of some sort, that the elites are compromised in America?

RW: Yes, it was a very strange thing. He started his own blog. And from his whole trip to the United States, to speak to the United Nations and meet with world leaders, the only thing he put on his blog was this meeting he had with thirty of us from the Council on Foreign Relations. It was bizarre.

HH: Now given that his party won the elections this past weekend, his hand is strengthened. And they're not really elections. They're sham elections. Are they more of a sham or less of a sham than Egyptian elections, Robin Wright?

RW: Well, that's a very good question. There is a veneer of democracy in Iran. People, male and female, can vote from the age of 16. But the problem is that there is a vetting body that can prevent people from running for office. They can say you're not Islamic enough, or, you know, it doesn't have to be a criminal charge or something. It can be just the kind of whim of the group of people who make the decision. And of course, they barred all but a handful of the reform party candidates, and that gave an automatic edge to the conservatives and the hard liners. The interesting thing is that Iranians often find people who they can vote for who might do something to contest the status quo. And so there were some conservatives elected who are opposed to Ahmadinejad's economic policies and some of his argumentative and difficult language about the outside world.

HH: One of the people we've spent time with on the program with is Michael Ledeen. And he dismisses talk of there being factions within Iran, at least effective factions. I gather you disagree with him, in that you write the portraits of Abdolkarim Soroush and Akbar Ganji in a hopeful kind of way, that there are dissidents, they suffer for their dissent, and they work for change. What's wrong with Ledeen's analysis of oh, come on, they're all the same terror-sponsoring fanatics?

RW: Well, the reality is that Iran, after the revolution, had one party, but there was such division within the one party that it eventually was disbanded by Khomeini. He used to scold them, and say you know, how childlike they were behaving.

Today, there are over three dozen different parties running for office, so that yes, many of them are legal within the system, but they also advocate different policies. And then there are those parties who are not allowed to run, like the freedom party, that are quite different from those in power. Clearly, there's not the diversity we have in the West, or not the diversity you have in Israel. But there is diversity. In Egypt, the president, President Mubarak, when he ran and allowed for the first time opposition in a popularly elected presidential contest, he turned around after the election and arrested his chief opponent, and he's been in jail ever since. They both have their fraudulent aspects. I mean, you certainly wouldn't call them free and fair.

HH: Well yeah, but...I agree with that. The one, though, doesn't export terror around the world. I love the fact that you discuss in detail the indictment of Rafsanjani by the Argentinians, and you discuss in detail the work of the Quds forces, and the assassinations they've sponsored all over the globe. Iran is really a gangster regime, but they maintain this veneer, this bizarre system of the two sides. Any chance of that, really, any chance of that changing absent violence, Robin Wright?

RW: I think the Iranians do not want a second revolution, that between the upheaval in 1978-1979, followed by the Middle East's bloodiest conflict with Iraq, in which there were over a million casualties, Iranians are not looking for more bloodshed. But the reality is that the younger generation, which dominates Iranian society, up to 70% are under the age of 25, there is a real sense that the regime has not delivered. And life is more difficult than it was during the Shah in the sense that a lot of families have two and three jobs. Women have gone to work not because of women's rights, but because of family necessity. And young people are not able to get married, they can't get into tenant housing. There's terrible gas rationing at the moment. The most interesting dynamic of change in many of these countries may be economic, in being unable to provide for the young, which is where the votes will come from, where the political activism will come from. And the end of the day, the Soviet Union and Apartheid in South Africa both crumbled in part because they were no longer economically viable ideologies. And that may be a decisive or a major factor, anyway, in many of the Middle East countries as well.

HH: Any sense on your part, though, that there's a way to have regime change that's imminent? It seems to me that it's as repressive as it needs to be, unlike the Shah, that they'll mow you down.

RW: I think that's true, and they'll also arrest you and hold you in prison. But I think that Iran is a vibrant society, and that so much has changed, even though we're cut off from it, and have been now for almost three decades. Whether it's the young women and the fashions they wear, and the red nail polish, whether it's the philosophers like Soroush who argue that there's not one single path, but there are many paths, and that he says to be a true believer, you have to have come to your religion of your own free will, even if you embraced it because of family, community or country. To be a believer, free will has to have been involved. And therefore, free will precedes religion. That's a revolutionary idea. There are lots of ways in which there are challenges to the rigid, theocratic regime that was first created in 1979.

HH: As we exited the last segment, Robin Wright, you were talking about Soroush, the philosopher of Iran, who's attempting to introduce some sort of reformation thinking into Islam. And in Morocco, you detail how feminists have said, "Look, we've got to introduce some interpretive techniques into Islam." It seems to me that this goes right back to Benedict XVI's speech at Regensburg about whether or not Islam has it within it to reinterpret its holy scripture. [It's the biggest...] and how to interpret jihad. It's the biggest debate. You touch on it repeatedly. Are you an optimist about that?

RW: Well, I think it's quite interesting that last week, the Islamic Conference Organization met, was hosted by the president of Senegal, in which he said that the time of jihad and wars is over, and Muslims must make sure they do not engage in conflict or provocation that leads to wars with other religions. There's an awareness that Islam, Islam itself is part of the big issue in the region. And can you blend the ideas of Islam and the values of 21st Century democracy in a way that will give people a sense of not abandoning their traditions, but also being part of the 21st Century and globalization. And I find that there are a lot of people, women, for example, in Morocco who organized a million signatures to get the king of Morocco, an absolute ruler, to change family law, which is the greatest restriction on women across the region. And she forced the hand of the government to open up so that women now enter a marriage as equals with her husband.

HH: Is this Latifa Jbabdi?

RW: Very good, Latifa Jbabdi. [And she,] the petition led the government into a debate. They made one proposal, it wasn't good enough, they went back, looked at it again, and women no longer need the signatures of their husband to get a passport to travel or to work. They enter marriage as equal partners. They leave not by a man divorcing a woman simply by saying it three times, but by judicial authority. Women have better rights of custody, an older minimum age for marriage. It's just changed an enormous amount about women's rights. Another one of the women activists in Morocco was born into a harem. Every other woman in her family was illiterate. The father hid the radio, locked it behind closed doors, Fatima Mernissi, and to keep the women from getting access to news from the outside world. They had a man whose full time job was to prevent the women from going outside or from outsiders getting inside to see the women. And she convinced her mother to convince her father to hold a family council of all its men to decide whether she could go to school. She ended up not only graduating from high school, she went to the Sorbonne, and she did her PhD at Brandeis. And she is today the Arab world's leading feminist, writing...

HH: She wrote the book, The Veil and the Male Elite. That sounded like an amazing woman. But where does she live now? Does she live in Morocco?

RW: She lives in Rabat. Yes, and I went to see her there. I've known her for a long time, but it's quite interesting how she's changing the debate for women, and looking at how many of the traditions that have restricted women were actually added centuries after the religion was founded.

HH: [Well, that's what...] when you brought up her writings and the writings of Jbabdi, they are trying to get Islam to reinterpret itself. And that's what I go back to, and that's what Soroush is trying to do, and others that you mention throughout this. But is it succeeding, because you pointed out that they mobilized 300,000 people in 2000 in Morocco to march for a different interpretation. And then the Islamists turned out a million in Casablanca. It doesn't seem to me like you've got the population on your side, or...go ahead.

RW: But the government did change the rules. And the reality is, we in the West went through the Christian reformation, which gave birth to the age of enlightenment, and then the birth of modern democracy. And that's a process that's played out over the last four hundred years. And I'll tell you as a woman, it's not over, that we're asking the Islamic world to go through a political transformation and a reformation within their religion at the very same time. It's an enormous amount to try to handle. This is not simply trying to bring down something like the Berlin Wall. This is a transformation, overhaul of ways of living and ways of religious belief that date back to the 7th Century. That's asking a lot.

HH: Well, sure, that's like when Ahmadinejad is asked at Columbia about gay men, and he says we don't have them here. It's a denial of a fundamental reality about how humans function. You met with Khatami, the former president, a couple of times. He's supposed to be the big reformer. Did he have a substantially different view of women, of gays, of sort of the Western idea of liberty than...

RW: Oh, absolutely. But at the end of the day, remember, Khatami was a product, or a byproduct of a movement that already existed. People wanted change, and he was a candidate that represented more change than anyone else. So it was the movement that put him in power, rather than he leading a movement. And he failed the movement, because he was unwilling to stand up to his brethren. And that's one of the reasons that people voted for a non-cleric. The big debate in Iran today is the turban, representing the religious, versus the hat, the secular. And for the first time since the revolution in 1979, people voted for a secular official, not knowing what Ahmadinejad stood for, but believing that he was not yet another one of the corrupt clerics.

HH: But he's wildly popular, isn't he? I mean, he's a rock star.

RW: I don't think so. [I think that there are,] he clearly has a base within the Revolutionary Guards who are an ever more powerful force in not only the military, but also in the economy. But I think that among the young, among the women, that he is not an overwhelmingly popular figure at all.

HH: Well, let's talk a little bit about the end of the chapter on Iran. You point to the pattern of aggressive action. Not only export of deadly projectiles, I talked with John McCain about that yesterday, it continues, they're killing Americans, but also the British hostage-taking, and then the serial American hostage-taking. Iran seems intent upon, and it looks like the Revolutionary Guard seems intent upon provoking a major confrontation with the West. True?

RW: Clearly, they're trying to send a strong signal that they will not broker meddling in Iran, or challenges to Iran. I think one of the reasons the American-Iranian dual nationals were picked up, or were detained, was because it was a way of sending the signal in opposing the U.S.' allocation of $75 million dollars to promote democracy inside Iran, and that many of these actions are, as they perceive it, I'm not saying it's justified, but as they perceive it, their response is to think [that they] think we initiated when we of course think just the reverse.

HH: And in terms of who controls the Revolutionary Guard, is that Khamenei and only Khamenei, Robin Wright?

RW: At the end of the day, the supreme leader in Iran controls every branch of government. He has ultimate say. And that's why at the end of the day, the big debate in Iran is over how much power he should have.

HH: Robin, I hate to disagree with you this, but I'm going to. I firmly believe…I was so expecting you to say it's been hard, it's been brutal, but the Arab people deserve the right that the American invasion has given them, that we would never has ousted Saddam, and his mad as hatter sons would have been a disaster for the region. But you didn't. You seem to believe it was a mistake to have invaded Iraq.

RW: Yes, I think that history will look back on the invasion of Iraq as the greatest foreign policy mistake the United States ever made for a variety of reasons. First of all, we didn't know what we were getting into, we relied on exiles who hadn't been there for decades, we had no good planning, and the steps we took at the early stage to disband the government were serious mistakes. I think there's universal agreement on that. That includes disbanding the army, leaving 400,000 people without jobs, without being able to support their families, and no alternatives in place. Disbanding the Baath party was also a mistake, because a little bit like communist regimes, to get a job as a schoolteacher, any kind of civil service job, you had to be a member of the party. And that put a lot of people on the streets, or disqualified them from getting any kind of job at a time there were no alternatives. And that set us up for an insurgency. I think the military action itself, we did not commit enough troops to pull it off in a way that would have prevented the insurgency. We didn't do the kind of international homework to ensure the international community was with us. We could have waited longer at the United Nations to win some kind of agreement. But we were in a hurry, because we didn't want our troops to languish there for a long time. We wanted to get in and fight a war before the hot summer set in, and we had our own election schedule to think about. There were a lot of things that were just miscalculated. And if you could reverse all that, change all of that, maybe the outcome would have been very different, and my judgment would be different. But my fear is the long term tragedy is that it made people in the region even more nervous about change. People who are willing to put their lives on the line are now worried about democratic openings, because they fear it will lead to instability, chaos, death, insecurity, fewer jobs, limited electricity, and on and on.

HH: Now it's possible to agree with a lot of what you said, that we didn't know a lot, we didn't plan well, we made serious mistakes with the army and the Baath, there weren't enough troops, we could have waited, it's possible. But also, to step back at the end of the day, and say, as John McCain said on this program yesterday, it is working now, the Iraqi Army is in place, democratic institutions are stabilizing, people are going about a normal life without fear of being disappeared. And most importantly of all, he didn't say this, but [I think it's the most...] Saddam is gone, and as Robert Kaplan has said on this program, he never would have been gone, he would have been replaced by his crazy sons, it would have gotten worse. And as your friend, Charles Duelfer's report said, he was intent on reconstituting his weapons of mass destruction as soon as sanctions were lifted, Robin Wright. So on balance, admitting everything that's bad that you articulated so well, isn't the region better off today than it was five years ago?

RW: Iraq is better off without Saddam Hussein, but the price that everyone has paid for this invasion, and long term intervention/involvement in Iraq, is horrendous. And I would love to be wrong. I promise you, I would welcome the opportunity to be wrong. My fear is that the surge, which has turned things around, will not last once we begin to pull out troops. We can't sustain it indefinitely. The greatest success in Iraq, which has led to the kind of stability we're seeing now, is not our responsibility, it's the result of some of the people I write about in my book. Sheik Sattar in Anbar Province, who mobilized his tribal compatriots to take a stand against al Qaeda, he had personally lost his father and two brothers to al Qaeda murders. And he then mobilized 90,000 Iraqis in Anbar Province to serve in the police and the military, so they could ensure that al Qaeda was pushed out of Anbar. That's critical, and I think that reflects a growing awareness throughout the region that al Qaeda doesn't provide answers to the daily questions of life anymore than Saddam Hussein did.

HH: We're going to a break, Robin Wright, but is it possible that you're wrong, and that in ten years, you'll look back and say despite the horrendous costs, and I haven't even articulated the 4,000 Americans who are not coming back, and the tens of thousands who are wounded, is it possible you'll end up saying, "Yes it was worth it?

RW: I hope so.

HH: I want to assure you, we've only scratched the surface of this book. You really have to sit down and read it as I did. You'll probably do it in as few sittings as I did as well, because it is riveting, and it fills in a lot of the gaps. I'm going back to Iraq right now, particularly Kurdistan with you, Robin Wright. I've got a pal over there now. His name's John Agresto. John's been there with the Coalition Authority. He's back. [He's intent on...] he loves the Iraqi people. And I spent all Friday with Pete Hegseth of Vets for Freedom, and a number of the American military who've returned who love the Iraqi people, and they're all optimists about Iraq. [That's what, that's what...] I'm a little bit disconnected from the tone of your book when it comes to Iraq, because they think the tide has turned decisively, and I guess you don't.

RW: Well, I don't think so. I think we still have to see that play out. The surge provided us with an opportunity, but the Iraqi government, frankly, has not taken advantage of dealing with the issue of provincial elections. It has gone back on some of the earlier agreements it made. They were all interconnected, and therefore, they have to kind of start from scratch, and seeing if they can come to common agreement on all of them. We had thought six months, [or...] and it's now been much more than six months of the surge, that they could take these basic steps that they'd been promising to do for years, and they still haven't. There is still deep discord, and the government of Prime Minister Maliki remains very weak. So I'd like to believe that they can pull off a miracle, but I think you'll find that when General Petraeus and Ambassador Ryan Crocker report to Congress in the early week of April, that they will say that we need to establish different kinds of benchmarks in judging progress in Iraq.

HH: But if they come back and they say we've done a great work in thirteen months, and we need to stay and not draw down troops because it can work, ought the Congress to believe them, Robin Wright?

RW: Well, the problem is we have a logistical issue with just how long can we keep how many troops there. You know, we can't keep them there on an open-ended basis. The military is on the verge of breaking, so it would be nice to have the luxury of keeping troops in either Iraq or Afghanistan so they could help get rid of al Qaeda and help the Iraqis train and create an efficient military so they could take over from us. But it's just not that simple.

HH: But now, the guys I was with on Friday down at the Midway in San Diego, and many of them are active duty and taking their vacation to make this, they dispute the idea that the military is close to breaking. They do point out, and as Senator McCain said yesterday, it's hard, it's very hard on the families especially, and of course, it's terrible for the families of 4,000 people who are dead, and the thousands who are wounded, but that the American military reenlistment rate, McCain pointed out, the 3rd Infantry Division's year-long enlistment goal has been reached now, and that enthusiasm and morale is extraordinary. Are we ignoring, or are we caught in a narrative that ignores the reality of what's going on there, Robin Wright?

RW: I think there are a lot of problems with post-traumatic stress syndrome, that we don't know the human cost in the fighting, those who come back with their bodies whole, but their minds are in trouble. I think there are a lot of costs in this conflict that [we have not,] have not yet been calculated. And that's maybe a side issue to the issue of can we achieve military victory and pull out of Iraq. I'd like to see us be able to do that as soon as possible. I suspect that we are going to be there indefinitely. I doubt a hundred years, as Senator McCain suggests, but I think we steamrollered in, and there's a little bit of a danger in also steamrolling out simply because we're tired of it or we think it's too expensive. The problem is we are now responsible for Iraq, and unlike Vietnam, it's not going to be easy to simply walk away. We will be paying the price for any instability there. There's some of us in Washington who already talk about the danger of Gulf War II, in having to go back in if we pull out precipitously, and Iraq begins to implode, that we have to go back in the same way we did in Afghanistan, because we can't afford a failed state.

HH: Well, that's what I come back to, is that the stakes are so high, and the alternatives so few, that we really have to have success in Iraq, we do have to stay if it takes a decade, or two decades, because of all the countries you surveyed, the most hopeful one to me is Iraq. I mean, Lebanon looks like Nasrallah's going to win, Syria is not changing, Egypt is on the brink, you don't even deal with Saudi Arabia, because it's a lost cause, Morocco's still a monarchy. The only one that seems to have a chance of peaceful evolution towards something that might be a model for the region and export a different ethic to the region, is Iraq, Robin Wright.

RW: I hope you're correct. I really do. I just, I'm a pessimist by nature. I'm not the one who says is the glass half full or half empty. I'm the one who says is there really any water in the glass at all. And when it comes to the Middle East, I've normally been right in my pessimism. But I want to be wrong about Iraq. I want Iraq to work. I think every American, after what we've expended, put our own economic health in doubt, jeopardized the futures of so many young men and women, really want to feel that this is a place that will work, and will be, as the Bush administration promised, the model for the future of the region. My sense is that there's so much instability now, people still five years later only have nine hours of electricity in Baghdad a day, that life is pretty tough.

HH: Let me ask you if you were to have an hour with the president of the United States, and he asked Robin, you've been over there a lot, what do you think we should be doing? How do you answer that?

RW: You mean just in Iraq? Or…

HH: No, no, just in the region.

RW: In the region, well, I think that one of the realities after Iraq is that we cannot push too hard or be seen to be trying to impose any form of government on the region, because there's already such deep suspicion about what we really want, and that we're often going to have to let change be more homegrown than it has been in Iraq, that we need to use our economic resources, when it comes to aid, for less propping up of regimes and helping their security apparatus, and more to help non-governmental organizations, help people get access to computers, help with educational exchanges, and help build and provide the tools that are necessary to introduce change, and then let people act for themselves.

HH: You know, that is remarkable, 140,000 web sites in Iran after the revolution, after Khatami was elected. That's a stunning statistic.

HH: Robin Wright has been my guest this entire program, talking about her new book, <u>Dreams and Shadows: The Future of the Middle East</u>. Robin, first of all, thank you for spending this much time. I very much appreciate it.

RW: Oh, it's always a pleasure to be with you.

HH: Now to conclude, as I read this, I developed an admiration for your doggedness. Do you think of yourself as courageous?

RW: No (laughing).

HH: You go a lot of places that a lot of people wouldn't want to go, especially women. Have you developed a sixth sense about how to do this.

RW: No, I'm just as nervous about going to any of these places as anybody else would be. But I guess I'm a student of history, I'm an historian by training, and I'm just a very curious creature. And the opportunity to see extraordinary history play out is such an opportunity that I consider myself very lucky.

HH: Are your books banned in many of these countries?

RW: That's a good question. I don't know. I know that one of them was actually, the first one, Sacred Rage, was taught in over 150 universities, including Hebrew University in Israel, and the University of Tehran in Iran.

HH: Okay, my last question, you covered Khomeini, the man who started it all, in many respects, extensively when he was still alive. If he was alive today, would he be satisfied that it was going his way, Robin Wright?

RW: Probably not. I think there are so many problems in Iranian society that he would be troubled by some of the practices of the regime. But he would also be proud of the fact that it's still an Islamic republic. Probably a mixed bag.

HH: And Hezbollah? Has that worked out as he hoped that it would?

RW: Oh, I think so. It's become an even more powerful force than I think the Iranian Revolutionary Guards ever realized.

HH: Robin Wright, once again, thank you, a real pleasure talking to you. I look forward to having you back, good luck on the book tour.

RW: Thanks so much, Hugh.

HH: My pleasure.

End of interview.

Chapter 6.

The American Intelligence Community and State Department and the American Military: Interviews with Timothy Weiner, John Bolton, Douglas Feith and Robert Kaplan

W hen the recognition of the long war could no longer be post-poned or misunderstood –September 11, 2001 guaranteed that if only for a season there would be clarity—two questions arose in many forms.

First, how could we have been so blind to the threat?

Second, could the American military adapt, respond and defeat the new enemy, and if so, how?

The New York Times' Timothy Weiner had long covered the Central Intelligence Agency, and as the CIA "celebrated" its 60th year among the wreckage of many intelligence failures, Weiner's **Legacy of Ashes** provided a comprehensive and compelling overview to the agency's history and how that history left it wholly unprepared for a new enemy with an ancient creed, completely unlike the spooks' first adversary –the Soviet Union. Understanding how the agency failed both in not seeing the attack on America coming and then in erring in the run-up to the invasion of Iraq is dispiriting but completely neces-sary background for moving forward against the enemy.

So too is former Ambassador to the United Nation's John Bolton's memoir of his life in and around the career bureaucracy of the United States Department of State, <u>Surrender Is Not an Option: Defending America at the United Nations</u>, and former Undersecretary of Defense's Doug Feith's detailed history of the years of Pentagon and State Department warfare following 9/11, **War and Decision**. These are the only first person memoirs I include on the "Necessary Bookshelf," because they are the only two to date which simply overwhelm via detail and documents any suspicion that they have covered-up the real story of the American government's response to the attacks of 9/11, an often hopelessly confused and self-defeating one when it came to career bureaucrats at the Department of State.

The Atlantic's Robert Kaplan, by contrast, has provided American readers in recent years with two inspiring accounts of the American military's response to the post 9/11 world. His <u>Imperial Grunts</u> and <u>Hog Pilots</u>, <u>Blue Water Grunts</u> have earned for Kaplan the sobriquet of the American military's Kipling. When in danger of flagging in hope, readers/listeners should repair to my conversations with Kaplan.

When feeling safe or confident, they should revisit the conversation with Weiner.

Interview with Timothy Weiner
September 27, 2007

HH: A special couple of hours straight ahead. We have with us the author of a brand new book, <u>Legacy of Ashes: The History of the CIA</u>, and let me welcome Tim Weiner to the program, a New York Times reporter, winner of the Pulitzer Prize. This is an amazing book, Mr. Weiner. Thanks for joining us.

TW: I'm so glad to be with you. Thanks for having me.

HH: Now last night, I told a member of Congress that this has got to be distributed to every member of every committee, because frankly, I'm astonished. Do most people come away from this book that you've talked to shattered in their illusions about the CIA's competence?

TW: I think some do. I think that if the book has a value, it's that it's all on the record, that it is not ideologically right wing or left wing. This is an American problem. It's about the CIA, but it's bigger than the CIA. It's about whether we, as a nation, can project our power around the world, whether we can be a superpower. And in order to do that, we need good intelligence. We need to know what's going on in the world. In a phrase, we need to know the enemy. And we've been at this sixty years now, the September 18th, 1947, sixty years ago, the

CIA was founded. And we are still trying to figure out how to run a secret intelligence service in our open democracy.

HH: And failing often in the process, as is detailed in <u>Legacy of Ashes</u>. Let me start with a recent headline to see if maybe the upswing has begun. Over the weekend, I read that Michael Sulick has returned to the Central Intelligence Agency, along with Stephen, I hope I pronounce this correctly, Kappes, and General Michael Hayden is reassembling a lot of the experience that had been lost in the Porter Goss interregnum. Is that good in your eyes that the veterans are returning?

TW: Even better, even more important is the fact that the present chief of the clandestine service, Jose Rodriguez, is changing his job from running America's spy service to recruiting, recruiting people to work. That is job one right now, because the CIA today faces some of the greatest challenges in its history, and it also has probably the least experienced workforce in its sixty years.

HH: We'll go through some of that history. Just to give people a taste they cannot possibly get even in a two-hour radio broadcast, the complexities in this book and the riveting detail, and I don't encourage them to do that, they've go to read it, but I do want to get through some of the history. But first, to set the stage, if you assume the best intelligence agency possible, and that means the brightest people, good funding, cutting edge technology, and you factor in that intelligence agencies will always makes mistakes, even if it's the best agency out there, if that's the best possible agency and it represents 100% of what could reasonably be expected of an intelligence agency, what percentage of that agency does the U.S. have functioning today?

TW: This would have to be a very rough guess. I would say that in terms of technology, we're somewhere above 50%. I would say in terms of human capability, somewhere below.

HH: Wow, and that just doesn't make sense after sixty years, as we'll find out. If we recall the Rumsfeld famous metrics memo that he sent out, one of his snowflakes about how do we measure success in the war on terror, how do you measure? What are the metrics for judging the CIA specifically, but intelligence agencies generally, Tim Weiner?

TW: One, can the United States, through the CIA, successfully recruit foreigners as intelligence agents, to get them to, in many cases, betray their country, because espionage is illegal everywhere, to help us gain the facts about what's going on in the world? Can we recruit agent from inside al Qaeda, from inside international jihadist organizations? That is a metric. Life is made more complicated in that realm by the fact that the public image of the CIA, and the public image of the United States today, is not at a high ebb in the Islamic world.

HH: It doesn't seem as though they have had any successes. But as you quote in the book, there's an old saying among CIA veterans, dating back to the Bay of Pigs fiasco, that the public only sees the failures, not the successes of the Agency. Is that true in the current war against Islamic jihadists?

TW: Well, there's a lot that we won't know for another thirty years, until the documents are declassified, if they are. I think we can say that we know we haven't been attacked again since 9/11. Whether that is the consequence of better intelligence, or whether it's the consequence of the interrogation of prisoners in the so-called black sites secret prisons, we don't know, and we can't know. We do know that this is not a war that's going to be won with fighter bombers or tanks or submarines. This is a war of intelligence, of information and ideas. And we will not succeed if we don't have better diplomacy, if we don't use our military more wisely, and if we don't have better intelligence.

HH: In this first segment, I want to cover the weapons of mass destruction fiasco, and I want to make clear to the audience, which is a center-right audience, that this book is not an apology for George W. Bush in any way, shape or form. But it's also very, very blunt on the WMD. I want to go to Page 491, and this paragraph. "This was not a selective use of intelligence. It was not cherry-picking. It was not fixing the facts to fit the war plans. It was what the intelligence said - the best intelligence the Agency had to offer. Colin Powell had spent days and nights with George Tenet, checking and rechecking the CIA's reporting. Tenet looked him in the eye and told him it was rock solid." That cannot endear you to some of your friends on the left, Tim Weiner, but it's very, very blunt.

TW: This is what happened. And then Colin Powell went to the United Nations and the world, with George Tenet sitting over his shoulder, I think we all remember that, and said these are hard facts. This is our best intelligence. Iraq is teeming with chemical and biological weapons. And we went to war, and George Tenet had to come back to Colin Powell, not once, not twice, but several times and say you know this central pillar of the argument we made? It looks like it might not be so solid.

HH: And there are a couple of fascinating aspects in this chapter. Quoting on Page 490, "The CIA as an institution desperately sought the White House's attention and approval. It did so by telling the President what he wanted to hear." You also talk about George Tenet's deeply-ingrained desire to please. It's disconcerting to think of the CIA as acting like an approval-seeking child.

TW: Well, you know enough about how Washington works to know that power flows from proximity to the President. And if you are the guy in there briefing the President every day, you have power. You have even more power if what you're telling him enhances or empowers his policy. Now there's a reason that the guy who runs the CIA is not the President's daily intelligence briefer anymore. There's a reason that the office of Director of Central Intelligence was disestablished two years ago. And it has to do in large part with the disaster of the WMD reporting.

HH: This is a hard question to answer, but speculate please. Would a different CIA director have made the same mistakes that Tenet did, so that George Bush's retaining of Tenet proves to be one of his greatest fiascos?

TW: That is very hard to say. Look, I know George Tenet a little bit. He's an extremely decent human being, and he tried his damndest to fix a CIA that he described, at the point where he inherited it in 1997, as a "burning platform." I mean, imagine you're on an oil rig in the North Sea in the middle of the night, and there's a storm, and the rig is on fire. That is how he describes the CIA he inherited ten years ago in 1997. He tried his very best, but it turned out to be not good enough.

HH: You describe his memoir as a bitter book. Is his bitterness justified, Tim Weiner?

TW: In part, because he had to, in addition to receiving a medal around his chest, take a lot of spears in the back.

HH: You also write on Page 489, this is another shocking conclusion, again, most people assume a New York Times' reporter, Pulitzer Prize winner's going to be a man of the left, [and that you're going to run into...] but I want my audience to understand you just call them like you saw them. Page 489, "Saddam wanted the U.S., his foes in Israel and Iran, his internal enemies, and above all, his own troops to believe that he still had the weapons of mass destruction. The illusion was his best deterrent, and his last defense against attack." That's why I asked about Tenet. Do you think that Saddam would have fooled everyone? Anyone in that job?

TW: No, the problem is that the best intelligence the CIA had at the end of 2002 was four or more years old, and dated from the time when there were weapons inspectors in Iraq, some of whom were CIA officers. After they were withdrawn in December, 1998, the intelligence kind of dried up. And so we were left with defectors like the infamous Curveball, who told the CIA what it wanted to hear, I mean, through the German service. And we just didn't have the facts on the ground. That's why you need spies, that's why you need espionage, and our efforts weren't good enough.

HH: As I said when I had Lawrence Wright on when The Looming Tower came out, I know a Pulitzer Prize winning book when I read it. Legacy of Ashes: The History of the CIA is one of those. Tim Weiner, let's go back to the beginning. Wild Bill Donovan enjoys a lot of hazy approval through the years.

Maybe Bill Casey contributed to that. But the OSS, it wasn't such a successful group, was it?

TW: Look, it was…after World War II broke out, after we were attacked at Pearl Harbor, there wasn't any question that we needed an unorthodox group of intelligence gathering people, and clandestine service officers. It was a desperate need, in fact, and the OSS at full strength was never more than 13,000 strong. But the analysts in it who did research and reporting, really quite useful. The operations side, very mixed record. There were daring people who did incredibly brave jumps behind enemy lines to hook up with, for example, the French resistance in occupied France, and then there was a lot of blind stabs in the dark.

HH: You know, in my years in D.C., I got to know a few Agency people, and no one ever said they didn't have courage. But dropping 22 two-man teams into Germany, 21 of whom are never heard from again, or how many agents did they drop into North Korea, Tim Weiner? I don't have my note on that.

TW: Well, this is now during the Korean War.

HH: Right, right.

TW: This is CIA, which was stood up in 1947, sixty years ago. Hundreds upon hundreds of foreign agents, Koreans, Chinese, Russians, Eastern and Central Europeans, were dropped behind enemy lines, behind the Iron Curtain, and behind the Bamboo Curtain in the early 1950's, because the CIA thought they could operate in Eastern Europe, and behind enemy lines in the Korean War, the way they had operated in Western Europe during World War II. And that turned out to be a terrible mistake.

HH: [Well that…] what I'm getting at is that OSS legacy of daring, and dropping teams into Germany, seems to me, from reading your book, never to have matured in the Agency, and that the reckless expenditure of human lives, in many instances, has been, well, it's astonishing, especially that North Korean example. Is that still lingering in the Agency, this almost…

TW: I think not. I think that the first phase of the Agency's history really runs from its foundation in 1947 until the Bay of Pigs in 1961. And when Allan Dulles ran the Agency, as he did throughout the Eisenhower years, '53-'61, there was a kind of derring-do and devil-may-care spirit that persisted from the OSS. But as a result, a lot of scattershot and harebrained operations resulted. And the ultimate one was the Bay of Pigs.

HH: We're going to come to that later in the broadcast. At this point, I would like to take a moment to introduce some names to people that they may not be familiar with, Allan Dulles, Richard Helms, Frank Wisner, and James J. Angleton. These are sort of the four horsemen of the Agency. Can you tell us a little bit for the audience who have not yet read <u>Legacy of Ashes</u> about Allan Dulles?

TW: Allan Dulles was a very prominent figure in the OSS during the War, operating out of Switzerland, brother of John Foster Dulles, who was Secretary of State in the Eisenhower years, became Director of Central Intelligence under Eisenhower, and these two brothers, one running the foreign policy of the United States, the other the secret intelligence service of the United States, they really have no equal in American history as a team that enjoyed enormous power, and really operated out of their vest pockets quite a bit. Sometimes, they told the President what they were up to, and a few times, more than a few times, they didn't. And the consequence, ultimately, was uncoordinated covert operations, for example, an attempt to run a coup in Indonesia in 1958 that was so not secret, that was so overt, and so miscalculated, that it really contributed to the growth of the Communist Party of Indonesia, which became the third largest such party in the world by the 1960's. Angleton, another OSS figure, brilliant, strange, became chief of the counterintelligence staff in 1954, and ran it for twenty years. This is the office that's responsible for both protecting the CIA from penetration from communist spies, and trying to penetrate. It's the game inside the game, spy versus spy.

HH: And Soviet-oriented for so long, and we're going to come back to this, because the Nosenko...well, the whole thing is fascinating. What about Wisner? I think he's probably the most obscure of the four.

TW: Frank Wisner, another OSS veteran, became the first chief of the clandestine service in 1948, and ran it for ten years. Brilliant, driven, undiagnosed manic depressive, and toward the end, had to be hospitalized several times for nervous break-down, finally blew his head off with a shotgun in 1965.

HH: Now I know you couldn't have spoken with Wisner and Dulles, [but it appears to me...or Angleton, maybe Angleton,] but it appears to me that you did have many conversations with Richard Helms over the years.

TW: We spoke when I was covering CIA in Washington. I was able to, during the 1990's, I was able to speak to him both in person and on the telephone. I have a great respect for the man. He died not quite five years ago at the age of 89, and in my estimation, probably the best director of Central Intelligence the country ever had.

HH: And why?

TW: Because he truly believed in espionage, as opposed to covert action.

HH: Explain that distinction, if you would for people.

TW: All right, espionage is spying, is trying to figure out what's going on in the world, the careful, patient development of sources of information, recruitment of foreign agents, until you get inside the enemy's head, you know, the enemy, okay? You can shake hands with a foreign intelligence service and pick its pocket at the same time. Covert action? That's Wisner's school, and Allan Dulles', to a greater extent. Not so much to know the world, but to try and change the world, and to swing elections, run coups, change governments, change the course of history to make it conform better with the goals of American foreign policy.

HH: But Richard Helms, did he downplay covert action when he was...

TW: He did not, but he was the most consistent advocate for an espionage service, a real espionage service that the CIA really ever had running the show.

HH: We've got about a minute to the break. Was he political at all? Did he come from an ideological base? Or was he simply an accomplished spy?

TW: He served one president at a time, and he was not a political man. Richard Nixon, when he came to power, he was director of Central Intelligence under Johnson and Nixon. Johnson came to respect him enormously. Nixon did not, because Richard Nixon, God bless him, hated the CIA.

HH: I'll be right back. He's right about that.

HH: I want to go just a couple of bits back to Georgetown, to the Wisners' home, when he becomes the head of foreign operations, covert action. And there really was such a time in Washington, D.C., it doesn't exist anymore, when people would gather together around a Sunday night dinner table and basically form the world.

TW: It is hard to imagine today, but in the years immediately following World War II, there was a fairly small circle of people who knew each other, many of them had been to school together, many of them had served side by side in the Second World War, who were really the intellectual movers and shapers of American foreign policy. Remember that President Harry Truman had come to office upon the death of President Roosevelt in the closing months of World War II, and he was not, you know, the world's greatest foreign policy expert. He was very good on domestic policy, but he didn't really know the world. So the elites of Georgetown included among their number people who did know the world, and they knew it from the perspective of fighting the War in Europe, and fighting the War in Asia, and being diplomats, charge d'affaires in Moscow during the War, and through long service to this country and diplomacy, and in the military, and in the OSS, in intelligence. These folks helped formed the foreign policy of the United States in the late 1940's, and the beginning of the Cold War.

HH: It's so intimate. It's really astonishing how small the circle was with George Kennan and George Marshall. But Wisner made his stamp on it, and it's a boozy, breezy, almost comic book approach to foreign affairs. They basically would decide who to kill over dinner.

TW: Well, kill is a bit strong, [but...] because the CIA never assassinated a foreign leader during the Cold War. It wasn't for want of trying.

HH: What about the 200 people at Mosaddeq's house, and we'll come to that, but...

TW: All right.

HH: ...a lot of bodies left in Iran that day.

TW: True. Foreign policy is sometimes a very messy business.

HH: We're going to come back to that. You know, my first job out of college was working with David Eisenhower on the book he wrote about his grandfather, and I knew a lot about Walter Bedell Smith. I've got to confess, though, I didn't know anything about his impact on the CIA. He's a remarkable man, he's largely forgotten. How did he fit in with this Georgetown elite, because that's what doesn't work for me. It's like the square peg in the round hole.

TW: He kicked their rear ends. Walter Bedell Smith had been General Eisenhower's chief of staff throughout World War II. He was a no-nonsense, hard as nails man. He did not suffer fools. And when Harry Truman asked him to take over the CIA, in the national emergency of the first days of the Korean War, he saluted smartly, and found that he had inherited quite a mess. The CIA was only three years old, remember, and it was really a series of sort of independent fiefs squabbling with each other. Well, General Eisenhower, when he became president, organized the White House as a good general runs his staff, with clear chains of command. And throughout the Korean War, General Walter Bedell Smith, as director of Central Intelligence, tried very hard to organize the CIA. And he gave it the shape, really, that is has today, out of a very messy and tangled organizational chart. In the process, he came to believe that both Frank Wisner and Allan Dulles, who had become the number two men at CIA, were pulling the wool over his eyes, and deceiving him about the conduct of covert operations overseas, particularly in Korea. Strangely, at the end of his eight years as president, I believe President Eisenhower came to the same conclusion.

HH: Interesting. [Did the...] do you rank Smith just below Richard Helms in terms of successful leaders?

TW: Walter Bedell Smith is one of the great forgotten figures of 20th Century American history, a truly amazing man, and he sweated blood to make the CIA work, and he really put it into a kind of organizational shape. There remained one problem, one that never got solved, which is talent.

HH: And interestingly enough, Tim Weiner, how did you get into the intelligence reporting business?

TW: Well, I was sent on my first foreign assignment when I was 29 to cover an election in the Philippines that turned out to be the first great popular revolution of the era, and ended in the overthrow of President Ferdinand Marcos in 1986. That got me interested in covering the wider world. And in 1987, I decided I was going to go to Afghanistan, which was then under the brutal occupation of the Soviet Army, to look at what the United States, and in particular, the CIA, was doing to support the Islamic resistance in Afghanistan. I called up CIA, and said you know, I understand you do briefings for foreign correspondents going to strange countries. I'm going over to Afghanistan, may I come by? And they said no, we don't do that anymore, forget about it. So I went to Afghanistan, went hiking through the mountains with the Mujahideen, got bombed by the Soviet Air Force, and had a good, long trip. I spent time on both ends of it in Peshawar, Pakistan, and after about three months, came home. And gosh, I hadn't been back in Washington more than a day or two before the phone rang. It was CIA saying hey, Tim, how'd you like to come in for that briefing (laughing).

HH: (laughing) Well, that's good work.

TW: So that was the first time I set foot in CIA headquarters, and you know, I was fascinated from the get go.

HH: Now what I'd like to do is for the benefit of people who don't read the Washington Post and follow it, sort of set up what, how the CIA is organized, and how it now fits in the new regime. You mentioned earlier in the program the disestablishment of the Director of CIA, and the new National Intelligence Director. But if you can get below that, and tell them how does the Agency organize itself...

TW: Right.

HH: ...you know, intelligence, covert, and all that sort of stuff.

TW: Well, the office of the Director of Central Intelligence, and the CIA itself, were set up sixty years ago in 1947. By the time Walter Bedell Smith was done whipping it into shape at the end of the Korean War, it was organized pretty much the way that it was organized for the next fifty years, which is you have a clandestine service, the operations directorate. These are the people who do things overseas. You have the directorate of intelligence. These are the analysts, largely desk-bound people whose job is to pull together all the information, both secret and open, available to the government, and eventually, you know, present it to the president. You have a directorate of science and technology that makes everything from little, tiny microphone gadgets to, you know, they helped to invent the U2 spy plane.

HH: How good is that directorate today?

TW: You know, the great problem that they have is the great problem that also confronted the National Security Agency over the past decade, which is that, is the explosion of cell phones, e-mail, and encryption, publicly available encryption, of fiber optic communications as opposed to old copper wires. It's much more difficult to penetrate communications now. And it's so much like trying to get a drink of water from a fire hose, that it's very hard for the secret technology experts, the computer guys, the guys who make bugs, to try and figure out how to penetrate the communications of the enemy. That is the great challenge.

HH: I'm jumping ahead here, but at the end of the book, you talk about the privatization of intelligence, and a pretty interesting...and I hadn't thought about...

TW: Yeah, ten years ago, fifteen years ago, they were ten years ahead of the public domain. Today, I think they're behind the public domain.

HH: All right, so [back to the...] that's the third directorate. [Is there a...]

TW: Right, and then you have a directorate of support that is everything from file clerks to people who get you from point A to point B, who maintain CIA stations inside American embassies abroad, the tail in the tooth to tail ratio.

HH: Tell me if you can the rough numbers and budgets of these four directorates.

TW: All right, all classified, these are rough approximations, very rough. Today, upwards of 20,000, maybe as high as 25,000 at CIA, budget, again, very rough estimates, between $5 and $6 billion. As a rule of thumb, the budget of the CIA is roughly one percent of the Pentagon's budget, and there is a big story there.

HH: Yes, there is. Of the 25,000 CIA employees, how do they divide between operations, intelligence, and the other two directorates?

TW: Probably somewhere in the neighborhood, again, these are very rough approximations, because the numbers are classified, and I can't give you a sense of authority.

HH: Sure.

TW: Probably 10% of those are in the clandestine service.

HH: All right. And where does the Farm, about which so much has been written...have you been there, by the way?

TW: I have not, that is a classified location. It is outside of Williamsburg, Virginia.

HH: And where does it fit in this organization? And what goes on there?

TW: The training?

HH: Yup.

TW: Mostly of people who are going to work for the clandestine service. It has been described as everything between a boarding school and a boot camp.

HH: Finally, in this segment, if you could put the CIA in the web, that includes PFIAB, The NSA, the DIA, the State Department...

TW: The alphabet part?

HH: Yeah.

TW: Two years ago, after the disastrous experience of the weapons of mass destruction reporting, an attempt was made, a serious attempt by Congress to restructure American intelligence. And the Director of Central Intelligence post was abolished. That guy had been doing two jobs. One, being the CEO of the CIA, the other being the chairman of the board of all American intelligence. That's now two jobs. The CIA no longer is first among equals in the American intelligence establishment. There's one CEO of the CIA, and another guy, that's Mike McConnell, running, being the chairman of the board. And General Mike Hayden is running the CIA.

HH: And does it work better, in your view, with this new system?

TW: The consensus even among the people in Congress, and in the intelligence community who helped create this change, is that what we have done is add another layer of bureaucracy, fifteen hundred people in the Directorate of National Intelligence. And if we see changes, we will see them down the road.

HH: It's a short segment, Mr. Weiner. I just want to ask you about other foreign intelligence services. It's limbed out a little bit in the book, but does the CIA rank them in terms of their reliability? And we're taping this interview just a couple of days after Israel goes in and takes out a secret facility in Syria that may have had North Korean glow in the dark stuff, which looks like a pretty doggone good operation. Do they rank Mossad as the best of the best?

TW: You know, I don't think that there's a rating system. Each country's intelligence service is unique to that country's position in the world, their foreign policy problems...if we had a model that would be applicable to our American democracy, and our superpower status in the world, it might well be the British service in the 19th Century. Why do I say that?

HH: Yup.

TW: When the British were, for example, running present day India and Pakistan and Afghanistan, the Raj, their foreign intelligence officer and their military officers and their spies, their diplomats and their soldiers, went to India and they lived there. And their children grew up there. And their children grew up to be foreign service officers, diplomats, spies, soldiers. And they stayed on for generations. And they achieved a deep knowledge of the languages and the histories and the cultures of the countries they wanted to command and control and contain. We do two year tours.

HH: But you know, I'm curious, I've read Peter Hopkirk's books, the <u>Great Games</u>, they're wonderful books. But is it even possible for Americans, given the way that the world views us now, to try and immerse themselves in the way that Brits would go into Afghanistan or into Pashtun and hang out forever?

TW: Let me suggest to you that the war we are now in may last as long as the Cold War. And to quote Mike Hayden, General Hayden, the head of the CIA, this is an intelligence war. We are not going to win this war with fighter jets, or nuclear weapons, or aircraft carriers. We are going to win it with intelligence and information and ideas. If that is true, we need to cultivate a generation of Americans who know how to speak Arabic, and Chinese, and Korean, and Farsi, and Pushtu, the language they speak in Eastern Afghanistan, and Hindi, and Urdu. And those people need to know not only the languages, but the histories and the cultures of the countries where those languages are spoken. And then we can go out and win this war.

HH: Before we get started on our sort of postcards from CIA history segments, Tim Weiner, I've tried to sell the idea over the last year or two, a couple of people in the presidential campaigns, that we really need to have established the intelligence equivalent of the Naval Academy, the Air Force Academy, someplace where you can spend five years shaping an intelligence operative and analyst. Is that ever going to happen in the United States?

TW: Well one, I couldn't agree with you more, and two, it would require a long term commitment by whoever our next president is, and whoever is in control of the next Congress, and the folks who run our intelligence services, and our universities, to agree that we need a crash program in this country, just like we were curing cancer, which in a way, we are, to train many thousands of young Americans who are coming out of high school now, in those really tough languages like Arabic and Chinese that pull down your grade point averages. And really, it's a kind of intelligence ROTC.

HH: Yeah, they need a Rickover. They need someone who's going to build the equivalent of the nuclear program, [and do so on a...] you're right.

TW: Right.

HH: Because...

TW: And at the same time, those people can't go out and recruit foreign agents, that is foreigners who know what's going on in their countries, or in their political groups, and maybe in their terrorist organizations. They can't go out and recruit them when the public image of the United States is at a low ebb. It makes it so much harder. So we have a lot of diplomacy, a lot of work to do on that front, we have a lot of work to do in the intelligence front, and we have a ways to go in restoring the public image of the United States in the world.

HH: Now let's talk about the price of having a great reputation and a terrible record, as Donald Gregg once said about the CIA. Would you explain to people who Donald Gregg is?

TW: Don Gregg was George H.W. Bush's National Security Advisor, and before that, Ambassador to South Korea, and before that, station chief for the CIA in South Korea, and before that, a distinguished twenty year history, twenty five years at CIA.

HH: So he knows what he's talking about. And when he says the Agency had a great reputation and a terrible record, what's he referring to?

TW: That in the years before the Bay of Pigs, the arts of covert action and espionage were really new to us as a people, okay? We had not had a permanent peacetime intelligence service in this country. And the CIA made a lot mistakes. And you know, when intelligence fails, people die.

HH: Their great claim to success if, of course, the coup that removes Mosaddeq, the Iranian prime minister, and restores the Shah to his full authority. Do you, in retrospect, view that as a good action on their part, and a wisely calculated move?

TW: Well look, President Eisenhower authorized it. The operation was not quite as smooth as the CIA represented. It was quite a chaotic business. But in the end, a willing partner of American foreign policy, the Shah of Iran, was installed in power. And you can argue that 25 years of stability resulted. But 29 years of bitterness and instability has followed that. And the Iranian people, the people that we as Americans don't know a lot about, are not unaware that the United States overthrew their prime minister. And that breeds resentment and fear and hostility.

HH: [What was the...] why was the failure so great on intelligence in 1978? The overthrow of the Shah and the installation of Khomeini, probably the greatest foreign policy disaster to befall the United States in the last thirty years.

TW: Well, one of the biggest surprises.

HH: Yeah. What happened? Where was the breakdown?

TW: You know how many people there were at the CIA station in Tehran?

HH: No.

TW: Four, one of whom had deep experience with the country.

HH: Was that a Carter administration drawdown? Or was that bureaucratic bumbling?

TW: That was a drawdown that really began in the second Nixon administration, and continued throughout the 1970's, and it was part of the general diminution of American forces abroad toward the end of the Vietnam War.

HH: There's a book by Ali Ansari called <u>Confronting Iran: The Failure of American Foreign Policy and the Next Crisis in The Middle East</u>. He argues that the Iranian people carry the Mosaddeq coup on their sleeve, that this is going to define us for a very long time. But there was also a failure to understand the role of Islam in this. Does the Agency, has it begun its education on Islam, Tim Weiner?

TW: I think that we are now almost three decades distant from the rise of Islamism and jihad, that is holy war in the name of Allah in this world. And I think we have a much better grasp as a people, and that the CIA probably has a better grasp as an institution of some of the forces that drive it. However, we are in a bad position right now, because much of the Islamic world views our present situation in Iraq not a lot differently from the way they viewed, and I know this is a terrible thing to say, the Soviet occupation of Afghanistan. And that here is a non-Islamic power occupying an Islamic country, and it's not good for the public image of the United States right now.

HH: Oh, as I mentioned, Lawrence Wright's been a guest on this program three times, and clearly, the jihadists are portraying us as the new Soviet Union, and to what extent...

TW: Well, that's the last thing we want to be portrayed as.

HH: Right, right, and that's a call for the communication strategy of the United States to be a lot better. Let me go back to Mosaddeq, though. Two hundred people killed in the assault on his home in that botched coup that actually did work out to the stability side. And after that, as I read your chapters on Guatemala, and South America generally, 58 assassinations approved, you say in the Guatemalan takeover.

TW: Yeah, on paper.

HH: On paper.

TW: Yeah.

HH: But this is a bloody gang. This is a really ruthless group of people.

TW: Look, this was war. You know, the Cold War was not fought over negotiating tables. The Cold War was fought in a hundred different countries, often by proxies of the United States and the Soviet Union. I mean, my favorite image of the Cold War is a battle that took place in 1964 on Lake Tanganyika in the heart of Africa, when a boatload of our Cubans, and a boatload of their Cubans...

HH: Right.

TW: ...started shooting at each other.

HH: Do we have the stomach for that as a country anymore, Tim Weiner, because I'm not disapproving of the necessity of doing hard things, although some of these are really bloody things, but does the country have that stomach at all anymore?

TW: I'm not sure that we as a people have a lot more stomach for Americans losing their lives to shot and show overseas right now. We have an armed forces, we have an army, I should say, an army that is very tired, that has been fighting a war that has been going on, you know, longer than World War II, and that we can't fight the war on terror the way we fought the Cold War. We are not fighting a nation. We are fighting ideas.

HH: But as you know, when it was proposed, as it's detailed in your book, and in Wright's book, when it was proposed that bin Laden's farms be shelled, or bin Laden be tracked down with the emirs he was hawking with in the middle of the Afghani desert, Tenet and Dick Clarke wouldn't approve it, too many collateral casualties. And that sort of summed up for me what happened.

TW: No, Rumsfeld wouldn't approve a plan to hit Osama bin Laden's number two guy in Pakistan…

HH: But that goes back to…

TW: …in 2005. Why? Because it was going to be so big an operation, a DOD operation, that it was going to look like an invasion of Afghanistan. Hitting people is not necessarily the solution. You know, Osama bin Laden could get taken out tomorrow, and you know, God willing, someone will take him out at some point, get him off the stage. But it's a hydra. This is not about individuals. This is about a war of ideologies, of ideas, and of information.

HH: But as you describe in <u>Legacy of Ashes</u> after 9/11, the Agency went to a war footing that was stunning. They picked up a lot of people who did not deserve to be picked up, but they did capture a lot of al Qaeda people…

TW: Yeah, there was an international dragnet, and you know, they had to let some people go, probably nine out of ten.

HH: And was that kind of energy and that kind of ruthlessness, is that capable of repetition absent any other?

TW: Not right now, because Iraq has sucked all the air out of the room, of covert operations, and of the military. This is both the Army and the clandestine service of the CIA, run pretty ragged right now.

HH: Throughout those sixty years, Tim Weiner, Congress has done a bunch of things, vis-à-vis the CIA. It's helped destroy it from the left, the Church Committee's helped destroy it from the right, Porter Goss and his band of "reformers." What should Congress do, [after you've studied...] they can read the details in <u>Legacy of Ashes</u>, but how ought they to operate vis-à-vis this agency and intelligence generally?

TW: Things have changed. The CIA is no longer first among equals in American intelligence. Congress, in its wisdom, and the administration, changed the architecture of American intelligence two years ago. We now have sixteen different instruments in the orchestra, and a conductor in this new office called Director of National Intelligence. That's Mike McConnell. And McConnell, former director of the National Security Agency, has noted that he's working 18 hour days, seven days a week, trying to get these instruments tuned up, harmonized, and playing off the same piece of paper. The problem is do we want to have a secret civilian intelligence service in our open American democracy? We have gone sixty years now without solving this. If you're going to have a secret intelligence service, then it's going to have to be really, really secret. And as you may have noticed, it's awfully hard to keep real secrets in the American government.

HH: Does the American media, and hey, the New York Times has been involved in this, as has the L.A. Times, I've talked to Doyle McManus about it on air before, are they cognizant...I know they're doing what they perceive to be their job, but are they cognizant of how difficult it makes the intelligence gathering operations of the United States?

TW: Let's take a case study. I wasn't one of the reporters on this story, but not too long ago, the New York Times ran a story about a tremendous argument taking place in the Bush administration about how far the United States should go when it comes to spying on Americans in the name of the war on terror. And boy, the paper and its editors were called everything but a child of God for running that story – traitors, treason. But we now know that in fact, this argument was so deep that the Attorney General of the United States wouldn't go along with it, and you know, was confronted in his hospital bed by the White House Counsel and others, saying you've got to sign off on this, and he said no. And his deputy, the acting attorney general of the United States, said no. Now is that a legitimate story for us to cover, that there is dissention that deep in the administration over a question of spying on Americans? I would argue that it is.

HH: There is no compulsion in the world under our Constitution that restrains the New York Times from running that, but tell me about, since you cover this world, when the details of the banking surveillance are revealed, a program that had successfully helped obtain the arrest of one of the great Indonesian terrorists in Thailand, and it's compromised, and the New York Times puts it out there, it's compromised, Doyle McManus of the L.A. Times says yes, it's possible we may have provided information that would lead to terrorists escaping capture or killing.

TW: Right. [All I can do is to tell you what…] I can't speak for the New York Times, all right? But I can speak for myself as an American citizen, and a reporter who covered CIA for some years, I would never knowingly publish anything that I thought could get anybody hurt or killed, ever.

HH: [That is…] I think that's the standard I would love for everyone to have. Let's go back to the history. Diem and the Kennedy's. You're not going to be invited to the Kennedy Library anytime soon, I don't think, or maybe you are. Maybe they're pretty broad-minded. But this is a pretty awful picture of Bobby and Jack Kennedy that come across.

TW: I am parenthetically going to speak at the Nixon Library tonight.

HH: Oh, wonderful, in Yorba Linda. What time are you talking…oh, I'll talk about it…we're recording this on the 17th of September. I will tell people about that. What time are you speaking?

TW: 7 pm.

HH: Yeah, John Taylor's an old friend.

TW: Okay.

HH: And so I'll tell people about that. But what about the Diem story?

TW: Well, you know, President Kennedy installed a taping system in the White House in July of 1962, and he recorded his thoughts about his role and the American role in the overthrow of President Diem of South Vietnam, who had been president for nine years, and whom we were backing in what became a major war against North Vietnam. He said three days after the coup in which Diem was murdered, "We really shouldn't have done that." We bear a great deal of responsibility for it, and practically, this was eighteen days before his own assassination. Richard Helms, Director of Central Intelligence under President Johnson and President Nixon, I think put it quite succinctly. Let's leave, I'm paraphrasing Helms here, let's leave aside questions about morality and the brotherhood of man, and so forth and so on. The question of political assassination boils down to this. If you try to knock off another country's leaders, why shouldn't they try to knock off yours?

HH: Well, you do confirm in the book that the Kennedys repeatedly tried to take Castro out, but you do not weigh in on any kind of conspiracy theory. What is your thought on that? Did Castro...

TW: We'll never know.

HH: Okay, just wondered. So you're not buying...

TW: It's not knowable. Either...this is what it boiled down to for Helms, and this is where I come out. Either Lee Harvey Oswald, acting alone, squeezed off a million to one shot, or as Lyndon Johnson later speculated, Kennedy was trying to get to Castro, but Castro got to him first. And until the Cuban archives are opened, which will probably not happen in our lifetimes, and until the Soviet archives are opened, we'll never know. It's not knowable.

HH: Bottom line on the Gulf of Tonkin, was fake intelligence used to manufacture the incident that certified the conflict?

TW: Yes, and the burden there goes to the National Security Agency.

HH: Explain for our listeners.

TW: There were two ships in the Gulf of Tonkin in the summer of 1964. There was also a clandestine operation, sabotage operation going on onshore. The two ships believed that they were under attack from the North Vietnamese, but it was a dark night, it was a foggy night, and what they thought were torpedoes coming at them were in fact sonar images of their own shadows, of their own churning in the water. The intelligence that the NSA picked up of communications of the North Vietnamese was at first misinterpreted. And then when they discovered their mistake, they just buried it. They covered it up. They deliberately deep sixed the fact that there had been no concerted North Vietnamese attack in the Gulf of Tonkin on the night of the 4th of August, 1964.

HH: When did that become known?

TW: Well, the NSA...

HH: We've got about 30 seconds.

TW: ...to its great credit, the National Security Agency, to its great credit, published an unclassified or declassified history just less than two years ago.

HH: We have to stop at the Bay of Pigs. [They got...] the Agency had Cuba wrong from the get-go. They though the regime, the Castro regime, would collapse in a few months, you write at Page 155. They go with the mafia, they try to assassinate Castro, but the biggest fiasco of all, the Bay of Pigs. Did the CIA's will fail? Did the Kennedys' will fail? Could it ever have worked?

TW: The central problem was this. You had the covert operators, and the chief of the clandestine service at that point, Richard Bissell, shaping the intelligence for President Kennedy, who'd been in office only a matter of weeks. The analysts at the CIA were shut out of this. They didn't know squat about the Bay of Pigs. And it's like, you know, a hitter at the plate calling his own balls and strikes. I don't think that the president fully understood what the operation was going to be like, and I don't think Richard Bissell in his role as chief of the clandestine service really explained to him what it was going to be like. As one of Bissell's deputies on this operation, Jake Esterlein of the CIA, later reflected, Bissell was lying up to the president, and Bissel was lying down to his people at CIA.

HH: Wow.

TW: And the consequence, well, we all know the consequence, many dead in the Bay of Pigs, Fidel Castro is incredibly still standing, forty six years later.

HH: The description on Page 174, 1,189 captured, 114 killed, a massive foreign policy fiasco. Had the Agency improved its performance by the Cuban Missile Crisis? Do they get kudos?

TW: Well, I think the difference is that you had a new Director of Central Intelligence, John McCone, and McCone was a very forceful personality, very conservative California Republican, and he just knew in his gut that Krushchev was going to put nuclear weapons into Cuba, because that's what he would do if he was Krushchev. The CIA as an institution rejected this idea, said no, that'll never happen, but it did. And McCone argued very forcefully to get the spy planes up to look down, they found the missiles, and I think McCone is the unsung hero of the Cuban Missile Crisis.

HH: [Now the…] we keep coming back to strong personalities in this job, Bedell Smith did a good job, you're saying McCone did a good job, and you've got a lot of praise for Helms. So does Hayden fit into this successful…

TW: Well, I think he's certainly the most capable director since Bob Gates, our present secretary of Defense, ran CIA back fifteen, sixteen years ago. What he's got to work with? He has said himself it is probably the least experienced workforce in the history of the CIA. For every ten analysts he's got with less than four years experience, he's got one with more than ten years experience.

HH: Wow, that is such...

TW: And you know, by the CIA's own standard, those are trainees, people with four years or less in experience. So can this be turned around? Yeah. Was adding 50% more analysts and 50% more operators as the President commanded two years ago necessarily a good idea? We're going to have to wait and see on that.

HH: Does the popular culture, you've now been covering the CIA for twenty years, and we're talking the whole Len Deighton novels, nowadays, Dan Silva, Le Carre, The Good Shepherd movie, do they get the Agency? [Do they...] is there anyone out there who's succeeded in figuring out what it is to be a part of this organization?

TW: Well, this is a criticism of me as well as the people who write novels. I'm not sure you can know it until you've lived it. I have tried as an outsider to read the record, to interview some of the players, to read oral histories, to get a sense of what the job is like. I fear that most Americans and a notable number of presidents of the United States are more familiar with the myths about the CIA that are created by movies and TV shows and fiction, than they are with the actual capabilities of the CIA itself. And that's been a problem.

HH: I'm not debating journalism and stuff with him today as I've often done with people like your colleague John Burns, Tim. I'm just interested in this book so much. I'm amazed we won the Cold War. When you read...

TW: Well, thank God Soviet communism was such a rotten system.

HH: And thank God for Ronald Reagan. [But when we got...] they turned every agent, not every agent, they turned the Berlin office on its head right after it gets set up, they run us a counter operation against this Berlin tunnel, which I had never read about. Kim Philby is going to lunch with Angleton all the time. It's amazing we stayed in the game long enough for Ronald Reagan to win it.

TW: Our American democracy is stronger, more resilient, and more capable of change than certainly Soviet communism was. It blew itself apart.

HH: Ronald Reagan put the charge in.

TW: And I think that I want to try to make a very important point about Legacy of Ashes, that I think some of my friends at CIA have missed, because not everybody at CIA is happy about this book.

HH: Oh, I'm not surprised, yeah.

TW: ...to put it mildly. I think that espionage is a noble pursuit, not because I've been a foreign correspondent and I go to foreign capitols and say take me to your leader, what's going on here, all right? I think we have to know what's going on in the world to succeed as a superpower. And I also believe that there isn't a force on Earth, not jihadists, not terrorists, no nation, can every truly harm the United States. The only power on Earth that can harm us as a nation is us.

HH: Well, that's a big debate with which I disagree, but I want to get back to, before we go too long, you mentioned that they're not happy with you at Langley.

TW: Not everyone.

HH: What do they resent? The candor? Because I mean, you're obviously approving of their mission, and quite respectful of their courage, just their competence is at issue.

TW: I think that the history of the CIA is something that's been very jealously guarded at Langley, at CIA headquarters. The three successive directors of Central Intelligence, starting with Bob Gates, our Secretary of Defense today, vowed that they were going to declassify the Cold War histories of the big clandestine operations. And it never happened. And I started to wonder after a couple of years, this is in the early mid '90's, why not? And now I know, because I've done enough studying of the record, and I've teased out some of these histories, because they're horrifying…

HH: Yeah.

TW: …and they're embarrassing. And you know, if they had gotten out, both at the time they had happened, or at any point over the last thirty, forty, fifty years, it would have damaged the public reputation of the CIA, and the CIA cannot take that damage right now. They need to recruit a new generation of Americans who are willing to serve them. And the most important development there in recent days has not been the return of Mike Sulick, who was exiled under the Porter Goss administration to run the clandestine service. It's that the guy he's replacing as the chief of the clandestine service, Jose Rodriquez, is stepping down in order to recruit.

HH: Tell me why Valerie Plame is not mentioned in your book.

TW: Because it was a totally inside baseball Washington story that had nothing to do with the conduct of the CIA.

HH: But in your book is a theme that why do we exist if nobody believes us. The Valerie Plame affair has done a great deal of damage to people on the center-right, where I live and broadcast, in trusting the Agency. And there are others which you recount in here. It's a difficult thing to overcome.

TW: There was a larger story of which the Plame story was, in my estimation, an infinitesimal part, that I tried to recount at the end of <u>Legacy of Ashes</u>, which is this. This White House, run by a man who is after all, not only the son of a former president, but the son of a former Director of Central Intelligence, got in a war with the CIA.

HH: Yup.

TW: There was a lot of sniping going back and forth. And Lewis Libby was one of the casualties, took a bullet in the neck in that crossfire. Cheney, the Vice President of the United States, sorry, Dick Cheney, and Don Rumsfeld, the former

Secretary of Defense, had decided long ago during the Nixon and Ford administrations, that they didn't really trust the CIA. And that is reflected in this continuous sniping that's gone on since 9/11. And it's not a healthy state of affairs.

HH: And Tim Weiner, I've got to tell you, after reading this book, I don't blame them. You've indicted the CIA, and you've tried them, and presidents would be crazy to have trusted this Agency. And when they did, they got the WMD report.

TW: Yeah, but presidents also don't want to know the truth sometimes. And they don't want to hear inconvenient facts sometimes. And if you go back through the history of the CIA, there have been more than a few times when the CIA, for example, during the war in Vietnam, tried to tell Presidents Johnson and Nixon, look, this war is not going to be won by military means. This is a political war. Well, they didn't want to hear that.

HH: You know what you ended up persuading me, although I don't think you intended to, at the end, when you talk about Robert Gates seeing stars, and there are generals everywhere in the intelligence agency, and the Pentagon's war on the CIA appears to be successful, and it's taking over more and more, is that that's a good thing, that the competent professionals of the military are not the dilettantes who would gather in Georgetown, drink themselves under the table, and launch coups in Guatemala that killed hundreds.

TW: Well, you sound like you're channeling Richard Nixon.

HH: Well, I worked very closely with him for a long time (laughing).

TW: [The...] this takes us back to the original question.

HH: Yes, it does.

TW: Do we want to have a secret intelligence service, a civilian intelligence service, in the United States of America? If so, we better start getting good at it.

HH: But tell me if it's possible, [because one of the things... you also,] they all check out, Cofer Black leaves, they're all going to work for the new Beltway bandits. The military gets guys and they keep them, and gals, and they keep them. It's professionalism.

TW: Well, I'm going to quote Colin Powell on this, who in my estimation, is one of the greatest Americans to ever get a position of leadership in the government of the United States. Colin Powell has now warned us, this is an interview that Walter Isaacson did that'll be forthcoming I think in GQ magazine, against the formation of a terror industrial complex.

HH: That's fascinating. We'll look for that.

HH: I want to thank you, Tim Weiner, for spending this much time with me. It's a very important book. Are you surprised at how successful this is, and how much interest it's generated?

TW: You know, I'm surprised on a personal level, but…and pleasantly surprised, but I think when I step back and think about what it was like for me as a kid growing up, both of my parents are immigrants to this country. They both escaped World War II in Europe. And I want us to function as a participatory democracy, this country. An informed electorate, an informed citizenry, is crucial to American democracy. And I fear that many of my fellow Americans just are tuning out to what's going on in the world. And if the up and coming generation of Americans, kids coming out of high school and going into college now, tune out and turn off, and are not interested in what's going on in the world, we're not going to succeed, not as a participatory democracy, not as a free republic, and not as a superpower. So in part, I wrote this book to give people an idea about what happens when intelligence fails. The CIA has had successes over the years. But when intelligence fails, soldiers die. And we need to have an informed citizenry to help rebuild our capacity to do intelligence, to form strategy, to make American foreign policy.

HH: And not only soldiers die, but of course, thousands of civilians as well. There was an intelligence failure by the CIA leading up to 9/11, which is so well documented, that we really can't afford to be this blind. Let me close by asking you, are you staying in this business after this book? [Are you going...] what's the next project for Tim Weiner?

TW: Well, I hope to be able to write books in the future. I think that we're at a point in American history where we need to look at the structures we created in 1947, the office of secretary of defense, the CIA, the National Security Act of 1947, and the way it was amended two years ago, and really think about do these structures serve us now in the right way for this new war in which we're now engaged? Or do we really have to rethink the way in which we organize our powers, and the way we project power around the world. I think that's the subject I'd like to tackle in the years down the road.

HH: Does that mean...we've got 20 seconds, to study the Pentagon?

TW: Well, I think that Bob Gates, having served now both as Director of Central Intelligence and Secretary of Defense, would be a good person to start with.

HH: Fascinating.

TW: Are we organized properly to protect and defend the United States?

HH: Tim Weiner, a fascinating interview, a wonderful book. Legacy of Ashes: The History of the CIA. I'll be right back, America, don't go anywhere. I appreciate very much your time, Tim Weiner. Good luck in bringing this book to the attention of the public.

End of interview.

Interview with Ambassador John Bolton
November 5, 2007

HH: Pleased now to welcome to the Hugh Hewitt Show Ambassador John Bolton, former United States Ambassador to the United Nations. Mr. Bolton, welcome to the program, good to have you.

JB: Glad to be here. Thank you for inviting me.

HH: I'd like to spend a lot of time talking about <u>Surrender Is Not An Option</u>, quite a remarkable book, perhaps the most detailed diplomatic memoir published this soon to the completion of a tour of duty that I've ever read. Before there, a couple of quick questions, though.

JB: Okay.

HH: Can we persuade you to move from Baltimore and run for Senate in Virginia?

JB: (laughing) Well, I think a political campaign is not in my future, but I'm happy to help out candidates around the country. I've done that a little bit, and I'm happy to do more of it.

HH: All right. Number two, do you favor the ratification by the United States Senate of the Law of the Sea Treaty?

JB: I do not. I think that Reagan was correct to reject it during his administration. And as Ed Meese and Judge Clark pointed out in a recent Wall Street Journal op-ed, many of the reasons Reagan had to reject it remain valid today.

HH: And we have a very precarious position, a situation in Pakistan today, Ambassador Bolton, and we're getting conflicting signals, not surprising having read <u>Surrender Is Not An Option</u>, from the State Department and from the President. What ought to be the reaction of the United States to Musharraf's declaration of military rule?

JB: Well, I don't think it's anything we should celebrate, of course, but I think we have to be practical about this. This is a regime in control of a number of nuclear weapons, it's a regime we need to fight the remainder of al Qaeda and Taliban along its border with Afghanistan. And I don't think we ought to be pushing Musharraf out the door, or necessarily in a direction of coalitions with the likes of Benazir Bhutto, if he thinks it would weaken his position, because the alternative is not a nice Jeffersonian democratic government. The alternative to

Musharraf right now is an Islamo-fascist government in control of nuclear weapons, and that's definitely something to fear.

HH: Is there a danger that Musharraf could become Bush's Shah or his Diem?

JB: Well, I think that's entirely possible, and I think part of the reason is the State Department was pushing Benazir Bhutto on him, and I think it was a very foolish strategy, because you can't say take on some of the democratic opposition and not take on the rest of it. This trying to read internal Pakistani politics is hard for the Pakistanis, let alone for people at the State Department.

HH: All right, let's switch to the book, Surrender Is Not An Option, your new memoir. It's linked at Hughhewitt.com, available at Amazon.com, bookstores everywhere. First of all, it's very candid and detailed, as I said. How did you go about the recordkeeping that clearly underlies this effort? Were you doing daily dictation?

JB: Well, what I tried to do, particularly for the quotations that you see in the book, was either write them down contemporaneously or as soon thereafter as I could. And I did that, because I didn't want to be in a situation where I was accused of making up the quotes or anything like that. Those quotes are accurate. If a statement is not in quotation marks, it means it's a paraphrase, it's not a direct quote. I felt that was important to give the tone of a lot of the discussions we had, both in diplomatic exchanges and behind the scenes at the State Department and the White House. And for much of the rest of it, you know, I did a lot of public speaking, and speaking with the press. And much of the chronology is found in the transcripts of the press conferences.

HH: You know, when a Woodward book comes out that purports to detail internal conversations of the United States administration on these issues, it gets enormous play and a lot of attention. I haven't seen many people yet paying attention to Surrender Is Not An Option. Has it roiled the waters inside the Beltway?

JB: Well, I don't think it has yet, although it's just come out, and I'm sure it's roiling some waters in the State Department building. But this was an effort to tell, very candidly, how things happen behind the scenes at the State Department and the United Nations. And one person I quote in there is a career senior State Department official who said on occasion, if the American people knew how we made foreign policy, they'd be after us with pitchforks.

HH: Yup.

JB: And that's what I wanted to convey, because many people say how could the State Department come up with that position, or how could the U.N. come up with that decision. And really, what I wanted to show is exactly how it happens.

HH: [Well, let's start with...] I want to cover in detail four policies, five Americans, and a couple of foreigners. And the four policies are North Korea, Iran, U.N. reform and State Department reform. So let's start with North Korea, perhaps the most important pages in the book, Pages 100-117, on North Korean negotiations. You conclude it by saying, "The worst happened after I left, but was well in train by then." Are these alleged breakthroughs, and you know, they're just letting our inspectors into the dismantled plutonium plant. Are these all fig leaves on a completely out of control situation, Ambassador Bolton?

JB: Yes, I believe they are. I don't think Kim Jung Il has the slightest intention of giving up his nuclear weapons program voluntarily. He's very good at negotiating about giving up his program. He's even pretty good at committing to give up his program. He's done it four or five times in the last fifteen years. But when it comes right down to it, he never actually does it. He's happy to receive tangible economic and political benefits that help subsidize his regime, help keep it in power. But he's not going to relinquish those nuclear weapons voluntarily, no way.

HH: What about these inspectors and these technical experts who are going to [Pyongyang to...] not Pyongyang, but the...

JB: To the Yongbyon reactor.

HH: Yeah.

JB: Look, the Yongbyon reactor is probably beyond the end of its useful life. This is one of North Korea's negotiating techniques, to give up something of very little value. There's not much about Yongbyon we don't already know. The real issue is not what's going on there. There are several real issues instead. One is what were the North Koreans doing with the Syrians in the middle of the Syrian desert? Apparently, according to some overhead photography, perhaps building a clone of the very Yongbyon facility that is now being monitored. Where is the plutonium that they've previously extracted from that reactor? Where are the weapons that they fashioned from that plutonium? And tell us about the uranium enrichment program, the separate route to nuclear weapons that the North Koreans embarked on after they signed one of their previous commitments to give up the quest for those weapons, the 1994 agreed framework. Yongbyon, looking at Yongbyon is like looking at North Korea through a soda straw. It is a very small piece of the big picture.

HH: Well then, Ambassador Bolton, how do you think it came about that this is being trumpeted when you have obviously a very clear-eyed President Bush early in the administration saying exactly what should be said about Kim Jung Il, the nature of his regime, and the criminal enterprise there? [How has this...] has it fooled him?

JB: [I think...] I ascribe it in my book to the persistence of the bureaucracy. And I call it the risen bureaucracy. The policy that's being advocated now by the State Department is precisely the same policy that was being advocated by many of the same people on January 19th, 2001, the day before President Bush became president, and every day since then. They have never varied in any meaningful particular from the direction that we're now pursuing. Why did the President succumb to it? I don't know. I'm not a psychologist. I think it's in part because he's distracted with Iraq. I think in part, I don't think, I hope,

I guess I would say, he doesn't fully understand the agreement that the State Department has reached with North Korea. And I do live in hope that he will ultimately repudiate this agreement, and return to the principles that he previously articulated.

HH: Now Ambassador Bolton, on Page 112 of <u>Surrender Is Not An Option</u>, you quoted General Laporte as saying if, in fact, it comes to blows with North Korea, "We will kick his ass." However, if you go to a book called <u>Going Critical</u> by Dan Poneman and Robert Gallucci and Joel Wit, they say a million people will die in the first three or four days of that war. Who's got it right?

JB: Well, you know, nobody should want a war on the Korean Peninsula. Let's start with that proposition. And our goal ultimately should be the collapse of the North Korean regime short of war. And frankly, I don't think we're going to solve the North Korean nuclear problem until the North Korean regime disappears. This is not a case of regime case. This is a case of reunification of the Korean Peninsula, which has been our policy since 1945. But I do think it's important, and this will apply in the case of Iran as well, not to overestimate the threat that North Korea poses militarily. It certainly should not underestimate it. But we've got to try and get it right. This is a country where for the past several decades, the average height and weight of the population has been declining. And that is a remarkable statistic. So whatever military capabilities they have, and the regime has been pursuing chemical and biological as well as nuclear weapons, if we let them intimidate us, they win in effect without having been put to any kind of proof. Now again, I want to underline nobody should be looking for military hostilities on the Peninsula. But if you simply acquiesce every time North Korea demands something, they're prevailing simply by bullying, and not by any other reason.

HH: Last question about North Korea before we move onto Iran is that again, the Poneman-Gallucci argument is that every year that every warhead is delayed is a victory for non-proliferation. And we don't really know the extent of the uranium program. Do you expect that that uranium program, that second track, is actually operational now within the North Korean government?

JB: We don't know, but let me come back to the fundamental point that they're making about delay, because it's almost certainly the reverse of what is actually happening on the ground. It's true if you can delay proliferation, you're ahead. You're ahead of the game. But by and large, time actually works in favor of the proliferators. The more time they have to perfect the techniques they need to manufacture weapons, and to create ballistic missile delivery systems, the better off they are. So time is normally not on our side. And that's why dragging out these negotiations, dragging out the agreed framework over a long period of time benefits North Korea. It doesn't benefit us or the other nations like South Korea and Japan that are concerned about what the North is up to.

HH: Let's switch over to Iran now. Page 340 of <u>Surrender Is Not An Option</u>. The fact is, you write, that Iran will never voluntarily give up its nuclear program, and a policy based on contrary assumption is not just delusional, but dangerous. This is the road to nuclear holocaust. Overstatement? Or do you really believe we're lurching towards the use of nuclear weapons in the Middle East?

JB: Well, you know, the President himself believes that there's a risk of nuclear holocaust. And his recent remark about World War III was a public reflection of things that he has said and felt since the beginning of the administration. I think this problem of Iran was put very well by Dan Gillerman, who's Israel's ambassador to the United Nations, and a good friend of mine when I was in New York. He has said that President Ahmadinejad is denying the existence of the original Holocaust while preparing for the next one. And I think that's a very insightful assessment of what's going on in Iran, so that if we follow, continue to follow the course that we've been pursuing for four plus years, led by the Europeans to try to negotiate Iran out of nuclear weapons, not only will we fail, we'll end up in a worse position. It goes back to the point I made a moment ago. Time is typically on the side of the proliferators. And in

this case, Iran has very effectively used four plus years of negotiations with the EU to perfect uranium conversion, changing
uranium from a solid to a gas, and to perfect uranium enrichment, to get the U245 isotope up to weapons-grade levels. So
time has been used against us here in a very profound way.

HH: It is very agonizing, reading those pages on how the dith-
ering went on, but let me ask you if you're…

JB: It was agonizing to live through it, too. I can tell you…

HH: (laughing) I'll bet. I just…you know, on a side, I think
you've put out a book that will persuade most sane people
never to go to work at the U.N., because it sounds just the
most awful job ever. \

JB: (laughing)

HH: I want to go back to, though, your colleagues at the Mission
and at the State Department. When they hear Ahmadinejad
talk about the blue haze, and they read about the 12th Imam,
and they read what the supreme leader thinks, do they laugh
it off? Do they ignore it? How do they not understand this is
different from our previous peer competitors?

JB: Well, you know, when Ahmadinejad sent a letter, a long,
rambling letter in the summer of 2006, most people around
the world either took it as the sign of a delusional individual, or
saw in it references to Islamic teachings that were profoundly
dangerous for the United States. But many people at the State
Department said well, this give us a basis to negotiate. This is
the kind of perception by too many of our career foreign service
officers that everything is open for negotiation. And let me just
add here quickly, because I make the point in the book, and I
think it's important, I don't want anybody to understand that
I'm criticizing everybody in the foreign service, or all the civil
service people who work at the State Department. There are
many very good and effective diplomats who understand the
proper role of diplomacy. We need a strong State Department.
One of the things that I try to explain in the book is what we
need to change the culture of the State Department. And that's

something that the next president really needs to wrestle with. But the culture that's developed over the years is very firmly entrenched. So this is not an issue about this individual that I disagreed with or that individual. It's about an entire way of thinking that I'm sad to say pervades the building.

HH: And for those of you who are trying to find that segment, that's on Page 449, where he talks about the prototypical civil servant being excellent, and we'll come back to that. But before we move on, is there any awareness within the State Department, Ambassador Bolton, that they botched the first Holocaust, they held back on the refugee numbers admitted to the United States, they did not facilitate the distribution...in many ways, they were complicit in the launching of the Holocaust. Is there any burden that they bear, vis-à-vis the second pending holocaust as a result of that? Or has that gone down the memory hole?

JB: Well, you know, the answer is I don't think they have any recollection or burden in that regard, and it's a fascinating aspect of the State Department where one of the arguments for the culture as it is, is this deep expertise on regions of the world, and the nature of the problems. The historical memory at the State Department is actually very thin. I was shocked by that on any number of occasions in the various jobs I've worked in the Department going back to the early days of the Reagan administration of how hard it is to get people who can think back more than a few years. That's something, that's another problem that needs to be corrected, because each new person who comes onto the job approaches it as if everything that's gone before has not had the benefit of their superior wisdom, so they come in and think that they can immediately solve things, which is another dangerous risk we often run.

HH: Well, let's jump over U.N. reform, and we'll come back to it, and focus, since we're there, on State Department reform. In <u>Surrender Is Not An Option</u>, you quote the late Dean Rusk, successor to Alger Hiss, I thought that was very funny, and your predecessor, both of them...

JB: Right.

HH: …about his principal client. How do you fix clientitis when that client is understood to be other than the United States?

JB: Well, this is very interesting insight into how the State Department views its own problem, because they've misnamed it. Clientitis refers to the propensity of officials to take up the cause of the country whose affairs they're supposed to be dealing with. So if you're on the French desk, or if you're in our Embassy in Paris, and you sound like you're simply advocating French positions, that's called clientitis, being excessively deferential to the French. Well, if the State Department has any client at all, it's the United States. So if you're suffering from clientitis, it ought to be that you're accused of excessive zeal on behalf of the United States, which is very, a very, rare accusation at the State Department. Let's put it that way. They've misnamed the problem, because they fundamentally don't understand it. But this…the idea that too many people are advancing the parochial interest of the government or the region that they're responsible for is a problem that we pay for in our diplomacy every day, over and over again. And it is the kind of deeply rooted problem that has grown up over decades, and it will take a long time to correct.

HH: But now you talk about that, and I agree with that, and it's beyond the Department of State. It goes into the intelligence community as well.

JB: It certainly does. It goes in the military as well.

HH: But fixing it, obviously, the State Department and a lot of the CIA is drawn from East Coast elite institutions, much like media replicates itself. Are you proposing that the foreign service protections given to careerists be shortened, and that turnover be heightened?

JB: Well, you know, actually, I think one of the benefits of the foreign service, and we've now seen it called into question by the objections some people have of going to Iraq, one of the benefits of the foreign service is that they do turn over assignments. There's another form of clientitis, a form of parochialism, that the civil servants have, too. And you can see this in many domestic U.S. departments of people who have been engaged in one particular program for so long, they simply can't see anything wrong with the program, they're immune to trying to change it. For example, at State, many people who work in the non-proliferation area are just absolutely convinced that the International Atomic Energy Agency is the greatest thing since sliced bread, and they won't brook any criticism of it. That's a form of clientitis as well. The foreign service, at least, has the benefit of moving around, and you get more of a chance to bring a fresh perspective on things than you do in the civil service in State and many of the domestic departments. And that's why this recent controversy over going to Iraq is so interesting, because foreign service officers have plusses and minuses in their job. When anybody makes a career decision, they have pros and cons they have to weigh. And there are many, many attractive aspects of working in the foreign service. One negative aspect, though, that you take on from the outset is to agree you will be available for immediate worldwide assignment. And that's a conscious decision. And people understand that that doesn't mean you're going to get a call one morning to say pack up and move to Paris for five years. So when you see the foreign service revolting, or part of it revolting against Secretary Rice's effort to send them to Iraq, that's another sign of a broken system, basically.

HH: Now you've worked at Justice, as I have, and you know that career prosecutors never lose their allegiance, they don't go over to the Mob, and you've got FBI guys who don't go over to organized crime. What is it about the culture of Justice that keeps career prosecutors and AUSA's on the beam that is different from that at the Department of State that sees them go native or go hostile to the administration?

JB: I think Justice is different from State in so many, many ways. You've certainly named one. I'll give you another that I think is tied in. The State Department is consumed on a daily basis with turf fights among the different bureaus. The economics and business bureau fights with the Asia bureau over policy. The non-proliferation people fight with the European bureau. One country desk fights with another country desk. At the Justice Department, while there were certainly disagreements on various policy issues, the bureaus and offices and divisions basically ran on their own. There was very little turf fighting, compared to the State Department. So I think what's happened is that at State, there's an excessive devotion to process at the expense of substance. Now both process and substance are important. They both have to work to have an operational policy. But at Justice, I think people focus on the policy objective and substance, which is indicting and convicting criminals, whereas at State, they're consumed with process, and that is another aspect of the cultural problem that needs to be fixed.

HH: Two more questions, and then we'll move back to U.N. reform. You write about the battle fatigue capture problem of political appointees at State. How long do you think a political appointee should stay max at State Department to assure that they don't go over to the careerists, and that they don't get worn down by the constant turf battles?

JB: I wouldn't put a particular time limit on it, but what I would say is that you to have a clear sense from the very top of the State Department, from the secretary on down, clear reinforcement, and not just for the political people, but for the career people as well, so that policy which comes from the top is carried through and implemented all the way through. If you had an effective leadership from a policy perspective at State, and this is especially true in Republican and conservative administrations, I think people could go on for much longer than they do. The problem is that the bureaucracy is so sophisticated, so seductive, so effective, the political people are so isolated that they get picked off one by one. And if you could avoid that problem, I think people could stay a lot longer, and they'd be a lot more productive. Can I just say one thing on this?

HH: Sure.

JB: I know this discussion probably sounds bureaucratic to some people, but I want to tell you that this is the front line of where policy is made. Back in the Reagan administration, people for the first time said and understood personnel is policy. And at the State Department, that's true in spades, and that's exactly what we've been talking about here.

HH: Now you do not, except by implication, discuss the NSC, the National Security Council, in the same terms as you do State. Now obviously, the President can replace every single person at the NSC, unlike the foreign service. They're serving at the pleasure of the president over there. Is the NSC as broken as State?

JB: Well, I think today, the NSC is simply an adjunct to the State Department, and I say this with all due respect to Steve Hadley, somebody that I know and am friendly with, have a great deal of professional respect for as a lawyer, and a foreign policy expert. But we have not had as powerful a secretary of State since Henry Kissinger. And the NSC, as then during the Nixon administration and the Ford administration, is no longer serving the kind of role that it should serve as an honest broker for the president. It's just another branch of the State Department. I think that's unfortunate. I do think the best way for the NSC to function is not to be colonized by the career services at State, the CIA or the military. I think a president's got to have...if he can't have his own team at State, he certainly has to have his own team at the NSC.

HH: Let's go back to U.N. reform now. In the book, the most compelling case study is that of the outcome document by way of setting this up. This is sort of the successor document to the World Summit, which was one of the many summits, Rio Summit, Cairo Summit, Women's Summit, blah, blah, blah.

JB: They were everywhere.

HH: They were everywhere. And so you turned the tactics of the U.N. against them when you become the Ambassador, so that when the ash and the trash comes at the end, it's our version of the ash and the trash, because you ran the clock out on them. Why don't we do that every time?

JB: I think because…there are two reasons for this, I think. The first is many people will say these documents are utterly irrelevant, and therefore, it's not worth the time and the effort. And I would have to say in the great scope of human history, they are irrelevant, except that they creep over the years like a corral reef. Each new document, one lies on top of the other, and pretty soon, you find after years have gone by, this massive wall of documents that somehow or another, the U.S. has agreed to, which we always find being used against us. That's why we have to fight these mind-numbing battles against this sort of thing time and time again. But I think more importantly, the only way you're ever going to get people's attention at the U.N. to the way the U.S. sees things, which is fundamentally different, in many ways, even from our friends in Europe, is to fight over these issues. And when I say fight, I don't mean in an unpleasant way, I mean simply saying we're not going to accept this garbage, and pretend that it's smoothing over differences when it contains language that's ultimately going to come back and bite the United States.

HH: Were you better at this because you were a litigator first, and that you're not unwilling to go as long as it takes in a deposition or a trial?

JB: I think that there's certainly an element here of being prepared to face the consequence, the possible outcome of no document at all. For most people, most foreign ministries, the idea you have a meeting and you don't have a document that the meeting produces is a kind of heresy. But there's a circularity here. You need…people want documents to advance their agenda, and therefore, they have to have a meeting. And if you have to have a meeting, you have to have a document. So the whole thing just kind of goes in circles. And it's very hard for diplomats, American diplomats included, to be isolated. They don't like being isolated. It's not fun at the cocktail parties and dinners that follow the day of negotiations. I couldn't have cared less about being isolated, and I couldn't have cared less whether we had an outcome document or not. I think that strengthened my hand in the negotiation, and I think it would strengthen our negotiators to take that kind of attitude in a wide variety of other negotiations as well.

HH: In the summary of your six years in the Bush II administration, you write we withdrew from the ABM, the biological weapons convention verification procedure draft was tanked, you unsigned the Rome treaty on the International Criminal Court. You got some focus on resuming nuclear testing, you foiled international gun control. But it's like Lucy in the chocolate factory. They just keep coming. This international Law of the Sea Treaty has got a general authority in it which looks like the General Assembly to me.

JB: Well, I think your analogy is a good one, and the Law of the Sea is a particular problem. You know, we've learned from experience there are not just the problems the Reagan administration saw in the Law of the Sea treaty. We know from the international criminal court that when you set up these adjudicatory bodies, internationally, you're turning over potentially enormous grants of our sovereignty to them, so that the problem is actually worse than we originally saw it. And that's why I thought in the early days of the Bush administration there was so much promise, because he was prepared to reject the Kyoto protocol, withdraw from the anti-ballistic missile treaty, unsign the international criminal court treaty, and a variety of other things, all of which we've left behind in this...now this push to support the Law of the Treaty shows the completely 180 degree nature of the turn that they've taken.

HH: Well, that leads me, though, to the idea that don't we need a moratorium on international agreement of a generation, [even, in order...] you argue for voluntary contributions as the effective solvent on U.N. craziness. But I'm thinking we can't win at this game, because there aren't ever going to be Boltons every year, or Kirkpatricks or Moynihans. We're always going to have periods of lassitude followed by periods...we just can't win if the United States...and I'm not one of these North American Union nutters, where they're worried about agreement that don't exist. But can we play in this arena and ever advance the American interest abroad?

JB: Well, I think we can if we could get the State Department on track. And I would say there are two elements of this front of international agreements. One is the front of traditional international negotiations, the International Criminal Court, the Land Mind Convention, the Comprehensive Test Ban Treaty, all of which are bad ideas. The more pernicious front is the kind of treaties that people have been proposing about gun control, about the death penalty, about family issues, abortion and the like, because not only are these agreements contrary to our principles, but they are efforts to reach into what are fundamentally domestic political questions. At least you can say on the Comprehensive Test Ban Treaty, bad idea that it is, that it's a subject of international, legitimate international discussion. Whether the United States has the death penalty or not has no legitimacy for discussion in the international arena. That's what we decide democratically in this country, if we want it or we don't, as other countries make their decisions as well. And part of what's happening here is that the international left, and abetted in many cases by American non-governmental organizations, seeing that they can't win on gun control or abortion or this issue or that issue, they can't win in domestic American politics, and they're trying to internation-alize it, and that is, I think, a phenomenon that we're going to see more of in the future, especially if we get a Democratic administration after next year.

HH: Let's pause on that for a moment, because one of the revelations of <u>Surrender Is Not An Option</u>, your memoir, again for people listening, the European Union is not a neutral in this. They're attempting to norm European Union standards of domestic politics through these international agreements. And our left wing is abetting them in that. Is there hope in your view for the EU's reform, either through Britain's refusal to participate, or the new Europe coming in and saying to the old Europe no, this far and no farther? Or is the EU lost?

JB: I don't think it's lost, but I think a lot will depend on what happens with this new mini-constitution as they call it, an effort to take European integration one step further, and basically, to reduce European parliaments to subsidiary bodies of European commission and other institutions in Brussels. I think this is a critical moment for Europe, and I don't know what the outcome is, but I do know that the discontent in Europe over the increase in what they call the democratic deficit is growing. But make no mistake, if that persuasion loses, we do face a more difficult situation, that the U.S., I like to describe the U.S. as the most libertarian country in the world. We're not completely libertarian by any stretch of the imagination, but we love liberty and our form of democracy very intently. There aren't a lot of Republicans or conservatives as you find in the U.S. in very many other countries. So this strategy of leftist NGO's to internationalize our domestic questions inherently puts them in a more favorable political terrain than trying to debate them in this country. And that's why although it seems counterintuitive to go global on these things, it's really a very shrewd political strategy from their perspective.

HH: In the 15 minutes we have left, Ambassador Bolton, I want to cover some of the people and the portraits you've got here. Let's start with the President, George W. Bush. There are two Bushes in this book like there are in so many people's understanding. There's the not so eloquent Bush, and then there's this very firm, very focused colloquial Bush of the private meeting, funny but also as pointed as pointed can be. And again and again, he'll use you as a foil, he'll make you the guy who's delivering the message, but he knows what he wants. Why is there this divergence between the Bush we see in the Rose Garden or the Oval Office, and the Bush who sits down with Kofi and starts giving him a hard time, and uses you to advance that?

JB: Well, it's…frankly, it's a matter that just makes me heartsick, because I think the President's instincts have been and remain largely correct. I think he is being talked out of pursuing his instincts perhaps by Secretary Rice, perhaps by others, in a way that I think will leave him very damaged in history. He's got one year left, and I think he would be far better continuing to pursue the policy he is in Iraq, but reverting to many of the policies that he pursued in the first term very successfully for our country. We're going to have a debate about many of these issues in the upcoming presidential election, and I think a stronger more consistent President Bush would go a long way to shaping that debate in a better fashion than we're otherwise likely to see.

HH: Do you think the moment of decision, vis-à-vis the Iranian nuclear weapons and military force will be reached over the next year prior to the election, Ambassador Bolton?

JB: I think it's possible...if you would have asked me a year ago what I thought President Bush would do, I would have told you that he would not leave office with Iran on the verge of acquiring nuclear weapons. I have to say today, I don't know where he would come out on the question, unfortunately, and I just don't know what he's going to do on it.

HH: Secretary of State Rice is the subject of a lot of commentary in <u>Surrender Is Not An Option</u>. Page 318, Rice started off her tenure as Secretary of State following a tough line on Iran. By late February, 2005, however, she began to wobble, largely because of Nick Burns. Why the because of Nick Burns?

JB: Well, this is an example of the culture of the State Department taking over the policy. And although I deal with individuals in the book, you have to, because policy is not made by vast, impersonal forces in the sky. It's made by individuals. What I'm really talking about is the State Department's culture. And the culture is defer to the Europeans, if the Europeans want to negotiate, defer to them. We want to keep close ties with the Europeans. We don't want to break with them. This is, in effect, the same thing as Senator John Kerry's global test, so that here's another case where process triumphs substance. It's better to keep the Europeans together with us than to achieve anything and stopping Iran from achieving nuclear weapons. And for whatever reason, I think Secretary Rice bought that perspective.

HH: But this goes to a much more deeper point. I've been running around these circles, although I haven't had the pleasure of meeting you, for 25 years, since the beginning of the

Reagan administration. And Nick Burns has never been a part of any of this. What is he doing in the number two position at the Department of State?

JB: Well, I tell the story in the book that it may be apocryphal, but I've heard it a lot of times, that before the 2004 election, Richard Holbrook, one of my predecessors at the U.N., introduced Nick Burns as the person who would be his undersecretary of state if Kerry won, and if Holbrook became secretary of state. And of course, Kerry didn't win and Holbrook didn't become secretary of state. But Nick is still the undersecretary for political affairs. And I think it's a reflection of the astuteness of the building and the culture of the foreign service that even in a Republican administration, this is able to happen.

HH: Does Nicholas Burns understand the Iranian threat, John Bolton?

JB: I don't think he does. I don't think Nick really appreciates what proliferation is all about. He's a perfectly pleasant individual. I had, I think, pleasant dealings with him, and I don't want to turn this into a personality issue, because I think he is simply what the culture at State throws up. This is the consequence of decades of the problems that I identify and discuss in the book.

HH: You know, I do want to pause and note the tone here is never personal when you're talking about people who you have a policy opposition to. But on Page 455, you write that it is personal, vis-à-vis the left versus Cheney, Rumsfeld, Wolfowitz, Feith, Libby, you, and that they've adopted sort of the politics of personal destruction. Are we going to have to go that way, Ambassador Bolton, in order to prevail?

JB: Well, I hope not, because I think one of the consequences of the battles that are going on in Washington now over, for example, the confirmation of Judge Mukasey as the new Attorney General, which I think is now likely to go through, is that people will say I'm not going to serve in the government. I'm not going to put myself and my family through this kind of torture, which is designed to pick people apart and not disagree with them on policy, but just find ways of preventing their nomination from being confirmed. And that will leave as a class of governors people who have never done anything except work in the government. And I think that's destructive for the United States, it's destructive when people spend their whole career in politics. They ought to have a life other than politics. And I think senior officials ought to have a life other than government.

HH: You know, Rumsfeld's gone, Wolfowitz's gone, Feith's gone, Libby convicted and commuted, you're gone. Only Cheney's left. Have they dented Cheney?

JB: [Well, I don't...] he is a very determined individual, and one thing that we really don't know, and may never know, is exactly what his conversations with the President are, because he has, I think properly, refused to comment on what he says to the President and when he says it. But if you look at the score-card, it's a vastly different array of policies in the national security area in the second term than it was in the first term. Now I still have the hope, as I mentioned a moment ago, that the President may turn around again and come back to his original posture. And if in fact that happens, that will be because Dick Cheney never relented.

HH: Let's go and talk for a moment about your confirmation fiasco. I was there for the Agresto one which launched all these, and then through the Bork one as well. I'd like to apologize for Voinovich, since I'm a son of Ohio. [But I'd also like to take...]

JB: But he came around at the end, so...

HH: He did. But I'd like to take credit for helping to beat Lincoln Chafee like a drum. I'm wondering about the people who opposed you. Did you get the sense that they ever had an idea of the details of these policies, [that they really...] did Lincoln Chafee for a moment understand the Iranian threat, the North Korean proliferation, the counter-proliferation initiative, did they get it?

JB: I don't think so. In his case, I think he was just scared of what was going to happen in the election, and as I quote him in the book several times, assuring the White House that he would vote for my confirmation, he had before, he said he would do it again, and then he faced a very tough primary fight in the Republican primary, and then lost in the general election. And I think [that's what it...] it was a question of political fear more than anything else.

HH: What about Republicans running things? Bill Frist is a friend of the program, been on a number of times, but throughout the whole tenure as majority leader, I thought they operated at 33rpm when they needed to operate at 78. And <u>Surrender Is Not An Option</u> proves that they were postponing votes all the time, they never pushed, they never acted like it mattered.

JB: Well, I think my experience, going back when I was at Justice and worked on Bob Bork's nomination to the Supreme Court, is that neither in the legislative branch, nor frankly in the executive branch, do people appreciate the difference between a confirmation struggle and a struggle over enacting legislation.

HH: Agreed.

JB: Confirmation is up or down. It's one vote. You can't amend a confirmation, you can't trade something for something else. And what we have in Washington today is that important or controversial confirmation fights are political campaigns. They're not even legislative efforts anymore. They're political campaigns. I think the Democrats and the left understand that. I think they've become expert on it. I don't think we understand it enough. We'll get a chance here to see if Democrats elected in '08, whether we've developed the political skills to handle that. But right now, conservatives and Republicans are far behind in that struggle.

HH: Let's turn to the most complete portrait in the book other than your own, and that is of Secretary Powell. "I am slow, but I always get there," he says, and you call it his finest hour of state when he dumps the verification of the biological weapons draft protocol. Is that true that he was slow but he always got there?

JB: Well, you know, I tried to write this book objectively. I know some people will think that's self-serving, but I didn't set out to portray anybody in a particularly unfavorable light. I tried to write this as it happened, as I recalled it at the time, as in fact it played out, without trying to fit each episode into a preconceived pattern. And I have to say a number of people who have read the book say how surprised they were that in the contrast between Secretary Powell and Secretary Rice, Secretary Powell actually came out looking better.

HH: Yup.

JB: Now he may not feel that way, but quite honestly, I wrote it as I saw it, and in many respects, although I disagreed with Secretary Powell on various issues, he did come out the right way in surprising areas that we have not seen in the second term.

HH: On Page 316, you write about his press conference in the jungle when he speaks at length about Iran's attempt to weaponize their nuclear capacity. That's a star. That's a good day. But then you write, and would you explain to the audience, what the Marshall Legacy Project was?

JB: [Well, another...] I think this is another Washington problem. Everybody, at some point in their tenure in their jobs, starts thinking about their legacy. I think this is a pernicious practice that we've got to stop generally. But in Secretary Powell's case, he wanted to go out on a high note, and to leave behind certain achievements that he could point to. I think he was obviously disappointed in the Security Council speech on Iraq's weapons of mass destruction, but the way he went about building the George C. Marshall Legacy, picking as his model another former chairman of the Joint Chiefs of Staff who became secretary of state, the way he was building it was in opposition to the President, and in a number of respects, on Iran in particular, at the end of the first term, that I found very unfortunate, very disturbing.

HH: Now I have spent almost no time, none, actually, on the Secretary-General of the U.N., because Kofi Annan's such a sad sack. But my question is, can anyone not be a sad sack in that job, given what that job means? Can there ever be a great, historically significant secretary-general, Ambassador Bolton?

JB: I don't think so anymore. I think what we need is a secretary-general who doesn't fall prey to what Kofi Annan fell prey to. You know, in the last years of his tenure, he had his aides go out and say to the press that he, and indeed the position of secretary-general, was a lot like being a secular Pope. Now many people will hear that and just break out laughing. But I can assure you, they were serious when they said this to people. And I was determined to make sure he didn't perform as a secular Pope when I got to New York, but also to make sure his successor didn't view his role in life that way. And one of the criteria we looked for was for a person who wouldn't get up one morning and conclude he was God's gift to humanity. And I'm very hopeful that the new secretary-general, Ban Ki-Moon, is immune to that way of thinking. I don't think he's succumbed to it in his first ten months in office. I hope the last four years and two months will be the same.

HH: What about this insufferable anti-American Canadian whose name I can't put my hand on right now, who would pop off in public speeches, and lecture the United States? Is he still there?

JB: Well, this is...I think you're thinking of Mark Malloch Brown...

HH: Yes.

JB: ...who's actually a Brit.

HH: Oh, I'm sorry.

JB: ...and has been made a member of the House of Lords, and put in Gordon Brown's sub-cabinet.

HH: Oh, no.

JB: You know, this is another phenomenon that pervades the U.N. secretariat, unfortunately, of people who think they are apart from or superior to the member governments. They've forgotten they're international civil servants who work for the member governments. They're not their bosses. It goes the other way around. We have examples of that for…in the IAEA, the International Atomic Energy Agency, with Mohamed El-Baradei, who has for the past several years been an apologist for Iran. The Security Council has passed resolutions mandatorily requiring Iran to give up uranium enrichment. And El-Baradei's out there saying he doesn't think it's a bad thing if they continue. This is what drives Americans crazy about the U.N. system, that these bureaucrats think that they're actually more powerful than the countries that pay their bills.

HH: Ambassador Bolton, I want to finish with some politics here. Obviously, you got an education in tough politics many times, but certainly in Florida, 2000. Who are you supporting for president in 2008?

JB: Well, you know, I haven't picked anybody yet, in part because I wanted to write the book, and I didn't want to be a burden to a campaign. I didn't want to inhibit myself in writing and telling this story. I do think, though, that on the Republican side, we've got a much stronger field in the national security area than perhaps people have considered. I am not so pessimistic about our chances next year. I think this is going to be a very consequential election for America in the foreign policy field. I think it's important to have this debate have a higher priority in the election campaign. And I think our top tier candidates are all capable of carrying that debate.

HH: Some people think you've signed on with Giuliani. Is that simply wrong?

JB: I have not. No, I've had the privilege of talking to most of the candidates, I guess, and I'm happy to talk to them and their advisors and what not, and I'm glad to do it. But I've not signed on with anybody in particular.

HH: I think it's a two person race between Romney and Giuliani. Would either of them represent the United States well, in your opinion, Ambassador Bolton?

JB: I think they both would, and I think Senator Thompson and Senator McCain would as well. I really am quite pleased with the top level in the national security point of view. I know there are a lot of areas of important domestic policy where they disagree. That's what the primary will resolve. But looking forward to the general election, you can see from the Democratic debates that they've got a very different worldview than our candidates do, and that's why it's so important that that worldview not carry itself into the White House.

HH: Do those Democratic debates encourage Iran in their proliferation and their ambitions, in your opinion, Ambassador Bolton?

JB: I think they do. There's little doubt in my mind that both in North Korea and Iran, they've seen the polls, they've heard the commentary about the dissatisfaction with the Bush administration, and I think they're looking for that happy day when the Democrats return to power, Madeleine Albright clinking glasses with Kim Jung Il in Pyongyang, apologizing for CIA-directed coup in the 1950's in Iran. They can't wait for that crowd to get back in.

HH: Ambassador Bolton, last question, it's not covered in Surrender Is Not An Option, your memoir. Looking ahead, if the Republicans retain the White House, give me four or five, six names of people you would want to see in senior positions in the Department of State, Department of Defense, NSC, to be confident that the team going forward would build on the successes, and avoid the pratfalls of the Bush administration.

JB: Well, you know, there are a lot of great people. J.D. Crouch and Bob Joseph, two people I worked with very closely, talk a lot about in the book. I think there's a younger generation of people out there who got bloodied in the Bush administration and ought to come back, Steve Rademaker, Mark Gesper, Marshall Billingsley, [just a...] Jackie Sanders, Mark Wallace.

[I mean, these are people,] and many others that I can't name, we've got a very good bench. And with the right leadership in the White House, we could have a very strong and effective foreign policy after next year's election.

HH: Well, I hope during the transition, if it's a good one, they pass out <u>Surrender Is Not An Option</u> as sort of a Bible for going forward. Ambassador John Bolton, a pleasure making your acquaintance, and a pleasure for having this conversation. I appreciate it.

JB: Well, thank you very much for having me on. I do appreciate it.

End of interview.

Interview with Douglas Feith
April 23, 2008

HH: Douglas Feith is the author of <u>War And Decision: Inside The Pentagon at the Dawn of the War on Terrorism</u>. He was number three at the Pentagon for the four crucial years that began the Bush administration, saw the beginning of the war. He joins me now to talk about this controversial and compelling account of what went on in the Pentagon and the Bush administration from 9/11 forward. Douglas Feith, welcome, it's good to have you today.

DF: Thanks, good to be with you.

HH: Let's start by explaining to people what the undersecretary of defense for policy did. That was your job, and just generally, even before the war, what's the scope of that office's duties?

DF: Well, the undersecretary is the main advisor, I was the main advisor to Secretary Rumsfeld on defense policy, and the international affairs of the department. So I ran the office that was sometimes referred to as the little State Department within the Pentagon. And also, I supported Secretary Rumsfeld for the work that he did in National Security Council meetings. So the briefing papers for him, for the meetings when he would meet with the President, the Vice President, Secretary of State, and others, those briefing papers were the responsibility of my office. And when he would go to those meetings, I usually accompanied him.

HH: And I'm going to get into chain of command at the Pentagon later. But in the book, you're very careful to lay out the chain of command. By the way, it's a very good book. It's a very compelling read. I've been with it for the last week, and it's fascinating on many levels. But give some folks a sense of who Douglas Feith was before he arrived at the Pentagon.

DF: Well, I had served before in the Reagan administration. [I started off,] I was trained as a lawyer, but then went into the Reagan administration as a Middle East specialist on the National Security Council staff, and then moved over to the Pentagon, and was deputy assistant secretary of defense, and I worked on arms control negotiations, U.S.-Soviet issues, in the Reagan administration. And then I left and I started my own law firm, and practiced law for a number of years, and was part of the former Reagan national security officials network, and worked with my former colleagues on a whole range of national security issues throughout the 90's. And then came back to the government in 2001 as the undersecretary of defense for policy.

HH: Now you are widely understood to be one of the deep, dark circle of neocons. Do you wear that badge as an honor or as something that's a misjudgment of who you are?

DF: Well, the term neocon has gone through a lot of changes. There was a time when I think it was a very useful term, and that was in particular during the Reagan administration. There were two main groups that it was useful to distinguish between. There were the people who had been the lifelong conservative Republicans, and who supported and loved Ronald Reagan, and then there was a group of people, including myself, who started their political lives as liberal Democrats, and mostly throughout the 1970's, had found that the Democratic Party had drifted substantially to the left, leaving us behind, and we became strong supporters of Ronald Regan and his policies of peace through strength, and his emphasis on the importance of ideas in international affairs. We had the view, for example, that the Cold War was not a clash of great powers the way some people referred to it, but was in fact, in an important way, an ideological war between totalitarian communism and liberal democracy. And so those people who had started off left of center, started off as Democrats, and who supported Ronald Reagan, and who viewed Ronald Reagan, by the way, as a neocon, because he himself had started off in life as a liberal Democrat, we were distinguished from the lifelong conservative Republicans by the terms new conservatives, or neocons.

HH: And I think the left today uses that term primarily to attach to people who are staunch supporters of Israel, and people who are open to the use of American military power to achieve important objectives. Do you think that's a fairly safe assertion as to when neocon gets thrown around?

DF: Yeah, I think the term neocon went through a change, and I talk about this a bit in the book…

HH: Yeah.

DF: …that originally, it meant what I said. It was [this,] basically people who had been liberal Democrats, and who became Reagan supporters. In recent years, it's been cheapened and distorted, and some people use it just as a bigoted reference to Jews or Israel supporters, and some people use it just to mean, you know, people who they consider to be too hard-line, or too pro-military. [And I mean] now, you hear people describing Dick Cheney and Donald Rumsfeld as neocons. And you know, if they're neocons, then the term has no meaning anymore.

HH: Because they've always been Republicans.

DF: Sure.

HH: And they've always been sort of mainstream, orthodox Republicans, but that's always meant different things at different times. I just wanted to put that out there early, because I'm often called a neocon, but I've never been other than a

Republican. And so I just wonder what utility it has, and I guess we agree that it doesn't have much. But I do think there's a category, and there are a lot of them in the book, of professional Beltway savvy operators, and they would include George Tenet and Richard Armitage, maybe even Colin Powell, about whom it's impossible to assign an ideological assessment, Doug Feith. Is that fair?

DF: Yeah, there are people who tend to be, [they tend to be, I would say,] crisis managers rather than strategic thinkers, people who don't think systematically about world affairs or about government policy, [and who are actually,] who don't have a lot of patience for people who do think more philosophically or systematically. And they tend to view a philosophical outlook as just ideology. I mean, there were a lot of people who were very uncomfortable with Ronald Reagan, for example, because Ronald Reagan always talked about ideas. And that makes some people very uncomfortable. They don't like people who approach public policy or world affairs with an emphasis on the importance of ideas. They think it's rigid and ideological. And I happen to think, by the way, [that I mean,] it is possible to be rigid and ideological, and that's not good, but I don't think that everybody who thinks systematically about these things, and who takes the kind of philosophical approach that Reagan took, is an ideologue.

HH: I'm so struck by the deep division in the Bush administration first term, between those who think ideologically, and those who are often called realists, pragmatists, whatever. It's a deep, deep division. That's the revelation of <u>War And Decision</u>, that the media's been sniffing around this for a long time, Doug Feith. But it was profound, it had enormous consequences for the war thus far.

DF: It did, [and I mean,] one of the points that I make throughout the book is that [almost everything that...] almost all the key elements of the conventional wisdom that people get from the mainstream media are [...almost all those elements are] inaccurate. And part of the reason that they are so widespread and have become the conventional wisdom is that they came from people within the administration who did not support the President.

HH: Right, right, and that's very important. And the distortions in the public record, which we're going to go through, are many and important. But I want to start with a more global question, that <u>War And Decision</u> answers in a sort of backwards way. Six and a half years after 9/11, five years after the invasion of Iraq, does the American public, Doug Feith, have a good grasp on the network of jihadists, and the threat they pose?

DF: Well, we have some grasp of it, and I think in some respects, we have knowledge, and we've had some accomplishments. But as Secretary Rumsfeld used to emphasize all the time, we've got a thinking enemy. And so as we get on top of issues, the enemy adapts.

HH: Well, [I think...] my question was the American public, not our decision makers, but generally speaking, the average man or woman in the street.

DF: Oh, no. There, I would agree with you. [There is, I think,] I think that there is not, in general, an appreciation of the nature of this problem. And partly, it's because the administration decided, and that this is I think one of the things that is most to the President's credit, the President decided immediately after 9/11 that our main goal was not retaliation, but preventing the next attack.

HH: Yup.

DF: And he developed an entire strategy, with multiple aspects that I'm sure we could talk about at some length if you want to.

HH: We will be, yeah.

DF: And the goal was to prevent the next attack. It is interesting, as you pointed out in your question, that here we are six and a half years later, and we have not had another 9/11-scale attack. And one of the consequences, which is [you know,] ironic but important, is that because we have been able to prevent the next attacks, there are many people who think that the whole problem of jihadist terrorism was overblown.

HH: Doug Feith, there are a lot of personalities in this book which I have to cover, because personalities drive policy. But before we get there, a couple more sort of overarching questions, why is it so long after the fall of Baghdad that so much in the material from Saddam's regime and years is untranslated and unpublished?

DF: I'm amazed, and I think it's a terrible failing on the part of the government. We should be knowing what's in that material. [And I take] your question, it's an important question, and I don't know why the administration has not devoted the resources necessary to making sure that we can read through the enormously important material that was found in Iraq. There's a lot of stuff that hasn't been translated yet, or studied yet, and I think it's partly the result of something that I talk about in the book, which is the administration made a decision somewhere along the way, some months after we went into Baghdad, and we failed to find the WMD stockpiles that the CIA had said we would find. It appears that people at the White House made the decision that the President is going to focus his attention and his comments on the future and on democracy promotion rather than on the past and the actual rationale for the war, the focus on the threats that came from the regime. And that knocked the priority down for examining things like the historical record. And I think the administration did itself and its whole war effort enormous harm by making that decision to kind of turn its back on the past, and try to focus only on the future.

HH: I'll jump ahead in my question sequence, because the Duelfer Report is a great part of the book, War And Decision. And in fact, as you point out, he discovered that Saddam had the capacity to reinitiate massive weapons of mass destruction programs, but the administration abandoned the effort. They didn't even try to make a case that that mattered almost as much as stockpiles. Strategic error on their part, Doug Feith?

DF: Yes, I think it was. And what the Duelfer Report, the so-called Iraq Survey Group Report found was that Saddam had purposefully put himself in a position where he could manufacture chemical and biological weapon stockpiles in three to five weeks. [And I mean,] this was an enormously important finding, but the Iraq Survey Group report was done under the control of the CIA. And when the report was issued, it was three volumes. It was almost like three inches of paper. And the CIA put it out to the press without so much as a one page sheet of bullets saying here are the key findings. So what did the journalists do when they were all of a sudden handed three inches of paper? Many of the key reports, the first reports came from the wire services, who have to write about something within an hour or two, they got a three inch report, and all they wrote was no WMD found. And so the whole world got the impression that the only thing that was of significance that was found by the Iraq Survey Group was no WMD. Now the fact is what the report actually found, and I quote it at length in my book, is they found that Saddam had facilities, they found that he had personnel, they found that he had material for chemical and biological weapons. The found that he had the intention to have it, they found that he had purposefully built dual-use facilities that could produce military and civilian items, so that nobody could pin it down as specifically military, even though it could be used for military purposes. And as I said, they found that he had purposefully structured his programs so that he could have chemical and biological weapons production within three to five weeks. And these were the things that if the CIA had put [those] in a fact sheet, a one page fact sheet, the whole world's perception of the Iraq WMD threat would be different.

HH: I'm going to get to the CIA a little bit later. But this is a good jumping off spot for a broader point you make repeatedly. You're critical throughout of the information efforts of the administration, the Pentagon, the CIA, State Department, all of it. Who's responsibility, Doug Feith, is it? Is it the President's fault that this communication strategy has been so badly, terribly managed?

DF: Well, it's been very sad to see, because I think that a lot of very good and important work that was done for the country in good faith, with careful analysis, was misunderstood by the American public, is not supported by the American public, because these efforts have been so bad. [I mean,] ultimately, of course, I mean, the President is the, as the saying goes, the captain of the ship, and he has responsibility for the fact that his administration hasn't done a professional, proper job in explaining what the administrations is doing in the national security field and why. [I mean, what I do in the book is,] it's hard for me to know exactly who within the administration is actually responsible for that, which office...I mean, it was not what was done within the National Security Council. I mean, there were various people who were doing strategic communications and political kinds of things in the administration, and I don't know where some of these key decisions were made that turned out to be so harmful. But I do know in the broadest sense that they were enormously harmful, because the public does not understand what the administration was aiming to do, or why it was doing it, what kind of activities are going on around the world. And as you pointed out in your earlier question, there's a widespread lack of understanding of the nature of the threats that we face.

HH: You know, the communication effort with the American people has been so random, halting, almost feckless, Douglas Feith. It's as though the people in the administration are the only ones in America who don't know how to sell anything. People who have to sell things go on radio and television...you know, if you've got a book to sell like War And Decision, and someone says hey, come spend three hours with me, they're there. But they were trying to sell an idea, a strategic concept, and no one...I mean, Rumsfeld's been on this show twice in his tenure, Dick Cheney maybe four or five times. But it's always ten, fifteen minutes. Did anyone ever sit down with the Secretary of Defense and say you've got to take this seriously?

DF: [Well, yeah,] I know that...when I was reviewing my notes, and this is one of the comments that I make in the book, when I was reviewing my notes from the years that I was at the Pentagon, [I mean,] I found literally hundreds of references by Rumsfeld, by Cheney, by General Myers, and others, saying our strategic communications are terrible. We have got to get on top of this. And this was not for political reasons.

HH: Right.

DF: This was because the administration had difficult, expensive, costly in lives and blood efforts underway, in Afghanistan and Iraq and elsewhere, and there was an appreciation that the American public has to understand these things if it's going to support the effort. And there's also this extremely important point that in fighting the jihadist extremist problem, a major part of the fight has to be at the level of ideological warfare.

HH: Doug Feith, I want to go back to the strategic communications collapse, because there's one very interesting story in War And Decision. There are many, actually. But on Page 463 or thereabouts, you're talking about Paul Bremer, who is running the Coalition Provisional Authority, and he's off the Pentagon reservation, never was on it, really, and Rumsfeld makes a decision to try and sort of bring him around to the idea that the CPA's got to be dissolved. And so Rumsfeld, as you point out, invests enormous time in doing so. He has him to his home on Sunday night, then two full days and a dozen meetings with senior staff. And Bremer is finally persuaded of the right position in the view of the Pentagon, as to the Coalition Provisional Authority's sunset date. [But you know...] so he realized he had to persuade him, and it took time to persuade him. But no one's ever taken the time to persuade the American public in the way that they try and persuade individuals. It's like they don't understand it's a country of individuals, each one of whom has to be approached like Paul Bremer was approached, and made to see the reason. I just don't think that perception exists within the Bush administration.

DF: Well, I agree with you, and I think it's been one of the major shortcomings of an administration that I generally support. And it was a great source of sadness and frustration for me, and a major motive for me in writing this book. [I mean, I think, and] I've had this reaction from a number of people who've read the book, I think that this book explains in detail, for the kind of people who want a more serious and detailed explanation than you can get from just a presidential speech that lasts for a few minutes and is generally fairly general. This book, in detail and in a specific way, walks people through the actual strategic analyses that motivated Rumsfeld, Cheney and the President, and the administration in general in deciding how to fight the global war on terrorism, how to fight the Afghanistan campaign, and how to fight the Iraq campaign. And I really wish that the administration in general had been devoting as much attention to presenting the case, and presenting it at multiple levels of detail. I mean, some people don't want detail. Some people want the five minute version, or the version that you get in a presidential speech. But then there are other people like you that are willing to spend hours probing an issue. And those people deserve a proper answer. And I wrote the book to try to provide a proper answer to people who actually want to know more than you can get in a one paragraph summary in a daily newspaper.

HH: And that's why it's on what I call the necessary shelf. I've got what I call the necessary shelf of books. It's got The Looming Tower on it, it's got The Crisis Of Islam by Bernard Lewis on it, it's got The Nuclear Jihadist by Doug Frantz on it. It's got Faith, Reason, and the War Against Jihadism by George Weigel on it. Now, War And Decision's on it. But there are a couple of things I wish you had spent a little bit more time on. One, for example, how big of a threat, how many jihadists are there? I remember Rumsfeld, and you cover this in War And Decision, sent the famous snowflake saying what are our metrics? Are we winning or losing? And you talk about the madrassas, et cetera, but Doug Feith, I ask any number of administration officials how many are there who are willing to die for the cause of jihad, and nobody has an answer. What do you think that number is?

DF: Well, I don't have an answer, either. I mean, we have intelligence services that are supposed to come up with estimates, and the one thing we know for sure is that those estimates get revised all the time, and they seem to be wrong. I mean, you remember at the beginning of the war in Iraq, the CIA was talking about the number of jihadists we were facing in Iraq, and they were saying it's 5,000 at most. And then our military kept reporting that they were killing more people than that, and yet the insurgency was growing. So it was clear that our intelligence community just didn't have a handle on that problem.

HH: It's clear…Tim Weiner's been a guest on this program, his Legacy Of Ashes book, combines with War And Decision. It's clear the CIA is just no damn good at this. And I mean, they're great people, I know a lot of agents, both covert and overt, at the Agency for many, many years. They're highly dedicated and selfless. But my gosh, they told you the Iraqi police, this comes through in War And Decision again and again, would be a force for order and a respected institution in post-war Iraq. They were thugs and killers.

DF: That's right. [And I mean, there were…] and I also want to add the same kind of observation that you made. A lot of people at the CIA are very dedicated people, and they have a very hard job to do. But the fact is, especially when it came to Iraq, on issue after issue, they revealed that they knew very little. And one of my main frustrations, which I highlight in the book, is that not simply that they knew very little, but that when they talked about Iraq, they pretended to know a lot more than they knew. And they pretended it to policy makers.

HH: Oh, that's right. We are going to come back to that, because they also tried to make policy. That's one of the lessons of War And Decision.

HH: I'm in so much trouble, Doug. I've got five pages of notes to ask you, and it's a 528 page book, and it's got another hundred pages of detailed notes and appendices, and source notes, et cetera. And I'm one half of one page through my five page outline, and I'm almost at the end of the first hour. So I'm going to have to giddy up a little bit. But I want us to go back to the CIA. You quote Wolfowitz as leaning over to you in the course of one of your very early meetings on the war, and saying to you, "What's going on here? The CIA is making policy recommendations." And you know, that struck me like a brick. That's not their job.

DF: No, it's not. [And it's...] to do national security policy, you need people who have a clear understanding of the line between intelligence and policy. And one of the points that I make, there was a lot of controversy about politicization of intelligence. And one of the points I make in the book is you don't want intelligence politicized, and you don't want it politicized from the policy side of the line, and you don't want it politicized from the intelligence side of the line.

HH: The CIA, I think, was engaged at some level, many people in the CIA, in a war against the war. Part of that war against the war turned into leaks against you and the offices underneath you, having to do with assessment of intelligence. And I want to just make sure in the first hour we put out there, that's just hooey. That's not what you folks were doing. And you were questioning intelligence, but you were not producing it.

DF: That's correct. [And we were challenged by...] people in my office challenged the quality of the work of the CIA. And it was a perfectly proper thing to do. We challenged their methodology. And the people at the CIA we criticized resented that challenge, and attacked us in the newspapers, and said that we were trying to get them to change their position for political reasons. That's absolutely untrue, and I explain that story in the book.

HH: And that's a very important, it's something of a sideshow to the strategic war that we're involved in, and to the tactical decisions that you made. But it's very important, because the war against the war is part of the war. And we'll come back to that. I also wanted to get your reaction on this past Sunday. The New York Times put out this long avalanche of an article.

They call it a reporter's dump, really, of everything in his note-book onto the table. And it's about the Pentagon's hidden hand, influencing the talking heads. I had to laugh, given how badly the Pentagon has been at influencing the talking heads. Did you have a chance to read that, Douglas Feith?

DF: I saw it, I was out of town, I didn't have a chance to read the whole article. But I was struck by the irony that for an administration that's done such a poor job of informing the public, to be accused of Svengali-like manipulation of the public debate is really too ironic to bear.

HH: That's exactly my reaction, so we'll just leave it there. Now I want to go to the first of the portraits, Rumsfeld. I want to quote from Page 509 that you write, "Rumsfeld wielded a courageous and skeptical intellect. He challenged preconceptions and assumptions, including his own, and drove colleagues as well as subordinates to take a long view, and to evaluate honestly whether their work was actually producing results. His ideas and ambitions for the Defense Department and the U.S. were high-minded, his contributions extensive and influential. But his style of leadership did not always serve his own purposes. He bruised people. He made personal enemies who were eager to strike back at him and try and discredit his work. Losses and disappointments in Iraq gave an opening to those who wanted Rumsfeld out, which led to his resignation in November, 2006. At his early remove," you write, "from the events in question, it would be feckless to venture an overall judgment of his role. But I never cease to admire him, even when he did not handle matters as I thought best." Now it's no secret to this audience I am a huge fan of Rumsfeld. And so the question to me is not, "Did he make mistakes?" Everyone would. The question is, could anyone have done better, given the difficulties of war, the intrigues inside of the government, the nature of the enemy, the terribly flawed intelligence, would a Robert Gates who followed him, or a Bill Cohen who preceded him have run up a pretty similar record in your view, Douglas Feith?

DF: I think that he did an extraordinary number of things that his predecessors and his successors wouldn't have even tried to do, things that were actually very beneficial to the Defense Department and to the country. He, Rumsfeld was willing to break from the ordinary, and was willing to consider things that were brand new and innovative and imaginative. And I think that contributed in an important way to the success that we talked about of reaching the point six and a half years after 9/11 when we haven't had another 9/11-style attack. [Now at the same time, and] I think that's an important credit to Rumsfeld, at the same time, as much of an admirer of him as I am, and I say so openly as you quoted, I try to be a critical admirer. And so throughout the book, I make observations of things that where he handled them differently from the way I would have handled them. And you know, he's a complex person. And he gave openings to people who didn't like what he was doing at all, and they were eventually able to take advantage of those openings and get rid of him.

HH: But the question I'm trying to get at is really one that looks to the future and tries to inform the future by asking who makes the best secretary of defense? Is it a Rumsfeld? Or is it a Robert Gates, who's sort of a technical and very quiet guy? Or a Bill Cohen, who's a political figure? What are you looking for in that job?

DF: Well, one of the things I think that one should be looking for is somebody who can at least to some extent get the bureaucracy [to]work for him, as opposed to what a lot of so-called leaders do, which is they come into a bureaucracy and they follow their subordinates. And if you follow your subordinates, you can become highly popular. But if you try to lead your subordinates, then you can grate on a lot of people. And one of the things that's essential to our democracy, I mean, we elect only two people in the whole Executive Branch, the President and the Vice President. And if we're really going to have a democratic country, then the President and the Vice President have to be able to guide and steer the Executive Branch. But the Executive Branch is a bunch of enormous bureaucracies that don't want to be guided or steered. And so it takes somebody with the kind of drive and intellect and personality of Rumsfeld to try to give some direction in support of the President's policies to an enormous bureaucracy.

HH: That's a very, actually, profound observation.

HH: Doug Feith, this is a short segment. Why did you leave when you left?

DF: Well, I had been in my job for a little over four years. And I mean, we were really working around the clock. It was exhausting, and I have four children, and I just decided after four years that it was time to go.

HH: Did you regret leaving when you left?

DF: Well, no, I didn't regret leaving when I left. I mean, I left under my own steam. Nobody asked me to leave. On the contrary, I was asked to stay. But I just was really exhausted. And I mean, what I regret is there were a number of very important projects that I had launched that I would have liked to have carried farther forward in the government. For example, the creation of a civilian reserve corps, to do stabilization and reconstruction operations abroad, and reform of our foreign and security assistance, and some other major projects that I launched and started in my office. But you can't do everything, and I thought that the summer of 2005 was a good time for me to leave.

HH: Do you think that the Pentagon has been transformed by Rumsfeld and his team? They came in talking defense transformation. Was it?

DF: Well, I think there were some things that Rumsfeld was successful in getting changed. It's a lot harder than anybody can imagine to move an enormous bureaucracy. A lot of people in a bureaucracy look at the political appointees, they know that they're only going to be around for a while, they know that if they delay things, they can wait them out. And a lot of people, all they want is [they want] the inertia to continue. They want to continue doing things the way they've always done them, and how they're comfortable doing them. And so there's a lot of resistance to adapting the government for future problems instead of just keeping it on autopilot, dealing with things that we've been dealing with for the last fifty years.

HH: The successors, an interest to the Rumsfeld team, are they on basically the same course that Rumsfeld set?

DF: On some things, but there also have been...I mean, there have been efforts made to undo some of Rumsfeld's transformational initiatives and reforms, and some of them have gotten undone, and some of them are continuing. So it's a mixed bag.

HH: More detail on that when we come back.

HH: Doug Feith, I want to begin this hour by going back to something I asked you earlier, because it's really one of the missions of this program, is to make sure people understand the nature of the jihadist threat. And you said the government doesn't have a number, and the numbers keep changing about the number of jihadists in the world. And by that, I mean either Shia or Sunni fundamentalists willing to use violence up to the point including suicide, and whose purposes, as you point out in War And Decision, massive destruction. They're not political theory people. They're intent on killing as many non-ideological brothers as they can. How do you put as an order of magnitude the number of people in that camp in the world?

DF: Well, the way I would see it is the number is hard to pin down, but the ability of these people to cause mass destruction is I think unquestionable. What they have learned how to do is to basically skip over the armed forces of various countries like ours...I mean, once upon a time in earlier eras, if somebody wanted to do really large scale destruction of the United States, they'd have to defeat our military.

HH: Right.

DF: What the jihadist threat represents, and what 9/11 drove home, is that people who could just bypass our military can come in, in relatively small numbers, and do something as absolutely mind-boggling as destroy the World Trade Center towers, both of them, knock them down, destroy the west side of the Pentagon. And what we were concerned about in the days right after 9/11 is what are the other follow-on attacks that might occur? And what would be the effect on American society if there had been a series of them? It doesn't take enormously large numbers on the part of the jihadists to pull this off.

HH: It doesn't take enormously large numbers, but it does underscore for America the nature of the threat, if, in fact, there are enormously large numbers. If it takes twenty jihadists to make a jihadist picnic, how many jihadist picnics are out there? And head of MI5 outgoing in Britain said there were 5,000 active plots in London. That got some attention. Did the Pentagon never sit down and say okay, the CIA doesn't know, but let's try and count up the number of people who've been through the camps, who expressed themselves on the Web, or are involved in various cells we know about, and it comes to 100,000? 500,000? Is there any order of magnitude, Doug Feith?

DF: Well, the kind of analysis that you're talking about was in fact done, and I think, I assume, I've been out of the government for more than two and a half years, but I assume it continues to be done. What I don't remember seeing was the kind of focus specifically on numbers that you are making. [That just, I think is just,] what I saw was that was beyond the capability of our intelligence community to come up with a really good handle on those numbers. But you're absolutely right to be focusing on the magnitude of the threat.

HH: And that's what...I don't know that that's been communicated. And I think part of it, it's sort of like a conversation... a debate I actually had in the Oval Office with some other talk show hosts with the President of the United States about whether or not the number of jihadists killed in Iraq ought to be publicized. And it's an off the record conversation, so I can't tell you what his position was, but the Pentagon, if I understand correctly from other sources, the Pentagon's always resisted putting out the number of jihadists killed in Iraq because it heightens back to Vietnam body count days. Were you a part of that conversation?

DF: Yeah, I heard that conversation, and I do know that one of the things that Secretary Rumsfeld and others talked about was whatever it is you measure tends to improve and increase. And so if you focus people on a particular metric, you'll get a lot of effort on that metric. And in Vietnam, when people were focused on body counts, it led the military to produce enormously large body counts, which wasn't necessarily the main thing that they should have been focused on from a strategic point of view. And so that was, as you rightly point out, a major part of the reason why the Pentagon decided that it was not going to make body counts a major part of its public discussion.

HH: Did you agree with that?

DF: Yeah, that sounded right to me, [because that, our main... we did have, in a more focused fashion,] we did have early on, for example, a list of key terrorist leaders. I believed that leadership was really crucial to the terrorist network. And early on, we put together, I mean, the government put together a list of all of the known leaders of al Qaeda. And there, an effort was made, and that was an important metric to go down that list and capture or kill as many of those leaders as we could.

HH: And that's in <u>War And Decision</u>. It's very impressive, although bin Laden, of course, and Zawahiri are at large, it's a very impressive devastation wreaked upon al Qaeda.

DF: Yeah, it was something like 75% of the people who were early on identified as the top leadership of al Qaeda were then captured or killed. Now of course, in the meantime, they're generating more people as you and I have discussed. This is a dynamic situation. But nevertheless, it's pretty darn impressive that the intelligence community and the Pentagon came up with this list, and then systematically attacked it, and produced a very good result.

HH: It is, but the downside, though, is for example, today, the Iraqi Security Forces are engaged in a battle with the Sadr army, Sadr militia, and nobody knows how big the Sadr militia is. Or if they do know, they're not talking. And the special militias, the Iranian Revolutionary Guard trained and assisted militias other than Sadrites, nobody knows how big that is. And I think it's hard for Americans to get a sense of a scale of threat, if they don't know things like that, Doug Feith, and if they don't know even how big the Iranian Revolutionary Guard is.

DF: I think you're right, and I think it's a challenge to the administration to come up with, you know, if you're not going to talk about those larger numbers, then what are the reasonable measures of progress and success? And I agree with you completely. This administration has done some important work, but it has completely fallen down on the job of explaining to the American public what they should be focused on, what they should be looking to as measures of success. And they've allowed critics of the administration, for example to come up with the setting of various benchmarks, so that Nancy Pelosi and others in Congress can then say that the Iraqis are not making progress because they're focused on benchmarks that turn out not to be the most sensible way of looking at what's going on in Iraq.

HH: Absolutely right. Let me tell you what was the most dispiriting part of <u>War And Decision</u> for me. Your account on Page 388 of the Jay Garner set up ORHA. What did ORHA stand for? I didn't write it in my notes here.

DF: The Office of Reconstruction and Humanitarian Assistance.

HH: Yeah, in Iraq. And he sets this up, and he begins to go around and get folks to fill the positions, and he takes a list into Rumsfeld, and said here's all the people I want. And Rumsfeld takes a look at it and says too many State Department people, and he strikes the list down. And then State goes crazy, and you write at Page 386-389 about this. And at one point, you go over to the situation room, you sit down with Mark Grossman, your counterpart from State, and you quote here, "I had gotten out no more than a sentence or two when Grossman stood up and walked out of the room in protest, saying over his shoulder something like, "I'm not going to listen to this." And I put the book down and I thought my God, we're in the middle of the war, and we've got, it's like high school between State and

Pentagon. And I can't tell you how disappointed I was to read that account, Doug Feith.

DF: Well, I was disappointed to live through it. And I mean, what I tried to do in the book is I talk about some things at the level of strategy and concepts, but you're also talking about human beings. And I tried to give some flavor of what it was actually like to work, what the interpersonal relations were among the people. Sometimes, there was cooperation, sometimes there were quarrels, sometimes the quarrels were very petty. And sometimes, even the very petty quarrels had strategic significance, and did real harm.

HH: That's what's scary, is that they did have strategic significance, like this debate over the externals which I'm going to come to in the next segment. Before I get there, though, one of the most famous petty quarrels, or big quarrels, isn't even in the book. Eric Shinseki is not mentioned in this book. Why?

DF: Well, in my book, I tended to focus on the things that I knew about, and had a substantial role in, so that I could give first person accounts that don't appear elsewhere. And [I just wasn't,] I just wasn't a player in that particular controversy. And so all I could have done there is recycle things that have reported on elsewhere.

HH: Okay, that's an adequate explanation, but given the centrality of the Shinseki mythology to the left's critique of the war, isn't that like one of the exhibits number one?

DF: It is. I must say, you know, I wrote a book that's, as you pointed out, about 530 pages with over a hundred pages of notes, and there are people who are going to say it should have been a longer book, but...

HH: How did I notice that Shinseki wasn't there...(laughing) Yeah, I know.

HH: Douglas Feith, one of the interesting things about <u>War And Decision</u> is the very, I think, complimentary portraits that emerge of the military professionals in this book, though not without critiques, and we'll come to Tommy Franks in a minute. But you're in Moscow when 9/11 happens, and you fly back with John Abizaid. General Abizaid's been a guest on this program when he was in command in Iraq. And the others, David Petraeus has been a guest on this program from Iraq, these are wonderful, extraordinary individuals, Myers, Pace, et cetera. Generally speaking, at that level of the general officer corps in the Pentagon, what's your assessment of the ability of the American military to keep turning out a bench of leaders like that?

DF: Well, it's crucial for the country. I was very impressed with the quality…I mean, not just their quality as human beings, which is extremely high. I mean, people who are honorable and honest and courageous, and have really golden personal qualities, but also their thoughtfulness, their kind of farsightedness, their willingness to consider broader strategic considerations beyond just their particular military responsibilities. And I mean, I overall found the quality of the top military leadership to be very impressive.

HH: Now in there is Tommy Franks, and the portrait that emerges of Tommy Franks in the book is of a brilliant and driven commander who just absolutely did not care for civilian input at all. Fair?

DF: Well, the point that I make is he was extremely impatient with civilian input, but he was also extremely impatient with the input that he got even from his fellow generals. And you know, this is really the answer to your Shinseki point. When people say that General Shinseki as the chief of staff of the Army was arguing for a different approach to the war in Iraq, and people say Rumsfeld ignored him, the point that I make in my book in general is that those people, top military people who argued for a different approach in Iraq, the real problem was not that they failed to persuade Rumsfeld, it's that they failed to persuade Franks, because Franks was the general responsible for the war plan for Iraq. And he clearly would have gotten any resources that he said that he needed for that operation. When he talked to Secretary Rumsfeld, Rumsfeld certainly pressed him hard, do you need everything you're asking for. [But while…and] I think that was a proper role for the Secretary of Defense, because we had a lot of requirements for military resources all around the world. And the Secretary wanted to make sure that we were not making wrong decisions as a government about the allocation of resources. But there was never any doubt that if General Franks said that he needed more troops or more other resources for the operation in Iraq or Afghanistan or anywhere else, he would have gotten whatever he asked for.

HH: What's very interesting in the book, and it's the first time I've seen it, I've only read parts of the Franks memoir, not the whole thing. I have read the Tenet memoir, and I've not seen this made, the argument before that understaffing the Army or keeping...that's a judgment, keeping the invasion force at the level that it was helped achieve an element of strategic surprise very difficult to achieve in the situation that was there because of the long telegraphed punch, as was Turkey's decision not to allow the 4th I.D. to enter from the north, and then launching before they had actually gotten into theater. In other words, Franks' tactical brilliance here was in somehow reclaiming a strategic surprise he was not entitled to have, given the long telegraphed punch.

DF: [Yeah, there was...] that is a very interesting topic. There was a general assumption that Saddam knew we were coming. And so the question was if we can't get strategic surprise, can U.S. forces at least get tactical surprise? And one way to try to achieve that, Franks and Rumsfeld worked out, was if we could start the war with a much smaller force than Saddam would think we would need to initiate the operation. And that's in fact what happened. And one sign that it worked was Saddam had put wires and explosives at various key points in the country to destroy infrastructure, like bridges, oil equipment and the like. And we know that he had done that back in the Gulf War in 1990-91. And he put that stuff out this time around, but didn't hook it up. So it was clear that he was making preparations for a war that he thought was not going to start for a while yet. And so we were able to achieve an important degree of tactical surprise by starting the war with a smaller force than Saddam thought we would need.

HH: In fact, the picture that emerges from this is of a war that went very, very well after the first counterattack which comes on United flight 93, in fact, up through May, June, July of 2003, when the insurgency begins to get its legs on, so that the Pentagon's almost series of brilliant innovations, and we'll come back to the naysayers about Tora Bora and quagmire, et cetera. But it went very, very well. But then it goes to hell, literally, in Baghdad and in the country because of an inability to plan for what happened afterwards. We're going to go to break in two minutes, Doug Feith, but just give people your summary of what went wrong after Saddam fell.

DF: Well, there were a number of things that went wrong. What I think is the single biggest error we made was setting up an occupation government of Iraq when it wasn't necessary to do so, and when we had actually had a plan to do it otherwise.

HH: And that is the debate that I think consumes probably half of the book, the debate over what to do with post-war Iraq that has not actually made it into print anywhere, has it?

DF: No, it hasn't. There are several dozen books about Iraq out there, and not a single one talks about this enormously important question of what was the plan that the President approved for political transition in Iraq after Saddam. My book lays it out in detail, with extensive quotations from the documents, and I think it's really rather a scandal that this has never appeared in any of the other books that are talking about the subject.

HH: And in a nutshell, on one side, Armitage and the CIA arguing for, and Bremer, eventually, for a long occupation government run by the Coalition Provisional Authority. On the other side, the Pentagon arguing for the Afghanistan model. Is that a fair summary?

DF: Yes, it is.

HH: I want to go back now to the days after 9/11, and the fact that in the Afghanistan campaign, there became obvious a split in the government. And I'll put Powell and Armitage on one side of it, and Tenet and the Pentagon on the other side of it, as to whether or not to march quickly to Kabul. The reason I want to go back to that, because I think the need for speed seems to be constant in the Pentagon, and always debunked at the other agencies. What was the debate over Kabul, Doug Feith?

DF: The debate over Kabul was part of a broader debate about what we should be trying to do in Afghanistan. Right after 9/11, Secretary Powell and Richard Armitage, his deputy, and the CIA, were advocating that the United States focus narrowly on al Qaeda. And there was actually a proposal that CIA people made that when we go into Afghanistan, we should be focusing not on the Taliban, but on al Qaeda. And the argument that they made was if we attack al Qaeda, we can get Afghans from across the country to support us. But if we also attack the Taliban government, then since the Taliban government was mainly ethnically Pashtun, the people who live in Southern Afghanistan, that we would be laying the groundwork for a civil war between north and south in Afghanistan, and we would be driving all the Pashtuns into the arms of the Taliban. And that was the line that the CIA took. Now there was something to that. I mean, it was worth worrying about that, and making sure that when we fought the war, we didn't fall into those pitfalls. But what the President believed, and what Secretary Rumsfeld believed, and Vice President Cheney, was that the CIA position was missing the main strategic point of what we were trying to accomplish in Afghanistan. It wasn't merely to hit al Qaeda. What we were trying to accomplish in Afghanistan was to hit al Qaeda, but also to shock all the state supporters of terrorism around the world by showing that the Taliban, as the state supporter of al Qaeda, paid the ultimate price for the support that it gave to these terrorists who attacked us.

HH: Right. But even after it becomes clear that you're going to go after the Taliban, they didn't want to rush to Kabul. And it just doesn't seem to make any sense to me.

DF: Right, but I think that was an extension of this debate. What the CIA had argued for was they had said that it was dangerous for the United States to ally with the Northern Alliance against the Taliban government.

HH: Right.

DF: And in fact, that strategy, I think, was a brilliant success, because the Soviets had been in Afghanistan with 300,000 troops, and failed utterly. We went in there with around 3,000 troops, not 300,000, but 3,000, and we were able to overthrow the government and get a new government set up within a period from October 7th until mid-December of 2001.

HH: You also make clear, Doug Feith, that at the beginning, the delay that many people thought was a harbinger of a quagmire, was because the CIA couldn't get their operators, very brave, extraordinary people, on the ground to call in air strikes, and that Rumsfeld was going crazy over this.

DF: Well, that was a frustration for both the CIA people trying to get in, and the Green Berets, the military guys trying to get in. And it took about twelve days before we could get the people on the ground, and the first so-called A-Teams of our special operations forces on the ground in Afghanistan. And you're right. Rumsfeld was exasperated, and he almost wound up having General Franks over that, because he was expressing his exasperation, and General Franks was on the receiving end of it.

HH: Now you had been gone from the government for twelve years, between the time you served in the Reagan administration in a senior Defense capacity, and when you came back. Were you stunned by the transformation of the American military's lethality over that period of time, Doug Feith? Or had it just never been on display before?

DF: Well, no, there had been a whole revolution in military capabilities that reflected the improvements in computerization, miniaturization. And the military had astonishing capabilities to do things with great precision that in early eras, they either couldn't do it all or required gigantic expenditures ordnance to do.

HH: Before we move on to the grand strategy, Douglas Feith, I want to just go back one more time to the CIA. As I said early in the show, they got so many things so wrong. Obviously, they and [other of…] the FBI missed the attack on America, they projected a relatively stable post-Saddam Iraq, they projected stockpiles of weapons of mass destruction, they thought that the externals, meaning Chalabi and others couldn't work with the internals inside of Iraq. They thought that the professionals who ran Iraq's police would assure order, et cetera. There's a guy named Michael Scheurer out there who's written a couple of books. Have you been following his post-CIA career?

DF: I know something about it.

HH: It's a little bit nutty. I mean, it's just very bizarre stuff. Is that representative of the intelligence side of the Agency, or the al Qaeda-assigned side of the Agency, as opposed to some of the covert staff that are working abroad in the various places around the world?

DF: Well, he was a CIA analyst, and an important figure in their al Qaeda work. And his basic view is that we do not have a fundamental, philosophical problem with bin Laden and the jihadists, that in fact our problem with them is more in the nature of a policy dispute. And if the United States changed its policies, and in particular changed our policy of support for Israel, we would not have the kind of problem that we have with the jihadists. Now I think that that's way off base. And I think that from my reading, and from the reading that many people have done of what the jihadists publish and what they say and how they act, and their whole record, that we do have a fundamental problem, and the jihadists basically believe that our form of government is a violation of God's sovereignty. I mean, their view is that a government where we say that the people are sovereign is to them, is to jihadist extremists, an offense against God.

HH: Yup, and that's brilliantly put forward in the book when we get to the ideological debate within the administration. It just seems to me that the other-worldliness of some of the CIA stuff is represented now, post-Iraq, by Scheurer on the outside. And I just wonder how endemic it is among the Agency's analysts. Do you have an opinion on that?

DF: Well, yeah. I mean, I think one of the things my book tries to explore is the CIA is full of people who spend many years studying a subject. And they develop their own ideas. They develop their worldview regarding that subject, and their theories, and their preconceptions. And many of these people are very serious and scholarly, and they have an attitude. And that's perfectly okay, but where it gets into a problem is when people like CIA analysts, who have an attitude and a worldview, filter or suppress information to the policy makers that is inconsistent with their theories and preconceptions. And that was precisely the nature of the fight that existed between the people in my office and the CIA on the Iraq-al Qaeda issue. You've pointed out that Scheurer has a view of al Qaeda that's really, I think, rather strange. But when these CIA people have those theories, and then instead of presenting all the information properly, they're shading, trimming, filtering the information to support their own theories, then the U.S. government can get in trouble.

HH: So far from the political figures in the administration manipulating the intelligence, the intelligence was being massaged, and I don't want to say manipulated, that's too strong of a word, it was being filtered through a worldview that led to distortions, from the Agency. Is that fair?

DF: I think so.

HH: Now I also want to ask you, this is a tough question. Did the President make a strategic error in retaining George Tenet, either at the beginning of the administration or after the 9/11 failure to detect the attack on America?

DF: [Well, I mean,] I think that what the President was trying to do, I suppose, I mean, he didn't consult with me on that subject, so I'm just like anybody else, on the outside speculating about it, but it seems to me that what the president was trying to do was sensible. He was trying to say we want important parts of our government functioning professionally, not polit-ically. And when you talk about our diplomatic service, the bulk of our diplomatic service is professional. When you talk about our intelligence service, it's professional. When you talk about our military service, it's professional. It's important that the government be political in a lot of respects, because that's democracy. But it's also important that parts of the government be non-political and professional. And I think he was trying to make that point by retaining Tenet as the head of the CIA, even though Tenet had been Bill Clinton's head of the CIA.

HH: Well, I understand what he was trying to do. But looking back...

DF: Looking back, my view is that I think that George Tenet was not a great leader of the CIA, and the CIA under him, I think, was particularly weak in the areas that I saw, and had dealings with in the analytical area. And I think that a lot of the problems of George Tenet's leadership are on very clear display in his own book. I mean, he wrote a 500 page book without a single footnote...

HH: Yup.

DF: ...full of errors.

HH: Yeah, you demolish that book in <u>War And Decision</u>. You demolish Bremer and Tenet books in <u>War And Decision</u>. You're a little bit more gentle on Tommy Franks. But I mean, those books are just revealed as unprofessional, myth-making.

DF: Well, I believe it's very important that people be accurate. I don't mind if somebody disagrees with me, but I think that it's really important that people be informed and accurate, careful, meticulous, cite their sources, don't misrepresent the views of their opponents. And I tried to do that in my book. But Tenet's book shows the kind of attitude that you really don't want to have in a person who is supposed to be in charge of the intel-ligence community.

HH: To set up the last hour of our conversation, Doug Feith, this is the short segment, why does everybody at the CIA and State hate Chalabi, the head of the exiled Iraqi National Congress, and many people believe to be, if difficult but nevertheless the most effective operator in post-war Iraq? Why did there develop such an animus towards him?

DF: Well, Chalabi had relationships with State and CIA going back to the early 90's. And at first, CIA people were pretty favorable toward him. But by the mid-90's, really intense resentments developed. Chalabi refused to act as an agent. He chose to act as an Iraqi leader. And he was happy to cooperate with the CIA and the State Department, but according to the report that was done in 2006 by the Senate Intelligence Committee, he did not want to act as an agent, and there were a lot of people in the CIA who resented that. Then, they got into quarrels about CIA support for coup activity against Saddam in Iraq. And Chalabi accused the CIA of incompetence. And it created enormous bitterness that went throughout the 1990's, and then became extremely influential in policy making in the George W. Bush administration.

HH: Did that in fact then poison the view of every Iraqi external? Or just Chalabi?

DF: Well, that's a very interesting question you're raising. I think that [there was…] it basically bled into a poisoning of the general attitude toward all the externals. We use the term external, by the way, because we wanted a term that applied to the Iraqi exiles and the Kurds. The Kurds were living autonomously, not directly under Saddam's control, but they were not exiles. So the term external was used to refer to both the Kurds and the exiles. And Chalabi was so detested, that people at State and the CIA did everything they could to block him, even at the expense of all of the externals.

HH: And it led to enormous distortions in how the occupation was organized, how long it went, and how the government of Iraq was finally agreed upon and set up.

HH: Doug Feith, I didn't ask you that in the first two hours. How's the book been received by reviewers and by the people that you served with?

DF: Well, the reviews are just beginning. It's a big, fat book, and it just came out. It takes people a few days to read it. But the reviews that have come out so far have been very positive. And there was an extremely strong one in the Wall Street Journal by Bret Stephens, and in the Washington Times by Frank Gaffney, and Michael Barone has had nice things to say about it, Victor Davis Hanson had some nice things to say about it, Rich Lowry, and so I'm looking forward to more comments and more reviews. [And I mean,] I hope that your readers will go out and take a look at it. I think they'll find it a very surprising book in a lot of respects, because it does challenge the conventional wisdom.

HH: I'm sure they will. I'm curious, did 60 Minutes ask to talk with you at length as they have those who have been eager to sort of attack the Bush administration strategy in the war? Have anyone in the book returned fire at you yet?

DF: No, [I haven't gotten,] and I'll be very interested to hear from some of the people that are talked about in the book. And I've talked to some of my colleagues who've had very positive things to say about it. People that I'm a bit more critical of, I haven't heard back from yet, but I'd be happy to hear from them. There are going to be a few forums in Washington [coming up] in coming days where some former officials like Paul Wolfowitz and Dan Senor, who was Jerry Bremer's press spokesman, and Peter Rodman and Larry DiRita from the Pentagon, who was Rumsfeld's spokesman, and others are going to be on panels at the Center for Strategic and International Studies in Washington, and at the Hudson Institute in coming days, talking about the book, and I think that will contribute to the debate a lot.

HH: I hope those make it onto C-SPAN. Now let's get to the substance of this, which is at the start of the war, Rumsfeld developed a strategy that the President embraced. And I want to give you my condensed summary of what it is here – prevent another attack, focus on the state actors within the enemy's network, get local peoples to get rid of terrorists [so they can get...] and the regimes that support terrorism. And Rumsfeld says, you quote him on Page 82, "If the war does not significantly change the world's political map, the U.S. will not achieve its aim." That's, to me, the core of what we agreed as a government to do in 2001 after the attacks. Fair summary, Douglas Feith?

DF: Yes, it is.

HH: All right, are we still pursuing that strategy?

DF: Well, I think we are to some extent. The problem is the war in Iraq didn't go as well as we had hoped. And we have run into precisely the problem that I talk about in the book when Secretary Rumsfeld put together this memo in October of 2002, warning of all the things that could go wrong...

HH: The Horribles memo.

DF: ...in the eventual war in Iraq.

HH: Yeah, the Horribles memo.

DF: The Horribles memo.

HH: That was interesting.

DF: And one of the things he said is if the war goes longer and is costlier and bloodier than we now anticipate, we could wind up being preoccupied in Iraq at the expense of other efforts that are important in the war on terrorism. And I think that when we look at the importance of putting pressure on other key state sponsors, like North Korea and Iran, I think it's pretty clear that the problems we've run into in Iraq have persuaded the governments in Iran and North Korea that they can defy us.

HH: You know, I do not see in War And Decision, [it may be there, I might have missed it, I don't think I did, but I did not see in War And Decision] that anyone anticipated Iran to be the maligned influence it has become in Iraq. Was that part of the strategic thinking?

DF: Yes, it was. [It was, and we actually...] there are some references in the book to it. There is less of a major discussion of Iran in the book than some people hoped for, and the reason for that is that I wrote the book so that every major proposition in the book I could tie to documents that were written at the time.

HH: I noticed that you redacted a couple that mentioned which other regimes would be targeted by us.

DF: Right, and the documents about Iran remain very sensitive. And I did not want to write big sections about Iran that just read like op-ed pieces.

HH: Right.

DF: I wanted to write a serious piece of history, and since I didn't have the material that I could use that would be declassifiable, Iran just gets less of a discussion than it might otherwise have gotten. You know, I would hope that maybe some years down the road, I'll be able to revisit this, and write more about it, and be able to draw on the actual documents regarding Iran.

HH: And so it was clearly understood, though, at senior levels, that Iran might try and meddle in Iraq?

DF: Absolutely.

HH: All right. Page 86, "I never heard any Pentagon official say that the war on terrorism could be won solely or even mainly by military means, and I never heard anyone in the administration contend that the U.S. should try and fight the war where the campaign's in Afghanistan and Iraq alone." It seems to me that these are obvious to folks who understand this, but not so obvious to the critics of the war. They want to believe it was unilateralist from the beginning, and they want to believe it was military only from the beginning. Obviously, we can't produce the case here, but I wanted you to comment on that, because [that's such a...] some people are simply not going to believe you, Doug Feith.

DF: Well, I realize that, which is why I quote from the documents that prove the point. I quote from the documents that show what we actually had in mind at the time. It's not a matter of my saying now in 2008 that we had these thoughts in our head. I'm quoting documents from 2001 and 2002 that show that we had a strong intention to have as broad a base of international support as possible. One of the reasons that the Bush administration got accused of being unilateralist is to be a unilateralist, you'd have to be an idiot. I mean, no sensible person would think that the United States is better off operating in the world by itself, when there's an opportunity to get other countries to work with us. And nobody in the administration that I ever heard supported unilateralism. And our opponents accused us of it, because it's such a damaging accusation. If we were unilateralist, we would deserve to be attacked of it, and we would deserve to be scorned for it. The fact is, we weren't unilateralist.

HH: Doug Feith, we talked about CIA failures, but in the run up to Iraq, there are two major State Department failures. First of all, we lost momentum at the UN between the President's speech and the failed attempt to get a second resolution. And I wanted to know, in your opinion, who made that decision to get the second resolution? Was that a Powell decision?

DF: Well, when we negotiated the first resolution, there was a question of what was going to be in it. And the people who wanted to try to block the United States, in particular the French, argued that there had to be a mandatory second resolution before the United States could take action. That, we resisted, and that did not make it into the resolution, the first resolution. But Colin Powell did argue that we could put somewhat diluted language about anticipating a possible second resolution into the first resolution. And that turned out to be a very costly, [that turned out to be, I think, a very costly] compromise.

HH: Clearly it was, yeah. What about the State's failure to secure the opening in Turkey? [There's...] military historians will be arguing for a long time whether the failure to bring the war to the Sunni Triangle through Turkey led to the insurgency. And it's an interesting thing. Victor Davis Hanson's written about that as well. That was a State Department failure, and you write very compellingly in <u>War And Decision</u>, they didn't see it coming.

DF: [Yeah, it was...I mean,] that was an extremely costly diplomatic failure, and I think that the State Department deserves some criticism for that. I wouldn't say that it's entirely their fault, but it was a problem, and Colin Powell did not go to Turkey once to deal with it, to meet with the Turks. I mean, I think Colin Powell had a lot of stature, and he's a very capable guy. And had he wholeheartedly thrown into the effort, and gone to Turkey, and talked to parliamentarians, we might have won a key issue in Turkey that we lost narrowly, which was their approval of the right of the 4th Infantry Division to transit through Turkey so that they could attack the Saddam regime from the North.

HH: Did Rumsfeld go and try and make that argument? Did anyone from Defense?

DF: Well, I mean, there were people involved. The diplomacy was largely being handled by Mark Grossman, who was a former U.S. ambassador to Turkey, and had a very good reputation in Turkey. He was the undersecretary of State, and Paul Wolfowitz, who was the deputy secretary of Defense, and was known as a good friend of Turkey. But I think we would have had a better chance of winning this narrow issue, this issue that we narrowly lost, if our chief diplomat had spent the time to go over and talk to Turkish parliamentarians.

HH: Doug Feith, I think it's going to be studied at places like the Kennedy School of Government for years as a manual on how to reverse presidential decisions without reversing the President's mind when it comes to the Iraqi occupation, and the transition to Iraqi control of their own life. It's as though the President never understood what was going on to a decision he had previously made. Can you give us the thumbnail version of what your office argued for, what the President decided to do, and how it got reversed?

DF: Well, the President talked about, from the very beginning, a strategy in Iraq of liberation, not occupation. And the

question was, how do you take that idea and put it into operation? How do you operationalize the idea of liberation rather
than occupation? And so what my office did was it came up
with a series of measures that would have gotten the Iraqis
involved to a much greater extent in the pre-war work, would
have given the Iraqis a role in working with our military forces
during the overthrow, and would have put important political
power into Iraqi hands soon after the overthrow of Saddam.
And we wanted to avoid setting up a U.S. occupation government. I mean, the thing that your listeners will remember is
that in Afghanistan, when the United States overthrew the
Taliban, we did not set up an occupation government. And
so what my office argued is we should use the Afghan model.
And when we overthrow Saddam, we should quickly set up
an Iraqi government that would be able to work with the
United States as a partner, and not work under the United
States with the United States serving as the role of occupation government. We did a plan for political transition in
post-Saddam Iraq that was based on that idea. The President
approved the plan, but inter-agency disputes between basically the Pentagon and parts of the White House on the one
hand, and State and CIA on the other, inter-agency disputes
about the value of working with Iraqi externals essentially
killed the plan, because when, even though the President had
approved it, when Ambassador Bremer was appointed the
lead U.S. civilian in Iraq, he wound up, over time, adopting
the State Department position that had failed to persuade the
President back in Washington, but did persuade Bremer in
Baghdad. And as a result, we wound up having a government
of occupation in Iraq for fourteen months.

HH: It's clear that you don't want to say anything too bad about
Paul Bremer in this book, that he was courageous, he took on
a very difficult task, he stayed through to the end, but he also
answered to no one but the President, and he was supposed to
answer to Rumsfeld, at least on paper. That's not a good way to
run something, is it?

DF: No, it was extremely badly run. And as I say in the book, the inter-agency process did not work as it was supposed to, Bremer's reporting chain, which had originally been laid out very explicitly, and he was supposed to report to Rumsfeld, got undone rather quickly. Bremer established reporting lines directly to the President, to Condi Rice, to Colin Powell, and as I pointed out, if you have three or four bosses, you effectively have no boss.

HH: But now we have this very interesting situation where the Petraeus-Crocker partnership has been working, spectacularly well. In fact, some people believe he's understating his success there out of a caution, an abundance of caution not to oversell, but to undersell and overperform. Who does he answer to? Is he answering to Gates? Is he answering to the President? Or is he, in essence, MacArthur in the desert?

DF: Well, I'm not in the Pentagon now, and I don't know exactly how it works. [I mean,] certainly in principle, General Petraeus answers to the Centcom commander, who answers to the Secretary of Defense. [I mean,] that's the textbook answer to your question. [I mean,] I think that General Petraeus has done so well, and has been so impressive in his discussions, in his conception of his operation, and in the results on the ground, that he gets an enormous amount of deference from everybody in the U.S. government. And so I think he's very influential, as he deserves to be, because of his success, and he has forged an excellent relationship with Ambassador Crocker. [And I mean,] one of the lessons that comes out of this, as I think comes out of some of the discussions in my book, is when you have an area where you have a major military operation, as in Afghanistan or Iraq, and you have the lead U.S. civilian official, and the lead U.S. military commander in close cooperation, our ability to accomplish things goes up enormously. And when you have tensions between, as existed between Bremer and our military commanders in Iraq at the time, General Sanchez and others, or General Abizaid at Centcom, when you have tensions between the civilian and the military leadership, they can undercut each other. And that's what happened during Bremer's tenure. But what we saw with Petraeus and Crocker, what we also saw with Khalilzad when he was in Afghanistan with General Barno, or Khalilzad when he was in Iraq with General Casey, when you had much better civilian-military cooperation, we had much better results on the ground.

HH: So why did the Bremer-Abizaid, or the Bremer-Casey relationship not work?

DF: Well, I don't know if I'm the best one to ask about that. That's something that deserves careful study, and I think it will get a lot of study, and by people who are focused on civilian-military relations. What I saw was that it wasn't working. I mean, exactly why it wasn't working, I don't consider myself an expert in. But I saw the bad results.

HH: Did the Iraqis draw from this an assumption that they had to remain contingent? There's some of this in your book, War And Decision, that they just were not going to work with a provisional authority that was going to hang around for a few years, because they'd get blown up, and they weren't going to be the puppets of the Americans. But was it, were they also sensing that there were two parties at war here, and I don't mean shooting war, but working against each other in the American set-up, and they had to figure out whether or not Abizaid or Bremer was going to win?

DF: [Well, they acted...when various bureaucratic debates,] you're absolutely right. And I think you put your finger on something extremely important, which is the key to our success in Iraq was getting cooperation from Iraqis. And when we send mixed signals, when we send signals of irresolution, when we send signals of internal disorder, we're creating disincentives for the Iraqis to cooperate with us. And then what they all do, they run off and they're trying to hedge their bets, and they're trying to secure themselves rather than cooperate with us.

HH: Doug Feith, when you started the Policy Counterterrorism Evaluation Group, what was your intention?

DF: I actually had a very modest intention, and that was to get people who worked for me in the policy organization to review the mountain of material that the intelligence community had been producing for many years about international terrorism networks.

HH: You came to be accused of running a secret neocon intelligence agency. There's some pretty funny rebuttals here, especially your exchange with Carl Levin. But actually, it was very damaging. It was very damaging to the war. [They,] people thought you were the guy who was running around planning regime change in places.

DF: [Yeah, no,] there were false things said about my office that did turn out to be very damaging to me and to the administration, and I think to our war effort. And I try to right a number of those wrongs in the book. The notion that I was setting up an alternative to the CIA is just ludicrous, and I explain the story in the book. And I mean, what basically happened was I came into my job in the middle of July of 2001, 9/11 occurred a few weeks later, I asked some people in my office to review the existing intelligence that went back for years in order to propose policies and strategies that we could use against the terrorist networks. That is exactly what policy people are supposed to do, and I had people doing that, and various conspiracy theorists spun that into an absolutely absurd tale of the Defense Department setting up an organization that was supposed to substitute for the CIA. Well, this group that I had looking at it was literally two people.

HH: One of whom eventually becomes a member of Congress from the Democratic Party. I found that amazing.

DF: Exactly. Exactly right.

HH: Now I've got to ask a tough, sensitive question here. Were you suspect because you are Jewish?

DF: Well, there have been some people who have made some very bigoted comments, attacking me and my motivation on the grounds that I'm Jewish, and have a long history of writing about Arab-Israeli issues, and writing in support of Israel. And people have made completely groundless, and I think really foul allegations that my motivation in working on all these things was not to serve the United States, but to serve Israel.

HH: And I think that is really one of the worst things that can be said, and a terrible insult. But I'm actually going to a more sophisticated point, not the naked anti-Semites, or even the close to naked anti-Semites. But on Page 170, you write, "State Department officials would often comment on these issues by arguing that nothing of importance could be done to push back against jihadist extremism until we resolve terrorism's root causes." And of course, that always means the Palestinian-Israeli war. And I just get the sense that for some people, they can't see the world because they're focused on this one issue in the war, Israel-Palestine, and that anyone who wants to talk on other than that immediately gets branded as an Israel firster. It just seems to me a disease in the State Department.

DF: Well, I agree completely, and it is a disease, and it's at this point, I think a politically significant disease. In other words, it's not a disease confined to just a few people on the fringes of our public policy debates. I mean, some of this thinking, which a few years ago, would have only been found on the lunatic fringe of American politics, you now hear in circles that really used to be respectable.

HH: Are you concerned about what you see on the Democratic side of this presidential campaign passing for conversation about the foreign affairs challenges we face, and the war that we are in?

DF: Well, I'm disturbed by people who deny that we are facing serious challenges to our country, to our security, to our constitutional system. I mean, I think that people should be clear-eyed about the problems that we have in the world, and intent on defending the country, and protecting what's important from those problems, and from those threats.

HH: Doug Feith, one of the key aspects of this book is that you deal again and again with key sidebar issues like the treatment of prisoners, the Geneva Conventions, the scandal that was Abu Ghraib. And you make it clear from the beginning that despite the propaganda and the political effort to damage the administration, that the President, Rumsfeld, you, lots of people, all from the beginning, Richard Myers comes through as saying we've got to do this right in the interest of the United States, the interest of our military, and that rogue sadists in Abu Ghraib should not be allowed to destroy, I mean, the overarching methods that you folks decided to put in, and did put in place. But unfortunately, it has.

DF: [Yeah, no,] it's hard to overstate how catastrophic the Abu Ghraib scandal was. [I mean,] this was basically a bunch of sexually depraved crazy people doing awful things for their own private, pornographic reasons. And it was not involved in interrogation. I mean, it was just disgusting, private behavior. And it harmed our country enormously, and has completely overridden the public's understanding of what the actual attitudes of the leadership of the Pentagon and of the administration were toward the Geneva Conventions, for example. [We took, and] I recount this, and I quote the relevant documents in my book...

HH: Yes, yes, you do.

DF: We took an extremely strongly pro-Geneva Convention position in the Pentagon. And what I said when I briefed Secretary Rumsfeld on this, and briefed the President on it, is we have troops all over the world. There is no country in the world that has a stronger interest in promoting respect for the Geneva Conventions than the United States, and there's no institution of the U.S. government that has a stronger interest in that than the Pentagon.

HH: So why do you suspect Secretary Powell in this interesting anecdote was so shocked that you would make this argument in the presence of the President?

DF: [Well, I mean,] I had a reputation, personally, as somebody who was very skeptical about a lot of proposals for international treaties. And I had a record of opposition to treaties that were not in the national interest in my view, treaties with unreliable, dictatorial regimes that would violate the treaties. And so I had a record on that subject, and from that, people simple-mindedly assumed that I was anti-treaty. Well, I was only anti-treaties that I didn't think served the national interest. And I think that the Geneva Conventions are basically a good treaty, and they are a part of the law of the United States, they're treaties in force, and I thought the Pentagon had an extremely strong interest in promoting respect for the Geneva Conventions.

HH: [It's a fascinating...] we don't have enough time to spend going through it, but I encourage people who have a perverse view of what the administration's record is to get <u>War And Decision</u>, if only for that. A couple of quick questions, Vice President Cheney, is his role in the framing of the war and its strategy been overstated, understated, or just about right?

DF: Well, I think it's basically been overstated. I mean, he's presented in some of the now-widespread conspiracy theorizing about the war as a kind of Svengali in the government. What I found in my exposure to him was mainly just in meetings of the National Security Council and the principal's committee. [He was a very,] his influence, as I saw it, derived from the fact that he's a very thoughtful, careful guy who is very measured, and rather sage and experienced in his comments about important issues. And he had a lot of just intellectual suasion.

HH: What did you make of the witch hunt against Libby?

DF: Oh, I think it was, it's just an absolute disgrace. I know Scooter very well, and I am confident that he is a truthful person, and I think that what happened is just a shame.

HH: I agree with that, but why did Armitage not come forward? How could that have happened in the middle of a war?

DF: [I mean,] I can't even imagine what went through Armitage's mind when he told the Justice Department that he was the source of the leak, and then allowed the President to be uninformed that he, Armitage, was the source of the leak, and allowed the President to go around saying that the leak represented a crime, when Armitage did not believe it was a crime, and knew that he was the source. [I mean,] I just think it was reprehensible that he would have stayed silent and allowed the President to be confused on that very important subject.

HH: It's not in the book, obviously, it's outside the scope of that, but I've got to ask you, Doug Feith, your opinion of the President, has he been the same guy on the first day as he is today? Much of this you watch from inside, the last two years from the outside, is it the same strategy? Is he the same purpose-driven President?

DF: Well, I think he probably in his mind has the same strategy. He doesn't have the same political capital that he had, and so you know, he's operating with different circumstances. It's not the kind of bold, decisive kind of operation that you had earlier on when you had a different political configuration in the country.

HH: Do you think he'll strike Iran before he leaves office?

DF: I don't know.

HH: Do you think he should?

DF: Well, what I would say is Iran is an extremely serious threat. And it would not be in our interest or the interest of the world in general for the Iranians to get nuclear weapons.

HH: I understand that, but it always comes down to, if it's going to be, if someone calls you up, Doug Feith, and says you were there, you know what we're up against, they're on the brink of weaponizing their nuclear program, what do we do? What does Doug Feith tell them to do?

DF: Well, what I would do if I were in the government is at that point, I would convene a meeting, I would try to look extremely carefully at what our options are, what we think we could accomplish. [I mean,] a large part of the answer depends on what you could actually accomplish through a military operation. And if a military operation were justified, I would say that the stakes are high enough that it's right for the President, as he always says, you know, to keep military options on the table. But there are a lot of very specific practical considerations that you would have to have before you would decide that a military option makes sense.

HH: Doug Feith, first of all, before I run out of time, thanks for spending this much time. It's a very important subject, and not a lot of authors will do the full three hours, and I appreciate your being willing to do so.

DF: Well, [I appreciate...] you're doing this the way you do everything, with a real seriousness of mind. And I'm delighted to talk with you.

HH: I want to close by talking about the American media, because I know the administration has had its failings in strategic communications, but the American media, generally speaking, is a complete disaster with regards to this. Are there any reporters out there that you admire for the job they have been doing when you were undersecretary and since?

DF: Yes, [I mean,] I think there are a lot of reporters in America, and some are better than others. And some are better on given subjects at given moments than at other times. [I mean, what I...] I review a number of real whoppers that people made, and you alluded to one of them earlier in the show when we were starting off in Afghanistan, and we were no more than three weeks into the war, there were a number of reporters that declared that we were in a quagmire, when in fact, we were something like ten days away from overthrowing the Taliban in what turned out to be a lightning war.

HH: And we had another quagmire during the dust storm in Iraq.

DF: Right. And then in Iraq, we wound up actually overthrowing the Iraqi government even more quickly than we overthrew the Afghan government. And it was about 21 days, and yet when the war was about ten days old, there was a sandstorm that slowed down the advance of the Marines and the Army for three days. And during that sandstorm, there were various reporters who came forward and talked about Stalingrad, a quagmire.

HH: Well, here's my last question, though. Can a free republic persevere in this difficult [of a] long war with a media that not only gets it wrong, but gleefully publishes top secret material, and constantly looks for sort of Darth Vader at the Pentagon, and in the administration? Is it possible, Doug Feith, to really win?

DF: Well, what I would say is it better darn well be possible, because that's the world we're living in. And we have serious threats, we have a number of major impediments. The way our press operates is in fact a major impediment to the United States being able to do what it needs to do in the world, but our leaders have to adapt, because that's just part of the strategic environment nowadays.

HH: And you are in favor of a free press, as I am. I know that from the book. But it's just sort of responsibility goes with that kind of power.

DF: No, it's true, but rather...I think we could have interesting discussions as we are now about the question of responsibility of journalists. But in the meantime, our leaders have to get better at what they do in explaining things to the public, in respecting the democratic rights of the public to know what's going on. I mean, my book is an effort to try to educate people.

HH: And well done. Doug Feith, thank you for all the time. War And Decision: Inside the Pentagon at the Dawn of the War on Terrorism.

End of interview.

Interview with Robert Kaplan
December 28, 2005

HH: Joining me to begin the conversation about the year around the globe, Robert D. Kaplan. He is the author of Imperial Grunts: The American Military on the Ground. He is also a correspondent for the Atlantic Monthly. He has been a guest on this program before. Robert Kaplan, thanks for spending some time with us this afternoon.

RK: It's my pleasure to be here, Hugh.

HH: I love this book, and I want to tell the audience it's probably the most influential book of 2005, because it's the book the president is reading right now. That's always got to give you a little bit of a pause, doesn't it, Robert Kaplan?

RK: Yes, it does. Certainly.

HH: I also noted in the author's note that it had its origin not only with Cullen Murphy of the Atlantic Monthly, but also Michael Kelly. Michael Kelly used to hold down this slot every Wednesday on this program until he deployed to Baghdad, where he was killed in the march to Baghdad. What's the origin of this, and can you explain the project for the audience.

RK: Yes. This started as a group of magazine articles to the Atlantic Monthly, supported by Cullen Murphy of the Atlantic, and Michael Kelly. And Michael Kelly's best writing, I believe, was actually done in the days before he was killed outside Baghdad. He was reporting about the troops as they saw themselves. He had some phrase that it was their history, and somebody needed to tell it. Well, everyone has to do things in their own way, and I can't replicate him, of course. But what I tried to do as this project got going was I realized that the media was writing about...you know, especially after the insurgency began, as the troops as victims, as demoralized, in some very rare cases as war criminals, as complexified morally. And that all accounted for about 2% of the troops I met. The other 98% saw themselves as warriors for good. But they had no voice. So what I decided to do was [I would do] at least two books traveling around the world, living in the barracks, not just in Iraq and Afghanistan, but in Colombia, the Philippines, many other places. To kind of write a postcard for posterity about this impoverished tactical existence that these American troops were living at the turn of the 21st Century. And the only other correspondents that I really related to were people from earlier generations like Ernie Pyle and Richard Tregaskis, and others who used the word, the pronoun we, rather than they, when referring to the troops.

HH: You're also drawing on a tradition, though, that has ancient roots, whether or not it's Thucydides or Tacitus, about people who have been where the battles have been fought, and who reported back…and even Caesar's dispatches from Gaul. And there's quite a lot of classical references sprinkled throughout this book.

RK: [Yes, it's probably…you know,] without taking on airs, but you know, of all the classical writers, the one I admire the most is Herodotus, because Herodotus doesn't write about one subject. He describes landscape. He describes personalities. He give stories. He kind of recreates a world of what people believe. And what I tried to do was a travel book. And by a travel book, I mean something very specific. [I mean] you don't throw a microphone in front of a sergeant's face, and ask him a direct question. You reveal him to the reader as he reveals himself to you over days and weeks. Sometimes, I wouldn't even take out a notebook until I knew somebody for a week. In other words, don't define them on your terms. Let them define themselves on their terms, and their problems and frustrations on their terms, and you be the kind of vehicle to the reader.

HH: Now I will go back and forth through the chapters in the world that you have traveled. I want to give people a summary, though. You began not long after 9/11, and you have in this volume of your work, covered places as far flung as Yemen and Colombia. You've been to Mongolia. You've been to the Philippines, of course Iraq, Afghanistan, Pakistan, and the Horn of Africa. Was there any method to this travel? Or was it simply handing off the baton from one special forces or Marine officer to another who would accommodate you?

RK: The method was the people I met. One of the suppositions of this book is that Americans, and the American military, don't like the word imperialism. They're uncomfortable with it. But the United States does find itself in an imperial-like situation around the world, where much of what the troops do, especially training missions, governance missions, are best related to what the British, the French, the Dutch, the Portuguese, during their periods of high empire, did. And so, the method to the travel was that I would meet a major in Yemen, or a Coast Guard officer in Yemen, who would tell me about people he knew in Colombia. And then I'd go to Colombia, and I'd hear about this fellow in Mongolia. And in Mongolia, I'd hear about this operation in the Philippines. So the very method of my traveling was proof of a worldwide imperial-like military, where people had interconnections around the world.

HH: Last night, Robert Kaplan, at dinner, I was telling a United States Congressman about the manager of the Coast Guard in Yemen as an example of the extraordinary kind of people the American military produces...offered admission to Stanford. He couldn't afford it. He went off to the Coast Guard Academy, found himself retired after 9/11, called back to duty, and now, he's one of ourPro-Consulars, really, in Yemen, building a navy.

RK: Yes, one of the things that I think really kind of unnerved the elite, is that while there are all these conferences and discussions in Washington and elsewhere about should we support Afghan warlords or not, should we create an Afghan national army or not, what should our foreign policy be in Yemen or Colombia or in Iraq. I discovered a world of basically working-class people, who were operationally far more sophisticated and knowledgeable about all these issues, who spoke languages, who had personalities that didn't fit into any one neat division. They were evangelical, but they spoke two exotic languages. [People like that who...] so while all these discussions are taking place, foreign policy is being enacted on the ground by majors and sergeants and lieutenants, who are utterly oblivious to most of these discussions. And you know what? They're doing these things very, very well.

HH: And they're very clear-eyed. In Yemen, a U.N. retired special forces officer, working for the U.N. now, described his mission as doing favors for everyone until the day came he had to get his people out, and he would collect. That's very clear-eyed.

RK: Yes, and who is this U.N. officer? He's a retired American army special forces lieutenant colonel, and this is proof that I've seen this around the world, that when the U.N. has a real important tactical mission to do, it hires Americans, Australians and Brits to do it. And then the U.N. takes the credit.

HH: Robert Kaplan, before we get into the specifics of where you went and what you found there, does America have enough capacity...I'm [...I mean] overwhelmed, actually, by reading this book, how many places we are, and how many enormous tasks there are to do, and the burden on the military. Is it big enough, is it deep enough to accomplish this?

RK: It's an easy question to answer, Hugh. There's no imperial overstretch with 70-80 missions per week in like 50 different countries, because in each of these places, we have ten people, we have twenty, or we have fifty or sixty. We're dealing with small numbers. The big problem is Iraq, where you have 150,000. And that overstretches the system. So the system is not overburdened by being deployed in 50 or 80 countries, or the Air Force having missions in, say, 190 countries. But the system is overburdened when you have tens of thousands of troops in even one country.

HH: And so you've described how we were in the Garrison age, but we've moved to the Expeditionary Age, but Iraq is sort of a precarious mixing of the two?

RK: Yes, and [it's also...] you know, people say America's imperialist. It's bad because it's in Iraq. Actually, Iraq is a perversion of intelligent imperialism, rather than an accurate expression of it, because the British and the French and the others were at their best when they had small numbers of troops training host country militaries, so that the British were not overextended financially, or in any other sense. And so American military influence works best when we have the least...when our military footprint on the ground is the smallest. I've seen one man accomplish miracles in Mongolia. I've seen dozens do great work in Algeria this past summer when I was working for Volume II. I've seen hundreds do great work in the Philippines and Colombia, where treading water with ten thousand or so in Afghanistan, and 150,000, whatever one's views on Iraq, does constitute a mess.

HH: Thirty seconds to a break, Robert Kaplan. Is it fair to say that the American military, with whom you've been spending, is deeply discriminatory on a gender basis by necessity, and absolutely egalitarian as to race and religion?

RK: Yes, that's true. Relations between whites and blacks in the barracks, in religious ceremonies, are much better than in society at large.

HH: Robert Kaplan, I want to talk about three specific places that you mention in the book, in this order. North Waziristan, which someone described to you as the most evil place on Earth. I want to talk to you about the Philippines, where the Abu Saaef terrorists are just about as savage as they go, until I remember that back in Colombia, among the FARC, in the border region with Venezuela, you described atrocities that people simply would only consider fables if they were in ancient text. We're up against truly evil people.

RK: Yes, we are. Keep in mind that throughout the Earth, there are all these regional separatist movements with barbaric techniques. And a good deal of them have some kind of like overlapping, strategic affinity with the goals of al Qaeda. It doesn't mean they have the same objective. It means their interests overlap. So think of al Qaeda as kind of a loose, post-modern organization that's weak at the center, strong at the edges, that doesn't demand absolute affinity of views with a lot of its allies. So the U.S. military is in this position of going to the Afghan/Pakistan border, where North Waziristan is, going to the southern Philippines, going to the Colombian/Venezuelan border, and kind of efficiently using an economy of force, force multiplication strategy, of just a few teams of special forces training the host country military to do the lion share of the work.

HH: But the host country militaries...are they capable of absorbing the sort of training that the special forces are willing to give them, in as short of a period of time as we have?

RK: Yes, they are, because what we do is we don't train just recruits. We train their best units. And not only do we train their best units in Colombia or the Philippines, we train the trainers of the best units, so that our methods can be replicated and carried on within these countries. And it's important to keep in mind that we have U.S. military training missions throughout the world. There are so many of them that the Marines are taking the burden from special forces in many cases. As we speak, Hugh, the United States Marines are [training...] retraining the entire Georgian military to kind of consolidate the gains of the Rose democratic revolution in the former Soviet republic. And in every single case, we're dealing with legitimated democracies. We're not around the world propping up dictatorships. You know, that may have been true thirty or forty years ago. But the reality today is there was an explosion of democracies in the 90's, and you cannot have an age of democratization without an age of military professionalization. If we don't professionalize these militaries, they won't stay democratic for long.

HH: That, I think, goes to the core issue in Iraq. It's not just training an Iraqi army. It's training one that will not immediately go to a coup situation, but will in fact support a long evolving pluralism. Is that working?

RK: Yes. I mean, all societies, democratic or not, have to begin with some sort of professional security structure. Freedom is impossible without authority. And so what we are doing is we are training the core element of authority in Iraq, the army and the police. I just got back, as it happens, from a month in Iraq, observing this throughout the northern half of the country.

HH: I am fascinated by the chapter on the Philippines for a couple of reasons. One, my dad was stationed in Zamboanga sixty years ago...

RK: Oh, really?

HH: And then he went on to Japan to be part of the occupation army there. Japan has stabilized and transitioned. But the portrait you paint of Philippines, of the klepto-oligarchy, [and of this...this is a truly...] I had very little grasp of how insidious the Abu Saaef guerillas are. Are you an optimist about the Philippines?

RK: Not really. I'm not a pessimist, either. I think that the Philippines will be a more accurate barometer for the U.S.' ability to manage the world, than Iraq will be, because we've been involved in the Philippines going back a hundred years. We invaded the country. We fought a long, difficult counter-insurgency there a hundred years ago. We developed the country. There's strong ties with the U.S. and the Philippines islands. But there's very few other places where the Chinese are more active now, trying to displace us.

HH: Oh, how so? Explain to people...

RK: Yeah, so the Philippines is the ultimate barometer to [kind of...] the relative power between the United States and China in the coming decade.

HH: A sidebar, Robert Kaplan, because I want people to understand this. I don't think of you as political at all. I don't know if you're a Democrat or a Republican. I think of you as an observer. Is that fair?

RK: It's fair, but I do definitely have a classical conservative sensibility.

HH: [But you're not writing a political...] you're not laying out an agenda for the military here.

RK: No, no. And there are many places in the book where I do express strong points of view, but they're on tactical issues.

HH: Yes, okay.

RK: Yeah, very rarely on strategic issues. For instance, I'm very hard on the regular army for too much bureaucracy in Afghanistan. Things like that I come down with strong opinions.

HH: What do you hear the officers of the military say about Rumsfeld and Bush?

RK: It's important not to become polemical about Donald Rumsfeld. [He's done...] the bad things, the mistakes he's made in Iraq are well known. We don't need to belabor them. But a lot of the good things he's done are things that the military appreciates, but because we have a media establishment that hasn't served in the military, it's something they don't appreciate and aren't interested in. For instance, NATO and European command were for long decades always ruled by American army generals. They became regular army mafias, so to speak. Rumsfeld appointed a Marine to head NATO as the supreme allied commander in Europe, General Jim Jones. And what he has done is refitted NATO in a leaner, meaner form, for an expeditionary age, so that NATO will have a real purpose. Rusmfeld has tried to kind of end in a soft manner the big navy mafia in the Pacific command, by trying to appoint an Air Force general to shake things up, to give the Chinese something to think about. He didn't succeed for other reasons, but the writing is on the wall there. His emphasis when he got in on special forces, and a lot of small deployments all over the world, rather than a few big ones, are all things that had to be done. His tragedy is that he understood the world of the future, which is a world of more special forces, a regular army that needs to reform drastically if it's going to survive, but he got himself involved in a war where he required the very forces that he knew he would have to make obsolete twenty and thirty years hence. So that made him conflicted about the number of regular army troops he needed in Iraq.

HH: Robert Kaplan, do you regret, personally, that we went to war in Iraq?

RK: No, I do not. I've been going back to Iraq since 1984. The only way I can describe Saddam's regime is think of Eastern Europe before Stalin died in 1953. It was like the worst, darkest regimes in Eastern Europe in the late 1940's. Had we not gone into Iraq, the sanctions would have been lifted, all the scientists from the ex-Soviet Union, the nuclear and other scientists, would have flooded back there. The U.N. sanctions would have been lifted. And the problems we would have now would probably be equally as bad, though of a different nature.

HH: I have saved for this relatively short section of our hour, Robert Kaplan, the six minute section, a discussion about Colombia, because this chapter unnerved me. I've always been aware that we send troops and money down there, and I read the Tom Clancy novel. But until you describe what's going on, on the Venezuelan border, and how Chavez is actually trading drug money and guns to Arab terrorists, and how the FARC is just a maniacal organization. It really did not drive home the strategic importance of this front. Can you expand on what you saw there in Colombia, what Americans generally don't know about what's going on down there?

RK: Yes. [Colombia to me...] I've been all over Iraq. I was in the Battle of Fallujah with the Marines. I've never been to a place that felt as dangerous as Colombia. You can't go from one Colombian city to another without flying. And Colombia does more kidnapping than any country in the world, per capita. Colombian narco-terrorists are as brutal and cruel as the worst al Qaeda people. We have a great opportunity in Colombia. If you ask me, Hugh, who is the most impressive leader in the third world, I would say President Álvaro Uribe Vélez of Colombia. He has risked his own life. He is a constitutional democrat. He has made big in-roads against these narco-terrorists. His approval rating after six years in office is still 70%, in a fully democratic society with a feisty media. When a commando operation goes wrong, he takes full responsibility on television. And what we are doing is we are backing up this man, because it is the only chance we have. And President Chavez of Venezuela is trying to undermine Colombia. I've walked along that border. It's a very porous border divided by just a narrow stream in the middle of the jungle. The FARC controls large areas of the country, in almost like a sovereign manner. When you think of the ark of instability in the world, don't just think of the greater Middle East. It's everywhere, because Arab terrorist groups are active. They are there in Venezuela, in

Maracaibo, in Margarita, in islands off the Venezuelan coast. So there is like a strategic alliance with drug criminals and the Arab terrorists, because the Arab terrorists have...what [they have] is they have expertise in car bombs, things like that, where the narco-terrorists have money. Billions of dollars of it. And they also have sovereign territory, so to speak.

HH: Does the intelligence gathering the military is about every day backed up by the NSA and other intelligence...does that keep us ahead of them effectively? Or are we always struggling to catch up with a basically irregular army of guerillas, with much greater mobility and firepower than anything we've dealt with before?

RK: In terms of Colombia, we have linguistic advantages. It's not like the Middle East. Almost all special forces officers, whether they're of Latin descent or not, speak fluent Spanish. So we're really ahead of the game there. The problem is not getting intelligence. It's [getting...you know, like] sighting criminals or leaders of organizations, whether it's Zarqawi in Iraq or it's the leading FARC officers in Colombia. I saw this in Iraq, where there were a lot of sightings in the battalion in which I was embedded, of Zarqawi. You can get sightings of people. But the person who sights the person has to be able to communicate it in real time, and then there needs to be an operational element ready to like go out immediately.

HH: And is that lacking in some of the...

RK: Yeah. It's a real bureaucratic challenge.

HH: Yeah, you write that up in the Colombia chapter.

RK: A real military transformation is bureaucratic transformation. Wherever it is, Colombia and Iraq, it's about pushing power out to the edges of command, giving young lieutenants and captains and staff sergeants more and more power and autonomy.

HH: A quick glimpse. I want to jump over the globe to Mongolia, where you write the Mongolians, even though occupied for 80 years by the Soviets, are more afraid of the Chinese, and deathly afraid of SARS. Now probably Avian Flu. Why is this?

RK: First of all, there are very few Russians living in the Siberian border regions near Mongolia. But China is a demographic immensity that [is not only overwhelmed, it] threatens to overwhelm Mongolia. But it's overwhelming Soviet East Asia. China is this surging economy, surging population zone. Mongolia is only 2 million people spread over a vast area. A million of them live in the greater capitol city area of Ulan-Bator. Mongolia is part of the former Manchu Dynasty. It's the only part of the mainland Manchu Dynasty that the Chinese have yet to reincorporate.

HH: Mr. Kaplan, I said this as we were going to break. I want to talk to you about China and the American military. A couple of times, maybe three times, unprompted by me, you brought China into the conversation...

RK: Yes.

HH: ...about the Philippines, other places. They are also a full frontal challenge to the American military. They're building a blue water navy. What is going on with the Chinese military? What should the American person listening right now know about that?

RK: Here's the American challenge. For the last fifty years, the American Navy has been able to treat the whole Pacific Ocean as an American light. That is not going to be the case for the next fifty years. The Chinese Navy is pushing out asymmetrically. There's a tremendous emphasis not on across the board development, but on submarines, and on missiles that can hit moving targets in the middle of the ocean. The Chinese are obsessed with the ability to attack an American aircraft carrier. That doesn't mean they will. That doesn't mean they'll have any motive to even threaten it. But the very fact that they could do it will affect our carrier movements, will constrain our own carrier movements, and thus, affect the balance of power in the Pacific. So the big challenge is how to accommodate China's legitimate re-emergence as a great power, without a serious cold war or a hot war occurring, that could really disturb the peace of the world.

HH: And are you an optimist about that?

RK: Yes, I am, because I think that our military leadership in Honolulu, which is the headquarters of Pacific command, is far less ideological than people in Washington, D.C. They're not liberals, they're not neo-conservatives. They basically understand that the worst thing that could happen is if we provoke the Chinese too much. But they also understand that unless we set limits for the Chinese, we will have real problems with them.

HH: Now I want to conclude our time together by talking about the American military. I'm a civilian, but I married into a military family. My wife was born on Quantico. I was married on Pendleton. They've lived all around the world with the Marines. And you spent...one of your chapters in North Carolina with both special forces and Marines. And there's a lot of very interesting stuff in here, especially about the rhetoric we hear that the American military is tired and worn out. Your commentary?

RK: My commentary is that...and I just came back from Iraq, and I spent six months a year in the barracks, is that I've only met two kinds of Army Special Forces and front line Marines: Those who have fought in Iraq and Afghanistan, and those who are pulling every bureaucratic string to get deployed there. Morale has never been better. It's much better than in the 1990's, where the military was not really allowed to do anything. Front line combat troops are like artisan writers. They want to be active in their chosen profession. As I said, morale has never been better, and the one complaint I hear is we can get this thing done in Iraq. It may take a few years longer than people think, but the weakest link is the home front.

HH: You know, a few years ago, Thomas Ricks of the Washington Post wrote <u>Making the Corps</u>...

RK: Great book.

HH: ...that really interested me in the civilian/military divide that he worried about. Do you see that growing or narrowing?

RK: I see it growing, because this is the first time in history where you have an intellectual media governmental elite, [where people don't have anyone...] where [have] very few people who've served in the military within their own social circle. One of the things you see in Iraq, you see all these soldiers, Marines, private contractors, and they're all from the South, the greater South, the Mid-West, the Great Plains. And they all e-mail their families every single night about what's going on. And so people in other parts of the country are far more cosmopolitan and sophisticated about what's going on in Iraq now, than people on the two coasts of California and New York.

HH: Now what about the American military's rock-solid tradition [for...] since the country was founded, even before it, of unwaveringly listening to and following civilian orders. Are you ever worried, Robert Kaplan...you've spent a lot of time in both politics and military, about the temptation that overcame Rome, in the era of empire as well...

RK: Absolutely not. I am not worried at all about that. The one thing...in fact, and just to really bring this down, Hugh, to concrete terms. You know, I've heard conversations in the barrack...well, what if Hillary Clinton were elected? And people say well, if she's the commander-in-chief, she's the commander-in-chief. We'll respect her as much as President Bush.

HH: If, in fact, 9/11 had succeeded, and had decapitated American leadership, what would have happened, Robert Kaplan?

RK: If it had decapitated...well, that's a big question.

HH: Would the military have assumed control, and then given it back? That's the bottom line.

RK: Absolutely. Absolutely. In fact, the military now, another tactical frustration they have in Iraq, is they say, "Where is the State Department?" We want desperately to hand over responsibility to USAID, the State Department. Now, the State Department may be an unhealthy agency. It may be in desperate need of reform. The military knows it can do a better job than these civilian government departments. And yet nevertheless, they are very uncomfortable with their expanding role.

HH: Crucial question, Robert Kaplan. After all these years and deployments, and thousands of hours with American military, and summing it up, do you expect, do they expect that al Qaeda will successfully attack the United States again on United States soil?

RK: [They have...] you know, militaries have to think in worst case scenarios, or else they wouldn't be doing their job. And their assumption is that it will happen. And if they didn't assume that, they wouldn't be doing their jobs.

HH: And do you hear about weapons of mass destruction in the hands of these various evil forces that we've been talking about?

RK: All the time, because we live in a time of history, where weapons of mass destruction are in the hands [of very emotional...] or getting into the hands of very emotional people without the bureaucratic control mechanisms that say the late Soviet Union had. So wherefore the Soviet Union may have been evil and communist, it was also very conservative and responsible, bureaucratically, in terms of handling such weapons.

HH: So is it a tale designed to scare people? Or is it a reality of a nuke in the hands of people who would try to get it here?

RK: It's not a tale. It's not a fable. It's a reality that the U.S. military lives with.

HH: Robert Kaplan, when's the next one come out?

RK: Well, probably not for two or three years, Hugh.

HH: Well, it's a magnificent achievement. My hat is off to you. I mean, you've really reduced most writers to feeling like bystanders, but congratulations and enjoy the rest that...the military told you what? Take a few months off and then get back on the ground?

RK: That's right. Thank you so much, Hugh.

HH: Thank you. Robert Kaplan, author of <u>Imperial Grunts: On the Ground with the American Military</u>. I cannot, simply cannot encourage you strongly enough to read this, because it's factual. It's not written by the tubas of the media, in a seminar room on the Charles. It is the real story of the real challenges, and the real men who are fighting and facing them down around the globe, in the hands of a craftsman, Robert Kaplan.

End of interview.

Interview with Robert Kaplan
January 26, 2006

HH: Everything going on, but in the middle of all that, there's been one theme. I don't know if you've listened to it very closely. I keep bringing up a book. It's a book called <u>Imperial Grunts</u>. I've had its author on before, but now I'm rejoined by Robert Kaplan, because Robert, I want to talk to you a little bit about this. Welcome back. Thanks for making some time this afternoon.

RK: It's my pleasure to be here, Hugh.

HH: Now Robert, I asked the Vice President and the Secretary of Defense, and neither of them yet had the chance to read your book. But I asked them specifically about the idea that Special Forces at the forward operating bases, which you described in meticulous detail in Afghanistan and other places, are being constrained by a big Army, as you put it, at Bagram and other places, and they deflected the question. And I didn't have enough time to push them and go deep on this. They just were non-responsive. What do you think that indicates?

RK: Well, I think to be fair to them, it indicates how decentralized the system is. I'll tell you a story. I had a piece on U.S. Marines training in a country in sub-Saharan Africa,

Niger. And it reached the office of the Secretary of Defense, and some people said, "Wow, we had no idea we had people there!" And that would have happened if William Cohen was Secretary of Defense, William Perry. It's not a reflection on the Republicans. It's a reflection of how de-centralized the system is. Unless there's something uniquely controversial about the deployment, this is something that's going to be decided at the level of European command and Stuttgart, if it's Africa for instance. So let's get back to the Special Forces bases. These are issues that are basically decided, in the case of an Army Special Forces, a forward operating base, or fire base as they call it, in Afghanistan, it would be decided at the level of the two star general at Bagram, in Afghanistan, and would not go up to the Secretary of Defense. The Secretary of Defense may have like an overarching order that I want as little bureaucracy as possible. I want our people unconstrained. But the problem is that those are all general commands, which can be interpreted in so many different ways as you go down the chain. And the Vice President being further above, probably knows even less about this.

HH: That's remarkable. But it is a real problem. Is it getting remedied?

RK: See, this goes back to one of the main points in my book, that many of the policy discussions in Washington and New York are so ill-informed, because they often know even less than these people about how all this stuff is being carried out.

HH: Right.

RK: And the people who are best qualified to, say, write an op-ed is a staff sergeant somewhere, who would never even think of reading the editorial page of a newspaper, let alone submitting an op-ed.

HH: Right.

RK: My in-feeling is that things have gotten better.

HH: All right. Now Francis Harvey, Secretary of the Army, was also my guest in the last week, and I asked him where are we going with Special Forces in terms of numbers. He said 16,000 by '09. Is that enough?

RK: Right. Yeah, in the quadrennial defense review, which I think will be out next month, I expect to see a whopping increase in Army Special Forces. I believe right now there are about 9,000 Green Berets over about five active duty groups, and two National Guard reserve groups. So that's going to go up by about a third or so. But remember, you cannot produce Special Operations Forces overnight. It takes years to produce them. That's why they're special. So what it means is they will begin recruiting, in the hope of training and develop... and ramping up this force from 9 to 16,000 over the next two or three years or so. But again, let me emphasize that the real issue, in terms of our military is not Special Ops, it's the regular Army.

HH: Now Robert Kaplan, I want to again know the book is Imperial Grunts. I've linked it many times at Hughhewitt.com. Go to Amazon.com. And I've been through it now twice. It's really epic. And I want to ask this question particularly of you, because I don't think there's an American journalist at work today who has spent more time with the American military over the last three years. I think that's just an objective statement.

RK: Well, let me put it this way. There are a lot of great reporters doing great work, men and women, in Iraq and Afghanistan. But it's very hard to find people who even want to go to all these other places that I've been. And in many cases, it's not because they lack the curiosity or willingness. It's that they can't get their editors to assign them to go.

HH: Sure. But there are lots who don't exactly want to deploy from Kuwait across the Iraqi desert as you did in that last great wheeling motion with the Marines. That was fascinating, logistically.

RK: Yeah, well that's one of the advantages, Hugh, of being a magazine writer, and not writing on deadline, and having to file a great piece in three or four days.

HH: Right.

RK: You know, it's one of the advantages of being able to let a piece marinate and develop over weeks.

HH: Well, yesterday in the Los Angeles Times, a young writer, not so young, 35, by the name of Joel Stein, wrote a piece that began, "I don't support the troops," and ended with a declaration that parades should not be given for them when they return. Did you see that piece, Robert?

RK: No, I didn't. Frankly, I didn't.

HH: If you have a chance to, I would encourage you to read it and write something. And I actually hope you'll put it in the L.A. Times, because it needs to be answered by someone like you. But when you see someone who is esteemed by many as a fine talent and a writer, write "I don't support the troops," what are they missing?

RK: Well, first of all, I had a piece in the L.A. Times, to be fair to the L.A. Times, in late December, making the exact opposite point. And the piece basically said that the future of America is being written in Iraq, because all the future great politicians are right now captains and lieutenants in Iraq and Afghanistan. Because they will be the first greatest generation in history that will have real on the ground democratic governance experience, unlike previous war veterans that we've had.

HH: Oh, that's interesting.

RK: All right. Basically, what I think they're missing is that we frankly live in a society [that has been...] that is divided up into all these sub-groups, because of its size and complexity. We have not had a draft for a third of a century, so that the military is this mysterious kind of vestigial other. There's something like retrograde about it. People feel they have to say nice things about it. [It's not, you know, it's not...] in good polite company now, you always have to praise the troops. But deep down, particularly on the left, though obviously a lot of people on the left don't fall into this category, but a sizeable minority do. There's just this roiling kind of angst that they really don't support the troops. And the reason is because they have no real social connection with troops.

HH: That's actually how I...

RK: I mean, their social connection is limited to like watching a retired general on TV, or going to a seminar and hearing Wesley Clark or something like that, or maybe, if they're really, really curious, they'll hear a few colonels [at the Council on Foreign Rela...] who are always fellows at the Council on Foreign Relations, or who are always fellows at the Harvard Kennedy School. But of course, as you and I know, high-ranking officers, as high-ranking officers will tell you, is not at all what the military's about.

HH: Yeah, I was unfair to him when I had him on the air yesterday, because I pop quizzed how much do these guys make, and I'd read your book, so I was up to speed on everything.

RK: Yeah, you know, this is a reflection about how...like the military is a whole separate branch of society that a lot of policy people, intellectual...they're people they never encounter around the Thanksgiving dinner table.

HH: Last question, Robert Kaplan. And I hope before you deploy again, we'll talk to you at length, because I'd like to go chapter by chapter. The drone took out Zawahiri's buddies. That said to me that we're getting much more aggressive than when you were there. Did it say the same thing to you?

RK: It said something analogous, but different. It's that we've solved some diplomatic issues with the Pakistani government, that allows us to operate over the border in a way that we couldn't in '03 when I wrote that chapter. We've somehow come to some understanding in a very [like] unwritten, informal way with Musharraf, that there are things we can do now that we couldn't do a year or two ago.

HH: And that's what's going to be fascinating when you go back, is how our imperial grunts have seen the world change in front of them as they've deployed. When are you going back?

RK: Well, actually, I'm leaving Sunday for a month with the Air Force in Korea and Thailand. And...

HH: You're going to Korea in January?

RK: Yes. I've got to do it. I mean, a real traveler goes to places during the worst time of year.

HH: I'm trying to remember Chaim Potok's book about light. It's about a Korean guy, or an American stationed there in the Winter, and it made me freezing just to read it.

RK: Yeah. But in the Spring, I hope to be back in Colombia for the first time in three years, back in the Philippines for the first time in two years, back in sub-Saharan Africa for the first time in a year and a half, all with the same units.

HH: Whenever you get near a phone, Robert Kaplan, please call us and let us know if you feel like talking.

RK: Well, it's a pleasure you having me on, Hugh. Thank you so much.

HH: Thank you. Make sure you get that book, America. Imperial Grunts. If you want to fill in the knowledge gap, that's the place to begin. Imperial Grunts.

End Interview.

Interview with Robert Kaplan
September 20, 2007

HH: It's a long interview with an author who deserves a lot of time. Robert D. Kaplan is the author of the new book, Hog Pilots, Blue Water Grunts: The American Military in the Air, at Sea, and on the Ground. Previously, Robert Kaplan's been on this program as the author of Imperial Grunts and on a number of other occasions, on a number of other subjects. Welcome back, Robert Kaplan, great to have you on the Hugh Hewitt Show.

RK: It's my pleasure to be here, Hugh.

HH: You know, I want to begin in the 9th chapter of this, your second book on the American military, as you were driving out of Timbuktu, 11 hours beyond the gates of Timbuktu. Use that as a metaphor for what you were doing and why you went the places you have gone.

RK: Well, Timbuktu is not the edge of the Earth. The edge of the Earth is miles beyond Timbuktu, north into the heart of the Sahara desert. And I was with a company of American Special Forces officers, about twelve of them, all non-commissioned officers except for a captain. And you would think what is the U.S. military doing in the heart of the Sahara desert. Well, we're not only in the heart of the Sahara desert, we're all over the Pacific ocean, we'll all over South America, and all this is occurring while we are fighting a war in Iraq and in Afghanistan. And what I tried to do in the course of the years in which I embedded with the military was to show the whole thing. Not to ignore Iraq, but not to be limited by it, either, because one big deployment might overstretch us like Iraq, but dozens upon dozens of smaller deployments will do no such thing. So I was with a company of American Special Forces officers who were investigating just what was in the center of the Sahara desert in terms of al Qaeda movements, humanitarian, prospects for humanitarian relief, just getting to know Africa. Because [in] this global world war on terrorism, really is a global war.

HH: Now you're accompanied by, extraordinary in the course of this book, an extraordinary array of Americans, one of which on this particular trip is an Evangelical staff sergeant from Oklahoma who doesn't want to be identified, because he doesn't want his deeds to serve himself. I thought that was another metaphor for the extraordinary people you've spent the last many years with.

RK: [Yeah, the people I...what I did was] I didn't report on anybody in this book. I befriended a lot of people, and revealed them to the reader as they revealed themselves to me. And the best of these people didn't want any publicity, not because they were afraid of being written up badly, but because they were afraid of getting public recognition for anything they do. For them, the real sweet thing is to do it and not get recognition, if you can believe it. And this Evangelical staff sergeant, he drove most of the way through blistering sandstorms, he slept only six hours, which was interrupted by an hour and a half of guard duty, and he got up the next morning to fit little African children for eye glasses as part of a civil affairs project that this Special Forces A-team was doing. And just, you know, just dealt with one child, one woman after another throughout the morning without any complaining about lack of sleep or anything.

HH: Let me tell the audience, this is a remarkable read, you're going to want to get <u>Hog Pilots, Blue Water Grunts</u>, and just an example of detail, "Following sun up, Captain Tory, an Evangelical staff sergeant from Oklahoma, set up an eye clinic inside one of the ruins. They unpack little boxes of adaptable eyewear, an ingenious, low-tech device manufactured by the U.S. Agency for International Development. These were round, Harry Potterish horn-rimmed glasses of zero prescription which increasingly strengthened as you pumped a clear gel solution attached to the frame inside the glass. The SF, Special Forces guys called them, 'never get laid again glasses,' because of how they made you look." Now that has got an eye for detail, pardon the pun, Robert Kaplan, but I guess it is in those very small things, as well as the B-2's that we'll talk about later, that the genius in the American military lies.

RK: Yeah, it all lies in the details. For the price of one F-22, you could populate all of Africa with SF-A teams doing humanitarian relief. But that is not necessarily a criticism of an F-22, because I get that later in the book when I talk about the 8-2 and other expensive bombers, which are sort of an expensive form of health insurance to keep the Chinese honest about their intentions in Taiwan. But you know, we get bargains in our military budget, and we don't. The 8-2's, the F-22's, there's no bargains there. But in terms of what we can do on the ground in a place like Africa, we get a lot of bargains like this deployment that I embedded on.

HM: Now Robert Kaplan, having set the table and hopefully got the hook into the listener, and I don't think it's very hard to do with this book, I want to back up and tell them a little bit about you. Your bio reads you're a correspondent for the Atlantic Monthly, you're the author of 11 previous books on foreign affairs and travel, many of which are just riveting, some of which have brought you audiences like President Bush at the White House, and an appointment at the United States Naval Academy as the class of 1960 distinguished visiting professor in national security at the USNA. Tell me what your, what's your motive? Why are you doing this?

RK: My motive [is,] as I said earlier, is without this book, these people would not have a voice, Hugh. And by these people, I mean all of the sailors in the U.S. Navy who are aboard submarines and aboard frigates and destroyers, all these Special Forces officers who are on deployments in Africa, South America and Asia, all these forgotten deployments, number one. And even many of those in Iraq and Afghanistan, where all you read, often, is troubling news. And what I'm doing is I'm not whitewashing anything. I'm befriending people and letting them reveal themselves to the reader as they reveal themselves to me. Without a book like this, these people would stay hidden, they would be silent. And I really believe that they deserve, you know, they deserve their voice, their recognition, too. That's what's really motivating me.

HH: After the first break, I'm going to come back and talk about the plan you adopted to get this book and the future books done, and the one in the past, Imperial Grunts. But before we come back to the specifics of Hog Pilots, Blue Water Grunts, I want to talk and end the first segment about Iraq, because you have a chapter on Iraq, you were there before, you've been back, obviously. What is the impact of Iraq on the American military?

RK: The impact, it's strained it. It hasn't devastatingly strained it, but it strained it in the sense that every deployment where I embedded, whether in South America, Asia or Africa, there was always complaints about they didn't have enough planes, they didn't have enough equipment, that the best linguists were not there, because everything [was being sucked by Iraq, you know,] was being sucked up by Iraq. Now they came up with ingenious solutions to a lot of these things, but you could feel the impact on the American military throughout the world on Iraq. But there's something else here, Hugh, it's that if you set aside the manpower strains that Iraq has surely imposed, Iraq has also invigorated the quality of the American military to no small extent. A military is only as good as its staff colleges. And people have been coming back from Iraq and from Afghanistan with a horde of lessons learned to reinvigorate curriculums at West Point, many other places as well. It's really turned the U.S. military [into a,] the Army especially, into a lean and mean battle-hardened military that knows a lot more about the world today than it did several years ago.

HH: We'll spend some time talking about those specific lessons. But before we get to the break, there's a spectrum of opinion on Iraq that ranges from Thomas P.M. Barnett's view that we've just got to get out of the way of the inevitable Sunni-Shia slaughter, and until that comes, we won't get stability. And then there's the Victor Davis Hanson view that maybe what we are seeing is the 1864, the equivalent of the 1864 march on Atlanta by Sherman, and a turning in the war. Stepping back from the specifics on the military and <u>Hog Pilots, Blue Water Grunts</u>, what do you see unfolding, Robert Kaplan, in Iraq?

RK: What I see unfolding is that there will be gradually a very uneasy Sunni-Shiite armistice. But that will not be the end of it.

Iraq is going to have major repercussions on politics in Syria, Lebanon, Egypt, Saudi Arabia, Tunisia, Morocco. [It's really going to ...] what it's really going to do is in a very uneasy, messy fashion is going to usher in more openness and decentralization in the Arab world. The next generation of Arab autocrats will not be able to rule as autocratically as the current generation,because of a lot of the changes that Iraq will have imposed. In terms of Iran, I think that Iraq may turn out to be Iran's poisoned chalice, that the Iranians have been able to be spoilers in Iraq, but it's unclear that they can make a peace any better than we have been able to.

HH: At the conclusion of the chapter, you write, "Excepting the collapse of Turkey's empire, the creation of the state of Israel and the Iranian revolution, neither anything nor anybody in a century has so jolted the Middle East as had George W. Bush." 30 seconds to our break, is that a good thing in your view, Robert Kaplan?

RK: It's unclear yet. We've seen the bad effects of it. You can't erase tens of thousands of deaths and say, "Yeah, but it's been worth it for the sake of strategic positioning." But I think the ability to get al Qaeda to fight against its own Sunnis, to get Sunnis to revolt against al Qaeda, and to upset the complacency of Sunni Arab police states in Iraq and Saudi Arabia will turn out to be hopefully a good thing.

HH: Before getting into the tall grass of the book, Robert Kaplan, explain to people your project, and how it began with Imperial Grunts, where it's gone with this book, where it's going to continue, and how you chart your course in surveying the American military in the air, the sea and the [ground].

RK: Well, I wanted to take the traditional genre of literary travel writing and apply it to the American military, to go around the world and meet people the way I did for years with previous books, except this time, I would limit myself to American soldiers, airmen, Marines and sailors. So it was to take a genre not usually applied to the American military, and apply it as such. My plan was to embed in as many missions as possible, not limiting myself to Iraq and Afghanistan, but to include Naval missions in the Pacific, on surface and subsurface war ships, to embed with Air Force units around the world, and with a particular emphasis, and with the Army, with particular emphasis on Army Special Forces and Marines, not only in Iraq and Afghanistan, as I said, but in the heart of Africa, in South America, in Asia, and to kind of always cover things that generally didn't get covered much. In other words, we were having all these exercises, these Special Forces exercises in sub-Saharan Africa for years. [But] The media was invited to cover it, but it failed to. So I figured I would cover it. We always read about F-15 and F-14 and F-16 fighter jets, but we don't read much about B-2 bomber pilots, or A-10 Warthog pilots. So I figured I would cover it. My aim was to be a gap filler, to give voice to people who are ordinarily invisible to America, but are out there on the front lines all around the world. It really is a global war on terrorism. And to convey that, I had to travel the globe.

HH: Now you visited, and it's a very moving little anecdote, the grave of Ernie Pyle. For the benefit of our younger audience, why don't you explain who he is and why you went there. RK: Well, Ernie Pyie was a World War II newspaper correspondent [who had covered,] who had used the words "we" and "our" in his narrative to show that he was one with the troops. This was during World War II when such an attitude was not controversial. He traveled all over with the troops throughout World War II, and was finally killed, literally, in the last days of the Battle of Okinawa, the last big battle of World War II in the Pacific, and in fact, of World War II totally. Because after Okinawa, there was just the dropping of the atomic bombs on Hiroshima and Nagasaki. So [he had just, you know,] he was killed literally in the last days of the war, and he's buried at the military ceremony in Honolulu.

HH: Now are you approving of his style, and are you consciously trying to emulate it in this book?

RK: Well, you know, as a practical matter, when you're one American civilian embedded with 20 or 30 or 50 or 300 American troops, whether in Special Forces A-team, or on a destroyer, not to use the words "we" and "our" is very awkward. You know, it leads you into factual inaccuracies, because you're doing things with them. You're an American, they're an American, and so not to use "we" and "our" becomes a very awkward construction. But I think that seeing that they were Americans, I was American, I was following them around, I thought that adopting the style of correspondents like Ernie

Pyle and Richard Tregaskis and Robert Sherrod, and other World War II correspondents, was quite appropriate.

HH: Now tell me, what does it take to get the men, and some women, but [it's] primarily men of the American military to talk to you, and to genuinely be candid?

RK: Well, that's a great question, Hugh. I can tell you, it's not always that easy. I spent a month embedded with a Special Forces A-team in southern Algeria in the middle of the summer.

HH: It's an amazing chapter, by the way. We're going to spend a section on that entirely.

RK: Right, and I can tell you the first ten days, I almost got nothing in my notebook. And all the gold came in the last ten days of the month, after I'd been with them for three weeks. And the reason is they won't open up to you until they know you and trust you. And you can't get them to trust you by telling them to trust you. You just have to hang out and be one of the guys in this case, and show them, you know, the thing is to pass the asshole test, to show them that you're not an asshole. And all you can be is [be] yourself, because they will see through you very fast. You know, as I said earlier, I didn't seek to report on people or to interview people, but to make new friends, and reveal them in the pages of my notebook as they revealed themselves to me. So you know what it takes to get them to open up to you, Hugh? It takes time. Time is the critical factor. I f you're just embedded for three or four days, if you're on a tight newspaper headline deadline, you're not going to have the time, and you're not going to get the gold, usually. But if you have a month to spare, you can be relaxed about it, you're not in anyone's face, you're not rushing them, and it just all comes to you almost organically.

HH: Now Robert Kaplan, both <u>Imperial Grunts</u>, and I'm certain <u>Hog Pilots, Blue Water Grunts</u>, is going to be greatly revered by the active duty members of the American military. But does American journalism avoid this kind of journalism as a matter of cost, as a matter of ideology? Why don't they do this?

RK: Well, actually, because what I'm doing isn't really journalism in a way. It's more like old-fashioned travel writing, or it's more like journalism from fifty years ago. You know, American journalism, [you know,] in the Woodward-Bernstein age is about discovering problems. It's about revealing inconsistencies. It's about finding out the story, and the story has to be something that's gone wrong in some way, shape or form. But if your idea is not to find out what's wrong, it's just to kind of reveal people, to show them, to send almost like a postcard to the reader as to what it's about, [you know,] what these people are seeing, feeling, what their challenges and frustrations are, that's not really where American journalism is at the moment.

HH: And for the benefit of the audience who didn't hear our first interview about <u>Imperial Grunts</u>, and are just hearing about <u>Hog Pilots, Blue Water Grunts</u> for the first time, how did you develop the actual agenda? This is not the Pentagon saying Kaplan, go to Korea, and then we're sending you to Algeria, and then you can go to Mongolia. How did this particular order of appearance arrive?

RK: Well, first of all, I didn't deal with the Pentagon at all. I don't even have in my Rolodex the phone number of the public affairs office at the Pentagon. The American military is radically decentralized. People at the Pentagon have no idea when there's going to be a deployment to Senegal or Chad or Mauritania. All that's done at the level of the geographic area command, the combatant command. So you need contacts with middle and upper level, and an upper middle level officer is at European command, at Pacific command, at Central command. I constantly worked contacts at the level of major and lieutenant colonel, or lieutenant commander in the case of the Navy. Those were the people who got me where I was going. And I had to drive them. I had to constantly repeat I want to go on a submarine for a few weeks.

HH: And then it happens.

RK: And then it happened.

HH: Robert Kaplan, I want to read three paragraphs as a means of illustrating a common theme throughout <u>Hog Pilots</u>. These appear on Page 189 and Page 190 that concern Master Sergeant Butcher of Springfield. "Once we get our ammo tomorrow, we'll be happy," said the team sergeant, Master Sergeant Ken Butcher of Springfield, New Hampshire. Staff Sergeant Michael Hare of St. Paul, Minnesota, the 18 Bravo weapons specialist cut in, derisively. "Any soldier who doesn't like to shoot all the time should leave the Army. And unfortunately, there are a lot of those around." "Everyone in America should own at least five guns," someone else answered. More nods. Master Sergeant Butcher owned 38 guns. Everyone agreed that whenever you read in newspapers about a kid shooting someone with his father's gun, it was because the father kept a gun in the closet and told the kid never to touch it, which of course he would. Rather than a working gun, it served as a macho item that the father owned to show to all his friends. With one or two exceptions, these sergeants all owned working guns, and had taught their sons and daughters gun safety. "My son is too young to shoot," Ken Butcher explained. "But whenever he hands me his plastic cap gun, he knows to disarm it first." Ken Butcher has handled humanitarian and military emergencies in 73 countries in the course of 17 years in the Army. Accepted at Dartmouth, he enlisted instead and never regretted it. He never even wanted to go to officer's candidate school at Fort Benning, Georgia. He had worked with the anti-Saddam Kurds in northern Iraq. And then for nearly a decade, he was all over the former Yugoslavia interrogating local politicians and suspected war criminals, helping Romanian and Hungarian elements of the international security force, providing protection for visiting heads of state, and so forth. He was in Zaire in 1997 when it felt apart, in Liberia in 2004 when it, too, disintegrated. He was in Sierra Leone twice during mayhem there, and he had tutored the cabinet of Azerbaijan in disaster management. He had called in a JDAM strike in Spin Boldak, in Eastern Afghanistan, in 2001, helped Armenia recover from an earthquake, and traveled on horseback and snowmobile through Canada's Northwest Territories, among a plethora of other assignments, an experience that would make Harrison Ford drool. Months later in Mali, I had mentioned Butcher's name to an SF buddy of his, Special Forces buddy of his, who told me how Butcher had, 'MacGyver' a solution to a frozen fuel line in a snowmobile using only a Leatherman. This all was after guarding Pershing I1 nuclear missiles in Germany in the last days of the Cold War. Butcher's musculature seems slightly crushed in on account of years of rucking and parachute jumps. Under short, dirty blond hair, he had a blunt, ground-down, rural New Hampshire way of speaking that recalled the poetry of Robert Frost. This was enhanced by a no-bull blank expression that at proper moments turned wistful. It reminded me of tough and reserved kibbutzniks of yore. Butcher was happiest embracing the suck." You know, Robert, that's an amazing piece of writing, but it's also an amazing man, and I guess he's not all that rare.

RK: No, he's not all that rare, and getting him to reveal all this stuff was not the easiest thing, because he really didn't want to talk about it. You know, this occurred many, many days into my knowing him. You know, he's not rare within the Special Forces community. He would be a bit rare within the larger Army community. But if there's one thing that kept coming back to me, it was the amazing resumes of these non-commissioned officers.

HH: Yeah.

RK: They read like the resumes of our best foreign correspondents,

HH: Now you also make a couple of points [about general ...] I want to do before we go to these particular assignments. One is that Alaska and the frontier ethic is completely pervading our military, and the second is that good farmers have always made great warriors, and they continue to.

RK: Yes. And one of the things is that you know, the family farm is dying in America. But on many of the SF A-teams in which I embedded, the Special Forces A-teams in which I embedded, there were sometimes half of the team had grown up on family farms. So the number of farmers in SF detachments, and in the Army, too, is much greater than in the country as a whole. And I think there's a link between a rural existence and a good fighting soldiery. And we're certainly losing that as the family farm dies off, as we become more of a suburban and exburban generation. You know, the whole idea of something rural is going to disappear in American society.

HH: You know, Victor Davis Hanson, I'm sure, classicist and military historian, would agree with that. We've got 30 seconds to the break. What percentage of people talk about Alaska and the frontier in the military with wistful tones, Robert Kaplan?

RK: More than you would think. For instance, you would think, "Who cares about Alaska? It's one other place." But in fact, the best U.S. Army units that I've encountered, the ones that are closest to SF units, tended to be those from Alaska, the Stryker brigades based in Fairbanks and up near Anchorage, and I think it's because, [and we can go into this in the next segment, but] there's something about Alaska, the very brutality of its climate, that develops tighter unit cohesion, and thus, better soldiers.

HH: We went to break, Robert Kaplan, we were talking about one of those themes that recurs through your various deployments. You run into a number of American soldiers, sailors, airmen and Marines with a fondness for Alaska. Many have trained there. [Some have been ...] I know Alaska like many Americans do, from the side of a cruise ship saying boy, this is a big place. But there's a cult in the military of Alaska.

RK: Yeah, there certainly is. And the colder the better. They almost look down on Anchorage as too much like Seattle and San Francisco. They call Anchorage the banana belt, because it's so much warmer and more tropical than Fairbanks and the central part of the state. They like it because it's hard. They like it because the hunting is good. The Air Force loves it, because there are very few low level noise restrictions. And also, training in the Arctic cold is much harder than training or deploying in any kind of climate. Here's why. Hot countries, you're just uncomfortable with heat and sweat. But cold climate, below freezing climate, you're more than uncomfortable. You could actually die if you don't plan ahead, or get frostbite, or lose your fingers or your toes if you haven't packed, if you've forgotten your gloves or something, or you forgot to pack your long underwear or something. So the Arctic demands much better preparation, much better logistical preparation and planning, [so that it's almost as if ...] Alaska's where we're training a lot of the Stryker brigades for deployment in Iraq, where I've seen whole Iraqi Arab towns set up in the heart of the Alaskan tundra, complete with Mosque calls in Arabic, and street signs in Arabic, and training in that Arctic cold, doing everything with gloves on, it makes Iraq itself a little easier once you get there, because you no longer have to wear your gloves, you no longer have the cold. There are a lot of things you had to pack you don't have to pack. So it's kind of like walking with weights, and then taking the weights off.

HH: There's also I think a tremendous insight, which I'm sure the military already has internalized, even if they don't articulate it, which is if your logistics are the essence to success, the people who learn their logistics in the Arctic are going to perform much better when they have to do the same sort of thing in any situation. And so it improves the NCO corps dramatically.

RK: Oh, yes, it certainly does. It's just a much more intimate indoors interiority of a climate up in Alaska, which brings units closer together. And if you think about it, the Stryker brigade combat teams which have basically rescued Mosul ...you know, an update on my chapter in Mosul is Mosul's doing a lot better now. There hasn't been a major attack since last spring there. The Stryker brigades that rescued Mosul, that did such fine work in Baghdad last summer, were all Alaska-based brigades.

HH: Now I want to switch over to the seas now, to the Benfold, the destroyer on which you deployed and embedded for a long period of time. Now I think this is the ship that my cousin served on in the Iraq war, and it's the ship that does the complete staff change. Everyone deploys onto it, and so they can stay deployed for the longest period of time.

RK: Yeah, it's called a sea swap, Hugh.

HH: Yeah, they don't like that. He didn't like that, either. I see you noted that in your book. The sailors hate that. Why?

RK: Yes. [Yeah, because sailors ... once you go to the Navy and the Air Force, Hugh ...] you see, our soldiers and Marines, they're just plain warriors. But in sailors and airmen, they have their relationship triangulated by technology, meaning that they have a particular love for the air or Naval platform. They love their destroyer, or they love their submarine, or they love their 0-2 bomber or whatever. And when you just tell them that all destroyers are the same, you're going to serve six months on this destroyer, six months on another destroyer, [you really,] you're really undermining their very morale in a deep sense. And when I was embedded on the Benfold, there had been a sea swap. A lot of the sailors had come from the U.S.S. Higgins, which had served in Iraq, which had fired some of the first shots of Operation Iraqi Freedom, and the sailors had a particular love for the Higgins because of the name of the boat, because it was one boat, one ship, where the name was not based on a World War II or a Korean war Medal of Honor winner, but on someone who had died in Lebanon in the 1980's. The fact that it was a much more recent hero engendered a whole new meaning to these young sailors.

HH: Now on your time on the Benfold, you also report, and I tested this out against my friend Joseph Timothy Cook who's a Vietnam-era Naval aviator, flown off of carriers, that the chief's mess, and the aura of the chiefs is so real, and that no one goes into the chief's mess, and he said good eye for detail, Kaplan. That's an interesting aspect I had never heard of before.

RK: Yeah, you know, of all the non-commissioned officers in the US. military, none have quite the aura of Naval chiefs. And the word itself chief, it connotes authority. These are what I call the 1950's, prosperous, uber-working class type of guys. They're almost from an earlier generation. You know, they seem like the kind of people I remember from my dimmest, earliest childhood, people who had beautiful homes not because they were investment bankers, but because they were an electrician or a plumber, or something like that. And in the officer's wardroom, non-commissioned officers will walk in and out if they need to. But no officer will ever walk into the chief's lounge on a surface or sub-surface warship without being invited, because it's almost like a cult.

HH: Now you write also about Petty Officer Second Class Robert Contreras of San Fernando. '"he Navy made him the geek he was always meant to be." We've got a minute to our break for the second hour, Robert Kaplan. What do you mean by that?

RK: What I mean is he was always the science whiz in school, very, very bright, a lot going on in his mind, a bit awkward. You know, he was someone who would turn into [like] a geek who went to a top school or something, but he grew up in very modest circumstances with family problems. He got into trouble, he had disciplinary problems. So this geek side of him was hidden, almost. But once he was able to join the Navy, and they did all these batteries of tests on him, you know, these intelligence tests, and it turned out just how talented and brilliant this kid was, the Navy revealed him, it was able to reveal a whole new side to him.

HH: Robert Kaplan, we'll come back next hour and start with going below the sea on the submarine chapter. But let's finish up on the Benfold, where you were deployed on a destroyer. You say that the Navy, this sort of Navy is vanishing, but the next generation of ships may not even have outdoor platforms, and that this is odd, really.

RK: Yeah, when you look at the designs of the new DDX destroyer that, by the way, if they ever build it, it's going to cost about $4 billion dollars per ship, there's almost ... you know, the whole notion of a deck, of deck plates, is sort of gone. It's almost like when you look at the drawings of these things, they're like submarines that are on top of the water. Everything is modular, and so I pointed out that to be embedded on a destroyer in the early part of the 21st Century [was very,] I was very privileged, because I was on a destroyer while it was still a real ship, where there was still a deck life, you know, where you could walk around. And I can tell you, probably very few experiences I've had in my entire life were like crossing the Pacific on a destroyer back from the South Seas, from Southeast Asia, all the way to Hawaii. You know, you look at a map and you see how there's a lot of ocean in the world, but until you really experience it, you can't really appreciate it. There's so much salt in the ocean that just taking a walk on the deck on the Benfold, you put your fingers through your hair and it's full of these salt particles.

HH: Now you write, to close out this hour, "whereas the Marines are a cult, the Navy is a calling." You're not meaning to denigrate the Marines, but you're trying to distinguish. Can you expand on that a little bit in the minute we have left in this segment?

RK: Yes, there's just an intensity with the Marines. The Marines are like a successful **gang**. They're like a reformatory that works, that's really **reformed** people into better citizens. You know, they're a gang that works. The Marines take people, they break them down, and then they rebuild them up again as solid citizens. But the calling to be in the Navy, to go on ships or boats, in the case of submarines and aircraft carriers, really is a calling in the sense that the officers that I met were not always that physical. There was just something in them, some hidden gene, which was a calling to go to sea.

HH; I now want to get into the guts of the book and do a few deployments. And obviously, we can't recreate a 400 page book, Robert Kaplan, but I want to give them a sense of where you've been and what you've **done**. And I'll tell you, when you go on this USS Houston, **this** nuclear submarine, I got claustrophobia reading about this. **I don't** do well in MRI machines. But [this is ... how did ...] **is this the** closest to the most uncomfortable deployment you **had?**

RK: Well, in a way, it wasn't, because remember, you never sweat, you don't get dirty. As they say, on a submarine, it's 69 degrees and fluorescent every day of the year and all times of day. You can walk around in a T-shirt, running shoes. It's not like 120 degrees in Iraq, where you rot through your clothes. Also, in terms of the claustrophobia, that when you first get down there, you say how am I going to survive this. I mean, even the urinals and the sinks fold out from the walls. The chairs have hidden recesses in the back where you can put books and manuals. Every ounce of space is utilized. There's one exercise machine for 154 men, and it's squeezed between computer banks. So you say, how am I going to do this. I mean, your dirty laundry is in a slip on the side of your bed, so you're sleeping right next to your dirty laundry, because there's no other space for it. But as the hours and days go on, and you get used to this environment, and you figure out ways to save space yourself, and how to wiggle into this and wiggle into that, my nose was, when I was lying in bed, was about two inches from the pipes up above. It just becomes normal. I mean, you adapt. People adapt.

HH: You write, quoting one of the submarine sailors, 'It's like being stuck in the boiler room of your high school for several weeks." I understand you adapt, but as you also write, these guys are called to this. This is what they love to do.

RK: Oh, yes, because it's very much an elite. The submarine service is a volunteer service within a volunteer service. Nobody's put on submarines unless they volunteer, and no pressure is put. It's very distinctly an elite. They tend to have the highest test scores, the highest math scores. I've never met more impressive non-commissioned officer than those in the nuclear power plant of a fast-attack submarine. So they feel themselves superior doing this. And [many of ... you know,] you meet people who have been underneath the North Pole like fifteen times.

HH: Now I want to talk about why the strategic element of the submarine service, and it's a theme throughout <u>Hog Pilots, Blue Water Grunts</u>, and a welcome one, from my perspective, which is China, China, China. Why this obsession with China?

RK: Because basically, what I found out, embedded in the military months at a time every year for the past few years, there are two overarching themes to our military deployment. One is the global war on terrorism, including Iraq and Afghanistan, and the other is facing up to the challenge of China as a new future peer competitor. Now that doesn't mean China wants to go to war with us, it doesn't mean the military is warmongering. But the military has to play the role of the constructive pessimist. So it has to accept the fact that China, for instance, is both buying and acquiring new submarines at five times the rate that we are, that it's developing anti-GPS satellite technology, that it's concentrating on missile technology that can hit moving targets at sea. The Pacific Ocean, Hugh, has been an American lake for the last sixty years. But the next sixty years, the American military, and particularly the Navy and Air Force, are going to have to adjust to a more multi-polar environment in the Pacific. And what this all boils down to is that the exercises, the constant combat exercises that are run on destroyers and submarines all the time, when they talk about Country Orange, or Country X as the adversary country, it's almost always China, though they don't admit it as such.

HH: Now Robert Kaplan, [you also ...] we've got 54 of these Los Angeles class fast-attack nuclear submarines. And I hadn't really quite ever thought about what they do all day, but you describe it in detail. They run exercise after exercise, drill after drill, to the point of, I don't know, is it maddening the repetition?

RK: I've never been so tired, and with things to do, than I have been when I was embedded on a fast-attack nuclear sub or an Arleigh Burke class guided missile destroyer. It's exercise after exercise. You know, they say every Marine a rifleman? Well, every sailor a fireman, because whether a ship is attacked at sea, whether there's an engine malfunction or whatever, it almost always results in fire. So sailors have to be expert firemen. So there are fire drills all the time that get quite real with smoke, with masks everyone has to wear, the hatches are sealed shut, parts of the ship are cut off from the other part of the ship. These things get really, really intense, and they last for a long time.

HH: Quoting from Page 147, "At several hundred feet beneath the surface, you might as well be in the Space Shuttle. Anal retentiveness was a matter of survival. Yet to know such a fact was not at the same time as appreciating it through a sustained close encounter. 'It's like being bad in 7th grade,' said one enlisted man. 'If you do something stupid, your crewmates never let you forget it.'" Does that cause bad humor or an excess of good humor, Robert Kaplan?

RK: An excess of good humor, because what it drives home every minute of the day is that these people are an elite, and they consider themselves as such, and they make things hard on each other. They challenge each other. Everyone is always challenging someone else on these ships and boats to be better, not to screw up, not to get this wrong, because the sea, seven hundred feet down, where the pressure of the water is like an elephant stepping on your finger, the sea that far deep is a zero defect environment, like space.

HH: Now occasionally, an American politician will step in it, and somehow insult the American military by suggesting they're in this because they can't get jobs elsewhere. I stand up now as an example from this chapter, Lieutenant Junior Grade Anthony Williams of Fayetteville, Georgia, graduate of Georgia Tech, a chemical radiological assistance in a reactor complex. "Lt. Williams," you write, "was very passionate about ideas as I learned during a discussion we had about the future of American democracy, about which he was deeply worried." Again and again in Hog Pilots, Blue Water Grunts, Robert Kaplan, these are very well read, deep thinking American soldiers.

RK: Oh, yes. [No,] especially when it comes to the Air Force and the Navy, a lot of these people, particularly the officers, could get much higher paying jobs elsewhere. They are there because of the feeling they get serving, and because inside the military, they feel like they're really doing something particularly interesting in their lives, that they're members of an elite, that they would not be in corporate America. But to say that these people don't have a choice is factually wrong. In fact, one of the reasons why the Air Force in particular offers such a cushy life-style to its officers and airmen, to a much greater extent than the Marine Corps does, is because they want to keep them. They know how a lot of their people are easily employed by corporate America, and they don't want to spend all this money training them just to see them leave.

HH: Now let's talk a little bit about the strategic significance of the submarine service. While the recent past had been carrier strike groups-centric, the future, you write, would emphasize force multiplication, get close real fast to a coastline to collect data or sink a ship when no one thinks you're there, perhaps even frightening away the enemy before he has time to muster his forces. And you go on to write about putting Special Forces ashore via submarines. These have become, well, the ultimate, as you write, "The sub was where the true intentions of a nation were revealed."

RK: Yes, that's true, because remember, throughout the Cold War, the war under the seas was quite high. We were getting right up near the Soviet coast. We were tracking the Soviet boomers, they were tracking ours. The most tense moments of the Cold War were under the sea. And in fact, what a submarine allows a president to do, you can have, for example, a Democratic liberal president with a multilateral foreign policy, but who can on the side, [he can] conduct a very unilateral foreign policy with his submarine fleet. So that's my point in saying that the submarine is where the intentions of a nation are revealed, because the submarine is really, in effect, the most secret part of our arsenal. I mean, there are leaks all the time from the CIA, or from the intelligence community. But there are no leaks, no information comes out of submarines. They are moving intelligence factories powered by nuclear reactors under the sea. They can pull down cell phone conversations on shore, and do a lot of other things.

HH: It's an amazing chapter.

HH: Robert Kaplan, I want to visit with you in this segment and the next one, a couple of places you've been before and returned to. One of them is the Philippines, and we go from these massively expensive tactical submarines and attack destroyers to a couple of guys embedded with the Philippine military. Tell us about Colonel Linder and what he's doing.

RK: Yes, well Colonel Jim Linder was the Army Special Forces officer who ran the whole special operations program in the southern Philippines, which is a Muslim community. Col. Linder basically had the following job to do. He had to convince the whole population of Muslims that American soldiers with American flags on their sleeves were basically the good guys hunting down al Qaeda. And he was able to do that quite successfully, because the whole context of operations in the southern Philippines is so different than it is in Iraq and Afghanistan. We haven't been firing any shots in the Philippines. We have been building health clinics, doing a lot of humanitarian work, and we've been empowering the armed forces of the Philippines, the Philippines' own military, to do the hunting down of terrorists on their own with logistical and training support, and with technical intelligence that we've been able to provide them. And Col. Linder himself was just one of these guys who exudes authority. He exuded quiet authority in the sense that you wanted to listen to him. And he was very much a warrior diplomat, because much of what he did was go around speaking and cajoling with Muslim politicians in this part of the country that was very weakly governed by the government, the Filipino government up in Manila.

HH: You know, you meet him in Zamboanga, and my ears perk up, because that's where my father was deployed in World War II. And I love this little speech he gave you and to crowds of Filipinos in Jolo and Basilan. "I will fortify the moral high ground," says Col. Linder. "People will attack me with stories about Abu Ghraib and the killing of Filipino civilians a hundred years ago by American troops, actions which I cannot defend. And I will respond that my troops can build a school, or fix a little girl's cleft palate at a med-cap, whereas all the guerrillas of Abu Sayyaf and Jamaa al-Islamia can offer is a suicide vest. I will build my fortress on deeds, because I know that the only force protection I have is the goodwill of civilians. All the guns in the world won't keep an IED from going off.'" Wonderfully put. Is it working?

RK: Yes, it's working very well. In fact, most of these small deployments are working very well. We should be careful not to draw generalizations from Iraq. It's working so well that in 2002, the United States military went into an island called Basilan in the southern Philippines, the most strategic island in the Sulu chain, all Muslim inhabited, the lair of Abu Sayyaf, the lair of al Qaeda organizations like Jamaa al-Islamia. And the Americans cleared it, they held it, they turned it over to the Filipinos [who ...] and since then, there's been very little, if any, terrorist activity on Basilan. And that was 2002. In 2005-2006, we went further down the chain and did the same thing on 3010. So this is an operation that's been working. It's been sort of a textbook success story.

HH: Now does the American military plan these things years in advance, because you've been here twice. When you were there three years ago, had they intended to be where they are now, or are they adapting as circumstances change?

RK: Well, they're much further along than they intended to be. They never thought for a moment that they would be able to subdue 1010, a real jungle environment, crawling with Abu Sayyaf and Jamaa al-Islamia Islamic insurgents. They always thought that Jolo would be too much of a challenge. But given the success they had on Basilan, they worked with the Filipino military on 1010, and now 3010's been completely turned around. So they're further along than they thought they would be.

HH: Now in the middle of this description of what's going on in the Philippines, you include, as you do often, a couple of meditations on why our military is where it is. This one occurs over on Pages 313-314 where you talk about what authority means, how you get it, and the frontier legacy in the American military. Expand on what that legacy is, and how that authority develops.

RK: Well, remember, the American military, particularly the Army, has had its culture, its personality determined by the fight to settle the American West, to wrest control of the American West from the native indigenous inhabitants. This is not a nice story, but it happens to be the history of the U.S. Army. And we built around a frontier fortress sort of ethos, much different than the British military, whose ethos has been much more naval-oriented than our own. [And this has given the Army, and because of this,] because we settle the frontier so fast, you know, a whole continent in just a few short decades, it happened mainly because of very clear and decisive command, so that there's a high element of simplicity in the way the Army speaks. So when you hear phrases like good guys and bad guys, and those kinds of things, I mean, it sounds corny, it sounds hokey. But this phraseology comes ultimately from the U.S. Army's struggle to settle the American West.

HH: I want to read the conclusion of the Philippines paragraphs. "The air of uncertainty prevalent in 2003 was now less so, to a point where big business in Manila, such as this restaurant chain, felt safe enough to invest. Basilan had now telephone towers, asphalt roads and bridges, more schools, higher agricultural production. Power outages occurred because of demand surge as a sign of uneven development, but of development, nevertheless. The Philippines," you conclude, "perhaps more than any other place in the world since 9/11, was a success for the American military. It wasn't a dramatic or a large-scale success, but something had happened that had a continuing upward curve, a significant and strategic island chain with a Muslim population which had been outside the law, and whose local bandits and insurgents were demonstrably linked to world terrorist organizations, was being reclaimed by a legitimate central government, a government that was in turn a U.S. ally and a democracy." You know, that's huge, Robert Kaplan. What it prevents, in terms of cost and disaster down the road, I don't think you can really quantify.

RK: No, what this is all about is get in early, get in fast, get in below the media radar screen, get in when you still have a chance to make mistakes, so that when you do make mistakes, it won't hurt your reputation so much, experiment with trial and error, and you can really have a success story. And we've been doing this in a number of places. [What it's about,] it's about taking on a challenge when it's still on Page 11, so that it never even reaches Page 5 or Page 1. You want to avoid future Iraqs, and the way to avoid future Iraqs is not to go isolationist, Hugh, but to be engaged in even more places than we have been.

HH: As I've said, I've got a very small bookshelf of indispensable books. On it is The Looming Tower, America Alone by Mark Steyn, Robert Kaplan's Imperial Grunts, and now this one goes on there, if you want to understand the world we live in.

Robert Kaplan, I used to tell people when I was recommending Imperial Grunts, that they had to read it if only to read what you wrote about Colombia, because we just didn't know. I didn't know what was going on down there, and how we were trying to stop it. You went back. Tell people about then and now, and what you found on your second trip to Colombia.

RK: Well, let me put it this way. Handicap for size the president of Colombia, Alvaro Uribe Velez. He's probably the most successful democratically elected ruler or politician on the Earth today. He's in his second term with a 70% approval rating. He's, more than anyone in decades, he's really taken the fight, and alleviated his country's suffering from narco-terrorists. When I was in Colombia in 2003, there were many parts of the country that I couldn't go to, because they were insurgent-controlled. By insurgents, I mean narco-terrorist drug armies. When I went back in 2006, I went to places along the Venezuelan border, along the Ecuadorian border, that I simply couldn't have gone three years ago, but these areas had all been reclaimed. He's managing to disband one drug army. He's got a second one on the ropes. And now he's facing up against a third. He's had like a Ronald Reagan foreign policy towards the drug armies, and a very liberalish domestic policy in terms of health care and other issues like that. He's really been an incredible class act, and we've helped him by deploying Army Special Forces in Colombia, and Navy and Marines to train his people.

HH: Now I want to emphasize the dramatic nature by a couple of sentences here from Page 325. 'The last place I visited in Colombia three years ago was Arauca ...

RK: Arauca.

HH: I'm going to mispronounce every single name in this book, but you come back and are very graceful in correcting it. 'In February, 2003, when I had been last there, Arauca province was considered the most dangerous in the region. To say there had been a dramatic change since then would be a serious understatement. Proper cafes were now open, storefronts painted, crowds flooded the street, at night, too. Rather than a rat hole, Arauca looked like a normally poor and unsophisticated provincial town." As I said last segment about the Philippines, this is huge, Robert Kaplan.

RK: Yes, it is. I mean, [I suppose that now, that] there's been a big turnaround in Anbar Province. For instance, I covered the original attack on Fallujah in April, 2004. And had I bought property then, I would have made some money, because Fallujah's a lot safer now than it was in 2004, and a lot more at peace. Well, the same thing has happened in Colombia, but even more dramatically so. I mean, there were towns in Colombia in 2003, whole sections of the country, where you had to wear body armor, you had to go around in full kit, full battle rattle, the whole way. Now, you can just walk around, sit, have coffee, take a stroll in the evening, and all this has occurred without nary a news headline or news story about it. And it wasn't accomplished by any quick fix, sophisticated new military solution that you could write home about. It was attrition of the same, over and over again, the classics lessons of counterinsurgency. Separate the population from the insurgents, give the population a stake in the outcome, provide them with security. It's working in Colombia.

HH: Now Robert Kaplan, across the border in Venezuela, a person that many refer to as the Mugabe of South America,

Chavez, is taking hold. Your Special Forces operators knew that three years ago. What do they say now?

RK: He's giving rest and relaxation. He's giving succor to the drug armies. They know that they have a safe rear base in Venezuela where they can regroup. So he's a real problem, because not only is he a problem with us, and his alliance with Iran and all of that, but he's been trying to actively destabilize the democratically elected government in Colombia. You know, there's some myths out there that I can't seem to dispel, Hugh, that we have all these military missions around the world propping up dictators and all of this. It couldn't be further from the truth. Congress wouldn't allow it. The moment a country stops being a democracy, our military aid program has to stop, as I found out in Nepal. But in Colombia, what we're propping up is an organically developed model democracy.

HH: We're going into the air now with the B-2 squad that you deployed with for a while. This is a very different chapter [than this other ... This is just] a very different feel. It comes through in the writings. These are the superdestroyers, Robert Kaplan, of our Army and military, I mean.

RK: Yes, it is. You know, keep in mind, a destroyer costs over a billion dollars, but it's manned by 330 sailors and officers. A fast attack nuclear sub costs over a billion dollars, and it's manned by about 154 sailors and officers. But an 8-2 costs over a billion dollars. It costs about the same as a submarine or a destroyer, but it's manned by only two people, [you know,] a pilot and a mission operator. So you know, if you divide by money, the amount of responsibility that anyone may have in the U.S. military, probably no greater responsibility is put on anyone in the US. military than on the pilots and mission operators of these B-2 bombers.

HH: Now can you explain for the audience the statement that I referred to in the last segment that the B-Z's, the 21 8-Z's, represent, "the most terrifying, frighteningly complex conventional struggles that might lie ahead."

RK: Yes. You know, each war is generally not a good predictor of the next war. Vietnam was not at all like Korea and World War II. World War I was not at all like the Franco-Prussian War. This war in Iraq is not at all like the first Gulf War of 1990-91. And therefore, the dirty land counterinsurgency we're fighting in Mesopotamia will probably give no inkling to what future wars may be about. And they won't be conventional, they won't be unconventional. They'll be a mixture of the two. They'll be about combining things like Special Forces A-teams, with a Marine unit, with a fast attack nuclear sub, with an 8-2 bomber, all kind of coming together like bees in a hive to execute an attack on a specific country, and then separating out just as fast. It's almost like a complex symphony in three dimensions.

HH: Now I want to take this opportunity, because you're with the 8-2 pilot, to talk more generally about the Air Force. There's a lot of inter-service rivalry, and understanding about each other that the civilian world never glimpses. Occasionally, I'll get an e-mail like the USAF v. USN by Bob Norris, which is fairly famous among aviators, discussing the difference in the cultures. But you spend some time explaining for civilians like me why the Air Force is just different. And I'd like you to expand on that for people, beginning with the fact that the academies of the other two are on the Coast, and the Air Force is in Colorado. It's just very different.

RK: Yes, remember, the Air Force is new. You know, the Marines, the Navy, the Army, go back to Revolutionary War times. But the Air Force grew out of the Army in 1947. It lacks the tradition. The Air Force Academy, on the front range of the Rocky Mountains in Colorado, has a very tubular, abstract architectural cold element, [whereas the service,] whereas West Point and Annapolis are completely different. The Air Force is really the technical service of the U.S. military more than others, you know, like spearheading the military's increasing involvement with outer space. And so the Air Force is open to change much more than the other three services, because technological change is really what defines it. It's what it's really all about. The Air Force also, you know, is very attached to its Vietnam role because of the pilots in the Hanoi Hilton. So [you know,] the Air Force doesn't have an earlier tradition like the Army and Navy and Marines. [So] it's really used Vietnam, and to a lesser extent, Korea, as a way to kind of create that historical tradition.

HH: Next hour, I'm going to talk in depth about your A-10 embed experience, but let's use this paragraph for the moment. "While the Air Force was run by aggressive F-series fighter jocks, witness who the top generals were, B-2 guys were, in a deeper sense, the ultimate Air Force pilots. This Air Force mentality can be explained through a comparison with Naval aviation. Whereas Marine pilots were primarily about close air support, and Navy aviators had the reputation of being screaming off the carrier deck daredevils, Air Force pilots had the reputation of being more operationally conservative. Navy aviators, alone in the ocean without having to bother about issues like noise restrictions, had fewer rules. Naval aviation is what you could do with an airframe. The Air Force was about what you couldn't. Begotten by big Army in '47, the Air Force had its character molded by the Cold War Strategic Air Command, the core of our nuclear delivery system, in the event of Armageddon. Because of its awesome strategic responsibilities, Air Force pilots were simply more by the book than their Navy brethren." Will they resent that, Robert Kaplan? Or will they nod in agreement?

RK: They'll do both, probably. You know, these are uncomfortable truths, but they're really basic truths that people can't disagree with.

HH: What about, when you write Kosovo in '99 was a breakthrough war for the Air Force ... I don't want to hear that, but tell me why it's a good thing.

RK: Well, it partly was, because we deployed 8-2...remember, the B-2 was not supposed to be about humanitarian relief. It was built in order to get the Soviets to spend themselves into the grave in order to counter it. But what the B-2 provided for President Clinton in Kosovo was an ability for part of his Air Force to deploy from the continental United States, refuel in the air several times, bomb targets from 35,000 feet at no danger to itself, and come back to the continental United States without the use of any foreign bases. So it gave the President an extra piece of leverage. It enabled him to fight a limited war, where he didn't want to go in on the ground, [and it showed that the B...] and it was also a breakthrough in the sense that it wasn't about many planes dropping bombs on targets. The 8-2 role in Kosovo was how just a few planes could hit many targets, because [it could drop up to,] each plane could drop up to about 80 bombs.

HH: Was there controversy about using one of ... I mean, there are only 21 of these things, as you point out. I mean, we're not making them anymore, they're phenomenally expensive. What about putting one of those at risk in one of these low conflicts?

RK: Well, you can flip that, Hugh. You can flip it by saying the very fact that we were willing to use it in Kosovo, and also in Afghanistan and Iraqi Freedom, we were sending a message to our present and future adversaries that we feel no compunction about using this platform. We'll use it all the time, so watch what it can do, because it can go in virtually undetected, it can drop heavy bombs into underground bunkers, and get out undetected. And most importantly, we use it a lot.

HH: You write, going back to the 8-23, Robert Kaplan, that the 8-2 and the F-22 keeps China from locking the U.S. out of the Taiwan Strait. How so?

RK: Well, because of their stealth capabilities, and the fact that they're forward deployed in Guam, or in Alaska, and places like that. What it does is remember, we've had a big war going on in the Middle East for years, but it's only had an indirect effect on stock markets. A war in Asia between the U.S. and China, for instance, even if it lasted just a few days, would completely roil Asian stock markets. We don't want a war in Asia. We never want to have to go to war with China. We don't want an accident or a series of mistakes to lead to a war. And one of the ways you do that is you make it clear to the Chinese general staff that we will defend Taiwan. That way, they don't even think of any military action to get control of Taiwan. You know, they'll just try to get control of its economy organically as the years go by. And one of the ways we show the Chinese that we're serious about Taiwan is our forward deploying of F-22's and B-2 bombers.

HH: And a last question this hour, we're going to come back with I think the most riveting chapter, is the Algerian chapter in <u>Hog Pilots, Blue Water Grunts</u>, but peppered throughout the book, Jack London, Jules Verne, Robert Service. Did you intend to set out to write about the people you most admire in the course of writing about the military you admire and report?

RK: No, I didn't. It just came to me. Remember, the books you read are heavily dependent on the people you meet, because if you think about it, you read a book because someone's recommended it to you. You met someone at a party or something who spoke very highly about a book. And the people I encountered in the U.S. military were aficionados of Jules Verne, of Jack London, of the Canadian poet, Robert Service, and others. So the military very much influenced my reading habits.

HH: You know, I have met many, many Marine Corps officers over the years, because my wife was born into a Marine family. They all know their Robert Service by heart. It's amazing.

RK: Yes, and it was Tom Wilhelm, an Army foreign area officer in Mongolia who I wrote a chapter about in my earlier book, <u>Imperial Grunts</u>, who really pointed out to me the joys of reading Robert Service.

HH: I want to go to Algeria with you, Robert Kaplan, because I found this to be the most striking chapter of many striking chapters. How did you get there? And what did you think ...give us the circumstance, physical first, of when you went there and how long you stayed.

RK: Well, I wanted to embed in a number of missions in sub-Saharan Africa that Army Special Forces were doing. And the European command had invited a number of top foreign correspondents from American media to go, but many of them couldn't go. They were willing to cover it from Senegal, in Dakar, as a overview, all of these deployments. But they weren't willing to invest a lot of time on the ground with any particular unit. So I was alone with twelve members of an SF A-team not just in Algeria, but in the extreme south of Algeria, meaning 1,500 miles south of the capitol of Algiers. I was closer to Nigeria and the Gulf of Guinea than I was to Algiers, even though I was still in Algeria. And you know, listeners should go to a map and just see how far south Algeria goes. This was the Sahara desert in the height of summer. It was so hot and so dry that I almost never used my towel to bathe, because the moment you turned off the water in the makeshift showers, you were [like] instantly dry and your hair frizzed up. That's how dry and hot it was. There were scorpions all around, [and it was ...] and everyone lived in the same tent. Now the Algerians were very gracious hosts. They had built several tents for us. But it was just amazing the way everyone congregated. We would rather be close together in one tent than to have just three or four guys in three separate tents. You know, that's an indicator of the togetherness of this A-team, and just how unified they were.

HH: Now the reason I was riveted by this is because I know the history of Algeria both in terms of the war against the French for independence and their own insurgency with an al Qaeda off-shoot. But if you could summarize for people why Algeria is of such strategic importance to the United States?

RK: Well, first of all, this was the first American military mission to Algeria since Eisenhower's Operation Torch in November of 1942, because after the War ended, Algeria shortly after had a war with the French for independence, where a million people were killed. Then Algeria became one of the most radical extremist countries in the whole Arab world. It led the third world movement, the anti-American, anti-Israeli third world movement. And so, relations with us were very, very low key for a long period of time. Then, Algeria had a civil war in the 1990's, and this was very instructive, because the Algerian military essentially fought a counterinsurgency against Islamic militants that was every bit as brutal as the one in Iraq, and they won.. They won, more or less, hands down. And the media rewarded them, with their victory, by just stopping to pay attention to the story. So it wasn't clear what had happened, it was just that sometime in the late 90s you stopped reading about Algeria as the media moved on elsewhere, because the Algerian government, for all intents and purposes, had defeated this particular group of Islamic militants. But the U.S. military had taken notice of Algeria's success. And because the Algerian government felt itself deserted by countries in Europe, by its own so-called Arab allies, it really led to a change of heart in the people in power in Algiers. And afterwards, they wanted a closer working relationship with the U.S. military. And this Special Forces A-team deployment was the ultimate fruit of all of that.

HH: Now Robert Kaplan, tell me if I'm wrong, but it strikes me that we have going in Algeria what we hope to potentially get in Iraq, eventually, a military and a government open to spreading stability and some transparency, while crushing extremist Salafist ideology at the same time.

RK: Yes. [No,] what we hope to accomplish in Iraq is what has been accomplished in Algeria, and has been accomplished in Colombia against another sort of extremist. The problem in Iraq is that we don't have the advantages that the Algerian government had. The Algerian government allowed in no media, number one, and it could get away with that, because it had no pretensions at the time to democracy, though now it's a democratically elected government. It was also dealing with its own people. This Islamic insurgency was an Algerian Islamic insurgency, so the government had no problem with language, it completely understood the culture, and so [it had,] it could block out the media. It understood the culture and language perfectly. And thirdly, its population was willing to put up with the cruelest of techniques that the government employed, so that the Algerian government was able to win,

Hugh, with methods that we simply cannot employ and should not employ.

HH: Right, but they also are able to teach us now, this is something that I thought was an amazing insight. You mentioned it in the first hour of our conversation today, that our staff colleges in the military are now benefiting from the return of soldiers, sailors, airmen and Marines who have deployed forward, and are learning how to fight this war. In Algeria, [they've been teaching,] even as our guys teach them tactics, they're teaching us the situational deployments of the bad guys, and they're teaching them how they set up camp and all this sort of stuff. Very much a two-way transaction.

RK: Oh, very much so. This was not like observing training missions in Mauritania or Mali or elsewhere. For everything we were teaching them, they were teaching us about how to infiltrate terrorist compounds, how to attack them. So it was very much a two-way street. Also, because the Algerian government was friends with all the wrong sorts of people during its decades of radicalism, it has real contacts in the Arab world, which have been very useful to us in Iraq. You know, Algeria has been a quiet provider of intelligence to us in our battle in Iraq.

HH: You also mention that in the Algerian army is a recurring problem in third world armies, that their non-commissioned officers are so far behind the American ... of course, the American tradition is extraordinarily successful and esteemed. But that's what they lack in the third world, the ability to make decisions.

RK: Yes, that's what they lack. Remember, our NCO corps [was] really started to be formed at Valley Forge during the winter of 1777-1778, when Baron Friedrich von Steuben, through his decentralization of command, established basically the principle of an NCO corps, which you find in Western militaries, the British, the French, you know, all have it. But you don't find it in a country like Algeria where the major, the lieutenant is overloaded with tasks to do, which means he doesn't perform them all that well, because he has to basically discipline his corporal, discipline his private, whereas in the American system, that is done by sergeants. It's things that the major doesn't have to deal with.

HH: Can the Americans convey that? Are they successful in conveying that to the Algerians?

RK: They're successful in conveying it, but an NCO corps, it's kind of like winning an insurgency. It's not a decision, it's a process. I mean, first of all, you need a lot of extra money you've got to put into it to raise salaries for NCOs. You have to establish training schools, you know, NCO schools, higher education, all this. You have to provide family support. If your NCOs are going to be talented and well-trained and confident, they're going to be the product of education and training academies. So it's a big investment for a military.

HH: Now before we move on to the A-10s after the break, I want to talk a little bit about these Special Forces operators, and their attitudes. One of them is they hate Al Jazeera.

RK: Yeah, they hate Al Jazeera. But let me point something out about Al Jazeera. I understand why the military, in fact, many Americans hate Al Jazeera. But remember, as to Arabs, Al Jazeera is provocatively pro-Western. You know, you're dealing with a culture and a society that for decades just had the dullest national media, which merely mouthed the pronouncements of the dictator. Now, you have a semi-independent television station which is prone to all the hopes, fears, conspiracy theories, prejudices of any society. And just like you see America through CBS or Fox News or CNN, you see a lot of the ideas prevalent in the Arab world through Al Jazeera. You know, the Arab world now really has a mass media that it never had before, but lo and behold, this mass media is going to reflect feelings on the street in the Arab world, some of which we're not going to like.

HH: A minute to the break here, just an odd question harkening back to the first hour. Do these guys like you, Robert Kaplan, by the end of your deployment? I mean, you're such a foreign presence to these people.

RK: Well, you never know if people like you, because you know, most people are very diplomatic. If there's something about you they don't like, they may not even say it. [But I felt …] the way you test it is will they still talk to you afterwards, like after they've seen what you've written, or two months later when you're no longer reporting. And I've developed quite a lot of friendships in the American military through this project.

HH: I'm not surprised by that. It's amazing reporting

HH: Before we leave Algeria, Robert Kaplan, as we were talking about last segment, the men and women of the military that you've served with have been obviously studying this new enemy, the Salafist extremists that they find in Africa and the Middle East and around Europe, as well as the Shia extremists that they have to keep their eye on in the Middle East. How much do they understand about the enemy? How often do they talk about them? And what motivates them, and how important it is to get inside their uda-loop, their decision loop?

RK: It's very important, obviously, Hugh. They don't talk about the enemy so much. The enemy is fairly abstract. You know, it's just something they have to do. They're concerned with more what I would call kinetic things. In other words, this is where the location is, this is what they have to hit, here's how they're supposed to carry it out. It gets really quiet and technical.

HH: You have a strategic element of the military, though, obviously, like David Petraeus, who we all saw last week testify, and redid the counterinsurgency manual for the United States. You mentioned earlier in the program that all the lessons that are being learned from all the places in the world are going back to the staff colleges. The grunts that you talk about, the pilots that you fly with, do they think about this changing in doctrine? Or are they just simply executing a higher command's doctrine?

RK: It's both. What you hear from a lot of junior officer and non-commissioned officers is that they didn't train me for this, but I'm learning on the job. In other words, I was trained to be an artillery officer, but now I have to meet and greet, and get to know my Iraqi police counterpart and work with him, and not get really angry if he's ten minutes late or twenty minutes late, or sometimes, he doesn't even show up. I have to find him.

HH: Let's switch over now to the Air Force, to some things they had to learn there like mid-air refueling. Hog pilots are A-10 pilots. Can you explain to the audience in a way that just summarizes, because I can't get into it, it's a fascinating chapter, who these guys are and their place in the Air Force hierarchy?

RK: Sure, it'll be a pleasure. It's officially the A-10 Thunderbolt 11, but they call it the Warthog, because it hovers low to the ground, it provides close air support. The Air Force wanted to kill the plane after the first Gulf War, so the Army said okay, you don't want it? We'll take it. Well, the Air Force quickly changed its mind. The A-10 Warthog, or hog, constitutes an argument against beauty, Hugh. It can loiter amid enemy gunfire, because it's tough. It's tough because it's got so much built-in redundancy, separate engines, separate hydraulic systems, double tails, double everything. If one part falters, another takes its place. You know, the engines are mounted high so that the wings shield the engine from ground fire. Because the engines are mounted high, they're less susceptible to foreign objects like gravel. That's one reason why the A-10 can work out of dirt landing strips. You know, the Air Force hates the plane because it's not high tech. It's low tech. It's Rudyard Kipling's cheaper man, Hugh. It looks ugly, it looks like something out of World War II, and in fact, I'll tell you, the A-10 pilots are the last of the old Army, World War II Army Air Corps pilots. They basically hate the rest of the Air Force, which is dominated by strategic bomber pilots and F-series fighter jocks. The A-10 pilots, though they're Air Force, they love the Army, they love the Marines. As far as they say, we're ground fighters. We just kill from the air.

HH: You know, I got a couple of particulars in this chapter, one, an A-10 really was a plane fitted to a gun, the GAU-8 Gatling gun, whose seven barrels fired 3,900 30 millimeter rounds per minute. That is quite a weapon. And how often are we using it in the global war on terror?

RK: We're using it a lot. First of all, to go back before the global war on terror, remember the highway of death in the first Gulf War, where a lot of retreating Iraqi soldiers were gunned down, leaving, running away from Kuwait? That was all A-10 Warthog. That was all hog, as they say. In Afghanistan, A-10 pilots are flying all the time, almost around the clock, the same in Iraq. You know, as more high tech we go, there's a lesson here. The more high tech you go, the more low tech you seem to need some platforms. This is the ultimate counter-insurgency airplane.

HH: Now I also want to talk about these people who met you in Thailand, this retired, I guess gunny sergeant, I can't quite remember. There's a cadre of Americans who are ex-military around the world who are actually running as our military, smoothing things along, so when A-10s arrive from Korea, it just works.

RK: Yes.

HH: I think that was a fascinating thing.

RK: Yeah, well, you're referring to a man named Dan Generet.

HH: That's it.

RK: Yeah, Dan Generet is an African-American from Walterboro, South Carolina, grew up in a poor neighborhood in New York City. He's a retired master sergeant in the Air Force. He's typical. He lives in Thailand, he speaks Thai, he's the private contractor as the U-Tapao Royal Thai Navy Station, so that the Thai military doesn't deal with the American military. It deals with Dan. Dan's the interface between the American and Thai militaries. So each have a degree of separation. And when American pilots fly into U-Tapao, Dan's the one who tells them what they can do, where they can stay, how much money it's going to cost. He keeps them out of trouble, and the Thais are very glad to have him there. And I'll tell you something, Dan may not be in the chain of command, Hugh, but he's more important than anyone in the chain of command when something goes down. Remember the big tsunami relief operation?

HH: Might be another one underway again.

RK: December, '05, January '06?

HH: Yup.

RK: December, '04, January, '05? Well, that worked partly because we were able to ramp up U-Tapao Naval Air Station very quickly as a major staging post. And that happened because of Dan Generet, a private military contractor. So with all the negative stuff you're hearing about private military contractors, it's a big field, it's a big area, and some of them are doing amazing work.

HH: But I can't remember where I read this in the book. You encountered a guy who just kept you cooling your heels in Kuwait [whoever] who was a private military contractor.

RK: Oh, yeah, there was a bad one

HH: (laughing)

RK: You meet good ones, you meet bad ones, Hugh

HH: Okay.

RK: This was a guy who took my passport, said I'll get it back to you in a few minutes, and I got it back like eight and a half hours later just moments before I had to board a C-130 bound for Baghdad. And because I didn't have my passport, I couldn't go into the DFAC, or dining facility, in order to get a midnight meal like everyone else. And he was very nonchalant about it. He was clearly hassling me. He was a private contractor, and who everybody disliked, by the way.

HH: Yeah, it's the ten percent rule. In any organization, ten percent of them are going to be people who have wonderful names we can't say on the air.

HH: I went to break, Robert Kaplan, quoting Captain Custer Kelly talking about the Sandy-1s and the Sandy-4s. Two reasons here, one, explain why that matters to him, and how general is this understanding of those who have gone before them to the modern American military.

RK: Remember, Hugh, that the Air Force is a new service. It only started in the late 1940's, it grew out of the Army. And Vietnam really gave the Air Force some real emotional tradition, because many of the people in the Hanoi Hilton, many of the prisoners of war, were Air Force pilots. They were real warriors. And A-10 Warthog pilots trace their squadron history back to Sandy search and rescue pilots. Sandy was a call sign like Misty was a call sign. The Misties were, [they were] fast area, they were fast facts. In other words, they set up the bombing runs, hovering in the air, searching for targets. The Sandies, another call sign, basically when a pilot was shot down in North Vietnamese territory, it was a squadron of Sandies that went in and tried to rescue him to keep him from being tortured or killed or imprisoned for many years. And there's a link, because a lot of these guys who are now A-10 pilots carry around a coin in their pocket. It's a Misty or a Sandy coin, which reminds them all the time of their forbears, two generations removed, who were rescuing Vietnam-era pilots. And they get real emotional about this. For many people, the war in Vietnam was just a cause. But for people in the military, it was a war with its bad moments, its positive moments, its horrible moments, its beautiful moments, and its very, very heroic moments, such as the risk taken by these Sandy search and rescue teams.

HH: Now I want to jump from there, and people have to read that chapter, to Nepal, because you ended up in Nepal with the Gurkhas.

RK: That's right.

HH: And this is just incredible to me. Tell people what you were doing in Nepal, and the Gurkha tradition, and how we're working into that in the new war on terror.

RK: Well, I was in Nepal to follow around an Army foreign area officer, an FAO, who was a specialist in Nepalese culture, who's there to assist the Nepalese military in fighting Maoist insurgents. And it was a very interesting trip, because people have this image of the U.S. military going all over the world as a busybody, propping up dictatorships. It's so false. In fact, the only regimes we prop up through training missions are of certified democracies, certified by Congress, which we have not imposed on them, that they've evolved organically on their own as democracies. And I was in Nepal at the time when the king curtailed parliament, parliament did not meet, so that our training missions there had to stop. They had to stop until parliament reconvened, because we could not even for a short period of time train or assist foreign troops who were not governed democratically. So this was a real indicator in just how under [such] a tight leash our training missions all over the world are that I covered. [The Gurkha tradition,] the Gurkhas refer to a town in western Nepal called Gorkha, and they're hill tribes. They're not an ethnic derivation; they're just a name that the British gave for the fighting hill tribes of Nepal, which the British allowed into their military, and fought with great distinction in many wars between the late 19th Century right up to Iraq and Afghanistan. And I was with an Army foreign area officer who was trying to assist a battalion of Nepalese soldiers in the Gurkha tradition.

HH: And what are we helping them to learn? They've been fighting wars a lot longer than we have.

RK: Yes, they have, but there are many things we know how to do with modern weaponry, troop formations, training that we can give them, communications.

HH: The idea that we are as far removed as Colombia is from Nepal is pretty astonishing, Robert Kaplan. Is this accelerating or declining?

RK: What? What do you mean?

HH: The number of deployments.

RK: They're fairly steady, several dozen a week in many of these countries. As I said, one big deployment that really over-stretches one particular service, the Army, like Iraq, can constitute overstretch.

HH: I have a couple of big questions to sort of wrap up our penultimate segment, Robert Kaplan. At the close of the book, you tell a little story. "At the 2006 Stanford commencement ceremony, a Marine general whose son was the lone graduating student from a military family said he was struck by how many of the other parents had never even met a member of the military before he introduced himself." This echoes a point made by Thomas Ricks and others that the civilian-military divide in this country is deep and getting wider, and that's very alarming.

RK: Yes, it is, and it's the result of almost a third of a century of a volunteer military that has evolved, Hugh, into sort of its own separate caste, the same way many other professions do, the same way plastic surgeons, lawyers, others … well, the military is separated on bases, it does a lot of work overseas of a highly technical nature, and so military families, and military men and women, live in a whole different cultural universe than the larger segment of society. And the result is that society at large looks at the military with a mixture of suspicion on one hand, and awe on the other.

HH: The awe is what I find, as well as the appreciation, more often than not. I also have lectured at the Naval Academy, and am lecturing at the Air Force Academy next month. I know a lot of the service members who get appointed there. And so I know they come from all over the country. How do you bridge that gap, then, if in fact it's a bad thing?

RK: Well, first of all, everything is relative. And our civil-military relationship, compared to that of Europe, is very, very good. Europeans look at their military as civil servants in funny uniforms, which they support for humanitarian and soft peacekeeping operations, but which they're loathe to support in any sort of combat operation, which is what militaries are about in the first place. So our civil-military relationship is full of tension, but I wouldn't call it altogether unhealthy. I think that one of the ways you can bridge the gap, because I believe that a draft is simply impractical in this day and age, because war has become so technological, so many things to learn, equipment to learn how to operate, that a draft wouldn't keep these people in uniform long enough to make this training worthwhile. So I think one of the ways you can bridge this gap that I mention is a stronger, more beefed up reserve and guard contingent.

HH: Let me also ask you about inside the military. "As for the combat arms community itself," you write on Page 378, "warrior consciousness will further intensify, even as the identities of each of the four armed service become less distinct. It's an exceedingly slow process, more noticeable at the top levels of command then elsewhere." But you also fret just above that about the loss of the warrior mentality. So what are you talking about? And how do you prevent it dribbling away?

RK: Well, you know, as societies become more prosperous, more upper middle class, more globally connected, they're less and less likely to support war, [to want to go ...] I mean, of course, you should never want to go to war. But they're less and less likely to feel any sort of tie to a professional military. They see it as sort of like an anachronism, something from the medieval age. So society as a whole [is less likely ...you know,] feels more and more disconnected from a warrior military, even as the military itself becomes more and more of a warrior caste. [The distinctions between ...] you know, there's more and more joint operations between the Air Force, the Navy, the Army and the Marines, more and more stuff is joint. Even the uniforms are starting to look more and more similar, so that the various services have more and more to do with each other, and thus, the distance between them sort of slowly collapses. So it's less Army, Air Force, Marines and Navy than it is more and more just purple warriors. I use the word purple because purple is the color of jointness. It's the overlapping of Navy brown, of Air Force blue, of Army grey, etcetera.

HH: Let me ask you two questions. Is the military big enough? And are we paying the enlisted ranks enough?

RK: We're not paying the enlisted ranks enough. We can always pay them more. And not only are they not being paid enough, we're not doing as much as we could to get them the education that they need, because we're going to have more, we're living in a world, in a media fishbowl world where the actions of a lowly sergeant or chief petty officer in the case of the Navy, can have strategic consequences. We've seen what happens when lower ranking Marines, et cetera, misbehave, or don't carry out something right. So we need to make these people as sophisticated as possible. It used to be that if you were a lieutenant or a captain, you were expected to have a college education. Well, we're going to need that for our sergeants and petty officers, too. It's not enough for a sergeant to have a high school education. In the future, he's going to have to have a college education, and he's going to have to know at least one foreign language.

HH: What about the size of the Army and the Navy, in terms of brigades and ships?

RK: Well, first of all, our Navy is declining. At the end of World War II, because of all the commandeered supply ships, we had a Navy of over 6,500 ships. That quickly went down to around 600 during the Cold War. Throughout the Cold War, the [size of] ships in the Navy were [hovered] around 600. Now we're down, throughout the Clinton 1990s, it went down to 300. And at the rate we're going, you know, former secretary of the Navy, John Lehman, claims that we're headed towards a 150 ship Navy, even as the Chinese are growing their navy, the same with the Japanese, the South Koreas, the Indians. [If you look at ships, numbers of hulls, you'll see ... and] I'll be writing about this in an upcoming edition of the Atlantic Monthly in November. If you look at navies and hull numbers, we're going from a unipolar American Naval world to a multipolar world.

HH: Oh, that's very, very troubling, and hopefully, it will be reversed.

HH: Thanks to my guest, Robert D. Kaplan, author of <u>Hog Pilots, Blue Water Grunts: The American Military in the Air, at Sea and on the Ground</u> for spending this much time with me. It's an important book, because the military's important. Civilians need to understand it. A couple of closing questions, Robert Kaplan. I was trying to think of a number of ways to pose this, and I came up with if your editor came to you and said you're going to have to do all of your deployments again except one, you can skip one of them, which one would you skip?

RK: I really can't say, because they were all so good. In each of them, I learned so much. And every one opened up a whole different world to me.

HH: Which was the least comfortable, most physically taxing of them?

RK: All right, well that was easy. That was Iraq during the first battle of Fallujah.

HH: Wow.

RK: Where you didn't bathe for days, weeks on end. You often had to run, dodge bullets. You were always cold or you were hot. You were never comfortable, because you couldn't just take off your body armor, and take off an undershirt or something like that. And body armor has this way of making you even hotter in hot temperatures, but doesn't keep you warm in cold temperatures. It's the worst of both combinations.

HH: Of the other men and women of American journalism who occasionally or often travel with American military, whose work do you respect and admire?

RK: I respect Michael Yon a lot, the blogger.

HH: Right, right.

RK: ... because of all the work he does staying there. And I respect Greg Jaffe of the Wall Street Journal

HH: And then finally, what's next, Robert Kaplan? Is there another book along the lines of Imperial Grunts and the new Hog Pilots out there?

RK: There may be, [but what ...]I'm going to keep writing about the military, about Medal of Honor winners in the future, and other things, because I think that there's just so much that the military does that doesn't get covered. We're too concerned with making victims out of them. Rather than cover technically what we do, we cover them [as if,] with a sense of pity, as if they're the latest victims. And you know, it's almost therapy ... we're covering the war for the sake of therapy for ourselves, rather than describing the war and what's actually going on tactically, technically on the ground.

HH: And are you staying at the Naval Academy? Or have you moved onto a different base?

RK: I'm still at the Naval Academy as a visiting professor this semester. It's my third straight semester there.

HH: Well, I look forward to talking with you about the Navy when the Atlantic Monthly article comes out.

RK: That'll be a pleasure.

HH: Once again, the book is <u>Hog Pilots, Blue Water Grunts</u> by Robert D. Kaplan. Thank you, Robert, talk to you again soon, thanks for your service to the military, and for a wonderful book.

End of Interview.

Chapter 7.

Understanding The Savagery of the Enemy: Interviews with Dexter Filkins and Michael Yon

Because relative stability has come to Iraq as a result of the surge and because the images of terrorism in far away Afghanistan and Pakistan just don't rivet the West as explosions and mayhem do when the civilian victims are Americans or Europeans, the public loses sight of what we are fighting: the barbarism of a medieval cult that thinks nothing of cutting off heads in video after video or of executing scores and hundreds of fellow Muslims because of the perceived necessity of provoking growing strife and war. The brutal nature of al Qaeda and of the Shia fundamentalists is almost impossible to convey to the average American.

Two extraordinary journalists have done just that in book/memoir form, detailing not just the brutality they have been told about, but the savagery they have seen and lived.

Interestingly, they could not come from more different backgrounds.

Dexter Filkins has labored for many years for the biggest name in old media, The New York Times. Like his colleague John Burns, Filkins is widely and deeply respected by the American center and right as a reliable, indeed an authoritative purveyors of true things —a very, very rare recognition in these days of an openly partisan, hard left American media that openly worked to elect Barack Obama for most of the past year.

When Filkins joined me on air, his memoir <u>The Forever War</u>, had just been published; and the surge's success was just moving from the tentative to the enduring stage. The book is crucial because Filkins began his reporting on the long war from Afghanistan before we were even generally aware that there was a war underway, and when the

Taliban were remote, Bhudda blowing-up extremists with a zero threat-to-us profile. Filkins would move on after the invasion of Afghanistan to the many wars of Iraq, leaving just before the surge had finally brought relative stability to the country and hope for its future.

Michael Yon, by contrast, is a citizen journalist, a former special forces warrior who yielded to appeals from his former colleagues still in uniform to come and report on the war for his blog, and thus began a series of reader-supported trips to the front which earned him a vast online audience for his courageous reporting on the many battles for Iraq. In 2008 his Moment of Truth in Iraq appeared to widespread acclaim, and within the book were accounts of al Qaeda's brutal nature that it will be a necessary read for anyone seeking to comment on the conflict.

Interview with Dexter Filkins,
September 19, 2008

HH: Welcome to a special edition of the Hugh Hewitt Show. In hour number three I'll talk with Congressman John Campbell from the Hill about the effort to calm the markets, which by the way, closed up more than 400 points on the Dow today. Lots of extraordinary stories behind the scenes, but the most extraordinary story in the world remains the war. And yesterday, the attack on the embassy in Yemen underscored, today the loss of seven American soldiers in a terrible helicopter crash in Iraq, underscores that while we focus on financial issues, it's got nothing to do with where the cockpit of, well, the future of the world is being decided right now. To discuss that situation with me, an extraordinary guest in studio, Dexter Filkins, who is the New York Times correspondent who you've often heard referred to on this program by John Burns and others as one of the preeminent war correspondents of our time. He has a brand new book out called The Forever War. It just came out. I've just finished reading it. It's linked at Hughhewitt.com. You should read this book. It's riveting. It's disturbing. Dexter Filkins, welcome to the Hugh Hewitt Show, good to have you here.

DF: Thank you very much.

HH: I want to start with some bio. Congratulations, by the way. It's an amazing book.

DF: Thank you, thank you.

HH: How long did it take to write?

DF: A long time. [God, you know, it takes,] I thought when I got back to the States that I could just sit there with all my notebooks and crank it out. But I just took a long time, because I had to relive a lot of this stuff. So a lot of it's not very pleasant.

HH: It's very troubling, it's very moving, it will bring a tear to many people's eyes if they know any soldier, sailor, airman or Marine who has died there.

DF: Thanks.

HH: And we're going to talk about some of them. But let's start with a little bio on Dexter Filkins. You're a young guy, because you're younger than me. How old are you? And how long have you been doing the reportorial thing?

DF: Well, I'm 47. I'm from Florida. Actually, I was born in Ohio.

HH: Which part?

DF: Well, born in Cincinnati.

HH: That's almost Ohio.

DF: Lived in Cleveland.

HH: Oh, you did live in Cleveland. Browns fan?

DF: Chagrin Falls.

HH: No kidding.

DF: Kind of Lake Louise.

HH: Yeah, I know Chagrin Falls well. I know the Falls well. I know the candy store above the Falls well, so go ahead.

DF: I'm more of a Dolphins fan, but you know, anyway, Bernie Kosar did a tour through Miami, I think at one point. But I grew up in Florida, and I was, as I mentioned as I was walking in the studio, I lived in Corona del Mar…

HH: California, down in Orange County, okay.

DF: '95, '96, '97, Marigold Avenue. And I was just wondering, yeah, we were just talking about what it looks like there now. I'm curious. And I did that. I went to India, and this is kind of when the book starts, I went to India for the L.A. Times in 1997. [And the opening scene of the book, of course, I started going to,] I was living in New Delhi, and I, part of my responsibility was this place called Afghanistan that nobody much cared about then. I didn't know much about it. And there I was on a Friday afternoon at the Kabul sports stadium one day watching a public execution and amputation. And the funny thing about that time was it didn't mean anything, you know? It was just who are these [kind of, these] really strange guys? They look strange, they act strange. And they were putting somebody to death here in a public execution and reading out of the Koran, but it didn't mean anything.

HH: I'm jumping way ahead here, and we'll come back, but you actually kind of make me sympathetic to Mullah Omar, who takes up his 13 Kalashnikovs and his 1 RPG, because boys are being sold between warlords. I mean, we don't like him, it's not a sympathetic portrait, but it makes me understand a little bit more about from which he came.

DF: Yeah, you know, basically, they're like a lot of movements, I guess, started out they had a noble purpose. They were totally brutal. But they were the biggest, baddest guys on the block, and they tamed everybody else, and they brought order to the place, which is all people wanted at the time. And they went bad. And you know, the last time before 9/11 that I had been in Afghanistan was 2000. I was there in the summer of 2000 and I was arrested by the Taliban and kicked out and expelled from the country. It was big, ugly scene, [but] which [actually doesn't, that little moment there] doesn't appear in the book. [But you could see, and] I remember I would have these conversations with my translators, with my Afghan translators, who almost uniformly hated the Taliban at that point, and they would say things like the Arabs are here and they're taking over. Osama bin Laden, [you know,] who was kind of known then because they'd blown up the embassies in Africa, [but you know, he'd say you know,] he's got a lot of money, he's spreading a lot of money around, and they're under the control of the Arabs. [You know,] they've got these camps outside of town. And again, back then, I think…

HH: You never ran into him. In your book, [you just,] once you ran into one in a supermarket, and you got the heck out of there, a drug store, I guess it was.

DF: You read the book very closely, thank you. Yes, and I remember he hustled me out of town. [The one,] we ran into some Arab women. [There was the moment in the airport where this bizarre scene in retrospect, of course, but it's only retrospect. At the time, I was thinking what on Earth does this mean.] But we were standing in the Kabul airport in the summer of 2000. It's a year before 9/11. And here are these women, head to toe burkas, and you could see their really, really nice high-heeled, probably Ferragamo shoes sticking out of their burkas, and they were complaining in Arabic about their jihadi husbands, my husband. You know, we could be in Paris shopping at all the stores. Instead, we're here because my husband has to be the tough guy jihadi.

HH: It's on Page 43. I made notes about this, because it's such a stunning anecdote. She says I could be shopping in Paris, but instead I am here in this awful place. Yes, my husband has to be the tough guy warrior fighting for Islam. We are stuck in this cursed place. And I was just in Venice a few weeks ago. Burkas in the Hotel Danieli, and I'm thinking to myself, who are these women, and they're imprisoned. And clearly, you caught the drift that they are imprisoned. [This is…]

DF: I think they know it, too. Yeah, they certainly did.

HH: All right. We're ahead. I want to go back to, was your first job in journalism with the L.A. Times?

DF: No, it was at the Miami Herald.

HH: Okay, so where did you go undergrad?

DF: University of Florida.

HH: Okay, so out of Florida, you just say you want to be a journalist, because I'm trying to get to where does a war correspondent come from? In the course of covering these wars, where did [that,] the light go on in Dexter Filkin's mind to say I want to grow up to go to these places and follow these soldiers, sailors, airmen and Marines?

DF: It's a funny thing you say that, because I was just thinking [of,] I went to a reading once of John Updike, [and I remember] he was talking, [this was 1987, and of course, our world has changed very much since then, but he said, I think I was covering the City Council in West Palm Beach, Florida then or something, and he said, he was talking] about why his books were so quiet, you know, they weren't Hemmingway. And he said I'm not Hemmingway. And he said we live in a very quiet time. And I was thinking my God, you know, we don't live in a quiet time anymore. But I went out to India not thinking of course anything. [I mean, I didn't,] I wasn't the war correspondent. It kind of just fell in my lap. But once it all started, and once 9/11 came, I knew that story pretty well. I knew Afghanistan pretty well, so I went back. And then kind of one thing led to another.

HH: You know, you're coming up on your 30th high school reunion. So Dexter Filkins goes back to Miami or wherever that is.

DF: Cape Canaveral.

HH: Cape Canaveral, and they say what have you been doing? And you say well, I've been watching MTV in a potato shed off of a generator with a 16-year-old Northern Alliance kid with a Kalashnikov. Did you have any idea that this is where you were going?

DF: [No, I mean, I think there were these moments…oh, at the time.] You mean when I was in high school?

HH: Yeah.

DF: Well, [I think] when I was in high school, [and probably everybody, I guess, but] I thought [yeah, I mean,] I want to do something interesting, you know? [And I could have gone,] I majored in government, and I suppose I could have gone to law school like the rest of my friends.

HH: Like I did, yeah.

DF: (laughing)

HH: Okay, careful.

DF: Got to be careful. [But I thought you know, studying,] I used to study in the law school, and I'd look and I'd see these enormous books called, things like torts and contracts, and I thought my God, what's going on in there? And so I decided to do, [I tried to do] something else. Actually, there was a moment in my life when the bell went off, [which was,] it was a long time ago, but I was studying for the LSAT to go to law school, and went to the movies that night, and I saw the "Year of Living Dangerously."

HH: Mel Gibson, Indonesia, Suharto, yeah.

DF: Yeah, and I thought Sigourney, Indonesia, the revolution, that's the life for me. [But I never thought, honestly, I mean I never thought, you know,] there was a moment in the book when I was in New York on 9/11, and of course, it was by 10 AM, everybody knew where this had come from. And then of course, it all sort of came together. [But…and then] I haven't really slowed down since.

HH: Are you addicted to it now?

DF: [You know, I think I was when I came out. I think it's not,] I don't know that you get addicted to the events. People ask me about the danger, and you know, it's a terribly dangerous place, and I'm very lucky that I've survived, [and] a lot of people haven't survived, a lot of people I know, people that I was with.

But to be able to watch history unfold right in front of your eyes, that's a rare thing, [and] it's an incredible thing to see, and to see the sort of tectonic plates [like] really press up against each other.

HH: But it messes your life up, doesn't it?

DF: Yes.

HH: I mean, you mention in the Afterword you lost what sounds like either your wife or your girlfriend in the course of this.

DF: Yes.

HH: And so looking back, are you glad that you have spent the last decade the way you have spent the last decade?

DF: Well, that's a very good question. I'd probably do it a little bit differently. But I think when I used to come out of Iraq, particularly in the beginning in '03 and '04, when it was so intense, [you know,] and every day was just, [God it was] so long, and the country would change 100% from one day to the next, and I'd come out of Iraq after two months and basically I would just lie on the couch for the first three weeks and just stare at the ceiling. [I mean, it's just not the same. I mean,] every decision you make when you're in a war zone like that, your life is on the line. Do I go down that road or not, [you know]? And then suddenly, you come out and it's like do I have Swiss cheese or cheddar cheese on my sandwich? And so it kind of whipsaws you.

HH: Dexter Filkins, I'm going over tomorrow to Las Vegas. I'm going to hang out with Bill Roggio, one of the milbloggers, all the milbloggers over at BlogWorldExpo. And people can still come over if they want to join us over there. And I think about Michael Yon and your colleague, John Burns, and yourself, who have been working hard to sort of tell the American people what has been going on in Afghanistan and Iraq for many, many years. When you come back to the States, you write this book and you're on a book tour. Do we understand what has been going on there? And I don't mean just me, I mean just generally as you walk around the United States, do they understand?

DF: You know, I hate to say no to that question, but I think what is most jarring to me is when I'm out in Anbar Province [hanging out] with the Marines or the soldiers, they're 19 and they're from Nowhereville, Kentucky, [for the most part.] And then I come back to the States, and if it's Manhattan or Cambridge or Los Angeles, [or…] it just doesn't resonate, [and I think because you know,] frankly, people who live in Manhattan, their kids aren't fighting in that war, [and L.A. for the most part. And so it's like,] and this is what they say, that the country is not at war, but the military's at war.

HH: Let me ask you about that. This is a patch for J.P. Blecksmith, who was killed in Fallujah, second battle of Fallujah. His dad's a friend of mine, a Naval Academy grad. Mark Metherell, I met his parents, Navy SEAL, dead, very extraordinary people in Southern California. I think of Mark Daily from Southern California, a UCLA grad killed in the war. I mean, there are lots of Americans all over the place. It's the officer corps, et cetera.

DF: Sure.

HH: So do you really think, it's not geographical so much as it is attitudinal, people who want to know. Do they figure it out?

DF: Good point. [Yeah, good point. I mean, the officer corps, I mean, I don't have to tell you this, but] the officer corps, you know, it's extraordinary. I mean, when you see these guys…I just came from Iraq, and I sat with General Petraeus, for example, for a couple of hours, and we just talked about…

HH: Were you there for the Times again? New York Times?

DF: Yeah, I just…

HH: Are you still with the New York Times?

DF: Yes, yes. I just went back for about a month. And we can talk about the specific changes, they're rather extraordinary.

[But I thought, you know,] General Petraeus has done 48 months in the country. Forty-eight months! You think of the sacrifice involved there, and that's four out the last five and a half years, and [those guys, you know, like] if you're a reporter, say, or a blogger, whatever, you go in for a couple of months, you leave for a couple of weeks. Those guys go over for, [they go over for] fifteen months, or seventeen months, and they don't go home, or maybe they go home for two weeks.

HH: How much time have you spent, let's just be clinical here, since 1997, how much time have you spent in Afghanistan? I mean calendar days, months, and how much time in Iraq?

DF: Well, a lot. I mean, I went back after 9/11. I went back pretty quickly to Afghanistan, saw the war there, the initial phase.

HH: With the Northern Alliance.

DF: Yeah, [yeah. God, it was insane. It was a crazy time, incredible time, though. I mean, it was just so dramatic. And we can talk about that, too, but I spent that time there. Then Kabul fell, and] I spent most of 2002 in Afghanistan and going in and out. He looked [like] there was going to be a war in Iraq, and I got ready for that. I moved to Istanbul and rented a Hertz Rent-a-car and a Ford Yukon in Kuwait City and drove in. Three or four years in Afghanistan and then about four in Iraq.

HH: Let me compliment you, and I want the audience to hear this. You do not discount or short-change the brutality of Saddam. And I think to understand fully what has been going on, and some of the critics of the war may actually not like your book because of this, when you tell the story of the record keeper at Abu Ghraib, who has kept count of the bodies that would be buried at night out of Saddam's prison, and then the families that would come to find them, it conveys…and you tell mad as a hatter boys, and what they were doing, the Saddam kids, there's a lot of criticism of the war effort in this book implicit in it, but there's also a great sensibility as to what went before, that Robert Kaplan shares with you. I don't know if you know Kaplan, but he said the country was so brutalized…

DF: Exactly.

HH: …that it's hard to imagine anything having worked in there. And so I appreciate very much that The Forever War pays respect to what went before. Let me ask you about Col. Sassaman. And by the way, we're on the air on Colorado Springs and Denver…

DF: Great.

HH: …so Col. Sassaman might be listening to this, lots of military across the country. You just mentioned David Petraeus, 48 months, extraordinary soldier. Col. Sassaman, extraordinary soldier as well…

DF: Absolutely.

HH: …but it gets to him. You kind of convey that it gets to him. How many Petraeuses, how many Sassamans, what's the division among the men and women of the Armed Service who have gone there that you've observed?

DF: You mean the division in terms of…

HH: In terms of it getting to them, and those who just get out, and those who accept it and thrive on it and learn from it, and embrace their sort of warrior calling.

DF: You know, when I was just there this last time, I thought about that a lot, because I think what you're seeing on the ground is the guys who were there, not just the 19 year olds or the 23 year olds who are on their fourth combat tour, you know, and have already had two kids and are divorced, but the officers. [I mean,] some of these guys now are in their third year or fourth year on the ground, and there's a learning curve, [you know,] and they're just way better at, they just get it totally, whereas before, I mean, reporters included, you drop into a country like Iraq that's just unbelievably complicated, and it takes a long time to figure it out. And so the guys who are there are totally committed to it, because if they weren't, they would have left. And a lot of them did, of course, but the ones who are there, it's a very, very strong corps.

HH: The Forever War concludes in '06, and of course it's now '08. And you just said you've come back from Iraq. How would you, would you ever guess we would be where we are in '08 from where you concluded the book?

DF: No, no. No. I didn't think that was possible anymore, frankly.

HH: What's it like at the Bureau now? You describe basically a prison, a fortress by the time you leave. John Burns has discussed that on this program as well. So what's it like there now?

DF: [Well, I mean at the Bureau, I mean, it is.] It's a sort of medieval castle surrounded by, [you know, we have] belt-fed machine guns on the roof, searchlights, the whole thing. Well, I'll give you an example of the Bureau. It's [a great, great example, is just the New York Times' Bureau is] on the eastern bank of the Tigris River, [just] in a neighborhood called Abu Nuwas. There's a park that runs along the river, it's about two miles long. [As I...there's a couple of moments in my book that as I left, you know...]

HH: These are your running trails, by the way. We'll get to this, because you're just insane to do this, but go ahead.

DF: (laughing) Yeah, it was like totally reckless.

HH: Yeah.

DF: But when I left Iraq in 2006, Abu Nuwas Park, there was like this kind of creepy militia checkpoint at one end, and these guys with guns and no uniforms. The Iraqi Army was at the other end. There was barbed wire in between. [I mean, it was just,] no one went there, no one. It was totally deserted. I went there every night when I was back this last time, and you know, the first night I got back, there were probably 2,000 Iraqis in the park.

HH: Wow.

DF: Yeah, incredible.

HH: Wow.

DF: I mean, parents with children, women walking around alone.

HH: Because the soccer games had vanished in the course of The Forever War.

HH: When we went to break, you were telling us, Dexter, about the change that you just saw in Iraq. And on Page 320 of your book, you quote Kharmut Hanoon, a 40 year old farmer who says, "I don't think things will ever go back to normal between Shiites and Sunnis." Was Hanoon wrong?

DF: I don't know if he's wrong. I think [there's,] there was a lot of extraordinary bloodshed there in '05 and '06 when this civil war, [or whatever it was,] got going. I think what's happened now is a kind of stepping back. [I mean, you can see, the nice way to say this is] when I step out into Abu Nuwas Park, and I see the parents walking with their children, you can see the relief on people's faces. I thought the city was dead. Well, it wasn't dead. Everybody was hiding. So you can feel people sort of exhale when they come out. But I think you don't get over something like what happened in '05 and '06 very easily. And so the Americans [have sort of erected these various arrangements which] are [kind of holding. I mean, they're] keeping the peace, like the awakening, for example, where we've got 100,000 Sunni gunmen on the payroll. You know, it's working. I mean, it's definitely working. But I think it's a very, very fragile relationship, and so I think those two groups, to answer your question, those two groups are kind of warily looking at each other. But for the moment, they're holding their fire.

HH: Let me bottom line it right now. Are the Iraqis better off than they were at this time in 2002?

DF: That's a tough one. That's a tough one. I mean, the suffering that they went through before then is kind of incalculable, you know? I mean, there's a moment in the book where I go into a torture chamber...

HH: It is. It's grim.

DF: [Well, you see something like that, and I can't, personally, I can't listen to the sort of, I mean, it's easy to forget what they went through. I mean, there were operating tables in that place, and there was a morgue out back. But you know, there's been a lot of bloodshed since.] And so I think the best way to answer that question is say let's ask it again in five years, and see how it's gone.

HH: How about Afghanistan? By the way, I completely bollixed up this interview. I've jumped all around. We're going to go back and try and resurrect it, because it's not the narrative I want it to be, which is sort of Iraq has to be experienced chronologically in the way that you lay it out in the book. And it can only be understood after Afghanistan from the perspective of Americans as well, so I appreciate the book that way. Let's go back and focus on Afghanistan. You talk about these young boys, these Northern Alliance fighters, very early in the book with [wolf-like monosyllabic,] wolf-like eyes, monosyllabic, no attention span. And I put the book down and I said I wonder where those boys are, and I wonder if this country can ever recover. You've just come back from Waziristan and Afghanistan. What's the answer to that?

DF: Well, I think those boys are probably dead. They were 15 years old, maybe 14, you know, sitting up on a hilltop, a hundred yards or half mile away were the Taliban, who came down the road a few months later. So I don't think those particular boys made it, but I think that's a brutalized country. [And I think, I don't know, because I remember back, and some of this is in the book,] when everything broke in 2001, and the Taliban collapsed, it was extraordinary. I mean, we'd roll into these towns, I was in Northern Afghanistan, and the music was going, and people were digging up their TV sets, and women were taking their burkas off, and there was joy in the streets, which is why, as I said, I expected that there'd be the same thing in Iraq. I did. Call me a fool. [And I think... but I think...] I was just in Pakistan, and it's so much more complicated because of that particular issue, right on the eastern border of Afghanistan, you now have the Taliban not just resurgent, but really, really strong. And they totally control now the western part of that country, which means that they have training camps, sanctuary, planning facilities, everything. And so…

HH: How alarmed should America be about that?

DF: Oh, I think it's going to make Afghanistan extremely difficult to stabilize. And I think that's leaving aside possibly the larger question, which is what's al Qaeda doing there?

HH: That's why I asked, because at this point in the election cycle of 2000, the Cole was bombed in Yemen. At this point in the election cycle this year, the embassy in Yemen has been attacked, though no one was killed. And a year after the Cole comes 9/11, and it came from that part of the world where there was no supervision or authority. Do people talk about that openly in Pakistan, that they could be exporting more jihadis towards America?

DF: Well you know, I had a really eye-opening conversation with a tribal leader…

HH: Hold on, that music means we're going to get the tribal leader when we come right back.

HH: Let's go back to the tribal leader's conversation you had about the threat that is growing in the ungovernable areas of the northwest territories in Waziristan.

DF: Really, it was an extraordinary conversation. I mean, this was a tribal leader from south Waziristan, which is where a lot of people think Osama and probably Ayman Zawahiri are. [And so we were talking, and we were talking about a lot of things.] We were talking about the Taliban and kind of what was going on there. And at one point, I said what about the Arabs. And he said we have Arabs here, yes. I said how do you know? And he said well, you can hear them speaking Arabic, and you can see the Arab fighters in the Bazaar. They come in, and you can hear the language. But then he paused and said but the important Arabs, the important Arabs are in the mountains. So I said, intrigued, I said important Arabs? And he said they have Arabian horses. We don't have horses like that in Waziristan. He said we take food up to them, you know, the people in my tribe. And he said they come to me, they tell me everything, I'm the leader of my tribe. He said those horses eat better, [those horses eat better] than the common people do in south Waziristan. And he said they've seen the horses. They've seen the Arabs. And so I said important Arabs – Osama? And he said I don't know, but they're important. They've got a lot of money.

HH: Dexter Filkins, [after…] are you an optimist about this war? I'm going to go back and get us to this, but what's…you know, there's a famous snowflake that Donald Rumsfeld sent, which said we don't have any metrics. The madrasas are turning out tens of thousands of people, this is in 2003, I believe the famous Rumsfeld note, we still don't have any metrics. We don't have Musharraf anymore. We don't know what's going on in Pakistan. They've got 90 nukes. What do you think generally about the trajectory this war is on?

DF: Well you know, I never thought I'd say this, that I would be more optimistic about Iraq, but having just come from there, and have seen what's happened there, I am. I mean, I think it seems to have stabilized there, you know, knock on wood. Let's hope it lasts. Boy, the other one, Afghanistan just seems very, very tough. I mean, the terrain there is extraordinary. You know, it's like you're walking around on the Moon. And they've got these sanctuaries, and you know, Pashtunistan is what they call it. It's sort of the Pashtun areas on both sides of the border. It's 45 million people. You know, it's gigantic. [And we don't, I mean,] what do we have there, 35,000 troops? It's going to be hard.

HH: Page 24, "In my many trips to Afghanistan, I grew to adore the place for its beauty and its perversions, for the generosity of its people in the face of madness. The brutality one could witness in the course of a working day was often astonishing. The casualness of it more so. The way that brutality had seeped into every corner of human life was a thing to behold, and yet deep down, a place in the heart stayed tender." Now that's a very ambiguous statement of what Afghanistan is, and there are lots of books that have been written over the years, <u>War at the Top of the World</u>, <u>The Great Game</u>, things like this, Hopkirk, Peter Hopkirk, et cetera. Does that Afghanistan ever change? Or is this just the way it's going to be and has always been?

DF: Wow, that's a really good point. [I think] what I was trying to get at there was [this kind of very ambiguous yin yang, it's] the yin-yang nature of the place. It's the only way to describe. They are capable of extraordinary brutality, [I mean,] which I saw up close, and kind of so casual about death that your jaw falls open. And yet at the same time, my God, if you're in their house, they'll take their shirt off their back for you. [And I mean,] I was literally in a place that was surrounded by the Taliban. This was in 1998, ten years ago. There was famine. It was in Bamyan when the statues were still up. And there was a famine, and every house I went into, unannounced, a stranger, dirty boots, they fed me, or tried to feed me every last crumb of food they had. And I think maybe that's why it's so difficult.

HH: Are they devout Muslims? Or are they…all sorts of different spectrum of Christians from those who are sort of Sunday Christians, or Easter and Christmas Christians. Are the people who extended you this hospitality acting as a result of Koranic injunction? Or is it the culture of…

DF: I think it's the culture. And I think likewise, it's the Pashtun culture as much as anything that we're fighting against. I mean, that's the hard core of the Taliban on both sides of that border.

HH: You talk about being up with, is it Dostum, the crazy guy in the Northern Alliance?

DF: Dostum, yeah, yeah, yeah.

HH: Dostum is just as brutal as they can be. That's not Pashtun, right? That's a different Tajik, and as a result, do they ever take over Afghanistan? Or are there just too many Pashtuns to do that?

416

DF: Well, that's a good point. [I mean,] I think that they've been slugging it out. The Pashtuns are about 45% of the population. [I mean,] they're Uzbeks and Tajiks and Turkmens, and Dostum is an Uzbek, and as brutal as they come, absolutely. But [yeah,] he's never going to take over. And so I think the question is [are they just going to,] can they cobble something together that works? [Or is it just going to be the...]

HH: Now we wouldn't care if they couldn't export it, right? We really wouldn't care. It's been that way forever, and it's going to stay that way, but they can export. That goes back to the question to the tribal leader. Can they export again like they did on 9/11, the terrible death that...you were in the ruins of 9/11 on that day.

DF: Yeah, you know, I had a conversation with Bruce Hoffman...

HH: Sure.

DF: ...who's a Georgetown University terrorism guy. [And I didn't realize this, but I mean,] he pointed out six terrorist plots to me, successful and unsuccessful, including the 7/7 attacks in Britain, the subway attacks that killed 52 people, six terrorist attacks since 2004, have been traced back to the tribal areas. So I think there's the answer.

HH: It used to be that they would come into Kabul and then go to the camps. They're now entering Pakistan and going to the camps. So they're ending up in the same place, the camps have moved around a little bit.

HH: Dexter Filkins, you just got back from Pakistan, and we were just talking about the export of terror. What was the conversation you started to say when we went to break?

DF: [Well, you know,] I had been there in the 90s, and I'd been to the madrasas before 9/11, and I saw what they were doing. [You know,] [I've] [got to] remember uncomprehending at the time, but walking into these classrooms full of, [you know,] 14 year olds being taught about the jihad.

HH: Memorizing…

DF: [Yeah, yeah,] and memorizing the Koran. I wanted to just take a peek and see, look in about the madrasas when I was just there in Pakistan a few weeks ago. And I went to the wrong madrasa, obviously, or went to the right madrasa. Went in, walked into a room, and in the room were a bunch of clearly non-Pakistanis, North Africans, probably Egyptian, maybe Sudanese, Arabic speaking. [It was, you know,] they let it be known pretty quickly that I wasn't welcome there. [But there it is. I mean,] I think the dilemma is for the United States is that we've been on these guys forever to shut these things down. Either they can't do it, or they don't want to do it, but they haven't done it.

HH: Is there a sense of change in Pakistan with the fall of Musharraf and the assassination of Bhutto and the replacement with her husband?

DF: [Well, I think. You know, I'm a little mystified,] I've always been a little mystified, at the [sort of] idealization of Benazir Bhutto, because I think she was a lot more complicated figure, and particularly her husband…

HH: Mr. 10%er.

DF: Mr. 10%er.

HH: Mr. 10%er, yeah.

DF: [Yeah,] and [you know,] the billion dollars that went missing when they were in power. But I think people actually had the middle class there, and the educated people had high hopes for them. And then when she was killed, I think that really set them back, and I think they're still reeling from that.

HH: Have you read Doug Frantz' book, The Nuclear Jihadist?

DF: Yes.

HH: Great book.

DF: Yes.

HH: Had him on for three hours, [and it just...] Pakistan is indecipherable. I don't know what we do with Pakistan. And did you, are you going to go back there? Is that where the Times is sending you next?

DF: I'll definitely go back if I can get a visa.

HH: Oh.

DF: It's funny you mention A.Q. Khan. [You know, I...or] Doug Frantz' book, which is of course about the nuclear program and A.Q. Khan, the father of the Pakistan nuclear program. When I was in Islamabad, I was running, [I went running a few times in Islamabad,] which was [you know,] kind of reckless...

HH: Stupid.

DF: Well, absolutely.

HH: Go ahead, we'll come back...

DF: You know, you get kind of crazy when you're holed up in these places. And I had interviewed A.Q. Khan twice before in the 1990s, when Pakistan tested its nuclear device. And you know, he's a very eccentric guy. [And I remember, you know,] he lives in this beautiful neighborhood in Islamabad, and there's these woods across the street, [and] that have monkeys in the woods. And I remember him saying [you know,] "I go out every morning and I feed the monkeys. I'm a humane man, I love animals." [And so I went for a run,] I remember where his house was, and I went for a run. And there he was, sitting on his porch, you know. And I waved to him, and he looked at me...

HH: The world's greatest criminal, if you read this book, The Nuclear Jihadist.

HH: Dexter, I want to cover a lot with you. But before we do, I will be remiss if I don't get to the story of Lance Corporal William Miller...

DF: Yes.

HH: Of Pearland, Texas, because it seems to me almost the central episode in the book. I might be wrong about this.

DF: Absolutely, yeah.

HH: But tell people the story about Lance Corporal, and the odd and unusual relationship of combat reporters and combat soldiers.

DF: [Wow, yeah. Well you know, I just,] I'll start this way. I remember, [you know,] I was embedded with a company of Marines, Bravo Company, the 1-8 Battalion, 150 guys that went into Fallujah in November, 2004, which for anybody who doesn't remember, [it] was just a horrendous battle. It was the biggest, probably the biggest battle of the war, about 100 American dead, maybe 600 American wounded, to retake the city from the several thousand jihadis that held it. [And somebody like me shows up, you know, and I,] these guys are 19 and 20 years old. They can do 20 pull ups and smoke a pack of cigarettes, and then run five miles. And they look at me, and they say is this guy going to slow us down? Are we going to have to go back out into the street and go into gunfire to save him? And so when you show up usually to embed, particularly in dangerous situations, they're a little worried about that, and I can understand that. And so I went into Fallujah with these guys, and it was intense, it was extraordinary. I'm still in touch with a lot of them. It just kind of binds you.

HH: You go to their memorial services.

DF: Yeah.

HH: You look them up. I found that very interesting, but keep going, tell us about Corporal Miller.

DF: [Yeah. I mean,] it's a shared experience that's kind of difficult to relate to other people. [So I was,] this is the 8th day of the battle. It's basically over, we're at the southern end of Fallujah, which looks like a movie set. I mean, it literally, the town ends at one street, and then it opens up on the desert. And so it was pretty quiet, and [there was,] we knew there was a dead insurgent at the top of a minaret. One of the Marines had taken a photo of him, and we thought naturally, let's go back and get a photo and take a look. [And simple as that, and] the captain of the company gave us a squad of guys, about 20 of us, and we went back to the minaret. And the photographer I was with, Ashley Gilbertson...

HH: Ash, yeah.

DF: Ash, yeah. [He, you know,] we stepped into the minaret to go, [and right at the last second, to go] up the winding stairs, and right at the last second, a couple of Marines, I didn't see them until later, put their hand out and said, "We'll go up first." So they went up first, there was a dead insurgent at the top, but there was also a live one, and he shot and killed Lt. Miller. It was a horrible, horrible scene.

HH: It's Lance Corporal Miller...

DF: Lance Corporal Miller. He was killed, stuck at the top of the minaret. [And one of the things that, you know, I had never really seen, I had seen it, but one of the things that if you're not in the military, it's difficult to appreciate,] Miller was stuck at the top of the stairs, and we didn't know if he was alive or dead. But we did know there was at least one insurgent at the top with a gun [who had shot, you know.] And my God if they didn't go up the tower, one after the other. They went up the winding stairs into the gunfire to get Miller out. They just don't leave their dead behind. And so they got him out, [and he was dead, and...]

HH: Ash is asking you please tell me he's not dead, and you tell him.

DF: Oh, my God, it's terrible. [Yeah, I mean,] Ash was [kind of] covered with blood, and [yeah,] he's [kind of just] delirious, basically, you know, my fault, my fault, my fault. And as this is [kind of] unfolding, the insurgents spotted us and surrounded the Mosque where we were. We came under attack then. So simultaneously, we had the body of Lance Corporal Miller, and we're surrounded. [And so] it was just a horrendous scene. And I remember [sitting there on the, or] standing there thinking oh my God, [the whole,] are we going to make it out of here for a picture, you know, for a photo? And I can't pretend it was anything other than that.

HH: You have sought out his parents, Suzie and Lewis Miller. Tell people about that.

DF: Well, they're a wonderful couple. [I mean,] they're wonderful. [I saw them,] I went to the memorial service at a gymnasium in Jacksonville, North Carolina. And I mention this in the book, but I was really struck by the memorial service. I flew in, Ash and [I flew in,] and we wanted to go. It was for all the guys who'd been killed in Iraq in that battalion. [And I don't know,] I was expecting a brass band and a parade, and all the local reporters and the whole deal. [And I don't know, I mean, they didn't even,] there were so few people in the gymnasium, they didn't even have to pull the bleachers out. [So it was, just] the whole thing was kind of crushing, and in big ways and small. And I saw the Millers there, and I introduced myself, and they have been so nice to me, and I have no right to expect that.

HH: [Now it is a,] it's an interesting bit of writing, I'm sure it took you a long time. Do you feel guilt about the death of Corporal Miller?

DF: Oh, yeah, absolutely. Sure. I mean, but for me, that wouldn't have happened. [I mean, there's no way around it.]

HH: But there's no way around the necessity of telling this story, either, is there? I mean, that's what the American people need to know.

DF: Yeah.

HH: I suppose it's a personal versus a corporate issue, but...

DF: [Well, no,] you're right, of course. [I mean, I think, and as] one of the Marines said to me afterwards, he said look, this is what happens in wartime. This is what happens. And it is what happens. [I mean, you know,] there's guys running around with guns trying to kill you. And so...

HH: Is this why you keep going back? Because you're carrying some sort of burden?

DF: No, [no. I...] you can become addicted to that, and I think to the story, [and] to [kind of] telling it and trying to figure it out, and [you know,] just wait for a resolution of it.

HH: What happens to people like you long term? And I don't mean you personally, I mean war correspondents? Do they become drunks in bars reliving...and there are some of them that I wonder about that.

DF: Absolutely. I think they do. [I mean, I have to say,] I went from Baghdad to Cambridge, Massachusetts. And it was the most jarring, [I mean,] I didn't want to be there for about the first...

HH: Did you do a Nieman fellowship?

DF: Yeah, I did a Nieman fellowship. [So I had, and I wanted to write the book, so] it was an easy place to land because I was being paid for being there. [But my God, you know, it was,] I went from listening to ten car bombs go off every morning before 11AM to, [you know,] the most consequential thing that happens there is, [well, I remember] listening to the marching band in the morning march down to the football stadium. [And that's, I think that's the part that you know,] as somebody who's been there, becoming a drunk in a bar? I could certainly do that.

HH: Have you become, I'm psychobabbling here, reintegrated? Because it seems to me you must be used to BS'ing everyone. You could be BS'ing me totally, because you have to, you're in Najaf with the Shiites. They want to shoot you, and you've got to talk your way out of it. So are you, can you ever turn off that...I mean, you've got to be constantly BS'ing people.

DF: In Iraq?

HH: In Iraq, and I would imagine it carries over to the U.S. and everywhere. I mean, it's got to be like a second self, isn't it?

DF: [Yeah, well,] let me think about that. I think when you're in a dangerous situation in a place like Iraq or Afghanistan, [I think that what separates it is most of those, you know, I had no idea what was going on when they were happening, so I mean,] the survival instinct sort of kicks in, and lucky for me, I made it out of all of them, you know, knock on wood. I had a lot of close calls. [But I think] when I came back, [I think] the hard part, and I wonder what, if you had a, say, Marine here or a soldier, if he'd say the same thing. It's just normal life seems kind of banal. I mean, it's just hard to get excited about anything.

HH: Why didn't they kill you in Najaf? What were you doing? You were with the Mahdi fighters before they tried you and then let you go. But you're in this alley with all these Mahdi fighters, and I think to myself, why didn't they turn around and kill the American?

DF: [Well, we had this, we used to, and again, some of these rules you make for yourself are incredibly stupid, and I think this one probably was. But] there was always a sense that we had, that however bad the Shiite insurgents were, they were never as bad as the Sunni insurgents. They were never going to cut your head off, they were never going to put you in an orange jumpsuit and make a video out of you.

HH: But you said they liked their, what was their accoutrement or torture they liked the most?

DF: Oh, electric drills.

HH: Electric drills. They have a drill thing.

DF: Yeah, yeah. Shiites do electric drills. It's just bizarre. And I mean, you go into the morgue, and it's all these bodies just drilled with electric drills. Where'd that come from? Someone told me it came from Iran, [but...] that they do the same thing in Iran, and I just don't know the answer to that. But yeah, so I talked my way out of that one. But what happened in that case was totally bizarre, [was] the Mahdi Army was surrendering that day, and it was at the Imam Ali Shrine. The Americans had basically fought their way up all the way to the gates of the shrine. They were told not to hit the shrine, and I swear, there were maybe two bullet holes in it, and they hadn't touched it. And then that's when we got grabbed by the Mahdi Army.

HH: And you're lucky you had a great translator.

HH: I totally botched this interview in terms of sequencing, and I'm just not going to try and save it now. But let me do a few subjects, because there are some themes in this book, one is the incredible bravery of the Iraqi people. [And I...] we went down and broadcast from Camp Pendleton on the day they had their elections, because they allowed the purple thumbs to go down there, and they were exuberant and ebullient. You tell the story, and I want to get her name right, of the woman who stands for election...

DF: Oh, my God, yeah.

HH Widjan Quzay...

DF: Yes.

HH: ...who among with other fearless people, "they went to the slaughter, thousands and thousands of them, editors and pamphleteers, judges and police officers, and women like Widjan Quzay. The insurgents were brilliant at that. They could spot a fine mind or a tender soul wherever it might be, chase it down and kill it dead. The heart of a nation, the precision was astounding." Are there any of them left?

DF: I think there are. I mean, remarkably, remarkably. [But you know, it's funny, because people,] I used to get e-mails from people, [you know,] friends, whoever, and people would say why can't they govern themselves? What's wrong with them? [How come they're not,] how come they don't get with the program? How come they're not grateful? And there's your answer. [I mean,] every person who stepped forward to try to make a difference was killed. [I mean, and] it just happened over and over and over again. But what I think is remarkable, what's really remarkable, is that they're still coming.

HH: Very poignant, before the first battle of Fallujah, much less the second battle of Fallujah. They try and do democracy American style, and they bring all the local elected leaders and opinion elites together in a big room, and then you wistfully sort of remark in the book, who knows how many of them are left, probably not many.

DF: Probably not many. Probably not many, yeah.

HH: So who's running Iraq now?

DF: Well again, and I try to touch on this in the book a little bit, no matter how bad it got. Whenever somebody said you know, the election's today, or sign up to run for the city council, or to run the city, or to be a police chief, they always step forward. And I think the lesson of that is, and it makes me think of a conversation I had with General Petraeus recently, and with General Odierno, who I saw as well at the Pentagon before he went over, which was the premise of the surge was always that there was small groups of bad people were basically wrecking it for everybody else, al Qaeda on one side, and the Mahdi Army on the other. The average Iraqis, you know, are decent people. They're not sectarian, they want to live together.

HH: Now when you were just back there in Iraq, standard operating conditions in which you are living now, you tell often in the book, and I'm a runner, slow, but you're a runner, fast, how you'd go running through Baghdad in these crazy situations. But it was a good indication of what the quality of life is, when you start running on the Tigris, you can, it's two miles, it's green, we re-sod it, we put up barriers and all that stuff, and the guards like you. And then by the end of the time you leave, it's really kind of a death wish to go running. It's like Central Park at Midnight in the late 70s. What's it like now, just the daily life, when you went back there? You saw the people in the park, but in terms of just an American in Baghdad?

DF: It's remarkably better, remarkably better. [And I mean,] I went all over the place when I was there. I went to Sadr City, I went to the old Sadr Bureau, which was the Mahdi Army's headquarters. It's still there. There's an Iraqi Army post that they built right next to it. I went to Adamiya, which was totally under the control of al Qaeda in '06. [I went there.] I saw a wedding there at night. It was just unheard of. [I mean,] a lot of places I didn't recognize. I went to Anbar Province. I actually didn't recognize where I was in Anbar Province. [I was standing,] I had been in Ramadi in 2006, and it looked like Grozny. [I mean,] it was completely leveled. Every building was flattened except for the government center right in the middle. And there I was, I was standing in the middle of this paved, freshly paved road, and I was looking right at the government center, and I swear I didn't know where I was. They put a façade in the building, a new façade, big seal, Anbar Province. Things have gotten a lot better there. [I mean, they really have, and I think again, you know,] the larger question is, [is it permanent, is, you know,] that's a trickier question. But they are remarkably better.

HH: One of the accounts that you tell here, it's about, I think, the same battalion in which Corporal Lewis served, and the buzz that got, maybe it was Col. Sassaman's, about the Arab mind. And I probably get a letter about the "Arab mind" once a month from someone who's read the book that we're referring to, The Closed Circle, I believe. And it's about, and you quote it disparagingly, that Arabs…and it seems to me that that was one of the perhaps the wrong lessons that we took out of the first three or four years. What is the relationship now between the international corps and the Iraqis in terms of trust, which you write in the end between the New York Times correspondents and their guides, it's ultimately an issue of trust. On a larger basis, it's going to be the same way with the West and Iraq. What's that situation?

DF: Also changed, totally. [I mean, if you think back, or] if you look back to '03 and '04, [when, and I'm thinking of Col. Sassaman who was in the 4th Infantry Division, which…and the commanding general was Raymond Odierno, who's now in charge of all the troops in Iraq,] they had one mission, basically – kill and capture, you know, which you can totally understand. [I mean,] they were, [like] in Tikrit, it was Saddam's hometown, they were in the heartland of the nastiness. And a lot of people look back now and say the 4th Infantry Division and the Americans generally in Iraq were so hard on people that they created the insurgency, they created enemies. [And] I'm not sure I really buy that, because I'm not sure what really would have worked. [I mean,] would anything have worked in '03 and '04 with the Sunnis? I don't think so, I mean personally. [I mean,] they didn't feel defeated, they hadn't been defeated, and they weren't going to go down without a fight. But now it's very, very different. [I mean now], the overriding goal of the American military is not to kill and capture. It's to protect the population from the insurgents, and it's to basically separate them from the bad guys.

HH: Would you unpack that a bit, because Victor Davis Hanson often on this program makes this argument that if you don't defeat an enemy, they don't go away. You have to actually defeat them. Have they yet been defeated? Al Qaeda's been defeated, but the Sunni insurgency?

DF: This is a gut feeling. I mean, I heard a little bit of this. I talked to a lot of sheiks, I mean, I talk to people. It's remarkable what's happened.

HH: Are you an Arabic speaker?

DF: No, no.

HH: Okay, so it's always translators.

DF: No, like ten words, I mean, like two words a year I learn there. But I talked to a lot of Sunni sheiks and tribal guys, Sunnis, who frankly had been blowing up Humvees eighteen months ago, and who aren't doing it anymore. [And what...] they all told me pretty much the same story, which is we didn't want the Americans here, et cetera et cetera, but al Qaeda came, and they wanted more. They wanted us to kill other Iraqis, they wanted us to blow up the government, and we didn't want to do that anymore. And I had an amazing conversation with a guy names Ali Hatam.

HH: Yeah.

DF: [And he said,] I said so did you go after al Qaeda? And he said yeah, we killed 466 of their leaders in six weeks. And I said 466? And he said yeah, we have a list.

HH: Oh, that's not in the book.

DF: No, no, this was just the last time I was there.

HH: Okay, okay. I would have caught that detail.

DF: Well, [it was just,] it was almost as if he was saying, [I mean he was,] was they've known where these people are the whole time, you know? And when they flipped, and when we did the deal, it was over for al Qaeda.

HH: You meet with an insurgent leader at one point.

DF: Yeah.

HH: And he's talking, I'm trying to find my notes here, and I've written it down, I have his name somewhere, and it's basically the turning. It's the point where they say this is it, these people are making us kill our own people.

DF: Yes.

HH: Michael Yon made the same point in <u>Moment of Truth in Iraq</u>. Do you know Yon? Have you met Yon?

DF: We know each other pretty well over e-mail.

HH: Yeah, and so he's got the same perspective that al Qaeda basically immunized Iraq against Islamist extremism. Why hasn't that happened in Afghanistan? When we come back, you can answer that question.

HH: When we went to break, **Dexter Filkins**, I asked you the immunization of Anbar against **al** Qaeda occurred in reaction to their extraordinary terror **and our** surge. Why hasn't that immunization happened in **Afghanistan**?

DF: [You know,] to answer **that,** [I think, in a word,] I'd probably have to say because it's **so far** along that the tribes have basically been wiped out by al **Qaeda** in Pakistan. I think it's a little different in Afghanistan, **but** my experience in Pakistan, which was really extraordinary, was that if you remember, what's worked in Iraq just by way of comparison, is we made a deal with the tribes, the tribes went in after al Qaeda, and [really, really,] if not finished them off, seriously degraded them. When you go to the tribes in a place like Pakistan, the Pashtun tribes, they have just been annihilated by al Qaeda. I mean, the tribal leader who I mentioned earlier, the one who told me about the Arabs, 150 tribal leaders have been killed in south Waziristan alone. They've just basically destroyed the tribal structure. And so here was a guy, my tribal leader that I was talking to, it took me three weeks to persuade him to come out of south Waziristan to speak to me. And you know…

HH: How did you do that? Via messengers?

DF: [It was just…you spend, God,] you just spend days and days and days doing this. Yeah, I had people talking to him on the telephone. Finally, he left his house at midnight, and he took a taxi so that he wouldn't be identified. And he came to me and saw me. And he was so nervous when he saw me. I mean, he didn't want to meet me in the lobby of the hotel. [I mean,] it was just extraordinary. But he's a tribal leader. [I mean,] he's a leader of a huge tribe. And he was horrified, and basically, as he said it, they've just killed one tribal leader after another. [So I think when we…]

HH: Why did he talk to you?

DF: I don't know why he talked to me. [I think he's,] they killed most of his family. They killed his father, six other members of his family. He's angry. He hates them.

HH: So they just come into the tribe and execute people? In Waziristan?

DF: [Anybody who challenges them is basically what's happened. And what, as he described it, there's a bit of, you know,] the tribal structure's very old, you know, it's hundreds of years old. And these guys, like he said, Batula Massoud, who is now the chief Taliban leader in Pakistan, in the tribal areas, he said he was a nothing. He said he was a weightlifter. He was unemployed. And this other guy he mentioned, a guy named Munglebah, he said his job was to clean buses. And he said these are the illiterate among us, and they've essentially risen up and have basically killed the elites.

HH: By brutal…

DF: Totally brutal. Yeah, I mean, when I was there, there was thing, these groups of tribal leaders had organized themselves into something called the Peace Committee of South Waziristan, and they wanted to try to do some good. They ended up all dead, shot on the side of the road.

HH: Well, this is grim, Dexter Filkins. When you come back, do you hear any American official, Pentagon, Congress, Executive Branch, who really has a grip of what we're up against there?

DF: Yeah, I think they do. I think they know. I think the problem with a place like Pakistan in particular, there's just not a lot of options. I mean, we're, we've given $10 billion dollars in aid to Pakistan since 2001, and yet at the same time, it's the military and the intelligence services in Pakistan which were supporting the Taliban at the same time. So it's this terrible sort of dilemma, but what do you do? I mean, if you cut off aid to the government and the government collapses, I mean, you could have the Taliban in control of the government, you know? So I think the options are just very, very few.

HH: You mentioned your experience in India, as your colleague John Burns has. What do the Indians say? Are the Indians afraid they're going to be facing a nuclear suicide state on their border sooner or later?

DF: I think if there's anybody who takes this threat really, really seriously, it's the Indians. [And] I was [just] often thinking about that, that the day may come, when the moment of truth comes, if it comes for the United States, if, say, the nuclear weapons that Pakistan has gets out of control, gets in the wrong hands, if the United States doesn't act, we're going to have a hard time persuading the Indians not to act, because they're right on the border.

HH: Now let me ask you about the segment of the book, <u>The</u> <u>Forever War</u>, about suicide bombings, and this will carry us over. "I think it was like porn for them. I think they got off on it. The insurgents made videos of their suicide bombings like they were making an amateur sex tape. There was a hint of nihilism in everything al Qaeda did." This is on Page 175. And you tell the story of this former Santa Monica lawyer, American-loving, hair gel-wearing lawyer who walked among the bikinis of Santa Monica, name's Raad al Bana. And he ends up blowing himself up.

DF: Totally bizarre.

HH: When we went to break, we were talking about the suicide culture and Raad al Bana. Is it on the rise or is it on the wane, Dexter Filkins?

F: [I think it's…well, I think it may have just,] the center of gravity may have moved over to Pakistan, I think. But what struck me then, [I mean, we used to hear these stories, and I mentioned these in the book, and these aren't the sort of stories that you can verify, so they're not stories I could write in the newspaper, but things like, I mean, somebody told me this story with, who I think sounded as if it was true,] that there were so many suicide bombers coming in, and this was about 2005, so many guys were coming across the border that they were literally giving them numbers and saying you're number 27. Go home and we'll call you when we need you, stuff like that. [I mean, there was…it's exactly,] it's a great term, the culture of suicide bombings. [I mean,] I think there was a manual that was found on the internet, a jihadi manual, it was called The Road To Iraq. And I remember it said it had these instructions on what you should do, and one of them was try to look like a Westerner, buy a Walkman, wear blue jeans, and eat donuts when you're sitting on the bus. But it said never tell them, never say you won't do suicide work.

HH: Why?

DF: Well, [I mean,] you can just see [the kind of, you can see] the fanaticism, you know?

HH: Never tell them that you won't do it.

DF: Never tell them that you won't do it.

HH: There's a passage which I found oddly optimistic in your Afghanistan chapter on Nasir, who you find dying in Mazar e Sharif Prison, and he just ended up there by accident. He comes from Riyadh, and he wants to do the jihad, but then they give him a gun and they send him on a…how often does that happen among these people, for example, last hour you were talking about the madrasas of Pakistan, you find North Africans. How many of them just end up in the current of jihadism that perhaps could be dammed and blocked?

DF: A lot. [I mean, a lot, inevitably, you know? I mean,] if you take somebody like Nasir, [he was,] it was a fool's journey. He's kind of a lost kid, he's a smart guy. [I mean, he's not stupid.] He gets talked into it, wow it's a great adventure, his life is without meaning, without purpose otherwise. And suddenly, he finds himself on a bus headed for the Afghan border. He didn't want to be there. I think he's dead now, but yeah, I think there are a lot of guys like that.

HH: But what about Raad al Bana, the other guy who's the Santa Monica lawyer? He's not an American, he's an ex-pat from, I don't know where he's from, but he ends up back in the jihad, and blows himself up. How many of those are there?

DF: Unbelievable. The American military has a term for almost everything, great jargon. And their term for the foreign fighters in Iraq was always that they were force multipliers, that one foreign fighter was worth a lot more because they were the fanatical ones. And Raad al Bana was the strangest story. I mean, I sat in his parents room, upper middle class home, everybody spoke English…

HH: In Jordan?

DF: In Jordan, [yeah, yeah, which is, you know,] Amman, Jordan is a very nice city. And the father sat there and spread out the snapshots for me. You know, here's Raad, he loved America, he loved America. There's Raad standing in front of the Statue of Liberty. Here's Raad standing in front of the Santa Monica Pier. Here's Raad on his mountain bike with the flowered shirt. He wanted to be American. He really did. And something happened somewhere, and he blew himself up in a gasoline truck and killed 175 people.

HH: Did you figure out what it was?

DF: His parents, who were deeply conflicted when I talked to them, thought it had something to do with the fact that he'd come to America a few times, and then after 9/11, his visa didn't get renewed. But you know, who knows? Who knows what goes through the minds of these guys?

HH: Let's conclude this segment by talking about Chalabi. I've interviewed him. Christopher Hitchens set it up, and said you've got to talk to Chalabi. He is the new Iraq, he is everything that Iraq is, he is every contradiction. And you certainly convey that in <u>The Forever War</u>. What a fascinating character, but a character.

DF: Yes, first.

HH: [Would you,] do you think he'll be there in ten years? Do you think he'll be the leader eventually of Iraq?

DF: I don't think so. He is just a fascinating character. He's brilliant, he's not trustworthy, he's funny, he's charming, he's warm, he's deeply learned, he's brilliant. It is astonishing. You couldn't invent him. When he went back to Iraq, he was a place where he literally had not been for 45 years. He cam to a country that he didn't recognize, and they didn't recognize him.

HH: Well, what upsets me, not upsets me but worries me about the long term is that you contrast, you don't intentionally do it, but you've got Mike from the CIA here as well, who's trying to work you to work sources. And Mike seems so ham-handed and unsubtle compared to Chalabi. It's like we don't have a chance when it comes to out-cheating these people.

DF: Well, I guess that I'd like to think that there's been a learning curve, [and I think] there have. [I mean,] when you can talk to, as I did on this last trip when I was there, guys who are former insurgents, who were blowing up Humvees eighteen months ago, and they're now, they've made peace with the Americans, as I talked to one of them who said the past is past, he was a police officer, in Anbar Province, keeping the peace, whatever else that is, and maybe it's doomed, and maybe it's fragile, but I'll tell you, it takes a lot of sophistication to even imagine doing something like that. And they are.

HH: What about the Iranians?

DF: That's always the $64,000 dollar question. I mean, you have to think, I mean, the Iranians overriding goal is a weak government, right? They want a weak Iraqi government, one that they can manipulate and control. And the Iraqi government's getting stronger. And the Iraqi Army's getting stronger. And Muqtada al Sadr, who they put a lot of chips on Muqtada, he's failed. And so...

HH: Is he gone? I mean, do you expect him to be a force again in Iraq? He's been out of the country for some time now, but...

DF: I think if he came back, it would have to be very, very different. [I mean, I went, as I think I mentioned,] I went to the Sadr Bureau, and [really,] I was literally [was] sitting with guys that were Mahdi Army commanders six months ago, no guns, sitting in their office, and kind of apologizing for the Mahdi Army. And at one point, one of these guys who, again, was a military commander six months ago, and they controlled Sadr City, three million people, protection rackets, everything, they were ruthless. And he said to me at the end of the interview, he said could you just do me a favor and not print my name, because you know, I'm a fugitive. [And so,] and there was the Iraqi Army post was fifty feet away, so I think it's changed. I don't know that they're defeated, but they're definitely down for the moment.

HH: Thank you very much, Dexter Filkins, for joining me... Let me close with a couple of quotes, Dexter Filkins, on Page 147. "As much as I hated arriving, I hated leaving more." You were talking about Iraq. "After so long, I'd become a part of the place, part of the despair, part of the death, the bad food and the heat and the sandy-colored brown of it. I felt I understood its complications, its paradoxes, and even its humor. I felt a jealous brotherhood with everyone who was trying to keep it from sinking even deeper." This was an echo of a couple of conversations I've had with your colleague, John Burns. It seems that if you spend time in Iraq, you grow attached to Iraq in a way. Will you be going back and back and back?

DF: Boy, I don't know. [I don't know. It's really hard.] It's really hard. The strange thing as I was trying to convey there was I never really wanted to go back, either. And once I got there, I didn't want to leave. And I think that's kind of what it does to you. It kind of tears you apart inside. When you're in the middle of something, a project as gigantic as this one, [where,] which is changing all the time, and it's so dangerous, and every decision you make is life or death, it does. It becomes addictive, you know, but it's also very, very hard. So it's a kind of paradox. I think I will go back, is the short answer, but probably not forever.

HH: What is your job now with the Times? Are you on leave still?

DF: No, no. I'm back. I'm back. I'm attached to the Foreign Desk.

HH: So they just send you where they want to send you?

DF: Yes. [Yeah,] the difference is I get to live in the United States.

HH: Can the newspapers survive? I mean, the expense of keeping you in the field...

DF: Oh, it's crazy.

HH: ...and keeping the Bureau open. I mean, I rag on your newspaper all the time. I don't do it when I'm talking with New York Times people, but I do recognize the expense of keeping people like you in the field.

DF: Oh, my God.

HH: Extraordinary. I don't know how they can afford to do this.

DF: It is insane. [I mean,] if you just take the Baghdad Bureau, [I mean,] I think it's $3 million dollars a year. We've got 45 armed guards. It's crazy. We generated our own electricity. We have two generators. We have two satellite systems. [I mean, it's just insane.] It's very, very expensive first, and that's why there's no reporters there. That's why there's hardly anyone left.

HH: Are your mom and dad living?

DF: Yes.

HH: What do they think of your job?

DF: They think I'm a little crazy.

HH(laughing) A little? A little crazy? And in terms of The Forever War, did it turn out the way you expected it to turn out?

DF: The book or the war itself?

HH: Yeah, the book.

DF: Yeah, I think so. [I mean, I think I wanted to,] there's a lot of great books on Iraq, and there's a lot of great literature, [I think.] What I wanted to try to do, which I felt like I could do, is try to convey to people what it feels like. I wanted to write about the blood in the sand and the sweat and the fear and the ambiguity. [I mean,] I wanted to [kind of] convey that emotional experience rather than an intellectual one.

HH: Well, let me conclude with a compliment that I never expected to meet Vida Blue in your book.

DF: (laughing)

HH: And I'm not going to tell people what the story is. Vida Blue is not in Baghdad, but it certainly did convey the experience of living with danger at every moment. Vida Blue, I hadn't heard that name, seen that name in 20 years. Dexter Filkins, a pleasure. Thank you.

DF: Thank you.

HH: Get the book, America. It's on the necessary bookshelf.

End of interview.

Interview with Michael Yon
May 7, 2008

HH: A special conversation with Michael Yon, I believe now America's preeminent war correspondent. He's an independent reporter. You can read about him at his online journal, but mostly, you should read his brand new book, <u>Moment of Truth in Iraq</u>. It is out now, it's been out for a month. Michael Yon, welcome back to the Hugh Hewitt Show, great to have you.

MY: Hey, Hugh, it's so great to be on the show, and to be, especially to be back in America. I'm back for a short period. I'm down in Florida right now, so if you hear any barnyard animals, there's actual animals around me, so please excuse me for that.

HH: Well, that's fine. Congratulations, the book is extraordinary, and I want to talk to you in detail about it. You may know that Townhall Magazine is giving away a copy of <u>Moment of Truth in Iraq</u> for every subscription to Townhall. That's how highly we think of it. By the way, the URL for that is www.townhallmagazine.com/truth. That's www.townhallmagazine.com/truth. How's the book been received, Michael?

MY: Very well, Hugh. The first print run of 30,000 was gone almost instantly. [The print date was, or] the pub date was April 23rd. So we went to another print run of 50,000. [So] it went out of stock in a lot of places for a while, [like] it got to number six on Amazon, I'm told, and then they went out of stock, and it got to number two on Barnesandnoble.com, and went out of stock. But we're back in stock now, and it's doing quite well.

HH: Well, it is linked at Hughhewitt.com. I'm sure it's going to soar back up as people learn about it, Michael Yon, because it so accurately portrays the long and very difficult, but at the same time inspiring effort of the American military to bring peace and stability to Iraq. I want to start with Farah. The cover picture is of little Farah who died in a terrorist attack, being cuddled by an American soldier rushing her to help. Tell people the story of Farah, and why you believe, as your chapter says in the middle, Farah did not die in vain.

MY: [You know, that's an interesting thing that you said that. I mean,] I took that photo on May 2nd of 2005 up in Mosul. A suicide car bomber had lined up to do an attack on some of our soldiers, and they were in Stryker fighting vehicles. And Farah, and about twenty other kids, had run out to…when they would hear the Strykers, they would run out and wave, and the soldiers throw them candy and that sort of thing. And Farah's mother later said that she ran out barefooted, you know, to wave and get candy or whatever, the suicide car bomber, who could have waited two or three blocks to attack our guys, or at least do it away from the kids, just [an right,] drove right through the kids and exploded, detonated right there, killed one boy outright, burned him up. And then, you know, Farah…a woman, I don't know if it was her mother, but a woman ran out with Farah, and came to the first American soldier she could fine. Walt Gaya, this is a pattern I've seen over and over, when Iraqis get hurt, they immediately go to American soldiers. And Walt was pushing out to a sniper position, [but…] and that's really where he needed to go. But when he saw Farah injured, he grabbed her and took her back to the medics. The medics started working on her, and then Mark Bieger, he's the major who's in the photo that's on the cover of the book, he picked up Farah, wrapped her in that blanket, and started to rush off to the hospital, grabbed up a few of the family members, and rushed to the hospital with Farah. But she, unfortunately, Farah died, so that's how that photo was taken.

HH: But you also write that shortly after Farah's murder, this picture published all over Iraq and over the world, had a devastating effect on the terrorists. Farah's death was not in vain. Is that still true? Because obviously, it did show the American military man at his finest, but also the cost of this war and its starkest.

MY: It sure did. It had a terrible effect on the enemy. I mean, that neighborhood, which was previously somewhat pro-insurgent, turned completely against them. And in fact, [I mean,] her family invited the soldiers to her funeral. They didn't go because, [you know, because] it just wasn't appropriate, but the intelligence community told me that, a couple of officers told me that when that photo was released, they got a huge amount of actionable intelligence. [And you know,] what we've seen there in Mosul, that was Nineveh Province, we've seen this repeated in other places like Anbar Province and Diyala Province, and down in Baghdad, where al Qaeda, in particular, does horrible things to people, and they just turn completely against them. [I mean,] the Islamic world and the Arab world are really turning against al Qaeda, and just for this kind of thing.

HH: You know, Michael Yon, I want to spend a little time on that. It's a little bit out of order, but I'm going to jump ahead in the book to Page 136 where you're talking about al Qaeda. [And] you've done a lot of work studying cults, you've done a lot of work studying gangs, all over the world. And you write on that page, "Iraqis love and greatly value their children. This makes children especially vulnerable as targets for terrorists. This is a brutal fact. The official had gone on to say that on a couple of occasions in Baquba, al Qaeda invited to lunch families they wanted to convert to their way of thinking. In each instance, the family had a boy about eleven years old. When the family sat down to eat, their boy was brought in with his mouth stuffed. The boy had been baked. Al Qaeda served the boy to his family. My repeated attempts," you write, "to verify this story failed to produce concrete proof, although many had heard similar stories. But the rumors showed how terrible al Qaeda's reputation for atrocities had become among the local people." And in another place, you write about exhuming a grave with Iraqi Security Forces, and in fact, you saw the evidence that they're just butchers.

MY: They are. [I mean, just a couple of days, or] maybe one or two days before I heard that story, I was at a village just north of Baquba. It's actually kind of contiguous with Baquba. [And] I published the grid coordinates of where this happened, [actually.] You know, al Qaeda had come in, the locals said it was al Qaeda, in the nearby places, and they had butchered everybody there. They had shot the adults, they had shot the animals, even, and beheaded the children. And I saw this with my own eyes. I photographed it. I made video and photos. It was unbelievable. I mean, they beheaded the children. [So this is the kind of thing, you know,] the Iraqis just have learned to hate al Qaeda. I mean, they are resurging, though, I mean, not all Iraqis. Not everybody's gotten the memo yet, or the message. But a huge amount of them have just turned completely against al Qaeda.

HH: Now Michael Yon, I want to go to the end of the book, and then we're going to go back and make a little more coherent your narrative there, which is very coherent in the book. I'm just jumping around to get some high points in at this first segment of our interview. At the conclusion of <u>Moment of Truth in Iraq</u>, you write that, "A powerful democracy in the Middle East is within our grasp, and nearly all the hardest work has been done." Amplify that, if you will.

MY: It sure has. [I mean, we came in,] of course, we made a lot of mistakes in 2003 and 2004. But we really started to improve in 2005. In 2006, of course, the civil war was taking hold, but with al Qaeda taken out of the equation by 2007, or [mostly, they're still there, but they're mostly,] they're not as big a factor as they used to be. We're [really] getting to the point [where we're getting down] to really building the country now. I mean, there's still fighting going on. We've seen this was a rough month, April. But what we can see now is the Iraqi Army is dramatically better now than it was in 2005. The Iraqi Police were more problematic than the Army are coming along, I see definite progress. And you know, I don't pull my punches. I've seen a lot of progress even with the Iraqi government, despite the fact that it's a corrupt culture. But I am very hopeful for Iraq.

HH: Let me tell people on the back of this book, the reason you can trust <u>Moment of Truth in Iraq</u>, the blurbs come from, of course people like Michael Barone and Joe Galloway, the author of <u>We Were Soldiers Once</u>, but unexpectedly from Brian Williams, from the Washington Post, from Thomas Ricks of the Washington Post, from the New York Times correspondent, Clifford May, from the Los Angeles Times, and of course, you've got General David Petraeus. So you have earned the respect, Michael Yon, I think because of your candor, of the entire spectrum of war observers both abroad and here at home. That's a hard one, but I mean highly estimable achievement.

MY: I was so honored by the type of blurbs that I got for the back cover. I got an e-mail from General Petraeus just a couple of weeks ago about the book. It was a very nice e-mail. [I just...]I [just] feel honored, because these people know, General Petraeus knows, I don't always write positive things about what's going on, and sometimes, I'll get messages from pretty senior people about that. But all in all, if you tell the truth, the good, the bad and the ugly, over a period of time... [and] I do want to win. I don't hide that fact. I do want us to do well. You do end up getting, let's say, some nice words coming your way.

HH: Once again, if you want to join with all these people in praising this book, you can get if for free if you order a subscription of Townhall Magazine, www.townhallmagazine. com/truth, or you can order the book itself over at Amazon. com. I've linked it at Hughhewitt.com. Now Michael Yon, people like Command Sergeant Major Mellinger, we'll come back to him, Lt. Col. Eric Kurilla, have they read the book yet? And what's their response to it?

MY: Oh, Jeff Mellinger definitely has, because I just had a barbeque with him, [actually], and his wife, Kim. He's up in

Alaska, [actually], salmon fishing right now. He's still on active duty. That guy has been in the Army almost 35 years. His brother was [actually] a sergeant major in the Marine Corps. But Jeff has read it, and I'm going to have another cookout with him, and probably Gary Sinise on about the 15th of May up in Washington, D.C. [But you know,] he's read it, and he said he enjoyed it, and he was very appreciative and thankful.

HH: How about Col. Kurilla?

MY: [Col. Kurilla, he's actually off doing his duty right now, and not to go into further, into that, but] his wife sent me a nice e-mail that Eric is off doing his job right now. So he's on his fourth combat tour since he got shot.

HH: Wow. All right, we're going to take a break.

HH: It's the best book, because Michael Yon has spent the most time at the tip of the spear, as the combat soldiers like to say, all over Iraq, also Afghanistan and the world, former Special Forces warrior himself. If you want to get a copy of it for free, all you have to do is subscribe to Townhall Magazine, www.townhallmagazine.com/truth. Or if you just want to get the book, it is linked at Hughhewitt.com. And if you want to read Michael's dispatches, it's www.michaelyon-online.com. One of the reasons I send you there is drop some coin in his tip bottle there, because he is independent of all the journalism institutions of the United States. He works off of your support, and we've got to keep him in the field. Michael Yon, let's briefly review for people your background in terms of the time, and what years you were in Iraq, so they know what you bring to this table when you reported this book.

MY: I first went to Iraq in December of 2004. I was a late comer, and I went after a couple of friends were killed in Iraq. One was an old Special Forces friend, Richard Ferguson, [was] killed on March 30th, 2004, in Samarra, and then another friend was killed, Scott Helvenston, was one of the Blackwater contractors murdered and mutilated in Fallujah. I went to high school with Scott. I went to their funerals, one was in Colorado, the other in Florida. And people at these funerals kept saying, military people, [you know,] you're a writer, you should go the war, and I said no, I'm not going to the war, I've got no interest in doing war correspondence. But then in April of 2004, the same month as the funerals, Abu Ghraib broke, and I saw these photos, and I remember just thinking [you know,] we may have just lost the war because of what has happened here with the way this looks. [And so,] but I still refused to go, but throughout 2004, I had one friend, another friend that I went to high school with, who was then a lieutenant colonel in the Army, Rodney Morris, and he was in Iraq, and Rodney used to call me up and e-mail me constantly from Iraq, you know, come over to Iraq, you need to cover this war. And I kept saying Rodney, love talking with you, but I'm not coming to the war. But finally, in November of 2004, when we did Operation Phantom Fury, which was the second attack on Fallujah, I could tell that we were in the middle of a horrible insurgency that was just growing, and we were adding fuel to the fire. So I went there in December of 2004, and I stayed most of 2005. Then I went to Afghanistan for a short time in 2006, and then I went back to Iraq in December of 2006, and stayed most of 2007. And then I went back for two months so far this year, and I'll be heading back again soon.

HH: So I just want people to know of which you speak. You have been there and done that, and I've got to tell you, I'm so thankful for this book for a number of levels, one of which is it caught me up short, had to stop, on Page 53. You tell the story of the patrol that was lost, of the Two-Seven, to the massive car bomb led by a Lt. Mark Daily. I know his mom and dad, had lunch with them, and I went to his funeral, and I'm glad you memorialized him. But my God, the stupid losses we've had in this war, for lack of a nail, as you write, Michael Yon. We just didn't do this soon enough. We didn't conduct the counterinsurgency soon enough.

MY: Right. [I mean,] we didn't. I just listened to an interview on NPR today, [actually it was taped, but] they were talking about counterinsurgency. And it's a very difficult type of warfare to wage. It's the most complex type of warfare there is.

And so in the beginning, firstly, we did not recognize that there was an insurgency, because those who called it an insurgency were basically branded as non-Americans for a while, because you know, we were getting the political spin from Washington that these were dead-enders, or whatever. But clearly, it was an insurgency. And so, until you recognize that you've got a fire, you're not going to show up and call the fire department. And it takes a long time to retrain your military to conduct this kind of war. Well, that's what [General Petraeus and] General Maddis from the Marine Corps, General Petraeus from the Army, [you know,] they set out to do with a group of very intelligent officers, wrote the counterinsurgency field manual, and then got that out there, and started to retrain the soldiers. [And now they've successfully,] they've been very successful at that. And now that General Petraeus, [well, he]'s in charge of Iraq right now, [but] he'll be taking over Central Command soon. We've just seen a tremendous turnaround in our military, and their ability to conduct counterinsurgency.

HH: Well, that's what I want to pause on, because people like Lt. Daily and Lt. Blecksmith, and 4,100 other Americans who've lost their lives there, and thousands who've been wounded there, they didn't do it in vain. They've won. This country is stable, and al Qaeda is pushed back to Mosul, and we'll come to that. But I want you to stress that, because you go there a lot, and you were just there recently. Explain to people in this audience, and especially to anti-war critics who are listening, and they are there, that victory's in hand because of these sacrifices by heroes like Daily, Blecksmith and all the other men you chronicle in this book.

MY: It's true. I mean, Daily was out there doing his job. I was there that day. [It was…] we had a bad day. But we were making tremendous progress. One battalion of Americans along with their Iraqi counterparts held Mosul for a year, which was incredible, because there were other things going on in other parts of Iraq. We couldn't sacrifice the troops to go elsewhere. But we have really crushed down al Qaeda to the point where their last vestiges are mostly in Nineveh Province up near Mosul.

They're trying to resurge in Diyala, but I mean, they're just being crushed down. We've made a huge amount of progress, the Iraqi government finally has enough breathing room that it can actually start making some real decisions, and we've seen recently when the Iraqi government…many Sunni, by the way, have complained to me for at least a year now that the Iraqi government, mostly Shia, would not take on the Shia militias. Well, they just did. And that's why we saw the increase in violence in April. I mean, they are clearly going heads-up with some of the militias. And so this is important. The progress is very real. [And it's…] we're making it step by step.

HH: Michael Yon, I've also got to compliment you. I had never heard of the 1920 Revolution Brigades until I read your book. And that's not because I'm ignorant, it's because I read all this stuff, it's just the detail in <u>Moment of Truth</u> in Iraq is at a level and a degree of explanation that's simply not out there. And I think it's because, other than John Burns and a couple of others, I don't think anyone's spent enough time in Iraq to really translate what's happening there to us until your book came along.

MY: You know, it takes a long time to develop the context. And unless you're willing to invest that time, [and it's tough, you know, that's why there's not so many folks that do it. But unless you're going to spend the time,] you can't develop the context. But the 1920 Revolution Brigades, they were a very effective enemy against us. They were mostly comprised of former regime elements, many ex-army officers and soldiers. They were very effective, they were serious fighters, [but] they turned, but they were more pragmatic fighters. They're not like al Qaeda in the sense that al Qaeda, you've just got to find them and kill them or capture them, demoralize them, do anything you can. But you're not going to ever negotiate with them, whereas the 1920's, [they had more…] the things that they wanted were more concrete. They wanted more power in the government, they wanted these kinds of things. Those are things that you can work with.

HH: Michael Yon, I like the fact that the theory of the war is in here, as well as riveting war reporting. And I want to go to one part of that, which is your criticism of the U.S. military as "politically dense and media illiterate." Is that changing? I think it is, because of the outreach I'm receiving from Iraq, from people like Major General Rick Lynch and others to come on the show live from Iraq. It didn't happen three years ago. It's happening now. I think maybe you've been a part of that turnaround on their part.

MY: They're definitely improving. There's no question about that. They [have really...] they're more agile than they seem. They've learned that the media is an incredible part of the battle space when it comes to counterinsurgency. And part of that is back home. You've got to explain to people why this takes so long, why we have so many difficulties, [and why...] give us time, we can make it. That's what they have to do. [And they're doing an outreach.] They've been reaching out, trying to get their message out, and they've been successful, increasingly successful. They were not very successful under Sanchez and what not. I mean, General Sanchez, they were not at all, actually. But now, under Petraeus, I just see great improvement.

HH: Now Michael Yon, I know you're not political. You avoid being political, in fact. I appreciate that. But yesterday, or on Sunday on Meet the Press, Barack Obama said look, after I'm elected, they get sixteen more months, and we're out of there. What's your reaction to blanket statements like that, whether from left, right or center, that, you know, a timetable?

MY: Wow, that's shocking that he would say that. He said yesterday, sixteen more months and we're out of there. Is that what he said?

HH: Yes.

MY: That's shocking.

HH: After he's elected. So he says then we will have been there a total of seven years, and if they can't stand up at that time, they'll never stand up. And I'm paraphrasing, but that's very true to what he said.

MY: That would be catastrophic. I mean, we spent a huge amount of blood and money over there, and we've seen a tremendous amount of progress. But if we did do something like that, it would be catastrophic. It would be a complete loss.

HH: All right, let's go back to the actual war reporting. I'll tell you, I was exhausted at the end of your recounting of the Battle of Baquba in Operation Arrowhead Ripper. You were right in the fray of this a lot. I don't think you possibly can convey this, but hat's off to you. But the exhaustion level among troops who fight in that heat in those close quarters, with such attention to avoiding civilian casualties, I love the fact you point out, they'll just fall down and sleep wherever they are for as long as they can.

MY: They would. [I mean,] you would come into a building that's been bombed out [and what not,] and there'd be soldiers laying on the ground, and it was hot, it was very hot. You know, this is June and July, and I mean, really, really exhausting heat. Soldiers were getting heat exhaustion, and had to be med-evac'd sometimes for the heat, and they would just crash down in their body armor, and weapon next to them, and fall asleep. Other guys would be on guard duty. And then they would get up and keep fighting.

HH: Let me compliment you on your eye for detail. Never go on a patrol with people with dirty windows. Explain to people why that is.

MY: Well, [you know, especially towards the end of their tours,] soldiers, [they] realize they have to be more alert toward the end of their tours, that the closer they get to the end of their tour, the more they start thinking about being back at home, and they start talking about girls, or going to the races, or something, [you know,] buying a new car if they're young soldiers, and they stop paying attention to what they're doing, and they stop…for instance, paying attention to the rooftops, and the places where a sniper might be, or a bomb might be. And you'll see, [you know,] when they've got dirty windshields, they're not looking for small wires across the road, which could set off a bomb that can obliterate them. [And so] you can't see these little wires when you've got dirty windshields. [And so] I've noticed over a long period of time, and so many countless missions that I've been on, that if they've got dirty windshields, you just have to say I'm sorry, guys, I've got pneumonia today. I'm not going on this mission. I've started to avoid missions with people that have dirty windshields.

HH: You know, I think that's why your book is going to become required reading in a lot of the commands across the United States for lessons like that one.

HH: Michael Yon, a couple of things here. The surge has been misunderstood as being separate or responsible for the entire turnaround of events in Iraq. It's a part of it, but also the Anbar awakening was part of the sheiks deciding that they'd had enough of this. Can you explain to people why the sheiks get some credit, a lot of credit, for what has happened here?

MY: Right. You know, when al Qaeda started doing their barbaric acts, which was early on, by 2006, and out in Anbar in particular, the sheiks were tired of it. They had reached out to us, they wanted our help to help them fight al Qaeda, [and they reached out to us,] and finally we joined forces with them. [So] that was before the surge. And then in 2007, when the surge began, early 2007, we had already pretty much ejected most of al Qaeda out of Anbar Province, which a lot of people saw as being a lost cause, even as late as 2006. [But so] then al Qaeda moved to places like Baghdad and Arab Jubur, Baquba, Mosul, [they really went to other places.] [And so] when the surge occurred, more troops came in, but we also used different tactics. We pushed those troops off of the bases, and out into the cities, to these COP's, or combat outposts, which were proving to be very effective, you would see, open up a new COP, and you'd start getting intelligence, the very first day, about where the bad guys are. [And so, I mean,] once the people realized you're there to stay. And then with the extra troops, we had the ability to conduct operations like Arrowhead Ripper, where on June 19th, we attacked al Qaeda in Baquba with the help of

1920's Revolution Brigades. And so all these things conflated, added up to a very serious turnaround.

HH: You also describe in detail some of the tactics that are required for the success of counterinsurgency operations. There's one vivid story, you're out on patrol with Staff Sergeant Lee, USMC, and there may be an IED in a culvert, and rather than ordering the Iraqi Army to go in and clear it, Staff Sergeant Lee goes in on his belly to do so, you follow him in, and the moral of that story is you've got to demonstrate to the Iraqi Security Forces that you've got the guts to do what is necessary to win the war.

MY: [And that's true, and that's where we see...you know,] in the beginning of the Iraq war, a lot of the Iraqis thought, for instance, that American body armor was air conditioners. [They thought that we had,] they still think, many of them, that we have cold pills, in other words, pills that you can take to keep you cool in the hot weather. So they thought that we were weak. [But they've seen over time that...] they had the impression that the only way that we could beat people was from missiles from afar, that kind of thing, and jets. But they've seen that our people on the streets, United States Marines and the Army, when it comes down to street level fighting, man on man, house to house, we are tougher, better fighters than they are, and just as courageous as anything you'll ever see.

HH: But also, I want to stress this, and very good men, I mean, just extraordinary men of valor, but also of honor and dignity and of tenderness and gentleness at the same time. It's an extraordinary portrait that you put out here.

MY: Right. You know, at first, they saw that as weakness. At first, they saw that as oh, you're tender-hearted, therefore you're weak. But over time, you can... [you know, you can] prove to somebody you're a bad guy in one minute. But it takes a long time to prove you're a good guy. And so over time, they've seen that our guys, our soldiers and Marines, are tough, capable fighters, but they're also very good to the Iraqis. [They love the...] I don't know what it is about combat soldiers and

Marines, but the more combat they see, the more they like kids. And you'll see them, the Iraqi kids are actually very easy to like, because they're always out there smiling, and they always want to say hello and whatever. So the soldiers and the Marines get along very well with the kids, and this has gone a long way to developing bonds also with communities. And so there has been a lot of intangibles that you really can't quantify in any kind of numbers, but we are influencing Iraq just because of the [incredible] credibility that our military brings.

HH: And the leadership style of teaching, Lt. Col. Johnson in the chapter Walking Tall – Tonto and the Mayor, about how to teach civilian leadership in Iraq to be leaders. I mean, it's an extraordinary lesson in how you've got to stand up and go in, and Lt. Col. Johnson, what a guy.

MY: He sure was. I remember that Johnson, he really had his work cut out for him – him and many others, actually. One day you're doing combat operations, and then later in that day, they're doing detailed negotiations or whatever, or tribal meetings. And one thing that we were trying to do [that point is, that] was Operation Arrowhead Ripper that you're referring to, when we attacked al Qaeda in Baquba, but the first thing that we wanted to do afterwards is open up the food distribution back to Baquba. It had been cut off from Baghdad because al Qaeda had controlled Baquba, and they wanted that food distribution open so that the people would see that the government is now supporting them. And Fred Johnson, I detailed some of the events in Moment of Truth, he did stellar work and got that distribution going.

HH: I also want to point out an observation, I should have known because I've been around military bases a lot, but you point out American military run bases all over the world, so they know civilian reconstruction, because they run little cities all over the world. And they show people how to solve problems. It's a remarkable sort of gift to the Iraqi people.

MY: It's true. I mean, the military is like a microcosm of America [insofar as...] listen, if you're going to be a commander who runs a military base, you have to know how to administer a city. You have hospitals to think about, you have school systems, you have police, military police, you've got judicial systems, you've got sewage and food distribution, electricity, you've got the whole gamut.

HH: Cooking…skill sets.

HH: Michael Yon, thank you for a great book, <u>Moment of Truth</u> in Iraq, and for a wonderful hour. Let me review for people, if you want the book for free, www.townhallmagazine. com/truth, buy the magazine, get the book. If you want to get the book via Hughhewitt.com, it's linked there, and you can always go to www.michaelyon-online.com to help him keep in the field. Michael, I want to conclude with General Petraeus. And some fascinating history in this book – I haven't touched on the Brits, I haven't touched on money as the ammunition in counterinsurgency, I haven't touched on the Battle of Mosul, the Battle of Baquba. There's so much I can't do, but I want to finish on what you call the prime directive of political war, drawn from General Washington's directive to Benedict Arnold, and how David Petraeus has internalized this, and demonstrated it, and just let you sort of explain why he has brought such momentum to the effort in Iraq.

MY: Well, the moral high ground is everything, and General Washington, [you know, way back] a long time ago, demonstrated that he had a clear knowledge of counterinsurgency. I mean, our nation was founded on insurgency against the British. [But] the moral high ground is very difficult to keep, but it's everything in this sort of warfare. That's why we have been able to turn the tide on al Qaeda and just start crushing them in Iraq, because al Qaeda doesn't care about the moral high ground, and we do. It's very difficult to keep. [And so] the U.S. military has become, I started to notice in early 2007, [it has become] the most trusted institution in Iraq. I mean, by 2008, it's very clear to me, as I travel around, that the Iraqis want to know what the local American commander thinks about something before they make a decision. And so this is all based on moral high ground, not just money. I mean, they want to hear what the American said, because they know he is good to his word.

HH: [I also,] there's so many stories in here about the disarming of the Iraqi police general who'd gone bad, et cetera. [There's a lot...] but you walk away with an unvarnished admiration for the American military veteran over there. When are you going back, Michael Yon?

MY: I'll probably go back in a month or so. I've got to take care of a few administrative things, for instance, with my taxes. I've got to get right with The Man.

HH: (laughing)

MY: [There's some things...] I've got to pay my dues back here, too. So just little things like that, I'll take care of, and then I'll head back as soon as I can.

HH: Well, I hope that your readers continue to support you. And does any of the mainstream media send you any money, any support now, Michael Yon?

MY: Oh, they support me tremendously, actually, with just giving me coverage. You know, the New York Post did a very nice book review recently, New York Daily News published something I wrote yesterday, the Wall Street Journal published an op-ed a few weeks ago. [So I mean,] insofar as they definitely increasingly give me a voice, but I would say you were one of the first, though, a long time ago, Hugh.

HH: Well, I still hope when you next get to California, I can buy you dinner, because we really do owe you a great debt of thanks, as do the American military and the Iraqi people. Michael Yon, great book, congratulations, talk to you again soon. Moment of Truth in Iraq, all the links are at Hughhewitt. com.

End of interview.

Chapter 8.

Looking Ahead: After The Success of the Surge and Before the Withdrawal of the Coalition from Iraq

~~~

The voices of many impressive authors are heard in these interviews, but I have also had conversations with three individuals that were not tied to any particular book, but which need to be included in this collection of crucial conversations about the war.

General David Petraeus needs no introduction, of course, and neither should the New York Times' John F. Burns or historian Victor Davis Hanson. Each man brings unique perspective to the ongoing war.

Interview with General David Petraeus
July 18, 2007

HH: Welcome, General. You took over command of the multi-national forces in February of this year, February 10. In the past five months, how have conditions in Iraq changed?

DP: Well, obviously, we have been surging our forces during that time. We have added five Army brigade combat teams, two Marine battalions, and a Marine expeditionary unit, and some enablers, as they're called. And over the last month, that surge of forces has turned into a surge of offensive operations. And we have achieved what we believe is a reasonable degree of tactical momentum on the ground, gains against the principal near-term threat, al Qaeda-Iraq, and also gains against what is another near-term threat, and also potentially the long term threat, Shia militia extremists as well. As you may have heard, that today, we announced the capture of the senior Iraqi leader of al Qaeda-Iraq, and that follows in recent weeks the detention of some four different emirs, as they're called, the different area leaders of al Qaeda, six different foreign fighter facilitators, and a couple dozen other leaders, in addition to killing or capturing hundreds of other al Qaeda-Iraq operatives.

HH: Do you think al Qaeda in Iraq is buckling, General Petraeus?

DP: Well, it's probably too soon to say that, but we think that we have them off plan. Now having said that, they clearly retain and have demonstrated, tragically in [recent,] the past week or so, the ability to continue to carry out sensational attacks. They continue to demonstrate the ability to counterattack against our forces, and those of our coalition partners. But the detention, or the capture or killing of the number of leaders that we have taken out in recent months, and weeks, actually, and the progress in terms of just clearing areas of them...as you know, Anbar Province has really become quite relatively clear of al Qaeda. Eastern Anbar still has some, and we are working in that area. We have recently cleared Western Baquba, which was almost al Qaeda central, the capitol of the new caliphate that they have tried to establish here in Iraq. So there has been considerable progress against them, but they do continue to receive foreign fighters through Syria, who become suicide bombers in many cases, and they do certainly have an ability to regenerate, to regroup, and to come back at us.

HH: General Petraeus, we've seen messages passed back and forth between al Qaeda in Afghanistan and Pakistan, and al Qaeda in Iraq. Do you consider them to be operating jointly?

DP: Well, there certainly is a level of direction that takes place, and there is a level of reporting from Iraq that goes back, and it does go back and forth. And periodically, you'll see one of those released. More recently, as an example of the kind of direction, actually given by individuals coming into Iraq, [there were the,] we announced the killing of two, and it turns out three, [actually,] al Turki brothers. These are, not surprisingly, from Turkey originally, part of al Qaeda leadership, spent time in Afghanistan in past years, and were sent into Northern Iraq to help shore up the network up there after it took significant blows, particularly in the Mosul area. And we've managed to get the final fifty meters, if you will, on them after [sort] of pursuing them for some months, and did kill them several weeks ago.

HH: Do you see any evidence, General, that al Qaeda is now operating jointly with the Iranian regime? There've been some reports that in fact, they are now based, in some respects, within Iran and operating across the border with Iran.

DP: Well, there is an al Qaeda affiliate, I think is the best way to put it. Certainly, they're under the overall banner of al Qaeda, an element formerly Ansar al Sunna, some of their members, another group affiliated with al Qaeda, that is located in Northwestern Iran, just east of the Iraqi border, east of the Iraqi-Kurdish province of Sulaymaniyah. They have come into Iraq. Our operators and Iraqi operators have conducted strikes against them. And we believe, in fact, that Iran may have actually taken some steps against them as well. They're not sitting there at the invitation of Iran, but it's a very, very rugged area, and a fairly substantial area as well.

HH: General Petraeus, some of your staff have talked in recent weeks about Iranian government support for various elements of the enemy in Iraq, in the form of sophisticated explosives, some training. Has the amount of material and training from Iran to the enemy in Iraq increased or decreased over the past half year?

DP: Well, it's hard to say. It certainly has not decreased, and it's hard to say whether it's increased or not, but it has remained very substantial. It's something we track, sometimes we're able to interdict some of it, sometimes we capture it or literally stop it. We captured, for example the other day, several dozen rockets that were all set up on timers, and aimed at one of our bases, and some of our air assets happened to see them, and we were able to defuse them, all clearly from Iran. Iran has indeed provided substantial funding, training, equipping, arming, and even direction, in some cases, to what are called the special groups or secret cells affiliated with the militia of Muqtada al Sadr. We captured the heads of the secret cells, as you may recall, several months ago, the Khazali brothers. And with them, we captured a senior Lebanese Hezbollah trainer, the deputy head of the Lebanese Hezbollah department that was apparently created to help the Iranian Quds force, the element that does provide this training, equipping, money and direction to the Iraqi secret groups, or secret cells.

HH: General, what do you perceive to be Iran's strategy in Iraq via that support and their other initiatives inside the new Iraq?

DP: Well, there are various theories on that, and one of those is actually that they may be somewhat conflicted. On the one hand, they should see a neighbor that is, that shares the same religious sect, fellow Shia, although Iraqis certainly are Arabs, and Iranians are obviously Persian. They should see a country that with which they actually already have considerable commercial trade and exchange, and great interest in, in that regard, but they also see a country that has certainly ties to the United States, and one whose democracy is very, very different from the form of government, of course, that you find in Iran, where the senior clerics actually run the country, as you know. And so they, there is discussion about whether they are trying, in a sense, to use certain elements to Hezbollah. Hezbollah is in certain parts of Iran. [If they just don't...or Iraq...] if they just don't want Iraq to do that well, perhaps, certainly want to give the United States a black eye, a variety of different motivations, we believe. And again, perhaps even a degree of confliction, given that a number of Iraq's senior leaders has close ties to Iran in the past, located in Iran during Saddam's day, and certainly have close relationships with various Iranian leaders, and share the religious sect of Shia Islam as well.

HH: Do you have the authority that you need, General, for hot pursuit, or to take the defensive actions necessary to protect American troops and the Iraqi government from Iranian intermeddling?

DP: Well, we certainly have the authority that we need to conduct operations in Iraq against anyone who threatens our forces or Iraqi forces. And in fact, we have done that, as I think you know…

HH: Right.

DP: We detained, for example, five members of the Iranian Quds force that were in Iran, and that we believe were tied into this greater network that has provided this arming, funding, training and direction to the secret cells or special groups associated with Sadr's militia.

HH: General, I want to go back to the surge. About how long have you had the full complement of troops that were necessary for the surge in place?

DP: Well, it's about a month now, Hugh. We received the final Army brigade, the Marine expeditionary unit, and the combat aviation brigade in June, and they all went into operation about the mid part of last month. So it's about a month that they've all been on the ground, and all of our forces have been engaged in what is a pretty comprehensive offensive operation in just about all of the belts around Baghdad, as they're called, and then in also several neighborhoods in Baghdad that are of particular concern because of the activities in those neighborhoods of al Qaeda, or in some cases, of militia extremist elements.

HH: Now you're due to make a report back in September, I don't know if it's early, mid or late September, General Petraeus, is that enough time to really get a fix on how the surge is progressing?

DP: Well, I have always said that we will have a sense by that time of basically, of how things are going, have we been able to achieve progress on the ground, where have their been short-falls, and so forth. And I think that is a reasonable amount of time to have had all the forces on the ground, again, for about three months, to have that kind of sense. But that's all it is going to be. But we do intend, Ambassador Ryan Crocker, the ambassador here, and I, do very much intend to provide as comprehensive and as forthright an assessment as we can at that time of the progress that has been achieved, and where we've fallen short.

HH: Now stepping back a little bit from the day to day, General Petraeus, how would you explain to the civilians listening, and hundreds of thousands of them at this moment, the strategic interest of the United States at stake in Iraq?

DP: Well, I think just first of all, we have an enormous responsibility, because of course, we did liberate this country. And so right off the bat, a lot of us feel, certainly, that degree of responsibility. Beyond that, obviously, Iraq has the second or third most proven oil resources in the world. It is blessed with other mineral wealth as well that is very substantial, and has enormous potential in the global economy. It sits astride several crucial ethno-sectarian fault lines, fault lines between Arabs and Kurds, fault lines between Sunni and Shia Iraqis, and also has substantial populations of other elements, Christians, Yazidis and some others. It is important in regional terms, needless to say, against surrounded by some neighbors that are Sunni, others Turk, and of course, they have, Turkey, they have a substantial Turkoman population as well. And then or course, Shia to their east. So there's enormous potential implications for some of the courses of action that have been considered out there, and certainly, a precipitous withdrawal would have potentially serious implications for important interests that we have in Iraq, in the region.

HH: Some have warned that a genocide of sorts, or absolute terms, would follow a precipitous withdrawal of coalition forces. Do you agree that that is a possibility, or a…and a significant one?

DP: Well, obviously, it depends on the conditions when we withdraw. I mean, eventually, we are going to withdraw. We cannot maintain the surge forever, as everyone knows. There's always been an intention that the surge would be a somewhat temporary endeavor. So it has to do with the conditions at that time. I mean, we saw the sectarian violence of late 2006 and early 2007, and obviously, that was very tragic, and really quite horrific in a number of Baghdad neighborhoods. It literally changed the face of Baghdad. It struck at the very fabric of Iraqi society in places like Baghdad, and in other mixed, sectarian areas. And again, unless the conditions are sustainable by the Iraqis, one would certainly expect that sectarian violence would resume at a very high level. That's not to say there's not still some going on right now, although the level in June was about the lowest in a year, and we're certainly trying to sustain that. I don't know this month whether we can, given the two horrific bombings that took place, however that is certainly what we're trying and fighting to do.

HH: General Petraeus, you wrote your PhD dissertation at Princeton on the lessons of Vietnam, analyzing in part the aftermath of an American military defeat. And obviously, that was horrific in Cambodia, and awful in South Vietnam. What would you expect the consequences of the defeat of America in Iraq to be, both there and in terms of our military posture and position around the world?

DP: Well, to be candid, that's a hypothetical that I'm just not prepared to address. We are determined to do all that we can, while we're given the opportunity to try to bring this to as successful as reasonable a conclusion as is possible, and that is really what is just what I'm devoting all my intellectual energy and physical energy to at this point in time, not thinking about what the implications of not getting it right are.

HH: You and Marine Lt. General Amos coauthored the new field manual on counterinsurgency, and it talked about counterinsurgency has to adapt to local conditions. How long does it really take, in your estimation? I see you saw the BBC yesterday, telling them that it could take nine, ten years to put a counterinsurgency down in Iraq. Is that an accurate assessment, a decade to get this thing contained?

DP: Well, it depends where you are in Iraq, what you're talking about, and so forth. What I was doing there was merely saying that historically, it's taken about a decade or so for the average counterinsurgency to be sorted out. Sometimes, it's taken longer. I mean, in fact, the British Broadcaster interviewer and I were talking about how long it took the UK to reach the position that they've now achieved in Northern Ireland, and that was actually several decades, as you know. In some cases in Iraq, the situation is somewhat resolved. Surprisingly, Anbar Province, all of a sudden, has become just a remarkable development, and a place where you can actually see how it could possibly evolve into a situation sustainable by the Iraqis. Other places remain very problematic, and there's certainly neighborhoods in Baghdad where we are still trying to refine the vision of what would be sustainable, and then determine how in fact to get to that point.

HH: How are the capabilities of the Iraqi security forces? You spent a lot of time training them in the first part of the occupation, General Petraeus. [What are their,] what's their effectiveness now?

DP: Well, frankly, it is uneven. There are some exceedingly good units. The Iraqi special operations force brigade, a commando battalion, a counterterrorist unit, some other elements, national emergency response unit, the intelligence special tactics unit, SWAT teams in just about each of the provinces, and a variety of other [sort of] high end units that we have helped develop, each of these is really quite impressive, and almost at the level, certainly in regional terms, of the special operations forces of our own country, again, in relative terms, speaking in regional comparisons. On the other hand, at the other end of the spectrum, there are still some units that have a degree of sectarian influence exercised within them, and some that are still being cleaned up after having suffered from sectarian pressures, and given into sectarian pressures during the height of the sectarian violence in 2006, and into 2007. [There's also,] there's a vast number of units, frankly, out there just doing what I would call a solid job, manning checkpoints, going on patrols, in some cases in the lead, in some cases alongside our forces, in some cases, following. But I can assure you that the Iraqi forces are out there very much fighting and dying for their country, [They,] in fact, their losses typically are some three or more times the losses that we suffer.

HH: General, what about the losses on the enemy? You mentioned that hundreds of al Qaeda fighters have been killed in the last couple of months, but are they suffering losses in the thousands every month? Or is it hundred, two hundred? What kind of force reduction's going on there?

DP: Yeah, as you know, we try to avoid body counting, but inevitably, obviously, it is something we keep track of, because we're trying to have some sense of the damage that we are doing to al Qaeda-Iraq, its affiliates, other Sunni insurgent groups, and also certainly to the Shia militia extremist elements. And the answer to that in a general sense is that they are losing many, many hundreds of their, of these different elements each month, certainly since the onset of the surge.

HH: And you mentioned foreign fighters infiltrating. Has that flow slowed or accelerated over the past five months?

DP: We do not think there has been much of a change in that. Again, it is something that is difficult to measure. Certainly, if you knew precisely how many were coming, or where they were coming, we'd obviously interdict them. And we do in fact interdict some, but not huge numbers. We do occasionally capture them in the act of preparing to, or trying to carry out a suicide attack or some other attack. In fact, we recently killed a fairly substantial element, 34 in one batch, some of which certainly were foreign fighters and had suicide vests and belts on, and were trying to re-infiltrate into Anbar Province and cause problems there. But we think the number of these foreign fighters, foreign terrorists who come through Syria, by and large, has remained roughly the same, and that is a big concern, because of those 60, 80, 90 or so who do come in per month, many of those end up being suicide bombers. And even though their numbers are relatively small in the grand scheme of affairs here, they can cause horrific casualties, indiscriminate death to Iraqi civilians, and really substantial damage, physically as well as psychologically.

HH: General, one of your colleagues, one of the high profile generals in this conflict, Marine Corps Lt. General Maddis, said in December of last year that the enemy had denied American media the battlefield, with some pretty damaging consequences. Is that still true? Are we getting an accurate picture of what's going on in Iraq from the American media? Or can they just not get out where the fighting's going on?

DP: Well, we have media out with us all the time. In fact, one of the items that I have certainly stressed in the commanders I'm privileged to lead here, and the troopers have all tried to do, is to be accessible to the media. I mean, that's why I'm talking to you tonight.

HH: Right.

DP: [And I think, I mean,] we look on a daily basis at who's doing what out there. I think you've seen plenty of our leaders and our troopers out there. I mean, all of our commanders, just about, go out in front of the press on a fairly regular basis. They have occasionally said things that seem surprising to some people. I mean, we've had commanders who've said they needed more troops. We've had commanders who said we could draw down at some point. We've had commanders who've said good things about their Iraqi counterparts, and occasionally have expressed some reservations. So we are trying to present as forthright and balanced and accurate a picture as we can. Our job is not to put lipstick on pigs, or to spin. Our job is, again, to try to convey to the American public, and then the public of all the coalitions, and those who follow the media throughout the world, as accurate a picture as we can of what is going on here. It really is our view, you know, an informed population can make the best decisions at the end of the day.

HH: Is the media doing a good job of taking that ample amount of information and transmitting it in an objective fashion in your view, General Petraeus?

DP: I think they generally are. I think it is difficult, though, in a sense, to get past the soundbytes sometimes. It is difficult to convey a nuanced sense of events. And certainly, look, at the end of the day, it is hard to get past the fact that a sensational attack is going to lead. And that's just a fact of life. And I think that occasionally, you know, folks will wince over here and say gosh, you know, they didn't get the ribbon cutting we did today, or nobody covered the job fair, or the opening of the new police academy, or whatever it might be, because a car bomb went off. Well again, that's reality, and terrible loss of life, sadly but realistically, is going to bump some feel good stories. So I think that's just something we have to come to grips with. It is again a fact of life, and such is life.

HH: Some of the arguments about Iraq in the United States argue that it's possible for American troops to withdraw to their bases and just strike at al Qaeda, sort of an Anbar only option, I guess. Does that make any sense to you at all, General Petraeus?

DP: Well, first of all, al Qaeda-Iraq is throughout pretty substantial parts of Iraq, and it is a significant enough network in capability that it is not going to be dealt with just by certainly, if you will, classical counterterrorist operations. Indeed, we are doing those. Our best operators in America and in the world are here in the largest number of anywhere in the world by several multiples, and conducting a very, very high operational tempo, and doing extraordinary operations. When I think back to the operations that we did, for example, going after war criminals in Bosnia, or something like that, you know, and one of those would be a big deal, and you'd dine off that for the next several months. On a nightly basis here, you know, ten or twelve serious operations are going down by those forces.

HH: Wow.

DP: And any one of those is far more significant than we conducted for decades. They are very sophisticated, very complex, very lethal sometimes, and very effective. Having said that, although they may be the most important operations, because they can take down, as they did the senior Iraqi leader in al Qaeda-Iraq, or kill the three al Turki brothers, or what have you, it is also the weight of the operations conducted by the, if you will, the regular special forces, the Green Berets and the others that make up the special operations task force, and operate throughout the country as a very high operational tempo, and of our conventional forces. I mean, it is conventional forces who cleared Western Baquba. Certainly, augmented by, again, our special forces and our special mission unit elements, but they're the ones that, you know, killed the 80 or 90 confirmed kill, and perhaps another 80 or so more, and captured a couple of hundred in addition to that as well. And they're the ones who will hold that area against attempts that have already taken place by al Qaeda and their affiliates to try to get back into those neighborhoods.

HH: [You know, that...] in the forward to that manual that you wrote with General Amos, it said you needed a flexible, adaptive force led by agile, well-informed, culturally astute leaders. You're just describing that kind of a force. Is it increasing in its lethality and effectiveness on an exponential basis, General? Has it become a more...

DP: It has very much so, Hugh, yes, very, very much so. In fact, people ask, you know, what are the big changes during the sixteen months that you were gone from Iraq? I left Iraq in September, '05, returned in February, as you noted earlier. And there were two really significant changes. One was the damage done by sectarian violence. It is undeniable, it was tragic, and it has, as I mentioned earlier, ripped the very society, the fabric of Iraqi society. It's caused very significant fault lines between sects and ethnic groups to harden, and it has created an environment that is much more challenging than before it took place. Beyond that, though, I typically will note that our leaders and our troopers get it about what it is that we're trying to accomplish here in a way that certainly was not the case at the outset, or even perhaps a year or two into this endeavor. The typical leader here now has had at least one tour in Iraq, some have actually had two. They have, during the time they're back in the States, [they] studied this. Of course, while we were back in the States, we revamped the counterinsurgency manual, as you mentioned, published that, revamped our other doctrinal manuals, overhauled the curricula of the commissioned, non-commissioned and warrant officer education systems in the Army, Marine Corps and the other services, completely changed the scenarios at our combat training centers, the one in the Mojave desert, the one in central Louisiana, the one in Germany, and also captured lessons learned, created the ability to virtually look over the shoulder of those who are down range through expanded pipes in the military secure internet, just a host of initiatives have been pursued, changed organizations, changed equipment, and have given us capabilities, particularly in the intelligence realm, and with the proliferation of unmanned aerial vehicles, much larger pipes, the ability to shoot much bigger data, if you will, down them, and so forth. All of this has enabled our troopers in a way that certainly was not the case when we did the fight for Baghdad, or even, frankly, when I was here for my previous second tour. And so again, our leaders get it, our soldiers get it, they are these flexible, adaptable, thoughtful, culturally astute, and by and large, leaders and soldiers and Marines, and they are showing that on a daily basis here. That is not to say that it is anything at all easy about this, that the complexity is anything but just sheer enormous, or that this situation is anything but the most challenging that I've ever seen in some 33 years in uniform.

HH: It sounds optimistic, General. I want to respect your time and close with just a couple of questions, one that Senator Webb this past weekend rightly denounced politicians who try and put words into the mouths of troops. So I'm going to ask you. What do you hear your men and women saying about this mission? Do they think it can be won?

466

DP: Well, I think they do. [I mean, I think...nobody...] look, everybody wants to go home. I mean, nobody was cheering when we extended from 12 to 15 months, and I wasn't, either, you know? This is my fourth year of longer deployment since 2001. My family would love to have me back home, and I'd love to be there. But we want to go back the right way, if you will, so that although every soldier's first right is to, you know, grouse a bit, and we all exercise that on occasion, I think everybody's very determined to try to do the very best that we can to accomplish this mission. I was privileged on the 4th of July to swear the oath with some 588 soldiers in one huge formation here at Camp Victory, who reenlisted for another tour in the Army, Navy, Air Force, Marines, and so forth. And it was extraordinary. And I can tell you, you know, it's not because of the bonus or anything like that. There is no bonus that can compensate for the sacrifices and the hardship in the selfless service that our soldiers are providing here. So again, I think individuals are doing all that they can to try to achieve success in this mission here, and that's the focus of the folks with whom I'm privileged to soldier.

HH: Last question, General. How can the American public support these troops most effectively?

DP: Well, I think the American public has been doing that. I think actually, regardless of the views on Iraq, the American public has supported our soldiers, sailors, airmen, Marines, Coast Guardsmen and the civilians that are deployed over here. And I think that that is wonderful. We all saw, some of us, you know, as we were growing up, a situation where that was not the case. And happily in this case, as I said, regardless of one's views, regardless on where one comes down on the issue of Iraq, there is backing for those great young men and women who are putting everything on the line here on a daily basis, in right now, 125 degree heat and body armor and Kevlar, against a barbaric enemy, in an exceedingly tough and complex situation. I think I mentioned to you before that when Tom Brokaw was out here with us one time, he said that surely this has to be the new greatest generation. And I very, very much agree with that. And as I mentioned earlier, I feel very privileged to be able to soldier with these great young men and women here in Iraq again.

HH: General David Petraeus, thanks for your service, thanks for your time today, I look forward to talking to you again sometime.

DP: Thank, great to be with you.

HH: Thank you, General.

End of interview.

Interview with John Burns
September 25, 2007

HH: We begin whenever we can catch up with him with the New York Times' John Burns, war correspondent, Pulitzer Prize winner, and often, whenever he's been on this program, extraordinary insight into what's going on in the Middle East. Mr. Burns, welcome back, always a pleasure.

JB: And for me, too.

HH: Before we plunge into the conditions in Iraq, and I want to talk about Blackwater in your article in the Sunday New York Times, Ahmadinejad, President Ahmadinejad of Iran arrived in New York on Sunday, has gone to Columbia. What is the understanding of Ahmadinejad inside of Iraq? Do they view him as an enemy, a rival, or someone that must be appeased?

JB: Well, it's very difficult to tell, because as you know, there are strong relationships between important figures in the present government of Iraq and Iran. But I don't think that they are very personal in the sense that those relationships were built up in exile by people like Nouri Kamel al-Maliki, the present prime minister of Iraq, who spent, along with other leaders, a number of years living in Tehran, but most of their ties led to other Iranian leaders. I'm guessing here, because they don't speak about this, but I think that they would find him, as so much of the world does, a difficult and volatile character, but a necessary, if you will, partner, because in any foreseeable future in Iraq, of course, they have to seek some kind of an accommodation with Iran, and there's this very strong relationship between the Shiites, the ruling Shiites in Iraq now, and of course the ruling Shiites in Iran. Beyond that, it gets very complex indeed as to exactly what that relationship presently is and where it's going.

HH: And in his recent book, <u>Confronting Iran</u>, Professor Ansari, who's a very great expert on Iran, and who lives up in Scotland, reminded me that Khomeini spent many years inside of Iraq. And was he welcomed there as representative of that Shia theology? Is Sistani an advocate of Khomeinism and the sort of Mahdism that Ahmadinejad embraces?

JB: Well, the second question is I think fairly clear. The ruling hierarchy, the Shiite hierarchy in Iraq presently led by Grand Ayatollah Ali al-Sistani, have made it very clear that they do not subscribe to the principle called Velayat e-faqih, which is the ruling principle in Iran. That's just very simply put, they don't think that the clerics should be directly and actively involved in politics. That said, Mr. Sistani is involved in politics without any doubt. He's an extremely powerful figure. He's simply less obtrusive about it. He remains in Najaf, the holy city in Iraq. He doesn't talk, for example, never has to American officials directly. His hand is deeply involved in many, many things. But he doesn't advocate clerics taking governmental positions in the manner that they have in Iran.

HH: John Burns, have you been able to interview the Grand Ayatollah?

JB: No, no. He won't see Western journalists, either. He's an extremely elusive figure, and he is, by the way, paradoxical or odd as it may sound, he's actually an Iranian. So you have an Iranian who has lived for many, many years in Najaf in Iraq, who is in many ways the most powerful figure in Iraq, and that tells you quite a great deal about the amount of Iranian influence that there is in Iraq. There always would be in Iraq, if you had a Shiite-led government.

HH: Well, it seems to me that the issue of the future of Iraq comes down to whether or not Sunni and Shia are going to be able to reconcile without coercion. And that depends on theology. What's your estimate of that, John Burns?

JB: Well, that's very difficult to say. If the question is, do the most powerful Shiite clerics in Iraq foresee an accommodation with the Sunni minority? I think the answer is yes, but I think the devil's in the detail here. It's what sort of reconciliation do they envisage? They envisage a situation in which the Shiite majority would be in very clear control, and the Sunni minority, who of course ruled Iraq for centuries, would have to accept that. And it's not at all clear to me at the present moment that any such accommodation is available, certainly not available on the side of the Sunni minority, if the Shiites continue to rule Iraq through, in effect, religious parties. There's the problem. If it was a Shiite secular government, or a secular government led by a Shiite, say, Ayad Allawi, who was in fact the first prime minister of the post-Saddam Iraq, a former Baathist Shiite, secular, then the Sunnis would be much more likely to accept it. I think what they're very unlikely to accept in the medium term or the long term is a Shiite religious-led government.

HH: Michael Totten just filed an amazing series of dispatches from Ramadi, and talking with the Sunni sheiks there, and they are very suspicious of the central government. Is it because, if I understand you right, the central government is overtly Shia religious parties, not the secularists of the Baathist background? And if the latter came to the fore, you could expect some kind of rapprochement?

JB: I think that that's the most likely rapprochement if there is any rapprochement at all, short of a full civil war. But how you get there from here, that's another question, because the Shiite religious parties dominated the two elections that were held. If there were a new election, they probably would do so again. Shiites have found, if you will, in their great majority in Iraq, a sanctuary after their decades of repression under Saddam Hussein. They found a sanctuary in their faith, and I don't think that the hold of the Shiite religious parties in Iraq is likely to be relinquished anytime soon.

HH: A lot of people are speculating that a soft partition is settling in. Do you see that, John Burns?

JB: I'm a little suspicious of that, because I think that the contending parties in Iraq are identified by one thing that they do have in common, which is that they view this as a winner takes all game. And although it's true, for example, that in Baghdad, one cause of the lessening of sectarian violence in Baghdad, one cause in my view, is the American surge, the additional American troops have been there. But another cause is that there has been so much effective partition within Baghdad itself as a result of ethnic cleansing over the last eighteen months. But that's a battle that is far from over. Neither Shiites nor Sunnis are likely to accept that as a status quo in the long term, and you only have to think of the people who have been driven from their homes, and I know dozens of them, many of our own employees in Iraq of the New York Times, have had to leave their neighborhoods in fear of their lives because of the sectarian killing. The only property many of these people have, the only asset they have is their homes. They're not going to give them up. This is a struggle which will not relent, and not relent for a very long time. So if we talk about an actual soft partition, I don't see that as a lasting solution.

HH: John Burns, I don't have your resume in front of me, but I seem to recall that you were the bureau chief in India for a while for the Times.

JB: I was indeed.

HH: And of course, India went through a partition, and it was Hindu-Muslim, not Shia-Sunni Muslim, and it was bloody and it was awful. But when you were there, had it passed, not obviously in the Kashmir, but in the day to day relations between Muslim and Hindus, did they carry the scars of that partition forty years later?

JB: They did, they did. And as late a time that I was there in the 1990's, there was still major upheavals and riots and killings which could be traced back to that partition. I think in some ways, India has been more successful in overcoming the aftermath of partition than has Pakistan, so I don't want to leave the impression that India's a country that remains deeply traumatized by it, but the 120, 130 million Muslims in India still have a restive relationship with the ruling Hindu majority in India, and a great deal of that restiveness goes back to 1947-48.

HH: And do you expect that that same sort of restiveness will endure, even if some kind of rapprochement is worked out over the next four, five, six years in Iraq, between Shia and Sunni?

JB: Oh, I'm sure it will. Hugh, we're dealing here with a problem that has its origins right at the very earliest stages of Islam, 1,400 years ago. And Iraq sits right on the fault line of that schism between what we now know as the Sunni and the Shia. What happened when the American invasion of Iraq occurred in 2003 was lifting the weight of terror which Saddam Hussein had managed to suppress that schism, if you will, has exposed it. And the notion that Sunni and Shia in Iraq can resolve differences which are so deeply rooted in history, as their more recent experience on the Shia side of repression, and on the Sunni side of seeing their ruling power usurped, the notion that that can be resolved in any brief period of time, I think, is entirely notional. I think it's going to be a very long time before there is what you might describe as a lasting settlement.

HH: John Burns, when we went to break, we were talking about the Sunni-Shia divide in Iraq, and I'm hoping, given how many years you've spent there, you can sort of explain to me and to the audience how…you mentioned that Saddam's weight of terror suppressed this divide. How palpable is that divide, even, say, among the employees of the New York Times? Does it rise up as say racial tension would have in the South in the 50's and the 60's? Or is it much deeper and much more concealed than that?

JB: [No,] you mentioned in the last segment the situation in India, and I think that you could say this in common about the two societies in sectarian friction and violence, which is that it's a manmade thing. It's a provoked thing. So let me tell you, for example, about the mood in the New York Times' compound in Iraq. I think among media organizations, we are the largest employer. We have more Iraqi staff than anybody else. And one of the most pleasing things said to me as I left a few weeks ago by one of the Iraqi staff was that, "You've made it possible for us within these high walls, the high blast walls with which we've had to surround our compound in Iraq to protect ourselves, and our Iraqi employees, you've made it possible within these four walls for us to be Iraqis, not Sunni and Shia. There's no sectarianism here." I have to say, I was extremely pleased to hear that. And it wasn't we who created that. We made it possible for Iraqis, decent, hard-working, conscientious Iraqis, the sorts of people we employed, and who contribute so heavily to our daily report in the New York Times on Iraq, made it possible for them to be themselves. And their natural default position, and I'm speaking now of the great majority of Iraqis, is one of peaceable intent and goodwill across the Sunni-Shiite schism, if you will. This sectarian violence has been provoked in the first place by al Qaeda and the Baathist underground as it became, that is to say the remnants of Saddam's regime, who for a very long time, in the fact of, I have to say, passive Shiite resistance, were killing Shiites in very large numbers in their Mosques, in their markets, on the streets, in their schools, with the sorts of bombings which Americans became so familiar with. It was really only in 2006 that Shiites began to strike back in a serious way with militia death squads of their own. But on both sides of this, it's extremists who have prevailed. I don't think that they represent, they don't represent the default position on either side. That said, of course, the fundamental question of power, and the division of power, is a thing that divides Sunni and Shia. At the New York Times, it wasn't an issue that we had to address, but it is an issue that Iraq has to addressed, and that's going to be an extremely difficult one to resolve, absent active religious friction.

HH: Did the Times and similar organizations, do they hire with an eye on the religious background of their Iraqis, with an eye towards balancing? Is it that obvious when you're dealing with a Sunni and a Shia? Or do you ask purposely in order to maintain a balance? How do you chart that very...

JB: Well, I have to say that in the early stages of our presence in Iraq, and I'm talking now in the period under Saddam, and the period after he was overthrown, and we began to build a bureau there, I didn't personally know whether many of our employees were Shia or Sunni. It only became relevant for us to know that much later on, when after a couple of years of the war, when outside our compound, these schisms, this sectarianism, this killing, had become so severe that we then felt that we had to maintain a rough balance. And it's not always easy to do. It wasn't because we saw sectarianism arising within our ranks, but we felt that in order to be able to have access to both communities, and for our reporting to be, and to be seen to be even-handed, it was important that we should maintain that balance.

HH: Now as we've seen the Sunni sheiks of Anbar turn against AQI, and go after the extremists who blew up, Zarqawi's people who blew up the Golden Mosque, who did these terrible killings, will the Shia radicals fade as AQI is driven back, and hopefully to the level that they can't mount operations? Do you expect that the Shias that radicalized in response to the AQI will deradicalize?

JB: I think it's inevitable that they will. Since the principal spur to the rise of extremist Shiite sectarian groups in Iraq was the bombing by al Qaeda, and al Qaeda-related groups, to the degree that al Qaeda is put on the back foot by the rise of this moderate Sunni, mostly tribal phenomenon in Iraq, I think you'll see that opinion in the Shiite community will moderate, and indeed there's a very important development just over the weekend, when the American military command announced that they were having considerable progress with both Shiite and Sunni tribal leaders in Diyala Province to the northeast of Baghdad, which has become one of the focal points of the war, and to which al Qaeda migrated in large numbers as the tribal alliance against them grew in Anbar. So you have now Shiite tribal leaders beginning to move towards the moderate center, and against the more extremist Shiite militia groups led by, notably, Muqtada al Sadr, the Shiite cleric whose Mahdi Army has been so deeply involved in this sectarian killing. And of course, as you know, Muqtada al Sadr has himself declared a six month moratorium on violence. He's done that sort of thing before. And the proof of that pudding will be in the eating. But there are some significant signs of a move towards moderation.

HH: Now…hard question to answer completely or even in a comprehensive partiality, but if you ask Iraqi Shias would they rather be working with Iraqi Sunnis or Iranian Shias for the future of their country…

JB: You know, this is a hunch based largely on, if you will, my own personal relationships with the Iraqi Shia. My sense is that in the medium to long term, it will be, if you will, the fact that they are Arabs, not the fact that they are religious Shiites, that will be decisive. It's worth bearing in mind that the majority of Iraqi troops who fought Iran during the eight year Iran-Iraq war in the 1980's, the majority of those Iraqi troops were Shiites. Of course, Iraqis did not have a great deal of choice as to whether they went to war or not against Saddam. But I know a number of them, that is to say a number of Iraqi Shiites, who spent many years in the infantry and in the tank corps fighting Iran in the most bitter and violent conditions along the Iran-Iraq border in those years in the 1980's, who never wavered for one second in that war, who absolutely then and still now felt that Iraq was justified. So my sense is that the natural, again, default position of Iraqi Shia places great importance on [their, if you will,] the affinity that they share as Arabs with Sunni Arabs in Iraq, that is to say, as Iraqis, more than it does in their identification of themselves as Shia.

HH: Mr. Burns, the Sunnis I know that you have as friends, has the rejection of sort of the Takfiris become complete, the Islamists who [sort of] breed life into the al Qaeda extremism? I saw over the weekend as well, there was a Saudi senior cleric, himself a Salafist, who denounced bin Laden for his many, many murders of innocents. Is that taking hold within even the most conservative Sunni precincts?

JB: You know, I would say that the quick answer to that is yes. I've never felt that there was a major political constituency in Iraq for the Takfiris, for the Salafists, for al Qaeda. What there was, was a major constituency among Sunnis for any formula that presented them with a possibility of regaining what they lost in April, 2003, which was political primacy. And it was on that basis, of course, that these extremist groups thrived, and it's of course because of that that political reconciliation at the center is so important. But I thought it was inevitable, absolutely inevitable, and I felt this as early as 2003-2004, that the Sunnis would turn away from al Qaeda, because the Sunnis, as I knew them, were in the main a secular people. They do not wish to return to an 8th Century caliphate. They do not wish to be herded back as the people of Iran have been to a sort of Middle Ages version of their faith. Iraq, you have to remember, under Saddam Hussein, which the many, many things that were evil and wrong about it, women in Iraq, for example, probably were more liberated, at least professionally and socially, than they were in almost any other country in the Middle East. So Sunni women, for example, you would find very, very few people, very few of them, who would wish for the kind of caliphate that bin Laden and his friends have advocated for Iraq. So I think that this change was inevitable. And also inevitable was the recognition that American troops in Iraq who of course took the brunt of al Qaeda's attacks for so long, that American troops in Iraq are in effect probably the best guarantor that the Sunni community has against, if you will, a kind of brute and overbearing Shiite authoritarianism in Iraq.

HH: Now I think it was Ambassador Crocker during the many days of fascinating testimony, who made comment, asked is there a Mandela in Iraq, that Saddam had killed them all. Are there, is there a new generation of political leadership, whether led by Maliki or others who are different in kind and charisma and talent that you [sort of] need to run a multiparty democracy?

JB: Well, let me put it to you this way. In the ranks of the Shiite religious parties, there are very many highly talented, highly skilled, and as I judge it, mainly secular people. I think for example, Sharistani, the present oil minister, a nuclear physicist by training, highly talented man, you could imagine Sharistani in other circumstances emerging as [one] the leader or one of the leaders of an entirely different kind of Shiite-led government in Iraq. In other words, there is tremendous talent there. The problem is that that talent is not mostly at the helm of the parties. The leadership of those religious parties passed during the years in exile, to people who have proved to be rather mediocre. But that's not to say that there aren't highly skilled, highly capable, highly educated people within those parties who could emerge in the future as the leaders of a much more responsible and indeed much more secular kind of government.

HH: We'll get to most of this after the break, and then to Blackwater. With about 45 seconds, but do you sense that the Salafist surge is still rising? Or has it peaked in Europe and other places?

JB: Well, let's hope that it has peaked.

HH: But I asked if you thought it had, not if (laughing)…

JB: Well, let me put it this way. At this late stage, at least if we look in terms of the politics of the United States in the war in Iraq, as American patience is exhausting, we are seeing encouraging signs of the extremists being driven onto the back foot in Iraq. And let's hope that that continues to flower, because the potential in all of that is very encouraging indeed.

HH: Mr. Burns, you wrote a very interesting piece about Blackwater USA, very fair, I thought, on Sunday, pointing out that no trip outside the Green Zone is remotely safe. These contractors, many of whom are highly skilled retired SEALs, Special Forces and Marine Recon people, are going at risk every time they go out on one of their protection missions. Are they being unfairly diminished in the eyes of the public, with sort of the tabloid journalism surrounding them?

JB: I think Blackwater, if one took an overview of this, a fair overview of this, is a victim in effect of the indemnity that was granted to them by Bremer when he was the chief American administrator in Iraq for fifteen months after the American invasion. I think most of us put in a position in a way we are not accountable, tend to exceed moderate restraint, and I think that's what happened. So I think you can say on the one hand there's a fundamental truth about Blackwater which is that they have managed to keep the American officials in Iraq, and their great majority, whether they're involved in reconstruction or in the Embassy, all the way up to the Ambassador, they've kept them safe. There've been very few, relatively very few, assassinations of American officials, and Blackwater deserves enormous credit for that. On the other hand, taking force protection, as the military calls it, and they're almost all former military people as you mentioned, Special Forces people, taking it as an absolute has led to, in many cases, to I think injudicious use of force to a kind of overbearing attitude, which places the protection of American life as an absolute, and of course, relatively speaking, diminishes the relative, [the] value of Iraqi civilian life. And we've seen a number of instances, not just this most recent one, in which Iraqi civilians have died from gunfire, and not just from Blackwater, but from other security contractors, mainly British and American, and I think that the time was long past due when the American and Iraqi authorities in Iraq should have come up with some kind of legal formula which placed this all under some kind of accountability and restraint.

HH: Now I assume that the New York Times, like every other media organization, has to also contract with private security firms, don't they?

JB: Well, it would probably be unwise for me to speak in a show like this about exactly what we do, but let me put it to you this way. We do have to protect ourselves, and we do travel with people who have weapons, under the authority, in our case, most of those people are Iraqis. But they are under the authority of former Western military people. And we, too, are in something of a no man's land. The laws are not at all clear, and we have had to fashion our own rules for all of this, and without going too much into it, our rule is to avoid at all costs, and we have managed to do so, so far, for four and a half years, at all cost, to resort to violence, and at all costs, even if forced upon us, to resort to deadly violence. That is to say we hope, we pray, that we continue to operate safely with people who will never have to actually fire their weapons. And if they did fire their weapons, would do so in such a way as to avoid fatalities or serious injury. And I have to say that in saying that, I'm kind of looking to the heavens...

HH: Yes.

JB: ...because the situations can so easily get out of hand, and no doubt, if you or I had been present at the circumstances that occurred ten days ago in the streets of Baghdad when these people died under gunfire, some of it from, one supposes, from Blackwater, I'm sure the Blackwater people would say you had to be there to know how that happened. Things get very, very quickly out of control once bullets start flying.

HH: What is the sense in Baghdad? Now I know it's still risky, very risky in many parts of the city, especially Sadr City, but is there at least in some significant parts of the city a lessening of that sense of risk?

JB: I think there is, and the American military have begun to produce some interesting statistics on the degree to which Baghdad is under control. It's far too early to get too encouraged about this, what they're basically saying is that something less than 10% of the city is really under control, that another significant proportion of the city is much more under control than it was, and that quite wide areas of the city are not under control. The problem with this is it's extremely difficult to know which area is which, and sometimes, it varies from day to day. I think the general rule, a general rule which I've always operated anyway, is to regard every street, every traffic light, every corner, every nook as being a place of potential fatality. It's still an extremely, extremely dangerous place to be.

HH: Now in two days, I'm going to be talking with your long time colleague, Tim Weiner, about his magnificent new book, <u>Legacy of Ashes: The History of the CIA</u>. One of the things that was so stunning about this book is how badly the Agency bungled the WMD, and really didn't have a presence in Iraq. To the best of your ability to tell, is the CIA building an effective branch there? Or is it still plagued by the problems that Weiner charts in terms of rapid turnover, and an inability to place anyone there who's comfortable being there.

JB: Well, I have to say that frankly, it's a subject about which I and most journalists know very little. If they are building a much more effective presence in Iraq, it's not something that we would know very much about. If we knew much about it, it wouldn't be very effective. It has to be covert. I'm sure that… the short answer to it is that they are. And I think it has to be said to be fair, that to build a covert underground in Iraq under Saddam Hussein would have been extremely difficult, because his secret police were so pervasive, and because the costs, since you would have had to have been working through Iraqis, you had to recruit Iraqis to do this, the costs were so high. You would be asking people not just to put their own lives as risk in being recruited into the CIA, but to put the lives of their entire extended families at risk. Even if they were extracted in extreme risk, their families would likely then to go under the hammer from Saddam, and die in the most appalling possible way. So the CIA's failure to build an effective human intelligence network in Iraq under Saddam Hussein I think has to be put into that context, [and I think it can be sure…]

HH: You're not in Iraq now, you're in Florida. What's the plan for John Burns? Are you going back to Iraq? Or are you heading to somewhere else?

JB: I have transited to be the London Bureau chief of the New York Times, but I'll be going back to Iraq from time to time. I don't think any of us who have worked in Iraq will asunder our ties there, and I certainly want to stay involved. I saw General Petraeus on his way through London last week, and my last words to him as he left to fly back to Baghdad was I'll see you in Baghdad, and I hope that that will not be too long in coming.

HH: [You know,] you know the General quite well. You had to have watched the political firestorm around his testimony, and the effort to blacken his reputation in some quarters. Fair or unfair? What did you make of that circus?

JB: Well, it's true, I do know the General very well. I've traveled with him a great deal. I have a great respect for him, and a great respect for the really difficult, indeed, one's inclined to think impossible, situation in which he's been placed, and I think that as you would expect of a four-star general of the United States Army, under that assault that he faced, I think he behaved with a great deal of dignity and restraint. You have to remember that you or I, Hugh, subjected to that, would be able to respond much more robustly...

HH: Yup.

JB: ...in many ways than he could, and I know he felt a little bit belabored by that. But he was in good spirits when I saw him in London, and he said looking forward to getting back to Baghdad. And I rather thought that what he might have meant as much by...that he wanted to get back to fighting the war in Iraq, was that he was happy to be escaping the war in Washington.

HH: You know, he began his testimony by saying this is my testimony, I wrote it, nobody's seen it except me. Do you believe him, John Burns?

JB: I do believe it. I do believe it, and I actually saw him on numerous occasions in the weeks that led up to that testimony, and I know that to be true. At least what I can say is that I know that he was deeply involved in thinking about and drafting, along with Ambassador Crocker, what they were going to say. And indeed, what they said on the Hill was what they had been saying to people like myself, mostly privately, off the record, for some months beforehand. So I think that that was a misnomer to think that he was up on the Hill as his master's voice. He wasn't. I mean, David Petraeus is a serious individual, as is Ryan Crocker. They are in the service of the United States of America, not in the service of the president of the United States. Anybody who knows either of them knows that to be their fundamental and overriding concern. So I think that that was true. That's not to say that they don't feel a loyalty to the commander in chief, and to the President. Of course they do. But I think in their own minds, they found a way to make sure that it's those two commitments, those two loyalties, do not conflict.

HH: John Burns, always fascinating. Thank you for your time. We look forward to catching up with you again sometime soon.

End of interview.

Interview with John Burns
June 4, 2008

HH: A special hour as we return to a conversation that we always enjoy having here with John F. Burns. He is currently the London bureau chief of the New York Times. But if you've listened, you know that he is twice a Pulitzer Prize winner for the New York Times. He's been their bureau chief all over the world, including India, Beijing, Moscow, and most recently, for many years, in Baghdad, Iraq. Mr. Burns, welcome back to the Hugh Hewitt Show. Great to speak with you.

JB: It's a great pleasure, Hugh.

HH: John, you left Iraq in the fall of 2007, and you haven't been back, it's my understanding. How have you been keeping track of events over there? And are you still in touch on a fairly regular basis with your colleagues in the Times bureau there?

JB: Well, an indirect way of answering that would be to say that leaving the war is a great deal more difficult than committing to it over the five years that I was in Iraq. And the withdrawal is difficult, and so part of what soothes one in a situation like that is to stay in touch with people. And my wife remains in Baghdad, continues to work at the New York Times bureau in Baghdad, so I keep in touch.

HH: What do you understand to be conditions in the country generally now, compared to when you left?

JB: Well, of course, it's compared to what? If you compare the situation in Iraq to 90% of the countries in the world, it's still a very violent and threatening place. But if you compare it to the Iraq of sixteen months or so ago, when General Petraeus took over the military command and the surge began, things have improved very greatly.

HH: And give us some sort of metrics by which you would measure that improvement.

JB: Well, the most important metric that comes to mind that's recent, and it's been in every American newspaper, I would imagine, in the last 24 or 48 hours, is that in the month of May, just concluded, was the lowest number of American troops killed, I think I'm right in saying, in the entire sweep of the war since the second phase of the war began in the spring of 2004, March of 2004. That's when the United States knew that it was going into a second phase of war in Iraq, after of course the first phase, the invasion. Only 19 U.S. soldiers were killed in Iraq in May. Now that's 19 families across the United States who have been absolutely devastated, and one has to be very careful how you address this problem. But if you compare it with the worst months of the war, for example, November, 2004, when there were 137 U.S. soldiers killed, if you compare it even with the sort of figures that were being reported in the early months of the surge, when those figures were well up into the 60s, 70s and 80s a month, it's a remarkable turnaround. The levels of violence across Iraq, depending on the metric that you use, are very sharply down. They're particularly, sharply down in Baghdad, where my wife tells me that it's now a very rare occurrence, something that was a very common occurrence at our bureau on the east banks of the Tigris in Baghdad, to hear a suicide car or truck bombing. You could almost time the day by the early morning suicide bombings that were going on there as recently as a year ago. Now, thank God, it's become a rare event.

HH: Are your colleagues, not just your wife, but all your colleagues, and not just at the New York Times, but in the media, enjoying what they consider to be a measurable improvement in their ability to report, and in the quality of their daily existence?

JB: Well, they still have to be very careful. I'd like to say that the New York Times remained adventurous and enterprising in its reporting throughout the most difficult times of the war, but we were, there's no doubt about it, there's no point of pretending otherwise, pretty constrained by the risks that leaving our compound and going out across the city of Baghdad, and into Iraq, entailed. Those risks are down, but it's very hard to measure that, of course, You know, you only have to be unlucky once for it to be a complete disaster. So we're not lowering our guard. Our guard is still high, I mean, both in literal and metaphorical terms. We protect ourselves pretty well when we leave our compound, because the risk of kidnap or ambush is still there, although the figures for those things have also gone down very seriously. But if you compare the kind of journalism that you can do in Iraq to the kind of journalism that you can do in Los Angeles, of course, they're two very different things.

HH: In terms of the observable, such as quality and quantity of food, electricity availability on a fairly continuous basis, medical care, entrepreneurial openings, how's Baghdad feel now compared to three years ago?

JB: Well again, what I can tell you about that is second hand, and I think you have to look at each individual thing you've mentioned discreetly. Enterprise, from everything I hear, and from what I saw myself before I left Iraq, is thriving. The markets are busy, the roads leading out of Iraq are heavy with traffic in both directions. You have to remember that Iraq is now earning vastly more money, as are all oil producing countries, from its oil. Saddam Hussein, I'm taking a risk here with the figures, but my recollection is that Saddam Hussein had very few years when he earned more than about $25 billion dollars in oil revenues, and that was when there was no war. Those revenues now are up in the $60-70 billion dollar range for a year. This is naturally feeding its way back into the economy. But if you talk about things like electricity and medical care, those things were so devastated by the last four years of warfare in Iraq, that it's going to take a very long time to have a measurable difference. I think there are improvements, but they're incremental improvements. And from everything that I hear, from my wife and my colleagues who are still there, and everything that I read, there's still very widespread dissatisfaction among Iraqis about the paucity of government services. And amongst those, of course, are the generation of electrical power and medical services and education are very high on the list.

HH: I'm talking with John Burns, London bureau chief of the New York Times, five years a veteran of the war in Iraq, where he served as bureau chief for the New York Times. Mr. Burns, stepping back and recalling the time when the surge got underway, and you have a very extensive relationship with David Petraeus, and from our previous conversations, I know you admire him quite a lot. Did you give him any chance to have achieved what has been achieved there? Or is this what you expected would happen?

JB: [You know, I don't think...] as speaking for myself, I was pretty skeptical, as I think most of us were. We had seen four years in which the situation at every turn that we hoped for a turn for the better appeared to turn for the worse. It's now commonplace in Washington, D.C., to say that the war was well on its way to being lost by December by 2006. And so you know, if you'd been a betting man, you'd have had to say that the odds were heavily against the kind of success that General Petraeus and Ambassador Crocker have had there. And it's not alone, of course, the fact that they've had an additional 30,000 American troops, which are now in the process of being withdrawn. But other factors, all of which, if you will, one connected to the other, but the fact that the Sunni awakening, the turning, if you will, of very important elements in the Sunni community that had been either tacitly or overtly in support of the insurgency, who have now turned around and are working with the Coalition forces, the Americans and the Iraqis. That's had a remarkable effect, as have had the ceasefire by Muqtada al-Sadr, the Shiite militia leader. There are many factors here, but however you measure it, the fact is that an enterprise which was attended by a great deal of skepticism when it began, a great deal of skepticism in Washington, D.C., in the Congress as you'll recall, has had a remarkable success, which remains, as I think the phrase that General Petraeus used on the Hill a few weeks ago, it's fragile and reversible. I think you need to put that into context. The American military command is being extremely cautious in what it has to say about these improved metrics in Iraq, because after all, and General Petraeus is on his third tour in Iraq, as are many of the commanders, as are many of the troops, they've seen situations before where things turned briefly for the better only to get worse. And they're very wary of the possibility that this could happen again. And the most recent example of this was the announcement that 19 American troops were killed in May, as I say, the lowest since March of 2004. And I noted that the American military command, in releasing those statistics, was very careful to say that we're not going to claim any great significance for this, because we have seen, and this is the American military command speaking themselves, we've seen before how these figures have gone down from 100 or more a month to the high 30s-low 40s in a month, only to reverse again and get worse. So they're being extremely cautious, as you would imagine they would be.

HH: Mr. Burns, last week I had Lawrence Wright of the New Yorker on, and I don't know if you know Lawrence Wright. [I assume that...]

JB: I do indeed.

HH: Yes, and so we talked about his most recent New Yorker piece, The Rebellion Within, the sort of struggle for the soul of al Qaeda. And I think a lot of it, he believes, and I believe, is because the Anbar awakening has sort of shattered al Qaeda's confidence in itself, and is causing many, many good things to happen around the globe. What's your assessment about the effect on al Qaeda of the strategic blow struck them in Anbar?

JB: You know, that is really a very difficult thing to hazard an opinion on, because al Qaeda, as you know, is a kind of holding company. It's very difficult to tell what the resonance of al Qaeda's declining fortunes in Iraq will be on al Qaeda elsewhere. There's not much sign that al Qaeda's activities, for example, in Afghanistan and Pakistan have diminished lately, even as their fortunes in Iraq have deteriorated so badly. But there's no question that they are on the back foot in Iraq, and that the principal factor in that is that the Sunni community has, in very important dimensions, turned against al Qaeda.

HH: Have you had a chance to read Michael Yon's new book, A Moment Of Truth In Iraq yet?

JB: I have not.

HH: He makes the argument that the deep brutality and cruelty of al Qaeda, and he details it in such a revolting way because he saw it happen for so long, as you did, had the effect of immunizing Anbar Sunnis against a recurrence of al Qaeda. It doesn't mean that we're going to have peace in Iraq, but that they really [have,] threw away their opportunity, if there ever was one there. What do you make of that, John Burns? Are they such bad people that they sow the seeds of permanent rejection wherever they have a period of time in which to nest?

JB: You know, I think the answer to that has to be pretty emphatically yes. My experience in 35 or 40 years reporting around the world is whilst there are many cultural differences among the nations of the Earth, ordinary people are pretty much the same everywhere. Nobody likes to live in the midst of a kind of mindless bloodshed that al Qaeda has visited on Iraq. And even in the worst times, when we sat around our dinner table at the New York Times compound in Baghdad, and we used to remind ourselves that there was a phenomenon at work that would be very hard to gauge, how powerful it was, or how powerful it could become. And that's the exhaustion of the ordinary people with the conflict. It happened in Lebanon, not as decisively as one would wish, as we can see from current events in Lebanon, but their civil war, which lasted fifteen years, when it did wind down, it had a great deal to do with the fact that the people of Lebanon were completely exhausted. They wanted an end to it. And you could certainly see that beginning to happen in Iraq two years ago. And I've no doubt that the success that General Petraeus and Ambassador Crocker and others have had in the last year has had something to do with that. And it gives one hope that whilst some of the other phenomenon are involved here could turn around, that that could be very decisive. If in fact the people of Iraq have decided that they've seen enough of this, then they have it in their hands, of course, to bring this to an end.

HH: What did you see when you were there, and what have you heard since you've left about the professionalism of the Iraqi military, and their ability to maintain the sort of professionalism that prevents yet another strongman along the lines of so many strongmen we've seen in that region emerging?

JB: Very difficult thing to say. I think there's no doubt from some of the things that have happened lately, that it is a very mixed picture. There are Iraqi military units, I think it's best to talk discreetly here about the Iraqi Army and the Iraqi Police. The Iraqi Police is a whole different and much less promising issue. But the Iraqi Army has on occasion, and particularly when they are fighting alongside the Americans, have done quite well. At other times, they've done very poorly. The attempt to retake the streets of Basra from the Shiite militias, as you know a few weeks ago, very quickly ran into trouble. American troops were summoned, the 82nd Airborne, and limited the amount of damage. And now there's reports that large parts of Basra are back under government control. The Iraqis are tough people. If they're properly led, properly equipped, properly fed and properly paid, and if they believe that they are on the winning side, the Iraqis will fight. They'll fight for themselves. They won't fight for us, they'll fight for themselves. They're capable of doing this, and I think there are some signs now that things are really getting better. And certainly when you talk to American officers returned from the war, they have their frustrations, but they very quickly close you down if you suggest that the Iraqis don't want to fight, because they'll tell you many, many a story of how brave and resourceful the Iraqis that they have fought with have been.

HH: Now what do you make of Prime Minister Maliki and his government, and their trajectory of competence?

JB: Very difficult to say. These are people who have never had any experience of governing. They're mostly people who lived in exile for 20, 30 years. They're a fairly motley crew. They've been deeply scarred and traumatized by what happened under Saddam Hussein. They were not, in short, people who were well-equipped to assume the government of a troubled nation like Iraq. But they, too, are on a learning curve, and are doing better. And there are some people in that government who are corrupt, venal, inefficient, and there are others who aren't. So it's a very mixed picture. But the most encouraging single thing that has happened in that respect, of course, in recent weeks, is the decision of Prime Minister Maliki, at last, far too late, to take on the militias, the Shiite militias, and in particular, Muqtada al-Sadr, who let's remember, was the political figure, al-Sadr, who put Maliki in his job. It was Sadr's votes in the parliament that put Maliki in the prime ministership. So for Maliki to have turned around now and have gone after Sadr the way he did in Basra, and currently in Sadr City, is a remarkable change.

HH: And what are you hearing about the Sadr city initiative? [Is that...] critics of the war say oh, that's just Sadr holding back, and proponents of continued support for Iraq say no, Maliki has broken his back. What do you hear, John Burns?

JB: Very difficult to say. Muqtada al-Sadr is an extremely cunning fellow. He has moved between politics and insurgency with tremendous deftness. At the moment, he's on the back foot after taking quite a pummeling in Basra, and in Sadr City, and he's switched back to his political mode, and has been prominent, for example, in demanding that the Iraqi government, Maliki's government, not sign a new bases agreement with the American forces, which the United States very much, very badly wants to be reached fairly rapidly in the coming weeks. So you can't count Sadr out, and you can be sure of one thing, that if he gets the chance, he'll have his men in black pajamas back on the streets, I shouldn't say black pajamas, that's Vietnam, but these black-shirted followers will be back on the streets. They still are there.

HH: Mr. Burns, when we went to break, we were talking about Sadr and his militia, and his desire to get them, you never can count them out. He is so deeply identified with Iran. While you were there, and since you have left, have you been able to discern what Iran's objective is here? Do they really think they can have a satellite state with a nation that they were so brutally at war with for a decade?

JB: Well, they certainly see it as a historic opportunity for Shiism to push, militant Shiism to push westward. There's no doubt about that. But there are different Irans, of course. There's Ahmadinejad, and there are other Iranians who are much more realistic. And as I think I've said to you before, if you look at the Iraqi Shiite community, it's crucial to remember that the vast, overwhelming majority of them are Arabs. They are not Persians. And nationalism is a real thing in Iraq. And whatever the Iranians' intentions may be, my feeling has been, and evidenced by everything I was ever told by Shiites in Iraq, that the Iranians could very quickly overreach themselves. The Iraqis are proud of their nation, they want it to be a self-standing, independent state. They do not wish to be a Satrapi, if you will, of Iran, and I think if Iran had that in mind, I think it's in for a major disappointment. But of course, what they mostly have in mind, I think, is to frustrate the United States, the great Satan. That's been a very powerful force in everything that Iran has done in Iraq.

HH: There have been some intimations in the media that the grand Ayatollah Sistani has decided that it is time to move to eject the Americans from Iraq. Have you seen that? What do you make of those, nothing in writing, just reports and rumors and innuendo, and I don't know how to assess it. What do you think, John?

JB: [You know, you could...] it's a little bit like Chairman Mao in China during the cultural revolution. Cho En Lai used to say for everything that one group of people claim that Mao wants, there's another group of people that can claim the opposite, because Mao, like Sistani, is so elusive. He doesn't appear in public, he doesn't make public statements, but very rarely. It's extremely difficult to tell where at any one time he stands on these issues, so I wouldn't hazard an opinion about that.

HH: Now let me ask you, next segment, I want to talk about the United States and its politics in Iraq, and I also want to talk about the UK. But just as John Burns, are you an optimist about Iraq as we sit here talking at the beginning of the summer of 2008, John Burns?

JB: Well, I think like most fair-minded people, I'm a lot more optimistic than I was a year ago, and I can see the potential for it going very wrong again. But I do think that there is the prospect now, if this is deftly handled, for a soft as opposed to a hard landing to the United States in Iraq. It won't be victory, they won't be throwing flowers at American soldiers again, but there is now the possibility that with careful navigation, the United States could draw its troops down and bring them home, not quickly, over a period of years, and that this will prove not to have been quite the disaster that a year ago it seemed likely to be. But it could equally well turn around, and it could yet again, it could become a situation promising nothing but catastrophe for the United States. Very difficult to tell, but certainly, there's a great deal more grounds for optimism now than there was twelve or sixteen months ago.

HH: Are there reasonable prospects that in the intermediate term, nobody knows the long term, that there might be a stable Iraq that is free, and at least in that region's terms, and if not an ally of the United States, certainly a partner on some things such that it's a contributor to stability and to the war on terror, John Burns?

JB: That's very difficult to say, what the trajectory of a future Iraqi government will be. My own guess is that it will not be a democracy. That, as you know, is a very rare and almost unseen thing in the Arab world. There's likely to be a strongman there. I think in the view of all that has happened, any credible government of Iraq will have to be fairly wary of the United States. In years to come, I think the United States could live with that. But yes, I think it's quite possible that you could have an Iraq that is not overtly hostile to the United States, and could eventually, with its oil wealth, once again become a stable state exercising an influence for stability in the region. That, of course, is, right now, is too far forward a thing to predict, but it's not impossible.

HH: Mr. Burns, you've spent a lot of time in the United States since transitioning from Iraq to the London bureau, and you've talked to a lot of people about Iraq. What's your sense of the viability of Iraq policy in the United States? Is it too far politicized to ever get to a common sense approach that's bipartisan here?

JB: You know, a foreign correspondent who's spent most of the last thirty years outside the United States is well advised to stay upwind of complex problems of American politics. But I can say this, that my sense, talking to audiences and individuals across the United States in recent months, is that there's been something of a convergence of opinion that notwithstanding a presidential election which by its nature is likely to be a polarizing event on great issues of public policy like this, that there's been a slow but perceptible move towards some kind of moderated position, that is to say a position which at least narrows the gap between those who want it out fast and those who wanted to stay the course. And of course, you know, the fact that the Iraq issue has, is no longer listed as the principal issue, or even perhaps the second issue in the presidential campaign, speaks for itself. Why? Because Americans have seen that things have improved substantially there. But it seems to me, listening to people talk across America, that there is a view emerging which could eventually be a more consensual view. We need to get out, we need to get out as soon as we can, but we need to get out in a way that's consistent with American dignity and honor, and the maintenance of the credibility of American power in the world. It's not impossible in view of the situation on the ground in Iraq right now that some kind of formula like that could be found by the next president.

HH: And do you see that formula requiring a period of three or four or five years? Or are you talking about twelve to eighteen months? There, it really is difficult to find out where people feel is an appropriate long term extension of American power here. What do you think?

JB: Of course, that's the really tough question, how quick. I would guess somewhere in the region of three to five years. If it were five years, that's to say the whole of the term of the new president, the United States by then would have been in Iraq ten or eleven years. The generals have always said that the average length of counterinsurgency undertakings in the modern world has been about twelve years, I think I'm correct in saying. So that would be, I would think not less than three, and hopefully not more than five. And it seems to me that whoever is president, and John McCain has recently spoken himself about his desire within the course of his first term to bring this war to an end for the United States, whoever is president is going to try and set a target of getting those troops home by the end of that first term.

HH: Do you think that we have fairly well avoided, or that the Iraqis have fairly well avoided the prospect of genocide at this point, John Burns?

JB: You know, it's much less talked about, but I don't think that you can completely, if I can use a phrase civil war instead of genocide, I don't think you can completely dismiss that as a possibility. If the things that have gone right in the last year, the trajectory turned around, and those things started to go wrong again, I think you could find a fairly rapid descent back into the kind of perfectly dreadful situation that Iraqis faced in 2005 and 2006. I think the odds of that happening, the odds against that happening are improving, but you can't dismiss it.

HH: Knowing what we know now, and seeing everything that we've seen happen, John Burns, do you think the United States ought to have invaded Iraq when they did?

JB: You know, I'm inclined to leave that, leave that to the historians, and history will surely deal with that question on the basis of what the outcome is, something we don't yet know. But I will say that, and I can speak here for journalists, not for policy makers, that before anything like this ever happens again, I think we're all going to have to pay a great deal of attention to history in a way that perhaps we didn't sufficiently in the run up to this war. We need to be more cautioned. It may be that history will judge this thing to have been a disaster, in which case it will clearly judge that the decision to go in was the wrong thing to do. But if against all the odds, the United States manages to get home from Iraq for all the quite horrendous costs that it has faced in sustaining this war, with dignity, and leaving behind it something of a stable Iraq, perhaps history will make a kinder judgment.

HH: Do you find Iraqis wishing that we'd left Saddam in place, and just left them about their business, given the chaos that has followed? [The difficulty to get here, do you think that they…]

JB: [You know, it's…] we certainly were hearing quite a lot of that in '05 and '06. But what I noticed was you heard that at times of tremendous stress in the aftermath of the most awful events, big suicide bombings, the things which were making headlines in the United States at that time. But if you talk to Iraqis when they were not in that distressed state, more calmly, the much more common view, I would have said the overwhelming view was they don't like to be occupied, but [they felt the United States,] they needed the United States to stay long enough to return Iraq to some kind of equilibrium, some kind of stability. This is not rocket science. What would you expect Iraqis really to think in the face of the disasters that have befallen them in the wake of an American invasion, that they would feel unable themselves to restore the state to a state of stability? They would expect the United States would do it for them.

HH: First of all, thanks again, John Burns, for spending this much time with us, very much appreciated. And I want to close by focusing on your current bureau. A few weeks ago, I had Liam Fox, shadow secretary of defense, in the studio for three hours. And we talked a lot about the jihadist pulse, whether it was quickening or slowing in London and the UK. What's your assessment?

JB: Difficult to tell, but there's no doubt that the United Kingdom has a serious domestic security problem, beginning with the fact that they have a very substantial population here, possibly as many as 2.5 million Muslims, the overwhelming majority of whom are peace loving people who want to get on with their lives just the way everybody else does. But there is a radical fringe, and it's not small, and virtually no day goes by, certainly no week goes by, without more evidence in court cases of some pretty dire things that might have happened had the British security forces, backed by American intelligence in many cases, not interceded to stop it happening. Now most recent case involving a group of young men, British young men, British born young men in the main, who wanted to knock down a dozen airliners over the Atlantic in a single stroke two or three years ago. The plot was discovered, and is now before the courts. So Britain has a problem with domestic Islamic jihadism in a way that the United States has not up until now faced.

HH: John Burns, let me close with this question. It's ironic, you went from the center of the hot war against jihadism, not only in Iraq, you were in Afghanistan as well for many years. I think you're now in the center of the cold war against it.

JB: (laughing)

HH: Do you think the West has an appreciation of the struggle that it's in yet?

JB: Very hard to say, very hard to say. I think people in the United Kingdom are aware of it, because of course, they had, on a much smaller scale, they had their own 9/11 in July of 2005, with the attacks on the London transit system, followed very quickly by another failed attack on the London transit system, followed by this plot to knock down airliners, and a dozen or more other plots that have been discovered. So I think people in this country, in the United Kingdom, are pretty aware that there's a serious long term problem. And the government, if they're not aware, the government has not been slow in telling them that this is a problem that is a matter of a generation or more to solve, it's not going to be easy, and [that there's,] the government ministers involved in this invariably say that future attacks are not just likely, they're certain.

HH: Wow. On that sober note, John Burns, thank you again, I look forward to talking with you, especially as we get closer to English elections, which seem to be inevitably going to go bad for some people that you may very well know, and I may know. So I look forward to that conversation, John Burns. Thanks.

End of interview.

Interview with Victor Davis Hanson
October 8, 2008

HH: A very special two hours ahead, a prolonged conversation about the state of the election, the state of the parties, the state of the world, the state of the war with historian and classicist Victor Davis Hanson. If you're just joining in, though, I remind you our good friend, Dean Barnett, is in the fight for his life right now in ICU in Boston, so any prayers that you can offer up for Dean and his treatment would be much appreciated on these special days. We'll keep you posted as we get word of that. Victor Hanson, welcome to the studio. I've probably talked to you a hundred times, a couple of times in person, but never in the studio. It's good to have you here.

VDH: It's good to be here, Hugh.

HH: Now you will be talking tonight at Biola University at 7:00 in Orange County, California, Southern California, about Obama V. McCain in the classical context. It's open to the public, I believe, and people can get there. And I will give directions a little bit later in the show. In a nutshell, in the classical context, what's the message you're going to be expanding on for that audience tonight?

VDH: Well, I'm going to try and look at foreign policy, the war against radical Islam, and take into consideration the meltdown on Wall Street, and what lessons we can learn about the human condition, what happened to our education system that didn't allow us to appreciate these developments, and then like it or not, we're back in the culture wars, and we're wrestling with this question – what is wisdom? [And after…] my favorite illustration of that dilemma is when I saw Barney Frank in the 2003 clip, the overseer of the Fannie Mae/Freddie Mac monstrosity, Harvard Law School, interrogate Franklin Raines, Harvard Law School, and he says, "Do you feel that you're under-regulated at Fannie Mae?" and he says, "No, sir." And Barney Frank says, "Why are we here? There's no reason to be here." And that summed up the best and the brightest got us into this mess. It doesn't mean that a Harvard Law degree is synonymous with ignorance, but it doesn't mean necessarily it's synonymous with excellence. And we're seeing people that we've put our trust in that were educated, highly-credentialed, certified, and yet they had no common sense. And does this involve Sarah Palin? Well, we saw that when she was debating Joe Biden, he was far more impressive with recall of apparent facts, and he seemed that he had gravitas from his years of experience. He was a law school graduate, she was the Idaho commoner. But the more the debate went on, we found out that it would be much better to have someone with common practical sense who knew a few things, and could talk to the American people truthfully rather than to make up a whole plethora of assertions which in retrospect, almost everything Biden said was false. Again, what is wisdom? Is it certification of a particular school? Or is there wisdom to be found having five children and snowmobiling and running a business? And I think at this time of uncertainty about Wall Street, these issues about culture are coming back to haunt us.

HH: Victor Hanson, how old are you?

VDH: I'm 55.

HH: In your…and then let's say in your 45 years…

VDH: Yeah.

HH: …of being aware of the world, do you recall a time as fraught with peril other than 9/11? 9/11 is of to itself, but other than 9/11, a time such as this?

VDH: I ask myself that all the time. I ask people, didn't they hate Reagan the way they hate Bush? Or didn't they hate Nixon, remember the Watergate, gosh, the Vietnam War, I remember I was walking across as a high school student at UC Berkeley. I went up to visit, and it was just almost a war zone. We're not having that. [But I don't think that we're still,] it's not so multi-dimensional with the war, with a cultural divide, with a hatred toward a sitting president, with this complex financial meltdown that nobody can make sense of. And then the sense that America is at odds with almost all the world, and there's these insidious pressures that are telling us here at home you're wrong, you're wrong, you're wrong, you've got to emulate the EU, you've got to emulate Africa, you've got to emulate Asia. And it's almost as if we're 5th Century A.D. in North Africa trying to resist a tide that we can't resist. And so I think you're absolutely right, it's a phenomenal time to be alive.

HH: [Now do democracies have…] we've got a lot of ground to cover, and I'm so happy to have a generous allotment today to try and cover this. But do you think democracies have an inability to see beyond their nose, and to always think they're on either the best of times or the worst of times, to overreact to everything?

VDH: That was the complaint, the classical complaint of thinkers as diverse as Plato and Aristophanes that democracy inherently would always try to satisfy 51% of the people, and it would have an instantaneous referendum in the heat of the moment, that great passage in Thucydides where they vote to execute everybody on the island of Lesbos, and they changed their mind the next day and sent another trireme to revoke that order, or to executing Socrates for gratuitous reasons. So that's the complaint. [But I have...and then] this is the hyper-phenomenon of that. It's energized, fueled by the internet, and this technology that we've gotten addicted to with cell phones and the internet and cable television. But that being said, I still have faith in democracy that the average person, if he's given enough time and enough information, will usually come to the right decision. After all, we rejected Carterism for Reagan, and we rejected a series of people, whether it was Mondale or McGovern or Dukakis, or Kerry who had a very different view of where America should be going.

HH: You know, I'm actually, along with Mark Steyn, one of the few optimists about this election for the reason you just mentioned. Now it's not much time. It's four weeks. But there's a lot of information about Barack Obama, there's a lot of information about his tax policies, his anti-trade policies, which align him with Herbert Hoover's misguided approach to the great crash of '29, that I think the American people are going to step back over the next four weeks. And we saw a little bit in a couple of polls, and say can we really entrust the United States of America to this very outside-of-the-mainstream political figure? Are you as much an optimist as Steyn and myself?

VDH: I am, and I get criticized by a lot of conservatives for that reason. I think you hit the nail on the head when you said time. I think people were mad at Bush, they were mad and confused by the wars and the economic meltdown. And then suddenly, they do not want to vote for Obama, but they feel that they have to to express their dissatisfaction. But that being said, the more they're starting to learn about all of these various manifestations of...I say manifestations, because we're talking about FISA, public campaign financing, NAFTA, town meetings, guns, abortion, capital punishment. You and I could go on and on of the things that he's flipped or moderated or adapted, rejected his former positions because…and the question is why is he doing that? And the fact is he had to go further to the center than almost any modern candidate. He was so far in that coterie of Chicago leftists. And then we find another disturbing pattern is that he only will disown these people when they come to the public attention in sort of a meltdown. So Reverend Wright, he could no more forsake Reverend Wright or give him up unless Reverend Wright is stupid enough to go to Ground Zero at the National Press Club and let the world see what an odious racist he is. Then suddenly, he's gone. Bill Ayers, this man was e-mailing and phoning Bill Ayers up until 2005 after everybody had known that Ayers had said these ridiculous assertions that he was not going to feel guilty, he was unrepentant. And when did he throw him under the proverbial bus? Only when he ran for Senate, or he was elected to the Senate and he was going to start this presidential run. So there's a very disturbing pattern that the people themselves intrinsically do not bother Obama. He feels comfortable with them. He only distances himself when he feels that they become a political liability.

HH: Victor Davis Hanson, we've got two minutes to our first break here. Would you define for the audience hubris?

VDH: Well, it's a classical concept, and it's over-weening arrogance. [And what it means is that when things,] it's a very complex idea, but it means when things are going good, the person feels somehow that those good developments, that positive feeling is because of something he did. And then does something in excess more and more. They have another word, koros, excess. And then this finally is sort of a self-delusional process, and there's gods in the world that egg this person on because he lacks, the word is sophrosyne or moderation. And then of course, he implodes, and the words até. There's a succession from hubris to até, destruction, and this is the result of Nemesis. There is a god, Nemesis, that deludes people into thinking that whatever positive things that have happened to them is entirely because of their own rarely-answered genius and not because of accidents or fate or luck. So we all, the Greeks tell us when things start going well, do not think that you necessarily, if you're a Wall Street financier or a Fannie Mae, that you are responsible, because you're going to just keep doing to excess. I think Obama's had that problem when things have gone well most of his life. He's been able, as he said in his memoirs, to talk people into trusting him, or to talk people into doing things they otherwise might not do given his record of achievement.

HH: Victor Hanson, let's talk a little bit about John McCain. As I watched last night, I shared a frustration with many conservatives that he did not articulate arguments. He almost simply referenced them as though the American public should know of which he spoke, should have the same frame of reference. And I thought to myself, this is very frustrating, but on the other hand, it's very noble. He just assumes the American people understands what he's talking about. Did he make a huge error in doing so?

VDH: Well, my problem is incrementalism, that incrementally, he seems that he gains ground on Obama because people in their natural states would prefer his approach. And he's not by nature mean-spirited or disingenuous. So he doesn't like to go negative. He assumes people have a certain level of common knowledge. But the problem is that events are overtaking him. The headlines about Wall Street, Fannie Mae, the whole Washington-New York in pretty much a cesspool, and so what happens is Obama shoots ahead because of the events of the day. And you said it a moment earlier when you said it was time. If we had eight more weeks of this campaign, and the focus on Obama, I suppose, McCain could catch up. But he's going to have a great deal of trouble catching up unless he decides to be much tougher, to draw distinctions between the Obama of Chicago, the Obama that voted the most liberal Senator in the U.S. Senate, the Obama who had a particular view of the world. It's no accident when Obama's wife, I don't want to pick on his wife, but when she serially says that she has no pride in the United States until her husband ran, or she's mad at the United States, or this is a mean country, all of that is, is just a reification of the type of people they met, the type of conversations that were going on, the type of worldview they had. And that has to come out, or McCain is going to lose. And he's going to have to tell people this is the biggest contrast since McGovern-Nixon in '72, culturally, socially, politically, economically. We've got a European socialist who believes in statism and collectivized health care, high taxes, entitlements, and we have somebody who doesn't. We have somebody who believes in world governance and deference to the United Nations, and utopian pacifism, moral equivalence, multiculturalism, oppression studies, and someone who doesn't. But if he's not going to walk the American people through that labyrinth and tell people very simply that if you vote for my opponent, the following is going to happen in your lives. And if you don't, this is what's going to happen if you vote for me. [He needs...] he needed to say in five seconds Freddie Mac and Fannie Mae are not the entire problem with the economy, but they were the catalyst that started this, and here's why, because greedy people on Wall Street piggybacked on the assumption that the federal government would back bad loans. Why did they back bad loans? Because Barack Obama and Barney Frank and this whole group of Democratic apparatchiks, under the guise of political correctness, lent money to people who had no business borrowing it, and who walked away from their obligations. And that caused a chain of events that now we're supposed to think discredited capitalism. And he needs to tell people how that started. And if he can't, then he's going to be into this, you know, gecko and Wall Street did this, and this is typical greed, [and this is,] it's not going to work for him. If he gets into that paradigm, the Republicans will be just blamed for not believing in regulation or statism, and he's going to lose. He needs to get back to what caused this meltdown in the very beginning, and that really disturbing circular process where somebody from a Democratic administration is given a plum sinecure, and that person, to keep his job, gives money from that quasi-public institution to the Congress, who oversee it, and then cooks the books so that he or she and their friends can take multimillion dollar bonuses. And once that's established at a trillion to two trillion dollars, then the ever-ready profitmongers in Wall Street see that, and they see the guarantees, and then they start to participate in it.

HH: [Now that argument is,] I've been making that argument for weeks now, and it's an argument I'm familiar with, because it's an argument against the elites of Manhattan and Washington.

VDH: Absolutely.

HH: And I've always been comfortable broadcasting from the West Coast, because I'm not part of the Manhattan-Washington Beltway media elite. But it seems to that that elite, that media elite, has been engaged in a cooperative cover-up that keeps accountability far removed from an elite that's really not a business, it's not a Republican elite, it's not a country club elite, it's a hyper-privileged elite, Victor Hanson. And as Kissinger said about a different argument at a different time, this argument has the additional benefit of being true. And I think it's intuited by the American people, but do they connect it with Obama?

VDH: Well, we all know that from all of these informal polls that hedge fund directors, for example, the people who deal in highly speculative and highly remunerative investments prefer Obama. Goldman-Sachs is a sort of liberal Democratic stamp to it. And so people who make the mega-profits, think about it. It makes sense. They're immune from worries about taxes. They're immune from worries about making a payroll. The Republican constituency is the guy who owns a hardware store, a paving company, sells cars, because he might make up to $250 or $300K, but to make that $250 or $300K, he's got to work eighty hours a week, he takes risk, he can lose everything. The man at Goldman-Sachs who takes a thirty, or Franklin Raines at Fannie Mae who takes a $30 million dollar bonus, he doesn't care if taxes are 50% or 70%. In fact, he feels better when they're higher because it gives him a psychological cover that he's liberal, that he's caring, that he wants the government to do something that he in his own life doesn't want to do. He doesn't want to live in the ghetto, he doesn't want to tutor a kid from the barrio. He doesn't want to contribute very much money. We saw that with the comparative charities of Biden V. Palin.

HH: Wasn't that shocking?

VDH: Absolutely, but it's been repeated again and again. We saw that with the Clintons when they gave their underwear and claimed them as deductions in the 90s.

HH: I think that was the Gores, wasn't it?

VDH: Gores, yeah.

HH: Okay, okay.

VDH: It's the same thing. It's a sort of remote control charity of feeling bad, feeling guilty as long as it's distant, and it's the government can do what the individual should.

HH: By the way, you're going to Europe in 2009…

VDH: Yes.

HH: …and leading a group of people that will be touring what, Athens and Rome?

VDH: Yeah, I do that every year. I take about 60, first come first serve, and then we have a waiting list, and we go to great battlefields. This year, we're going to do some places outside Rome, Sorrento, and then we're going to go to Crete and Chania, and talk about everything from the Minoans to World War II and the airborne invasion, and end up in Athens at Marathon.

HH: An extraordinary opportunity at www.victorhanson.com, and an extraordinary conversation continues because Victor Davis Hanson is in it. Don't go anywhere.

HH: Victor Hanson, how many times have you met with George W. Bush?

VDH: I think four.

HH: Have you ever been alone with him for these conversations? Or is staff always present?

VDH: Once alone, but not more than five minutes.

HH: At this juncture, at almost the conclusion of his term, how do you assess him?

VDH: Well, I agree with him that we're not going to be able to assess him until later on. I think that his chief achievement was that at a time when everybody thought we were going to be struck in succession by terrorists, he and he alone guaranteed that we would not by the things he was willing to do – FISA, Guantanamo, the Patriot Act. All of these are caricatured now that they had worked, and they've stopped terrorism. Had he not stopped terrorism, he would have been criticized for not doing enough. He took out the two most odious regimes in the Middle East. There's constitutional governments there. [And I think that's going to be his chief,] he's going to be like Truman. He's going to go out in the 20s approval rating, we're not going to like him for the next ten years. We're going to look back in the context that he really did dismantle al Qaeda. They're not able to repeat these assaults on us. And I think that's the way to look at it, because I think a lot of our criticisms of what he did, my chief criticism is the increase in domestic spending at twice the rate Clinton did. And I think the reason he did that is he was willing to compromise too liberally with Democrats across the aisle, because he thought that in those critical years, 2003, 2004, 2005, and he was right, they would not pull the plug on the effort in Iraq, and he was willing to sacrifice a domestic agenda in some sense for that. I had criticisms with him on his open borders policy originally. There's other things that I thought…I don't think that no child left behind was wise, or prescription drug…he didn't address the entitlement problem, he spent too much. All that being said, I think that there were very few people given the pressures of the office at this particular time and this particular place in history that could have withstood that pressure, and he did.

HH: There's an aspect of his character I want to throw out to you which I think is under-remarked upon, but will end up being a large part of his legacy, is that he has, though a victim of relentless fury and almost derangement on the part of his enemies, he's never gone in for that. He's almost a non-partisan president here at the end of his term, down to 25% approval, maybe even to the detriment of his party, he has refused. And I think it's because of the briefings he gets every single day, he understands the world, et cetera. What do you make of his character?

VDH: I think that he sincerely believes that history later on will justify what he did when history is given the same facts at he was. I think he actually believes that he gets this frightening intelligence every day. He talks to these leaders abroad candidly that tell him horrific things that could happen. He makes these decisions, and he feels either that people share these same anxieties that don't have the same information, or there will come a time when they'll be privy to this knowledge, and they'll see that he made the right decision. But even Saturday Night Live, if you've watched those skits the last five years, he's never portrayed as Machiavellian. He's always portrayed as sort of somebody that Nancy Pelosi or a Barbara Boxer or a Harry Reid is taking advantage of because he refuses to get down to the same level. He's not calling people communists in the way that people are calling him a Nazi or worse even. So I mean, this is a very strange time, Hugh. I can't think…in the last five years, think of every genre of expression. Novels, we've had Checkpoint by Nicholson Baker, who's theme was how to kill George Bush. We had the documentary, the Assassination Of The President.

HH: We have the new W film coming out by Oliver Stone.

VDH: Yes, absolutely. It was about how to kill a president. And we've had comedians, we've had people who've said the most outrageous things about killing him and harm to his person, and he has never retaliated, or he's never got angry about it, and I think that there's some kind of philosophical perspective he has that when everything is said and done, and on the rare occasions I've talked to him, that seems to be the theme, that Truman's evoked, Eisenhower's evoked, as people who…

HH: Lincoln has been evoked when I've been with him.

VDH: Lincoln, absolutely. And he seems to be cognizant of critical periods in American history, the summer of 1864, the winter of 1776-77, the period in 1950 after we were almost pushed out of Korea. At key points where a lesser person in office would have capitulated to the pressures and the demands of the age, and that he didn't, and the people of that age, whether it's a Robert Taft, or it's a Horace Greeley, we don't remember those people. We only remember the people who said no, I'm not going to cater to public opinion.

HH: Victor Hanson, if Obama maintains his lead and wins, and the pollsters are correct, he will be joined in Washington probably with a filibuster-proof Senate, or very close, led by Harry Reid, and the House of Representatives led by Nancy Pelosi. I cannot honestly recall a period in American history where three such extremely partisan and differentiated in terms of the extreme of their ideology, conservative or left, would be in charge. And I can't even come up with anything like it in Great Britain, excepts perhaps immediately after World War II when the Labour Party came in. Can you, and what does it portend for the country if in fact the pollsters are right?

VDH: I think there was a period in 1933 and 1934 where the Roosevelt administration felt that a socialist National Recovery Agency and things like that, a socialist approach, and they went with that pretty much, and it didn't really bring results until the War, and then the War sort of stopped that. And the Henry Wallace wing of the Democratic Party was shunted aside. But there was a period in the 30s where they were trying things that nobody imagined that Americans would try, and they didn't work. But they did leave, I think, a pernicious legacy. Same thing, I think, is going to happen here. We're going to go into a recession, probably. And if Obama's elected, we're probably going to see a cap taken off FICA for people over $250K, small businessmen will see their marginal rates and sales taxes in the states, and it'll give the green light, people don't remark on this, it'll give the green light to state governments and local governments that higher taxation is the answer for their own fiscal problems. And so I think that we're going to see something akin to what Europe did in the 80s, where you'll have slower growth, larger state bureaucracies, and you're going to see, if Fannie Mae and Freddie Mac frighten people, and they saw the people who were attracted to that type of government service, the elites, and the inefficiency, that model of a quasi-private-public partnership is going to be the model for health care. We're going to see an expansion of federal control of education. I'm worried about other things that people don't remark about. He's rarely said anything about his educational philosophy, but on the rare occasion that he has, it's quite frightening. He's said that we needed, for example, more oppression studies. He went to an ethnic school, and I think [it] in New Mexico, and said this is a model, a Chicano ethnic school.

HH: I think it was Colorado.

VDH: Colorado, yes. And then he, in addition to this, he called for reparations, and he quickly sort of sidestepped that issue. And you get the impression that right now in the United States, [the problem that we don't,] the problem is not that we have too much of a therapeutic curriculum. We have these courses – peace studies, ethnic studies, leisure studies.

HH: Gender studies.

VDH: Gender studies. And what's happening is the public, when they send their children to school, they can't be ensured that they're going to have philosophy, literature, reasoning, logic, writing. And so the public itself, and we're starting to see the deterioration in things as diverse as the post office to the DMV, we're not turning out an educated, competitive citizen. And the worst thing you could do is A) accelerate that process, and then add more envy, anger, grievance to it, because you're going to get somebody who will not be able to compete, and then get angry as if he should be able to compete. And I'm really worried about that.

HH: In terms of that dynamic working its way through the political system, though, in the Great Depression, people didn't get angry. The revolution was expected, it didn't come. It self-corrected in many respects. Do you see a rapid bounce-back against statist policies if in fact it becomes Obama, Pelosi and Reid? Or do you see a prolonged period?

VDH: I think that's what you were getting at when you asked the questions about hubris. I think that if you get Reid together, and Pelosi and Obama, and the people who surround them, the legal team, the people who are going to be in the State Department, the people that are going to be at the Attorney General's office, maybe right below the radar that the public won't immediately fathom, I think you're going to see an intensification of an ideology. They're going to get further and further to the left. And it's finally going to reach a critical mass, and people as they did in the Reagan revolution, are going to react. But I think that we're going to have to go through this catharsis, because rightly or wrongly, people right now are blaming the conservative movement, Republicans, for things that I don't think they're culpable for. And I've never seen a period in my lifetime where all of the engines of the media, PBS, NPR, New York Times, Washington Post, CBS, MSNBC, CNN, the New Yorker, the New Republic, all of these things that while they don't reach as many people perhaps in terms of talk radio or Fox News, they have enormous cultural capital, and they set the tone, and I've never seen them all together working in concert to such an affect, that they're saying George Bush is a Nazi, George Bush is a buffoon, Sarah Palin is a yokel, these people want to burn books, they want to cram down fundamentalist religion or else down their throat, and they're scaring the people in a way that I haven't seen in my lifetime in the United States.

HH: Are they scaring all the people? Or are they scaring what I think it looks to me like, is a combination of critical mass of the underclass, who have grievances.

VDH: Yes.

HH: ...and the uberclass, the academic class, with whom you've been associated for thirty years, and I've been doing it for fifteen, almost uniformly to the hard left, and that they're taking the margins off, but that vast center remains not at all aligned ideologically. Or have I just got on rose-colored glasses?

VDH: No, you're right, but I think the problem is that the 51% that we see in the polls that are for Obama, that coalition for some reason is getting larger of the underclass. And they're not really the underclass anymore. They're the people in the lower middle class who have grown up on the expectation of more and more entitlements, more educational loans, more home owners relief, more federal money. We're in a serious situation where 35% of the Americans are not paying any money when they file a 1040. And they're not necessarily poor. So we're getting to a situation where that nexus that you described is getting at least 50/50, and what I'm especially disturbed about is I don't remember what I would call the boutique liberal, the person making $200,000 or $100,000, who's so radically left on the expectation that all of his bromides won't affect him because of his capital, but he has a disdain for the upper middle class that it will affect.

HH: Victor, we're talking as though the Democrats are going to come in, and I actually believe a self-correction's already underway, and that some of the polls show that, and that the Senate races will resolve, and Norm Coleman will win, and John Sununu will come back, and that we'll have a filibuster even if Obama wins. But I want to stay on the prospect for just a moment. It really wouldn't frighten me if I thought that they had an agenda worth experimenting with. But I don't...when Reagan arrived, and I was part of that in 1980, he had a number of big ideas. The Heritage Foundation put out the blueprint for America. They wanted to do a number of things. I don't see the Democratic Party wanting to do anything that I can articulate other than punish and redistribute. Do they have ideas?

VDH: No, that's why they were so angry at Clinton in the primary. For all of the pathologies of Bill Clinton, you could see that he understood, maybe it was the process of triangulation under the guidance of Dick Morris, but he understood that welfare had gotten out of control, and that there were political benefits, for whatever reason, of having a balanced budget and a surplus. I don't get that at all from these people. I get the impression, as you said, punitive. I think they're going to try to have sort of war crimes trials, that they will have Senate and House hearings about the Bush administration. I am very worried about certain things in Europe. They're going to be closely aligned with European socialists. I think that they're going to inordinately defer to the United Nations, which after the reception we saw with Ahmadinejad was quite frightening as well. And I think they have a different idea about taxation. They don't believe the individual creates that capital. If you talk to these people, they believe that because of some nebulous, arbitrary process, somebody who makes $200,000 due to his intellect or his expertise or his value to the economy got lucky, or it was a rigged system in which someone, let's say, who paints a house and makes $40,000 deserves $200,000. I was recently in Libya, and I had a ruptured appendix, and I was operated on in a country in which by fiat, the person who cleaned the floor made the same as the surgeon. And as I watched the manifestations of that all through the economy, I realized that the reason that an oil exporter can't fill potholes on the road on the way to the airport was simply that there was no incentive for anybody to do anything. There was no distinction. There was no recognition of talent or expertise or luck or sacrifice. So that's what I'm worried…I guess it would be summed up under the rubric that people around Obama, from what they've said, seem to believe in an equality of result rather than an equality of opportunity. And anytime that happens in history, you know the results of it, human nature being what it is.

HH: Victor Hanson, the intellectual terrain of the United States over the last seven years was marked by the sudden appearance of people who understood the war, you among them. Mark Steyn also rose to preeminence, a number of people on the internet rose up, the Powerline guys, et cetera. There was a seriousness about the war which I think in recent years has been fully and almost completely eclipsed by anger that it's not over and we can't go back to the 90s, and to the party that was the 90s. But we haven't stopped writing, and we haven't stopped reading what you and others have written. My question is did it make a difference? Did that argument that we had, and that understanding that we reached, make a long term difference with the American understanding of the war that we're in?

VDH: I think so. If you look at what's happened in Iraq, all the things that Mr. Obama and his associates said would not happen, did happen. The surge worked, and not just the surge, but the change of tactics and the grassroots repulsion at al Qaeda by Sunni peoples, tribes. There was a reconciliation in the government. It's a constitutional framework. They're working out oil, they're working out district representations. Iran did not go in and take that as part of its fiefdom. It's now isolated. And in fact, Iraq could be as destabilizing to Iran as Iran has tried to be to Iraq. But more importantly, the question was after 9/11, where were we going to fight al Qaeda? We went into Afghanistan and properly so, and we found immediately they had this sanctuary in a nuclear Islamic country where they were untouchable. And it would risk, really, a type of escalation that we weren't willing to take to go in there, at least overtly as Obama wanted to do. So we went in and we got rid of somebody who had been a long abettor of terrorists in Saddam Hussein, and immediately our enemies announced this is the new battlefield. They flocked to it, and we killed them by the thousands, we discredited them, not only discredited them militarily, but we discredited them culturally, socially, politically, ethically in the eyes of their natural constituency, the Sunni tribesmen, right in the heart of the ancient caliphate. They suffered a terrible defeat, they're disorganized, and during this whole process, they were not able to come over and attack us, which they promised was going to happen in a serial fashion. And yet, and if you look at all of that, the obstacles to that, we tragically lost over four thousand, but this is like trying to conduct the one campaign in World War II in the Marianas or something, where we lost commensurate casualties. So for all the mistakes that were made, and there are mistakes made in every war, it turned out to not only be valuable for our strategic interest in the Middle East, but it had a direct affect in attriting and hurting al Qaeda in a fashion that we had no other theater of operations to do that in. And that's lost on the American public, I'm afraid.

HH: Not only lost, but the level of imbecilic analysis of Pakistan, for example, last night as I watched Barack Obama talk about Musharraf and the whole Pakistan situation, and I thought to myself, does he not know that we partnered with Stalin in the…Musharraf was not Stalin, that you have to take your allies when you can get them, and you can't overthrow your allies. It seemed to me to be imbecilic, Victor Hanson.

VDH: Absolutely, and we not only partnered with Stalin, we did so with Obama's icons who made that decision. It was the people in the Democratic Party, rightly so, who saw that we had to use an evil force to counteract an evil force. And the other thing that was striking in the debate last night, when he talks about Musharraf in being a dictator, we forget where did Musharraf come from? He didn't come from in the Bush administration. George Bush was ridiculed by an elite journalist for not having instant recall of Musharraf, while he was running for election. He had been installed during the Clinton administration. Where did they get the bomb? This was the greatest foreign policy disaster in the last fifty years. They got the bomb under the Clinton administration. What did George Bush do? He came in with a nuclear dictator in an Islamic country, and what happened? As we know now, Dr. Khan's nuclear laboratory was shut down, and we understand that as imperfect as North Korea, there is a mechanism to control it, and it probably does not have more than one or two nukes. And Libya gave up an arsenal. Contrast that with the proliferation that went on during the Clinton administration. I'm not blaming the Clinton administration, but I'm just suggesting that when Obama says these incredible assertions, he doesn't have any idea what he's talking about.

HH: You see, a question that went unanswered, because it's been such a dismal series, maybe Bob Schieffer will ask it, Libya opened their kimono and turned over the Khan network products after the invasion of Iraq. We got their chemicals, their biological, we got their nuclear designs, we got their operational designs for the warhead that Khan had sold them. It was a huge strategic victory to disarm Libya. I would love to see a candidate asked, both of them, to what do you attribute that retreat from brinksmanship on the part of Qaddafi, and did it have to do with the successful use of force. And I want to ask you first, A) do you think it did have to do with the successful use of force, and B) do you think Obama has any idea that that happened or why it happened?

VDH: I don't think he has any idea, and we know that Mr. Qaddafi called the Italian prime minister and said just what you said, that he didn't want to end up as did Saddam Hussein. And remember, it didn't happen just after the invasion. It happened about six weeks after the capture of Saddam Hussein, and that had a powerful effect on a similarly-minded dictator when he saw the fate of Saddam Hussein. That's when he made the decision. When I was there in April of 2006, I talked with a number of people in the Libyan government. And off the record, they all said that. These were very hard people. They were no-nonsense pragmatists, and they said basically that the government has switched positions, that it was allowing cell phones in, that it had this natural oil wealth, that it was tired of the embargo, that it didn't want to deal with George Bush anymore in a confrontational manner, and they said this to me, that we have more WMD arsenals than you'll ever find in Iraq, and they were bragging about it as if this will be a bonanza, and this will open up relations, and we have more. And one man said to me you know, we're only pumping a million three, and we can have four million barrels of oil a day, and it's going to work out great, because the price is up and this is going to be one...they were saying things that were absolutely incredible had you broached them in 2003. But the problem was that all this came in a context where George Bush was a unilateralist preempter, had done nothing good but make the world hate us. And yet when you look at the world and you don't listen to the BBC or read Le Monde in Paris, you start to see that a billion people in India appreciate free trade with the United States, that China is not necessarily anti-American, that Russia, to the degree that it fears us, it's because that we've stood up to them in a way that I don't think Obama will. So I don't get by this idea that because there's people in the Middle East and Europe that don't like us and they're far more vocal, that this is a referendum on the morality of the United States. I don't want to be liked by people necessarily in the Middle East. I don't really necessarily want to be liked by people in a Paris salon. And to the extent that George Bush is not liked by those people, it's not necessarily a bad thing.

HH: There's a choice in front of the United States, and it's McCain-Obama. And they will then direct the foreign policy of the United States. And people in Israel are watching this choice, and people in Iran are watching this choice, and our enemies in caves in Waziristan are watching. What do you see is those two paths? What will be different if we select McCain than if we select Obama vis-à-vis Iran and Israel? Will the path of history be different, Victor Hanson, in your assessment depending on the outcome of this? Or is the confrontation coming regardless of who we send in?

VDH: Well, the difference is it's easy to voice cheap rhetoric, as we saw in the debate last night. It's easy to say, as Obama says, it's a game-changer if Iran were to get a nuclear device. What does that mean, a game-changer? That's intolerable. What he's not telling you is that if I choose to make sure that they don't have a nuclear device, then that means that basically the United States is going to have to impose an embargo or a Naval blockade because the Europeans will still try to profit to the 11th hour, or even a military strike. I, Barack Obama, must be hated by people in Berlin. There's no more Victory Column great extravaganzas for me. There's no more fawning interviews with Der Spiegel. It's going to be hatred from those people. I'm going to be a unilateralist pre-empter, and I'm going to do that, and all the people in the Muslim world and the Arab world that love me and fawn over me are going to hate me as worse than you know what. Okay, I'm willing to do that for a principle. Do you think he's going to be willing to do that, or John McCain? I'm sorry, but I don't think that all of that cheap rhetoric about invading Pakistan and a game-changer in Iran is anything other than rhetoric, because I think the problem with Obama is he's bought into the idea of Vero Possumus, the new presidential seal that he's promulgating, that the seas are going to cease to rise, that the planet won't heat up, this is the change that we've been waiting for. And he really believe in this Messianic sense that people love him for himself. And he's not going to be willing to give up that easily.

HH: Let's go back to this conversation about Israel. Ahmadinejad has been here three years in a row. He says crazier things every time. At least this time he wasn't feted by Columbia University. I don't doubt that we're in for a confrontation. Do you?

VDH: No, I'm afraid that we are, especially when he feels emboldened enough to go to the United Nations just a few blocks away from the Wall Street meltdown, and for the first time not just say the Israelis are culpable, but Jews in general, and talk about in Hitlerian terms an international Jewish banking conspiracy. It's what he basically was saying, and he felt not only would he get applause, but there would be liberal people in the United States, as happened, that would take him out to dinner in congratulations for that speech. So I'm very worried. I've never seen this level of anti-Semitism, I've never seen this level of appeasement among our elites. And he's basically really read the Western mind. He's basically said do you want a nuclear Iran to threaten you? Do you want a missile that can threaten Frankfurt? Because that's what I'll do unless you are nice to me, unless you call off George Bush and Dick Cheney, and then we can live together. And then once we get into that mindset, it's going to be very easy to obtain that goal.

HH: Are you amazed that people immediately begin to discount him, and they say well you know, he's not really in charge of the government, that's the mullahs, and he's a figurehead, and there's opposition to him, and the reformers exist. We've seen this for eight years. He is an expression of the inner elite in Iran, though, regardless of whether he's running the Revolutionary Guard, and there's some question about his influence there. But he's a perfect expression of that mindset.

VDH: Absolutely, and it reminds me so much of the 1930s when Hitler was making these absolutely atrocious statements and making a fool of himself at Nuremberg. And what did the people in France and England say? They'd say you know, the Prussian Junker class is really running Germany, and these are the old Hindenburg-Ludendorff people. Or they'd say the industrial is corrupt and these people are really running Germany. [They wouldn't,] this man is not typical. And what they didn't understand was that these people thought they may, but they found out that A) he was either useful, or B) he was far smarter than they were, or C) and most likely of all, that Hitler was an expression of the resentments and the anger of a whole humiliated German nation in the way that Ahmadinejad has sized up the Iranian people's frustrations, and how they can be manipulated in a way that's even more effective than the mullahs themselves.

HH: So here's my question. You know, if we post the transcript and the podcast of this conversation, immediately voices on the left will attack you, and me for hosting you, and they will deny the reality of what's just been said, even though it's not deniable. They will invent a reason to deny it. Why is that? Is it fear that they just don't, that they can't understand what we're up against? Or is it ambition? Or is it just stupidity?

VDH: No, I think it's, [and it's] fear. I mean, who wants to face that awful reality that this man is unstable, and there's a slight chance that he might welcome a nuclear exchange, because then he could tell the Islamic world that the downtrodden Shia, of all people, destroyed the Zionist entity when the Sunnis could not, and that they are now with, in martyrdom in Heaven. So there's that fear that you might be dealing with something that right after Afghanistan, Iraq, this financial problem. Who wants to deal with it? It's the same mindset that after going through the horrors of World War I, you weren't going to ask the French people to say look, you didn't do that in World War I. You really didn't win. Now you've got a bigger problem with Hitler. They were not up to it. And it's very hard to do. I have empathy in some ways for the liberal left, because you're trying to say to them okay, Iraq is a mess, Afghanistan is a mess, in your way of thinking, the economy's a mess, and you know what? There's somebody out there who does not believe in the world court of the Hague. He's not going to believe in the United Nations, and you can't just do a Milosevic on him. It's a very fundamental problem, and he wants to destroy the survivors of the Holocaust. And we have to deal with him. We either have to get the Europeans and the whole world to stop commerce completely with him. And if we can't do that, we have to blockade his country and shut off his trade. And if we can't do that at the eleventh hour, we're going to have to use some type of military option. And boy, once you do that, you sort of negate the whole idea of peace and conflict resolution studies, dialogue, he's sane, look, he went to Columbia, we talked to him, and the United Church of Christ, Unitarian ministers, they all said you can deal with him. We've been there. It goes all the way back to Demosthenes and Philip. [Nobody likes, the left thinks that everybody wants to have a war with…] nobody wants a war with Iran. But what we don't want to do is have a war with Iran. And the only way you're going to guarantee a war with Iran is if this man gets a hold of nuclear weapons, and he has guided missiles, and he starts pointing them not only at Israel, but he starts to dictate the oil production levels, or the type of governments with large Shia minorities in places along the Gulf, or he'd start to tell Germany that he wants more favorable trade policy. And given what the Europeans have showed the last eight or nine years, [it's really,] it's very depressing, because it's a very amoral foreign policy that's based entirely on local and regional self-interest and real politick. And Ahmadinejad has sized up Europe as no other person has in years.

HH: In the 30s, Chamberlain was supported by a phalanx of appeasers. In that time, it was not a dirty word.

VDH: No, it wasn't.

HH: Samuel Hoare and you had Halifax, and you had a bunch of people who honestly believed that you could buy off Hitler, and you could even make common cause with Mussolini to buy off Hitler. They were not disabused of that until the very end when it was too late. But they were not fifth columnists. There were some fifth columnists in London, but they weren't part of the government. Are you worried that we have actually people who hate America so much in the ranks of the Obamians that they wouldn't mind strategic defeats delivered to this country?

VDH: [No, I don't think that we have people...] I think that there are people in the United States who would like to see, for a variety of reasons, radical Islam defeat the United States. And they live in the United States. But I don't think that necessarily they're in the Obama campaign. I think the people in the Obama campaign really do believe that all of the problems in the world today are caused by either a lack of communication or a bellicose stance by the United States. And what's scary about that is in a pattern of moral equivalence, they don't see anything exceptional about the United States. They don't think our Constitution, our multiracial Meritocratic society is any different than Indonesia or Brazil, and that's scary. [But I don't think that they want,] it's even scarier in a sense because they think by dialoguing and having this moral equivalence stance with our enemies that therefore it's going to enhance our popularity...

HH: I agree with you. I just wanted to get it out there that we are not attributing to them an anti-American...but I'm wondering, that naiveté, is it remediable? You know, he will sit down, if he is the president on the first day, he will get the CIA briefing, or preferably during the transition, and he will see what we're up against. Does he strike you as the kind of individual who can change and immediately understand that the world is not as he wishes it would be?

VDH: No, what worries me about Obama is that, and he said this in his <u>Dreams From My Father</u>, the first memoir, that he had an uncanny ability, he even couched that ability in terms of race, he said a black man like me could reassure white people because of the powers of his rhetoric. He believes that he's so charismatic and so rhetorical that almost anybody would see the logic of his ideas. That's what's scary.

HH: Victor Hanson, when we went to break, we were talking about the war. And now I want to focus on the American military with which you are very, very familiar. You've written a lot of military history in your time. And the American military has shown itself again to be an extraordinary organization. It's adapted to such a changing environment. Robert Kaplan's written extraordinary books about it. How do you think they view this election? And they're not political, and they will never be other than not political, I know too many, I married into a military family of five generations. They're simply not ever going to be other than apolitical. But how do you think they view this conversation?

VDH: Well, I think that first of all, they're a little astounded that people don't recognize the extent or the degree of their achievement in Iraq. I mean, they not only went over there into a foreign landscape, they understood Islam finally, they figured out the tribal system, they did reconstruction. And then what's never remarked upon, they went into the allies of Baghdad and Fallujah and Baquba, and tried to help people who were suffering, and did that simultaneously while fighting hand to hand against some of the most wicked people in the world, and defeated them on their own terms and their own turf. And it was an extraordinary achievement. And I feel that to the extent that they don't get credit for that, they harbor, the proper word's not resentment, but they feel a yearning. Why don't people recognize us? Why do they keep saying that Iraq was the worst decision, it was a mistake, it was terrible, that you go over there, and you see what they're doing, and you just don't get the impression that they're the Wehrmacht terrorizing people. I think that Obama said that all we're doing in Afghanistan is killing innocent civilians so that we're putting pressure on the government. We're not doing that. There's never been a more careful, more scientific, more surgical military than our own. And they did a wonderful thing in both Afghanistan and Iraq, and they did the near impossible, and that message is totally lost on the American people.

HH: I want to ask you, there's a patch here which I keep for J.P. Blecksmith who was killed in Fallujah on November 11th, '04, and I know his family, and I know how proud they are of the contribution he made. And I know the American people love their military. But does this in any way affect the willingness of people to serve in it, that we are so cavalier about the sacrifices rendered, and the achievements obtained?

VDH: I hope not. I've been there twice, and I went there with H.R. McMaster for a week, and we drove all over that Anbar Province and Baquba, Fallujah, that area. And just to talk to those people, they're just excited about having people come over, and they'll take you on a tour. And it was very eerie to walk in places, and I went with a Marine colonel, and he said look at this house. In 2005, this man was killed here. And then we went down a road, and he said this IED blew up here. And it was almost a ghost land of the accumulated experiences that all these brave people, and he said something I'll never forget. He said the surge worked, yes. The Anbar awakening worked, yes. Change of tactics was necessary, yes. Petraeus was a savior, yes. But please remember that in 2003, '04, '05 and '06, there were unknown Americans who went out with the wrong tactics, the wrong type of knowledge, and they still defeated the enemy, and they killed some very, very evil, powerful people. And their absence today allowed this to happen, and we want to remember them. And I think that was very poignant.

HH: [We do want to…] Zarqawi was killed before the surge.

VDH: Absolutely.

HH: And the number of people he would have killed had he remained and trained are numerous.

VDH: Yes, yes.

HH: What about the idea that we have had a deterrent effect? I remember your writing, your reporting at the time of the invasion of Iraq, and how you marveled as a military historian at how far and how fast we went. Do our enemies remember that? Or do they understand, as the North Vietnamese did, it's not really that capability that matters, it's the political will of the people behind it?

VDH: Well, every war, all war is an intensification of the existing status quo. So to the extent the United States is successful, that enhances our world prestige, and it provides greater deterrence. And to the extent that we're not successful or are perceived, it has the opposite effect. It's just intensification is what war is. And so after 2003 in that brilliant three week campaign, and up until December, then we had a deterrent effect, and you saw that with the Cedar Revolution and the events in Lebanon, and Libya, and Pakistan. And then when the criticism mounted and we were told that we were Hitlerian and we were losing, then it had the opposite effect. And now we're starting to see a restoration of the prestige of the United States, especially when people look at the U.S. military, vis-à-vis the NATO allies. Remember what Obama and others said, Kerry and Obama, that Afghanistan was the good war, Iraq was the bad war. That was the multilateral war, the allies were there, NATO was there. It was all the right war, that was where bin Laden…and we're finding out that Iraq was more solvable, and that the U.S. military was far more capable than its allies. And the problem with Afghanistan, in some cases, is Pakistan, it's insolvable, and also the nature of our allies in NATO. They're not really allies as we usually use that term.

HH: Victor Hanson, we were talking before the break about the war. Our enemies, and here I'm talking about al Qaeda, not Iran, we talked about them, how do you think they feel at this moment about their position in the world? I think they might actually be cheered by the idea of receding American power and their proximity to the nukes of Pakistan.

VDH: I think so, but that being said, if we try to quantify that question, we look at the Pew International poll, for example. We see that the popularity ratings of bin Laden and Dr. Zawahiri are at all-time lows, about 34% on the average in the Middle East, except in the West Bank. And we see the tactic of suicide bombing is at an all-time low vis-à-vis before Iraq, which is quite startling. In 2002, it was far more popular. That tells me that people in the Middle East, it wasn't necessarily an ethical question whether to like bin Laden or his suicide bombing tactics. It was whether it was successful or not. And now people are starting to see that it caused untold misery to themselves, and the United States is going to win in Iraq and probably in Afghanistan, and governments are starting to stand up to terror. And it's predicated on the notion that the United States is strong, and it doesn't really care to bow to critics in the Middle East. And so that's very important.

HH: There was, however, a moment of time when the West understood itself to be the West...

VDH: Yes.

HH: And there were a number of developments immediately after 9/11 and the invasion of Iraq, where the West said, and we have to defend, we have to be concerned with demographics, we have to be concerned with borders...

VDH: Yes.

HH: We have to be concerned...is that all gone?

VDH: I'm worried. That's what I'm worried about. I was getting to that. I'm more confident about our military because of the type of people in the military. The Petraeus mindset is encouraging. But what I'm worried about is, this was a war with a Western enlightenment and the forces of medievalism, if I could use that term, not that the Medieval period was necessarily all bad. But nevertheless, look at all the things in enlightenment. Publish a novel, not just Salman Rushdie, but Jewel of Medina. We're self-censoring ourselves. If you think of films, Obsession or Fitna, you can't even do a film in Europe.

How about journalism? We can…Jonathan Chait can write an article in a wartime entitled "Why I hate George Bush" in the New Republic, but you dare not make a cartoon mocking Islam. We're talking about religion. We're all worried about whether Sarah Palin burned a book. How about the Pope? All he did was quote, I think it was a 14th Century Byzantine treatise, a letter to an Islamic sultan in the Ottomans, and all of a sudden, people started dying. So if you look at the classic genres of the Enlightenment, in journalism, in religion, novels, film, we in the West are self-censoring ourselves because we're either afraid or we're so indoctrinated with the culture of multiculturalism that we feel that no other culture can be any worse than the West. And that's what I'm very worried about. We are afraid as Westerners to say look, look at the globalized world, look at constitutional government, look at capitalism, look at the stunning advances in technology in medicine. Whether you like it or not, it came from, only came from a paradigm that was political, economic, social, freedom, individualism, secularism, rationalism, constitutional government that came out of Europe, Greece, Rome, the Christian Church, et cetera. And if we're not going to defend and articulate that, that's what I'm worried about, and we're not doing it.

HH: Do civilizations get tired of the burden of that? [And you've studied…but] not this quickly, I hope, but do they just wear out?

VDH: I think the Greeks told us that, that they were like human bodies, that they are young and vibrant, and they mature and they're wise, and then they become old and decrepit. And the question was to which degree do they reproduce and that cycle continues? There's always that cycle going on, but each generation is a link in a large chain. And it just takes one generation to give up or to age or decline or to become incompetent, and suddenly the whole civilization is lost. What I'm worried about is, because of our educational system, we don't have a critical mass of individuals who'll say I'm a Westerner, of all races, all religions, it doesn't matter, but I'm a Westerner in the way I think, I'm an American, and I'm unapologetic about it. And it has given us not colonialism, racism. Those are the sins of mankind. Look at Islam. Look at China today. But I gave you the remedies for that. And only did this paradigm do that. And we don't have people in the universities, in politics, in journalism and in the media who are willing to say that.

HH: But Petraeus came from somewhere, and he's a great military commander. I don't know if he ever has any political ambition, but he's 54. He comes out of the Boom, sort of the middle of the boom.

VDH: He does.

HH: …so that opportunity remains. And there are other great leaders around the United States, many of them Democrats, by the way.

VDH: Absolutely.

HH: It's not political, [who have…] Jim Webb is an extraordinary, I think, inspirational figure, though I wish he'd lost to George Allen.

VDH: Yes.

HH: But nevertheless, they come out of this generation. So the question is, does the tide that is flowing right now as we see in this election context worry you that we've run out of gas to produce those sorts of people? Or is it just one of these ups and downs?

VDH: I don't know. I hope that we have more people like Webb and more people like Petraeus. I just don't see that they're as common on the landscape as the people who believe antithetically to them. And they're necessary. But you know, this country, we could have had this conversation in 1861, and all of a sudden, where did Billy Sherman come from, William Tecumseh Sherman? He was a complete failure until he was 39 years old, and suddenly, the right man at the right time. I don't know where Matthew Ridgeway came, but all of a sudden, everybody thought MacArthur was a genius, and Ridgeway saved Korea. So we always have been saved in our hour of need by people among us that we didn't appreciate in times of peace.

HH: Do you see any great political leaders out there who are not on the ballot right now who speak to you from a younger even generation than Petraeus and Webb?

VDH: I don't see them necessarily in the political landscape, but one thing I'm very confident, I spend a lot of time as a professor at the Naval Academy and going into Iraq, and then being involved with a security fellow program at the Hoover Institution. There are some absolutely brilliant colonels in the U.S. Army. These are people with PhDs, combat experience, and they're not just a dozen. They're in the very hundreds. And I see them of all political backgrounds, but they're absolutely brilliant. And their influence is expanding beyond the military. And they're saying and writing things in an American context that are absolutely phenomenal.

HH: Victor Davis Hanson, thank you. What is your prediction of the next four weeks?

VDH: I think that incrementally, if we don't have another complete financial meltdown, and I think you'll see that the American voter will see a structure emerging that will deal with this process better than, say, the European alternative, and the result of that will be they'll concentrate more on the difference between McCain and Obama, and you'll see McCain close the gap to about three points. If that happens, and I think there's a good chance it could, I don't see the Bradley effect, or racism involved, but I do think that Obama has a Messianic effect on people, and they tell pollsters, they congregate, they say they're for Obama. But in the privacy of the voting booth, three to four percent of them at a critical juncture won't think of race, but they'll think of experience, and they'll say you know what? I've got all the mileage out of telling all of my friends I'm for Obama. There's sort of a pet rock effect. But I really don't want to turn the country over to somebody who's going to raise taxes in a depression, and follow the dictates of Europe and the United Nations at a time of war. And I think McCain has a very good chance.

HH: What do you want John McCain to say over the next four weeks?

VDH: I want John McCain to say that you may not like George Bush, you may think I'm old, but look, we are in a critical time, and everything that in the past has worked in recession and depression I'm for, and everything that hasn't my opponent is trying to fawn on you. And we know that in times of war, you need a steady person who has confidence in American exceptionalism, and is willing to be unpopular to get us through this crisis, and my opponent defers too many times to too many people abroad, and he's not willing to lose that Messianic image of himself to make the hard, tough decisions. He'd rather be liked that do the right thing.

HH: And by this time next year, do you think we will have had a confrontation with Iran, either Israel as a proxy for the U.S. in the world or ourselves?

VDH: I hope not. I hope that we can do it with commercial pressures. But I'm very worried about the period November, December, January should Obama be elected, because I feel the Israelis will think that if he's president, they will not get the green light, and Bush is a lame duck, and then they will feel they have to preempt, and that's a very critical period we have to watch carefully.

HH: Victor Davis Hanson, thank you for an extraordinary two hours.

End of interview.

Chapter 9.

Conclusion

N o broadcast program can thrive with just a diet of the war and the debates around it. But no broadcast program deserves to thrive if the war and the debates around it are not accorded an amount of time and depth of conversation at least approaching the seriousness of the subject. I watch and listen in amazement as most television and radio host after host either refuses to discuss the nature of the conflict we are in, or misrepresents it, or simply lacks the curiosity or the capacity to understand what is going on in the world on which they are allegedly "reporting."

The war has sadly became politicized in the fashion that the Vietnam War became politicized, but hopefully not with the same result. George Bush may have held off defeat long enough and pursued victory strongly enough to allow Iraq to thrive as a free state aligned with the United States against both al Qaeda extremists and Iranian terror.

But that result is not guaranteed, and the desperate attempt to keep Pakistan from falling to the Islamists continues as does the race to stop the radical mullahs of Iran from gaining the nukes with which they will gladly threaten Israel and blackmail the West. Various Islamist groups continue their attempts to establish sanctuaries elsewhere and to carry their message into the urban centers of the West. Though the battle for Iraq may be behind us, other battles continue, and not just in Afghnaistan.

The next two years will bring many more days of crisis and, hopefully, crucial books of knowledge and wisdom, and voices of experience and candor and purpose, to help the West deal with those days. I hope there will be more volumes of interviews such as these, celebrating and illuminating not only the continued resolve of the West not to be overwhelmed by barbarism, but also the knowledge it needs to succeed in that effort.

Acknowledgments

Many people assisted me in the writing of this book.

As she has for eight of my nine books, Lynne Chapman oversaw the compilation of the manuscript and kept many of the interview transcripts from vanishing forever. Lynne has been my assistant since 1989, and twenty years of patience and incredible ability, focus and good cheer are deeply appreciated.

Snow Philip again cast her practiced proofreading eye across the pages. As noted in the book, the senior producer of my radio show, Duane Patterson, and its senior engineer Adam Ramsey, have been instrumental in fashioning the broadcasts and thus the book. Duane has been a part of the program since before it began, and Adam joined a week into its launch. Both are extraordinary professionals and true friends whose contributions are immense and valued.

Robert Stevenson and Dustin Steeve did an incredible amount of work in the booking of many of these guests, Moses Nolf and Anthony Ochoa are always at the ready to assist in the program's smooth operation, and many of the program's interns have assisted along the way: Darren Case, Bethany Hill, Andy Kosch, Steven Lackner, Aabria Lipscomb, Christopher Munekawa, Caryn Moore, Danny Rasmussen, James Skahen, Daren Sprawls, Andrew Swaim, Austen Swaim, and Barak Wright.

For the fourteen years I have taught at Chapman University Law School, first Dean Parham Williams and now Dean John Eastman have presided over a young, dynamic, and growing school. They have reflected Chapman University President Jim Doti's commitment to engaged scholarship in its many forms, including the broadcast variety. The reach of these interviews is vast because Chapman University committed to allowing me to engage an audience far beyond the physical classroom, and I am grateful to all three and to a wonderful set of faculty colleagues, many of whom have contributed on air and off to my thinking. Barbara Babcock and Gloria Davis have always been ready to help marry the demands of teaching, writing and journalism. My students have been gracious about sudden departures when an interview became available. I thank them all.

Salem Communications is the home of my radio show and of Townhall.com, where I am the Executive Editor. Before any other major media company understood the synergy between the radio and the web, Salem's founders Edward Atsinger and Stuart Epperson had, and they acted on it. The new media infrastructure that has partially liberated American politics from the handicap of a deep left bias which still permeates the now very far fallen titans of old media owes much to these two gentlemen and their colleagues within the management of Salem. David Evans, Greg Anderson Joe Davis and Jim Cumby have led the transition from a radio company to a new media company that includes radio stations, and in so doing have significantly altered the face of American media and continue to do so. Tom Freiling and Eric Jones have been of enormous assistance in taking the radio interviews and converting them into this book and CDs.

I have been especially grateful to Russ Hauth, David Spady, Russ Shubin, and Chuck DeFeo, and Jonathan Garthwaite all of whom love politics and public policy as much as I do, and who keep the business of broadcasting focused on the product and its purpose. My colleagues behind microphones, Bill Bennett, Mike Gallagher, Dennis Prager, Michael Medved and Albert Mohler are great friends as well as communicators, and the many other hosts within the Salem network have always been eager to publicize my books even when they did not agree with my points of view. It is an extraordinary company, and people who work within it do so because they view the mission of attracting, informing and activating America's citizens as crucial to the future of the country. Whether it is Tom Tradup and the Dallas team, a GM in a local market, or a sales staffer making the pitch that keeps us all on the air, Salem's people distinguish it among the media companies scrambling for eyeballs and ears. I especially want to thank those brave souls who regularly sit in behind the microphone for me when I am away: the late Dean Barnett, Carol Platt Liebau, Michael Steele and Emmett, the Unblinking Eye. Each sacrifices time and energy in the cause of entertaining yet informative journalism, and I and the audience appreciate them for the effort.

As with every other book, the most important person in its completion and success, even as she is to my life, is Betsy, without whom nothing would get done and nothing would be nearly as sweet.

Printed in the United States
215364BV00001B/1/P